THE DEATH
AND REBIRTH
OF THE
SENECA

The history and culture of the great

Iroquois nation, their destruction

and demoralization, and their cultural

revival at the hands of the Indian visionary,

Handsome Lake

THE DEATH
AND REBIRTH
OF THE
SENECA

Anthony F. C. Wallace

WITH THE ASSISTANCE OF SHEILA C. STEEN

Alfred A. Knopf · New York

1970

THIS IS A BORZOI BOOK
PUBLISHED BY ALFRED A. KNOPF, INC.

TO BETTY

PREFACE

THIS BOOK TELLS THE STORY OF THE LATE COLONIAL AND EARLY reservation history of the Seneca Indians, and of the prophet Handsome Lake, his visions, and the moral and religious revitalization of an American Indian society that he and his followers achieved in the years around 1800. It is not intended to convey in a formal manner my theoretical views on social movements, although the case of Handsome Lake originally led me to consider the subject in a comparative frame of reference. For my general writings on revitalization movements, and for studies of special aspects of the Handsome Lake religion, the reader is referred to the several books and papers listed in the bibliography. Nor does the book attempt to describe in close detail the Iroquois cultures. The interested reader may consult the works of Morgan, Speck, Fenton, Shimony, Lounsbury, and others listed in the bibliography for further ethnographic information.

Library and field research in preparation for the book were begun in 1951 and largely completed by 1956; writing and analysis have been done on and off during subsequent years. Thus the dates of reference for "recent" events on the Allegany Reservation are the early 1950's. Much of the reserve, however, is now gone, covered by the water behind Kinzua Dam; the people—and the religious center—have been moved to new locations. Several persons have been of great help in collecting materials and in achieving interpretation. In particular I want to express gratitude to Mr. Merle H. Deardorff, who gave freely of time, wisdom, and extensive files of notes and photostats, all of which have been invaluable both in the accumulation and in the understanding of data; to W. N. Fenton, C. E. Congdon, Oscar Nephew, and Paul A. W. Wallace, for illuminating discussion; to the Social

(vii)

Science Research Council and the University of Pennsylvania for, respectively, a Faculty Research Fellowship (1952–3) and a research grant (1953), which permitted the collection of data and much of the writing; to Sheila C. Steen for loyal and creative research assistance; and to Josephine H. Dixon and Marilyn Crill for patient and careful secretarial work. To my wife Betty I extend thanks for typing, discussion, and for helpful encouragement. And to many unnamed Iroquois people go my gratitude for instruction and hospitality and my admiration for their creation—the religion of Handsome Lake.

ANTHONY F. C. WALLACE

Philadelphia, Pa.

July, 1967

CONTENTS

PART III / *The Renaissance of the Iroquois*

· Contents ·

ILLUSTRATIONS

(following page 144)

Unfortunately, there is no known portrait that can be identified as that of Handsome Lake.

A Map of the Iroquois Country in the 18th and early 19th centuries and a map of the Seneca Reservations in 1797 appear on the two pages following.

(xiii)

SENECA RESERVATIONS
IN 1797

Miles

0   40

palacios

palacios

IROQUOIS COUNTRY
18TH AND EARLY 19TH CENTURIES

Miles
0   150

ATLANTIC OCEAN

N

Quebec

Three Rivers

Montreal
CAUGHNAWAGA

Lake Champlain

ST. LAWRENCE R.

ST. REGIS

Boston

Ft. Herkimer
MOHAWK R.
Ft. Stanwix
Albany
HUDSON R.
CANAJOHARIE

OSWEGO
ONEIDA
ONONDAGA
OWEGO
CANAWAGUS
CHEMUNG R.

New York

Lake Ontario

DELAWARE R.

Philadelphia

TUSCARORA
TONAWANDA
GENESEE R.

Wyoming
SUSQUEHANNA R.

Harrisburg

Baltimore

Ft. Niagara
GRAND RIVER
BUFFALO CREEK

CORNPLANTER
Warren
VENANGO
(Ft. Franklin)
ALLEGHENY R.

Washington

CATTARAUGUS

Lake Erie

Pittsburgh
MONONGAHELA R.

Lake Huron

CUYAHOGA R.

Ft. McIntosh

OHIO R.

MUSKINGUM R.

Detroit

SANDUSKY

Ft. Harmar

Lake Michigan

Fallen Timbers
MAUMEE R.

Greenville

MIAMI R.
Ft. Finney

OHIO R.

INTRODUCTION

1

THE RELIGION OF
HANDSOME LAKE TODAY

THE OLD WAY OF HANDSOME LAKE IS AN AMERICAN INDIAN
religion that is still practiced on Iroquois reservations in the
United States and Canada. It is not Christian, although it includes
some elements borrowed from Christianity; it is essentially an amalgam
of ancient tradition and the innovations of the Seneca prophet named
Handsome Lake. It was developed by several tribes of Iroquois who,
a century and a half ago, felt a need to lift themselves from defeat,
demoralization, and despair and to revitalize their communities. This
book tells the story of the origin of their religion: how the Iroquois
lived before catastrophe befell them; what the disaster was like; and
how Handsome Lake and his disciples designed for themselves and
their people a new way to live and brought about a renaissance of
Iroquois society.

· The Old Way of Handsome Lake ·

AMONG THE TWENTY THOUSAND or so Iroquois Indians living on the
several reservations in New York State, Quebec, and Ontario today,
there are perhaps five thousand followers of the Old Way of Handsome Lake.[1] It is impossible, however, to obtain an accurate census

(3)

of "Handsome Lake followers," or "longhouse people," or "the pagans," as they are variously called. The Handsome Lake religion does not demand that its communicants rigorously avoid all other denominational affiliations. Thus many "Handsome Lakers" attend church or mass at times, and at times the longhouse, deriving benefit from both, each in its proper season. Many Baptists, and Mormons, and Episcopalians, on occasion—particularly at the high festivals of New Year and Green Corn—drop in at the longhouse to listen gravely to the *Gaiwiio* (the "good word," the Code of Handsome Lake), to partake of strawberry juice and corn soup, and to smile gratefully at the antics of the False Faces soliciting tobacco. There is good in both, they say, in the Handsome Lake way and in the Christian way. Some of the Seneca prophet's followers even aver that Christ was one of the four angels who taught Handsome Lake the *Gaiwiio*, but doctrine is not settled on this point.

The Handsome Lake religion now, more than one hundred and fifty years after its conception, is embodied in an organization that has no formal name or address, as a Christian denomination might have, but that nevertheless functions in almost every way as a church. Its headquarters is on the Seneca Reservation at Tonawanda (near Buffalo, New York), where are kept the wampum belts of Handsome Lake himself—belts so sacred that, according to legend, no white man has ever seen them, so sacred that even the preachers may read them only once every two years on a sunny day when no fleck of cloud, even so big as a man's hand, can be seen in the sky. On each of the New York reservations (except Tuscarora, near Niagara Falls) there is a longhouse. The term "longhouse," used in its religious sense, includes the council house itself, where the Handsome Lake meetings (in addition to other community functions) are held; the general congregation of Handsome Lake followers; and the specific organization (including preachers and lay functionaries), which arranges the annual calendar of services. There are longhouses on the Allegany Reservation (near Salamanca, New York), on the Cattaraugus Reservation (near Gowanda), at Tonawanda (near Buffalo), at Onondaga (near Syracuse), at Oneida (on the Thames River in Ontario), at St. Regis (along the St. Lawrence River), at Grand River (near Brantford, Ontario), and at Caughnawaga (near Montreal). Handsome Lake himself did not design the organization that now carries on his work. He founded the religion; his followers organized its practice.

The Seneca Reservation on the Allegheny River, where Handsome Lake once lived, extends in a long, thin strip along the oxbow from the New York–Pennsylvania state line, east almost as far as Olean, and encompasses the city of Salamanca, whose white inhabitants lease their land from the Indians. It is about forty-two miles long and contains forty-two square miles. Driving through it in 1950, before the Kinzua Dam flooded much of the low-lying area, on a good macadam highway, one would see a scattering of old farmhouses, log cabins, and brightly painted prefabricated "ranch-style" bungalows with television antennas stretching skyward here and there to escape the mountain screen that rises on both sides of the river. At Onoville, Quaker Bridge, and Red House there are country stores, filling stations, and small clusters of houses. Many of the men divide their time between working for the Erie Railroad, which runs through the reserve, cultivating their gardens, and working around the house. The women are housewives; some of them serve as domestic servants, secretaries, and factory workers in Salamanca, Olean, or Jamestown. Many of the fields are growing up in weed and wood because farming, a century ago the economic mainstay of the people, is less profitable today than wage work. There are no real-estate taxes to pay. About eleven hundred Seneca people live on the reserve: white men in respect to their names, their manner of dress, and means of earning a living; Indians in their view of themselves as a minority group, separated from the surrounding world by the legal and economic arrangements that make up the reservation system, and identified with an Indian past. Great events in their history are not Columbus, and Plymouth Rock, and the Declaration of Independence. Rather, they remember, dimly and often not too accurately, the founding of the League of the Iroquois, the days of glory when an Iroquois hunter could walk safely from the Atlantic Ocean to the Miami River in Ohio, the dark days of Sullivan's Campaign, when their villages were burned, the disastrous treaties at Fort Stanwix and Big Tree and Buffalo Creek, the treaty at Canandaigua, which guaranteed their lands and which was overturned by Congress in order to build the dam, and the great revival led by Handsome Lake.

Thus, while to the casual eye these are only an American minority group, no darker in skin color than many southern European immigrants, and equipped (many of them) with television, cars, refrigerators, plumbing, central heating, and a high school or college education, the discerning eye sees a separate cultural world more ancient than memory.

The symbolic hub and pivot of this Seneca world is Cold Spring Longhouse: a one-story rectangular frame building, about fifty feet long and twenty wide, its long axis paralleling the road. It is of clapboard painted white, with a shingled gable roof, and it stands in a treeless field close to where Cold Spring Creek joins the Allegany River. Off to the side are an old log kitchen—said to be the remains of a much older longhouse that once stood near Carrollton, up the river—and a frame shed used as a dining room. The longhouse interior is sparsely furnished. At each end are two tiers of raised, grandstand-like benches, and two similar tiers stretch along the sides. Movable wooden benches, anciently painted and now almost bare, stand in front of the fixed seating tiers. These are arranged in various ways depending upon the use to which the longhouse is being put. In the center of the floor is a bench where drummers sit when there is dancing. Two iron stoves, one at each end, face each other; their stovepipes extend to the chimneys at the back walls. Six windows light the room, and two doors face the road: the one on the left, to the west, for the women; the one at the eastern end for the men. An invisible line separates the male and female halves of the longhouse, men and women entering separately by their proper doors and sitting apart. (But a newly married couple may be seen to separate as they enter and later on to sit touching one another across this sexual equator.) Special ritual equipment is kept in a loft, which can be reached by upending a bench and hoisting oneself from it through the trapdoor. In ground plan a longhouse looks like the drawing on the next page (the basic plan, with minor variations in the location of doors and windows and type of seating equipment, is to be found in all longhouses). This simple plan is little modified from aboriginal times, when instead of stoves there were firepits, and instead of chimneys a slot in the roof; when roof and walls were sheathed with elm bark, and there was no glass. As far back as the Seneca can remember, there has been a longhouse of one sort or another, where the people could assemble to discuss politics and war and peace or to worship the Great Spirit in thankful or penitent mood.

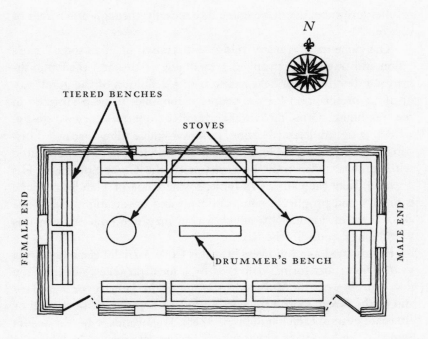

The heart of the Handsome Lake religion is the *Gaiwiio*, the "good word." This is the gospel—a gospel transmitted by word of mouth from preacher to preacher and memorized so that it can be chanted by a man standing in a longhouse filled with the noise of bustling people, slamming doors, and rattling stove grates, hour after hour, for the mornings of four days. Each preacher repeats a slightly different version, depending on which old man or woman he learned it from and on his own predilections and memory. Some of the preachers rattle off the *Gaiwiio* in a language so archaic that many of the words are meaningless to their own and their listeners' ears. Some tell the story of Handsome Lake's death—he was murdered by witchcraft—in awesome detail; others pass over it lightly out of consideration for the Onondaga tribe, on whose reservation he met his end as the victim of Onondaga witches. There is extant a verbatim translation of one preacher's version of the Code, edited by the anthropologist Arthur C. Parker and published by the New York State Museum. But this version has not supplanted the independent, parallel scriptures that have come down orally through other lines of speakers.[2]

The Code itself is many things: a narrative of Handsome Lake's vision and travels as a prophet, a catalogue of sins and their punishments, a description of heaven and hell, a definition of the good way of life, a prescription for the proper ceremonies to be performed in the longhouse. Drinking, witchcraft, theft, quarrelsomeness, gossip, wife-beating, adultery, abortion, jealousy—these things are evil. Husbands and wives are to love one another; children are to be treated with kindness; man must be reverent to the Great Spirit and His creation. Like the Christian's Bible, so the Code of Handsome Lake is history and prophecy, commandment and exhortation, and above all, a chart of conduct by which a man may live honorably in this world and happily in the next.

Handsome Lake followers hear this Code partially recited twice a year. This "short form," delivered by a local preacher, occupies the first morning of the Midwinter Ceremony in January or February and of the Green Corn Dance in August or September. In the fall of alternate years at each longhouse (except Tonawanda, where it occurs annually, and Sour Springs, which has an irregular schedule) the Code is recited in full by professional speakers at a religious "Six Nations Meeting." The full recitation occupies the mornings of four days. On the two former occasions the abbreviated Code has been grafted onto an ancient rite, but the Six Nations meetings are pure Handsome Lake and date from about 1845.

In October, 1951, a friend and I drove up from Philadelphia to see the "doings" at the Six Nations Meeting at Cold Spring Longhouse on the Allegany Reservation. We ate supper with an Indian family who were expecting us and had prepared a room in their comfortable old frame farmhouse. After supper we walked a couple of hundred yards to the longhouse to see what was going on. Visitors (the "comers") from the other reserves—Tonawanda, St. Regis, Caughnawaga, Cattaraugus, Onondaga, Grand River—were checking in. They had parked their cars in the field by the longhouse. As they entered, they were announced by the head of the reception committee and assigned a place to stay. (The delegates were asked their clan, and if they had not made other arrangements, a clan member was always ready to take them in.) Outside their end of the longhouse the women were running a food sale to raise money for the doings, which cost about five hundred dollars.

The first day of a Six Nations Meeting is called the handshaking. This is a formal reception for the visiting delegates. "There are no eats," as my informant said, "and only the faithful attend." The visiting delegates, after a few welcoming remarks by the head of the local reception committee, present their credentials—strings of wampum, consisting of half a dozen or so beads strung on a thong and attached to a notched stick, which identify the holder as the delegate from a particular longhouse. As each string is presented, the delegate in a long speech tenders the good wishes of each and every one of the congregation back home and details the composition of his party: the number of delegates, speakers, feather dancers, singers, and drummers. After all the strings are lined up on a bench, the hosts walk around the room, shaking hands with each of the twenty-five or thirty visitors. In the evening everyone, young and old, men and women, participates in social dances.

The next morning the real business of the meeting begins. The first part of the Code of Handsome Lake is recited by a guest preacher from another reservation. The preacher stands between the two fires in the longhouse. He is a middle-aged man, stocky, with a farmer's heavy hands and brown, lined face. Lank black hair straggles over his left eye. He is dressed in a baggy, threadbare, dark blue business suit with a blue workshirt and a brown string tie. On his feet, planted solidly and far apart on the pine flooring, are black, highly polished workshoes. As he speaks, his eyes are half closed and his head is tilted back, and he holds cradled before him in both hands a thick rope of white wampum strings. Behind him on a bench sits his assistant, holding the brown deerskin bag to which the wampum, carefully wrapped in a white handkerchief, will be returned when the preacher finishes speaking. The congregation are seated around the four sides of the longhouse: the women on his right, the men on his left. While he speaks, the men's heads are bare; but there is no ban against tobacco, and most of the men are chewing. Tin cans are scattered about on the floor as spittoons, and old-timers with expert eye use the hot shelf of the stove. From time to time men and women step outside to chat, to smoke, to visit the outhouses. Children are running in and out all the while, banging the doors. There is the constant rustle of feet, of whispers, of blue jeans sliding along wooden benches. A baby gurgles and is given the bottle. A man ticks reflectively on an "I Like Ike" button in his lapel. One of the deacons stamps over to the stove and rattles the grate. Someone begins to cough and cannot stop coughing and has to go out. But the speaker chants on, hour after hour, with eyes half closed, standing alone in the middle of the longhouse, holding in his hands before him the big shock of Handsome Lake wampum strings that serve as his credentials. The noise does not bother him, for it is no sign of irreverence. Now and then he stops to drink from the tin dipper of water his assistant fetches him. He finishes before noon, which is the meridian between sacred and profane time.

The first morning's recital tells the story of the death and rebirth of Handsome Lake. The Code has drifted, here and there, a little way off from the true relation. In one hundred and fifty years, tradition has accumulated small errors and illusions, and different preachers recite different versions. The preacher does not try to find and search through the old, mildewed diaries and letters of the Quaker missionaries or to compare differing versions of the tale in order to tease out the bare bones of history. "The beginning was in Yaikni [the lunar month in which the strawberries ripen], early in the moon, in the year 1800," he intones, and it does not matter that the year actually was 1799. For, in truth, it happened substantially as it is told: The early documents, the diary notations by one Quaker, the statements dictated by Handsome Lake himself, confirm most of the contents of the Code. The preacher repeats what old men remembered their prophet having said to them; the sayings, hoarded like jewels in the memory, have been only a little polished as they passed from hand to hand. Dozens of times have the listeners heard the same Code, delivered now by one, and now by another, of the many Handsome Lake preachers. Each one says it a little differently, but the substance is always the same, for the Seneca have cultivated, for hundreds of years, the techniques of verbal memory. An officially recognized speaker must have an almost phonographic memory: an ability to repeat, with proper inflection and emphasis, not only the sense, but even the exact words of treaties, of council decisions, of ambassadors— and of prophets. And so an aspiring preacher may, under the guidance of ambition, close his eyes and achieve almost total recall of the mumbled words of an old man reciting the Code by the fire, heard on winter evenings in his youth, forty years before. The speaker holds the *Gaiwiio* in his memory entire and plays it off for the people. In this way, even without benefit of written record, something approaching an imprint is handed down. One can even identify the "edition" of a particular speaker and trace it back through previous holders to the original disciple. This preacher is speaking from the "Blacksnake Edition," the version basically derived from Handsome Lake's nephew Blacksnake, who preached at Cold Spring on the Allegany Reservation and taught what he knew of the prophet's life and words to Owen Blacksnake, who taught it to Henry Stevens, who taught it to Edward Cornplanter, who taught it to the man now speaking.

After the *Gaiwiio* has been spoken, the Great Feather Dance begins. Two men straddle a bench in the middle of the floor where the preacher had been standing and hammer out the tempo on the bench with large turtle-shell rattles. The bench itself has been pounded by the sharp edges of turtle rattles for years; the wood is split and battered, and a ragged trough is hollowed out; soon it will need to be patched. The two men who lead the dance, which honors the Great Spirit, are dressed in elaborate, colorful Plains Indian headdresses, beaded shirts, trousers, and moccasins. They stomp and twirl, prance and rear and spin, while their followers—who include some of the most important men and women in the community—usually just shuffle.

After the Great Feather Dance everyone eats in the cookhouse dining room, where long tables and chairs borrowed from an undertaker have been set up with regular tablecloths, knives, forks, spoons, and china. The meal is substantial: salt pork, boiled potatoes, cold beets, cole slaw, applesauce, white pound cake, and green tea. It is paid for by the receiving longhouse, which for the last six months has been raising the money at cake-and-canned-goods sales, raffles, teas, and other "doings" where contributed items are sold.

In the afternoon there are two orders of business: the "interpretation" of portions of the text of the morning by various visitors who are responsible for the sacred part of the services, and "confession." In preparation for the confession two benches are arranged in front of the stoves, one for the women and one for the men. On this first day the visitors confess the local longhouse officials, first the three men, and then about six women.

This public confession is not a perfunctory matter, nor is it an ecstatic, "holy roller" kind of thing.[3] Each man begins confessing loudly, almost defiantly; then his voice subsides until it is almost inaudible; and then after a deep, shuddering breath he starts again. It is obvious that the participants are deeply moved. Cheek muscles twitch; sighs are heavy, spasmodic. As they speak they wheeze, they cough, they rub their eyes. Tremors course through the arms and legs of one man; he shivers as if with cold. They have publicly confessed their sins: one drunkenness; another quarreling with his wife; a third, the least upset, apparently, merely announces that he is sorry for the evil things he has done and is resolved to do them no more. They sit down, looking sheepish and relieved.

The women confess—most of them—more demurely, simply repeating the formula of admitting sin without specification, and repentance, and resolution to sin no more. One woman, however, is in the grip of a severe struggle. She waits until the longhouse matrons have all confessed and then climbs down from the spectators' gallery and sits with shoulders bowed on the confessional bench. She is silent for perhaps ten minutes, apparently unable to talk. She is a stolid-looking woman, but her face is turgid, almost blue in color. She looks at the floor, her face twitches, and she seems deeply depressed. When at last she takes hold of the strings of white wampum handed to her by the confessor, her whole body quivers. She speaks slowly, almost inaudibly, while her fingers stroke and caress the wampum as if it were her sole support. She confesses that she left the longhouse to become a Catholic; now she repents and wants to return to the longhouse. Tears roll down her cheeks; from time to time she dabs at her eyes with a handkerchief. The spectators listen very quietly, almost as if so much emotion were embarrassing to watch. After she stops speaking, the confessor, who had been standing in front of her, leaves and goes to the visitors' benches. She sits down trembling. A preacher from another reserve gets up and stands in front of her and harangues her for ten minutes. She slumps exhausted on the bench, her shoulders sagging. Then all the officials, local and visiting, and many of the congregation come up to shake hands with her. She goes back to her seat; two more preachers speak, and the meeting ends for the afternoon.

In the evening there are traditional social dances, consisting of the usual shuffling line winding around the singers' bench, always counterclockwise. There is a good crowd for this, and the mood is lively and jovial.

The remaining three days of the Six Nations Meeting follow the same pattern: the preaching of the *Gaiwiio* in the morning, sermons on the text, confessions and exhortations in the afternoon, social dances in the evening. During the morning *Gaiwiio*, on the second, third, and fourth days, strawberry juice in a bucket is handed around to the congregation and drunk from a dipper. There are several current explanations for the serving of the strawberry juice. Some say it is because the prophet's first revelation occurred at the time when the strawberries were ripe. Others say it is because there is a spring in heaven from which strawberry juice constantly bubbles forth. It is just a form of "blessing" on the people, according to a third view.

But the true reason is deeper than all these. Strawberries have been since ancient times, before the coming of white men, a special plant among the Seneca. The three angels first came to Handsome Lake during "the month of strawberries." In their first message they instructed Handsome Lake to call a council of the people, at which he was to tell them of his vision; and those who assembled to hear him the first time were to eat dried strawberries. This was shortly after the strawberries had ripened. The council was held, and the strawberries were eaten; and according to the story as it is told in the *Gaiwiio* today, every spring since that time there has been a Strawberry Festival, when the juice of the berry is drunk by old and young, and the Creator and His spirit-forces are thanked for the first fruits of the year and implored to allow all growing things to reach fruition. Whether or not Handsome Lake originated the Strawberry Festival, the sacred quality of strawberries is certainly older than Handsome Lake. The earliest of the wild strawberries are traditionally believed to have medicinal value and are searched out and devoured. Strawberries are said to sprout along the road to heaven, and a person who has come through a severe sickness will say, "I almost ate strawberries." In all probability, the fact that Handsome Lake's angels spoke to him of strawberries reflects the influence of the strawberry season on the content of his dream, and his subsequent endorsement of the Strawberry Festival probably emphasized a custom already old.

On the morning of the fourth and final day, the preacher completes his recitation of the *Gaiwiio*. When he comes to the part describing Handsome Lake's final agony and death, faces flush, and a few women weep and men dab their noses with handkerchiefs as the preacher sits down. Slowly and reverently the preacher's assistant folds the wampum and places it in the deerskin pouch. Men get up and stamp out. The Great Feather dancers peer shyly through the door. Someone comes up and shakes the preacher's hand. Two singers move a bench into the middle between the stoves. In the afternoon, after the last of the confessions, the "comers" turn the meeting back to the local hosts, and the chief of the Faithkeepers delivers a speech summarizing the doings. In the evening the last social dance is held; this is called "shoving off the canoes." And on the next day the comers depart, on their way to another longhouse, where the same ritual will be held.

Thus it is ended until the next time.

The doings of a longhouse are under the management and direction of four persons: a man and a woman from each of the two moieties, or "sides." These are called the Headmen and Headwomen. They are responsible for setting the times of ceremonies; for appointing persons to perform certain tasks such as preaching, managing the evening social dances, serving food, and carrying messages; and for arranging board and lodging for visitors. They function as a committee, and during a meeting one may frequently see one of them get up and cross the floor to hold a whispered conference with another. They combine the roles of the board of trustees and the minister, in his purely business administrative capacity, of a Protestant church. They are not usually civil chiefs or clan matrons; the religious longhouse organization is distinct and separate, in principle, from the political organization.

The terms "clan" and "sides" require some definition before further use. The population of many American Indian tribes is divided into anywhere from three or four to twenty-odd groupings which are technically called "sibs." The Seneca refer to them as "clans" in English. All the members of a clan are supposed, by tradition, to be descended from a common ancestor, even if available genealogical records cannot show a connection. But no one among the Seneca is very much concerned about the fancy of common ancestry. Clans almost always have animal names like Wolf, Bear, Heron, Sturgeon, Eagle. Among the Seneca there are eight clans: Wolf, Bear, Beaver, Turtle, Hawk, Snipe, Deer, and Heron. The newborn infant is automatically a member of his mother's clan unless he is "borrowed" or "adopted" by another in a formal ceremony. Men and women of the same clan ought not to marry, and still rarely do. Clan members are expected to maintain a generally friendly attitude toward one another, as if they were all members of one big and more or less happy family. When he is traveling, a Seneca may look first for lodging or food to other clansmen on a strange reservation where he has no particular friends. The clan, where the old order of chieftainships is maintained, is represented in national and confederate councils by its own chiefs, who are nominated by the clan matron, its oldest and most venerable woman.

Among the Seneca, the clans are classified into two "sides," or in technical jargon "moieties": Wolf, Bear, Beaver, and Turtle on one side, and Deer, Hawk, Snipe, and Heron on the other. The sides are not named; nevertheless they are extremely important in the structure of many ceremonies, for it is customary on many ritual occasions for one side to "give" the ceremony to another. The theme of reciprocal benefices between the two sides threads through all Seneca ritual arrangements. The Handsome Lake preacher and his assistant (the man who sits behind him on the bench holding the wampum, ready with a glass of water, available to prompt him if his memory fails) must be from opposite sides. The two sides literally sit on opposite sides of the longhouse on some reservations. At condolence ceremonies the bereaved moiety is condoled by the other side. Games like lacrosse and the Sacred Bowl Game may be played with moieties contesting. Whatever its origin, the moiety principle now provides a ready tool for the organization of reciprocal behavior on almost any ritual occasion.

Serving under the direction of the Headmen and Headwomen are the Faithkeepers. These men and women serve as the deacons of the longhouse: they fetch and carry, cook, serve at table, contribute money and labor, and generally perform lay services essential to the practice of ritual. Theoretically, the Faithkeepers should include a man and a woman from each clan, but there are usually some positions vacant. These assistants are the nucleus of the congregation, the most persistent in attendance, the most dutiful in confession, the most faithful participants in dancing, singing, and game playing.

The Headmen and Headwomen, and the male and female Faithkeepers, may also call upon persons who have no formal status in the longhouse organization to do minor jobs like waiting on table, lending equipment, drumming or singing, and dressing up as False Face dancers. The performance of these tasks merges gently into devout participation in the ritual itself, and in this sense every participant comes under the direction of those officials who are responsible for the proper conduct of this or that part of the ceremony.

The preachers—always men—have relatively little administrative responsibility. In this their role is very different from that of the priest or minister in a Christian church. The Handsome Lake preacher, a "holder of the *Gaiwiio*," has no other responsibility than to know the "good word" and to preach it effectively when he is called upon. Such men hold themselves somehow apart; they often strike the observer as a bit temperamental, tending to be a little vain of their knowledge, jealous of other preachers, somewhat patronizing in manner. They are the stars of the longhouse. Every longhouse has a string of these preachers, usually three or four, each of whom may know a slightly different version of the Code, varying according to the identity of the earlier preacher from whom he learned it, and to idiosyncrasies of memory, interpretation, and emphasis. Some of these men preach only before their own congregation; others have recited their version before a council of preachers at Tonawanda and are officially authorized to preach at other longhouses during Six Nations Meetings or on special invitation. The personal lives (including scandal) of these preachers, their manner of delivery, the peculiarities of their versions of the Code, are constant topics of discussion and comparison among the faithful. Since preachers are qualified by knowledge of the Code and not by purity of past—or even present—conduct, a famous preacher lives in a glare of sensational gossip. But it is also noteworthy that sometimes, by report at least, weak and wavering men who possessed a knowledge of the Code and were appointed preachers have through their identification with this role of great responsibility become transformed personalities, putting away such weaknesses as drunkenness, extreme shyness, or lecherousness to stand before the people as new men. The wampum of Handsome Lake does not rest lightly in a preacher's hands.

In addition to the organization of the local longhouse, there is an association of all the longhouses in a united religious body whose "head" is the longhouse "down below" at Tonawanda. Here are kept the wampum strings that Handsome Lake himself held as he preached; here the best preachers are qualified for interlonghouse speaking; and here, every fall, in September or October, delegates from each of the other ten longhouses (Cold Spring, Cattaraugus, Sour Springs, Lower Cayuga, St. Regis, Caughnawaga, Onondaga, Oneida, Grand River Onondaga, and Grand River Seneca) assemble to arrange that fall's itinerary of Six Nations meetings. Starting each time with a meeting at Tonawanda, the chosen delegates, led by an Onondaga master of ceremonies, spend a month or more on the road, visiting five long-houses where a Six Nations Meeting is held. Thus, in theory at least, each longhouse except Tonawanda has a meeting every other year; Tonawanda has one every year. And by the same token, every other year a delegation from each longhouse is supposed to take to the road and make the circuit of the others.

The annual calendar of the Old Way, however, includes much more than Six Nations meetings. In each longhouse there is also a round of much older ceremonies, long antedating Handsome Lake, which have been continued with only minor modification. Most of them are still performed in substantially the same manner as they were in pre-Columbian times. This cycle begins with the great festival of Midwinter, in January or February, five days after the first new moon following the zenith of the Pleiades. Next comes, by tradition, the Thanks-to-the-Maple, in early spring, when the sap rises and the maple sugar is running. In May or June, at corn-planting time, the seeds of garden vegetables are blessed, "our Grandfathers the Thun-ders" are asked to water the crops, and "our Elder Brother the Sun" is begged to be careful not to burn the young plants. June is the time of the Strawberry Festival, the first fruits ceremony. Late in August or September the second great festival is held: the Green Corn Dance, which rivals the Midwinter Festival in length and solemnity. And later in the fall, when the corn is dried and put away and the nation is pre-paring for winter, the cycle closes with a Thanksgiving Ceremony, which renders thanks to the Creator for the harvest and bids the corn rest for the winter while the people hunt.

These ancient pagan festivals, revolving around the universal themes of birth and death, love and hate, food and hunger, health and disease, were old when Handsome Lake was born. In their embrace he found solace, and theirs is the Old Way that his "new religion" recommends to the faithful. There is matter enough in them to give meaning to life. The drums beat in high, quick pitch; the dancers twirl and stamp the floor; the masked men cavort about the fire, sifting hot coals through their hands as if they were playing with cool dust; and the ancient words drone on, words about the deepest human hopes, longings, fears, and pain, words spoken by those spirit-forces that men may see in dreams, the elder brothers and fathers and grandfathers, even up to the Creator Himself. . . .

Let us now see how it all began, this new religion, which in itself was not all new, and which now is called the Old Way of Handsome Lake.

I

THE HEYDAY

OF THE

IROQUOIS

2

THE SENECA NATION
OF INDIANS

THE WORLD IN WHICH HANDSOME LAKE GREW TO MANHOOD, AND IN which he took his place as an active hunter and warrior, was the world of an unvanquished Indian nation: the Seneca, the most populous and the most powerful of the confederated Iroquois tribes. They numbered about four thousand souls, and their tribal territory extended from the upper waters of the Allegheny and the Susquehanna rivers, on the south, to Lake Ontario, on the north. The western marches of the Seneca territory were the shores of Lake Erie. On the east, beyond Seneca Lake, were the Cayuga people. The other Iroquois tribes—Onondaga, Oneida (and Tuscarora), and Mohawk—lay successively eastward almost to the Hudson River. The whole area occupied by the Iroquoian confederacy between the Hudson River and Lake Erie was compared by the Iroquois themselves to a longhouse compartmented by tribes; and in this longhouse the Seneca were "the keepers of the western door." They were guardians of that portal from which Iroquois warriors traditionally issued to attack the western and southern nations, through which Iroquois hunters passed to exploit the conquered lands along the Allegheny and Ohio, and on which other nations, in friendship or in war, must knock before entering the home country of the confederacy. Their warriors ranged from Hudson's Bay to the mountains of the Carolinas, and from the

Atlantic to the Mississippi, fighting against members of alien tribes and, on occasion, against the French and the English; their chiefs and orators sat in council, year after year, with Europeans in the colonial capitals, working out a *modus vivendi* with the invaders. To be a Seneca was to be a member of one of the most feared, most courted, and most respected Indian tribes in North America.

· *Villagers, Warriors, and Statesmen* ·

A SENECA VILLAGE in the eighteenth century was a few dozen houses scattered in a meadow. No plan of streets or central square defined a neat settlement pattern. The older men remembered days when towns were built between the forks of streams, protected by moats and palisades, and the dwellings within regularly spaced. But these fortified towns were no longer made, partly because of their earlier vulnerability to artillery and partly because times had become more peaceful anyway after the close of the fifty-odd years of war between 1649 and 1701. Now a village was simply an area within which individual families and kin groups built or abandoned their cabins at will; such focus as the area had for its several hundred inhabitants was provided by the council house (itself merely an enlarged dwelling), where the religious and political affairs of the community were transacted. Year by year the size of a village changed, depending on wars and rumors of war, the shifts of the fur trade, private feuds and family quarrels, the reputation of chiefs, the condition of the soil for corn culture, and the nearness of water and firewood. The same village might, over a hundred years' time, meander over a settlement area ten or fifteen miles square, increasing and decreasing in size, sometimes splitting up into several little settlements and sometimes coalescing into one, and even acquiring (and dropping) new names in addition to the generic name, which usually endured.

The traditional Iroquois dwelling unit was called a longhouse. It was a dark, noisy, smoke-filled family barracks; a rectangular, gable-roofed structure anywhere from fifty to seventy-five feet in length, constructed of sheets of elm bark lashed on stout poles, housing up to fifty or sixty people. The roof was slotted (sometimes with a sliding panel for rainy days) to let out some of the smoke that eddied about the ceiling. There was only one entrance, sometimes fitted with

a wooden or bark door on wooden hinges, and sometimes merely cur-
tained by a bearskin robe. Entering, one gazed in the half-light down
a long, broad corridor or alleyway, in the center of which, every
twelve or fifteen feet, smoldered a small fire. On opposite sides of each
fire, facing one another, were double-decker bunks, six feet wide and
about twelve feet long. An entire family—mother, father, children,
and various other relatives—might occupy one or two of these com-
partments. They slept on soft furs in the lower bunks. Guns, masks,
moccasins, clothing, cosmetic paint, wampum, knives, hatchet, food,
and the rest of a Seneca family's paraphernalia were slung on the walls
and on the upper bunk. Kettles, braided corn, and other suspendable
items hung from the joists, which also supported pots over the fire.
Each family had about as much room for permanent quarters as might
be needed for all of them to lie down and sleep, cook their meals, and
stow their gear. Privacy was not easily secured because other families
lived in the longhouse; people were always coming and going, and the
fires glowed all night. In cold or wet weather or when the snow lay
two or three feet deep outside, doors and roof vents had to be closed,
and the longhouses became intolerably stuffy—acrid with smoke and
the reeking odors of leftover food and sweating flesh. Eyes burned
and throats choked. But the people were nonetheless tolerably warm,
dry, and (so it is said) cheerful.

The inhabitants of a longhouse were usually kinfolk. A multifamily
longhouse was, theoretically, the residence of a maternal lineage: an
old woman and her female descendants, together with unmarried sons,
and the husbands and children of her married daughters. The totem
animal of the clan to which the lineage belonged—Deer, Bear, Wolf,
Snipe, or whatever it might be—was carved above the door and
painted red. In this way directions were easier to give, and the stranger
knew where to seek hospitality or aid. But often—especially in the
middle of the eighteenth century—individual families chose to live by
themselves in smaller cabins, only eighteen by twenty feet or so in
size, with just one fire. As time went on, the old longhouses disinte-
grated and were abandoned, and by the middle of the century the
Iroquois were making their houses of logs.

Around and among the houses lay the cornfields. Corn was a main
food. Dried and pounded into meal and then boiled into a hot mush,
baked into dumplings, or cooked in whole kernels together with beans
and squash and pieces of meat in the thick soups that always hung in

kettles over the fires, it kept the people fed. In season, meats, fresh fruits, herb teas, fried grasshoppers, and other delicacies added spice and flavor to the diet. But the Iroquois were a cornfed people. They consumed corn when it was fresh and stored it underground for the lean winter months. The Seneca nation alone raised as much as a million bushels of corn each year; the cornfields around a large village might stretch for miles, and even scattered clearings in the woods were cultivated. Squash, beans, and tobacco were raised in quantity, too. Domesticated animals were few, even after the middle of the century: some pigs, a few chickens, not many horses or cattle. The responsibility for carrying on this extensive agricultural establishment rested almost entirely on the women. Armed with crude wooden hoes and digging-sticks, they swarmed over the fields in gay, chattering work bees, proceeding from field to field to hoe, to plant, to weed, and to harvest. An individual woman might, if she wished, "own" a patch of corn, or an apple or peach orchard, but there was little reason for insisting on private tenure: the work was more happily done communally, and in the absence of a regular market, a surplus was of little personal advantage, especially if the winter were hard and other families needed corn. In such circumstances hoarding led only to hard feelings and strained relations as well as the possibility of future difficulty in getting corn for oneself and one's family. All land was national land; an individual could occupy and use a portion of it and maintain as much privacy in the tenure as he wished, but this usufruct title reverted to the nation when the land was abandoned. There was little reason to bother about individual ownership of real estate anyway: there was plenty of land. Economic security for both men and women lay in a proper recognition of one's obligation to family, clan, community, and nation, and in efficient and cooperative performance on team activities, such as working bees, war parties, and diplomatic missions.

If the clearing with its cornfields bounded the world of women, the forest was the realm of men. Most of the men hunted extensively, not only for deer, elk, and small game to use for food and clothing and miscellaneous household items, but for beaver, mink, and otter, the prime trade furs. Pelts were the gold of the woods. With them a man could buy guns, powder, lead, knives, hatchets, axes, needles and awls, scissors, kettles, traps, cloth, ready-made shirts, blankets, paint (for cosmetic purposes), and various notions: steel springs to pluck out disfiguring beard, scalp, and body hair; silver bracelets and armbands and tubes for coiling hair; rings to hang from nose and ears; mirrors; tinkling bells. Sometimes a tipsy hunter would give away his peltries for a keg of rum, treat his friends to a debauch, and wake up with a scolding wife and hungry children calling him a fool; another might, with equal improvidence, invest in a violin, or a horse, or a gaudy military uniform. But by and large, the products of the commercial hunt—generally conducted in the winter and often hundreds of miles from the home village, in the Ohio country or down the Susquehanna River —were exchanged for a limited range of European consumer goods, which had become, after five generations of contact with beaver-hungry French, Dutch, and English traders, economic necessities. Many of these goods were, indeed, designed to Indian specifications and manufactured solely for the Indian trade. An Iroquois man dressed in a linen breechcloth and calico shirt, with a woolen blanket over his shoulders, bedaubed with trade paint and adorned with trade armbands and earrings, carrying a steel knife, a steel hatchet, a clay pipe, and a rifled gun felt himself in no wise contaminated nor less an Indian than his stone-equipped great-great-grandfather. Iroquois culture had reached out and incorporated these things that Iroquois Indians wanted while at the same time Iroquois warriors chased off European missionaries, battled European soldiers to a standstill, and made obscene gestures when anyone suggested that they should emulate white society (made up, according to their information and experience, of slaves, cheating lawyers with pen and paper and ink, verbose politicians, hypocritical Christians, stingy tavern keepers, and thieving peddlers).

Behavior was governed not by published laws enforced by police, courts, and jails, but by oral tradition supported by a sense of duty, a fear of gossip, and a dread of retaliatory witchcraft. Theft, vandalism, armed robbery, were almost unknown. Public opinion, gently exercised, was sufficient to deter most persons from property crimes, for public opinion went straight to the heart of the matter: the *weakness* of the criminal. A young warrior steals someone else's cow—probably captured during a raid on a white settlement—and slaughters it to feed his hungry family. He does this at a time when other men are out fighting. No prosecution follows, no investigation, no sentence: the unhappy man is nonetheless severely punished, for the nickname "Cow-killer" is pinned to him, and he must drag it rattling behind him wherever he goes. People call him a coward behind his back and snicker when they tell white men, in his presence, a story of an un-named Indian who killed cows when he should have been killing men. Such a curse was not generalized to the point of ostracism, however. The celebrated Red Jacket, about whom the "Cow-killer" story was told, vindicated his courage in later wars, became the principal spokes-man for his nation, and was widely respected and revered. But he never lost the nickname.[1]

Disputes between people rarely developed over property. Marital difficulties centering around infidelity, lack of support, or personal incompatibility were settled by mutual agreement. Commonly, in case of difficulty, the man left and the woman, with her children, re-mained with her mother. A few couples remained together for a life-time; most had several marriages; a few changed mates almost with the season. Men might come to blows during drunken arguments over real or fancied slights to their masculine honor, over politics, or over the alleged mistreatment of their kinfolk. Such quarrels led at times to killings or to accusations of witchcraft. A murder (or its equivalent, the practice of witchcraft) was something to be settled by the victim's kinfolk; if they wished, they might kill the murderer or suspected witch without fear of retaliation from his family (provided that family agreed on his guilt). But usually a known killer would come to his senses, admit himself wrong, repent, and offer retribution in goods or services to the mourning family, who unless exceptionally embit-tered by an unprovoked and brutal killing were then expected to accept the blood money and end the matter.

Drunkenness was perhaps the most serious social problem. Two Moravian missionaries who visited the Iroquois country in 1750 had the misfortune to reach the Seneca towns at the end of June, when the men were just returning from Oswego, where they had sold their winter's furs, and were beginning to celebrate the start of summer leisure. Hard liquor was dissolving winter's inhibitions and regrets. At Canandaigua, the missionaries, who were guests at the house of a prominent warrior, had just explained the friendly nature of their errand when the rum arrived. "All the town was in a state of intoxica-tion, and frequently rushed into our hut in this condition," complained the white men. "There was every reason to think that fighting might ensue, as there were many warriors among those who were perfectly mad with drink." After a sleepless night the missionaries traveled on, reaching the outskirts of Geneseo on the second of July. "The village," said the observers in surprise, "consisted of 40 or more large huts, and lies in a beautiful and pleasant region. A fine large plain, several miles in length and breadth, stretches out behind the village." But the kegs of rum had anticipated them. "When we caught sight of the town we heard a great noise of shouting and quarreling, from which we could infer that many of the inhabitants were intoxicated, and that we might expect to have an uncomfortable time. On entering the town we saw many drunken Indians, who looked mad with drink. . . ."

Alas, poor Christians! They had to hide in a stuffy garret, without food or water. David, their devoted Indian convert and servant, stole out toward evening with a kettle to fetch his masters some water and was seen. "A troop of drunken women came rushing madly toward him. Some of them were naked, and others nearly so. In order to drive them away he was obliged to use his fists, and deal blows to the right and left. He climbed up a ladder, but when he had scarcely reached the top they seized it and tore it from under his feet." David barely managed to escape "in safety" from these playful Amazons. The missionaries decided not to wait the two days until the liquor ran out to meet the chiefs in council; they bent their prayers to an early departure. They finally managed to escape at dawn by jumping down from an opening in the gable and tiptoeing away. "The Lord watched over us in such a manner that all the drunken savages were in their huts, not a creature to be seen. Even the dogs, numbering nearly 100 in the whole village, were all quiet, wonderful to relate, and not a sound was heard. A dense fog covered the town, so that we could not see 20 steps before us. A squaw stood at the door of the last hut, but she was sober and returned our greeting quietly."[2]

But such drunken debauches were only occasional rents in a fabric of polite social behavior. Other missionaries were more favorably impressed than the Moravians. The Seneca, said a Quaker scribe, "appear to be naturally as well calculated for social and rational enjoyment, as any people. They frequently visit each other in their houses, and spend much of their time in friendly intercourse. They are also mild and hospitable, not only among themselves, but to strangers, and good natured in the extreme, except when their natures are perverted by the inflammatory influence of spirituous liquors. In their social interviews, as well as public councils, they are careful not to interrupt one another in conversation, and generally make short speeches. This truly laudable mark of good manners, enables them to transact all their public business with decorum and regularity, and more strongly impresses on their mind and memory, the result of their deliberations."[3]

· The Iroquois "Matriarchate" ·

DURING THE SEVENTEENTH and eighteenth centuries Iroquois men earned a reputation among the French and English colonists for being the most astute diplomatically and most dangerous militarily of all the Indians of the Northeast. Yet at the same time the Iroquois were famous for the "matriarchal" nature of their economic and social institutions. After the colonial era came to an end with the victory of the United States in the Revolutionary War, the traditional diplomatic and military role of the Iroquois men was sharply limited by the circumstances of reservation life. Simultaneously, the "matriarchal" character of certain of their economic, kinship, and political institutions was drastically diminished. These changes were codified by the prophet Handsome Lake. As we shall see later in more detail, the changes in kinship behavior that he recommended, and which to a considerable degree were carried out by his followers, amounted to a shift in dominance from the mother-daughter relationship to that of the husband-wife. Handsome Lake's reforms thus were a sentence of doom upon the traditional quasi-matriarchal system of the Iroquois.

The Iroquois were described as matriarchal because of the important role women played in the formal political organization. The men were responsible for hunting, for warfare, and for diplomacy, all of which kept them away from their households for long periods of time, and all of which were essential to the survival of Iroquois society. An expedition of any kind was apt to take months or even years, for the fifteen thousand or so Iroquois in the seventeenth and eighteenth centuries ranged over an area of about a million square miles. It is not an exaggeration to say that the full-time business of an Iroquois man was travel, in order to hunt, trade, fight, and talk in council. But the women stayed at home. Thus, an Iroquois village might be regarded as a collection of strings, hundreds of years old, of successive generations of women, always domiciled in their longhouses near their cornfields in a clearing while their sons and husbands traveled in the forest on supportive errands of hunting and trapping, of trade, of war, and of diplomacy.

The women exercised political power in three main circumstances. First, whenever one of the forty-nine chiefs of the great intertribal League of the Iroquois died, the senior women of his lineage nominated his successor. Second, when tribal or village decisions had to be made, both men and women attended a kind of town meeting, and while men were the chiefs and normally did the public speaking, the women caucused behind the scenes and lobbied with the spokesmen. Third, a woman was entitled to demand publicly that a murdered kinsman or kinswoman be replaced by a captive from a non-Iroquois tribe, and her male relatives, particularly lineage kinsmen, were morally obligated to go out in a war party to secure captives, whom the bereaved woman might either adopt or consign to torture and death. Adoption was so frequent during the bloody centuries of the beaver wars and the colonial wars that some Iroquois villages were preponderantly composed of formally adopted war captives. In sum, Iroquois women were entitled formally to select chiefs, to participate in consensual politics, and to start wars.

Thus the Iroquois during the two centuries of the colonial period were a population divided, in effect, into two parts: sedentary females and nomadic males. The men were frequently absent in small or large groups for prolonged periods of time on hunting, trading, war, and diplomatic expeditions, simultaneously protecting the women from foreign attack and producing a cash crop of skins, furs, and scalps, which they exchanged for hardware and dry goods. These activities, peripheral in a geographical sense, were central to the economic and political welfare of the Six Nations. The preoccupation of Iroquois men with these tasks and the pride they took in their successful pursuit cannot be overestimated. But the system depended on a complementary role for women. They had to be economically self-sufficient through horticulture during the prolonged absences of men, and they maintained genealogical and political continuity in a matrilineal system in which the primary kin relationship (not necessarily the primary social relationship) was the one between mother and daughter.

Such a quasi-matriarchy, of course, had a certain validity in a situation where the division of labor between the sexes required that men be geographically peripheral to the households that they helped to support and did defend. Given the technological, economic, and military circumstances of the time, such an arrangement was a practical one. But it did have an incidental consequence: It made the relationship between husband and wife an extremely precarious one. Under these conditions it was convenient for the marital system to be based on virtually free sexual choice, the mutual satisfaction of spouses, and easy separation. Couples chose one another for personal reasons; free choice was limited, in effect, only by the prohibition of intraclan marriage. Marriages were apt to fray when a husband traveled too far, too frequently, for too long. On his return, drunken quarreling, spiteful gossip, parental irresponsibility, and flagrant infidelity might lead rapidly to the end of the relationship. The husband, away from the household for long periods of time, was apt in his travels to establish a liaison with a woman whose husband was also away. The wife, temporarily abandoned, might for the sake of comfort and economic convenience take up with a locally available man. Since such relationships were, in effect, in the interest of everyone in the longhouse, they readily tended to become recognized as marriages. The emotional complications introduced by these serial marriages were supposed to be resolved peacefully by the people concerned. The traveling husband who returned to find his wife living with someone else might try to recover her; if she preferred to remain with her new husband, however, he was not entitled to punish her or her new lover, but instead was encouraged to find another wife among the unmarried girls or wives with currently absent husbands.[4]

· The Ideal of Autonomous Responsibility ·

THE BASIC IDEAL of manhood was that of "the good hunter." Such a man was self-disciplined, autonomous, responsible. He was a patient and efficient huntsman, a generous provider to his family and nation, and a loyal and thoughtful friend and clansman. He was also a stern and ruthless warrior in avenging any injury done to those under his care. And he was always stoical and indifferent to privation, pain, and even death. Special prominence could be achieved by those who, while adequate in all respects, were outstanding in one or another dimension of this ideal. The patient and thoughtful man with a skin "seven thumbs thick" (to make him indifferent to spiteful gossip, barbed wit, and social pressures generally) might become a sachem or a "distinguished name"—a "Pine Tree" chief. An eloquent man with a good memory and indestructible poise might be a council speaker and represent clan, nation, even the confederacy in far-flung diplomatic ventures. And the stern and ruthless warrior (always fighting, at least according to the theory, to avenge the death or insult of a blood relative or publicly avowed friend) might become a noted warcaptain or an official war-chief. The war-captain ideal, open as it was to all youths, irrespective of clan and lineage or of special intellectual qualifications, was perhaps the most emulated.

In the seventeenth century an Onondaga war-captain named Aharihon bore the reputation of being the greatest warrior of the country. He realized the ideal of autonomous responsibility to virtually pathological perfection. Let us note what is told of Aharihon in the *Jesuit Relations*.[5]

Aharihon was a man of dignified appearance and imposing carriage, grave, polished in manner, and self-contained. His brother had been killed about 1654 in the wars with the Erie, a tribe westward of the Iroquois. As clansman and close relative, he was entitled—indeed obligated—either to avenge his brother's death by killing some Erie people or by adopting a war captive to take his place. Aharihon within a few years captured or had presented to him for adoption forty men. Each of them he burned to death over a slow fire, because, as he said, "he did not believe that there was any one worthy to occupy his [brother's] place." Father Lalemant was present when another young man, newly captured, was given to Aharihon as a substitute for the deceased brother. Aharihon let the young man believe that he was adopted and need have no further fear, and "presented to him four dogs, upon which to hold his feast of adoption. In the middle of the feast, while he was rejoicing and singing to entertain the guests, Aharihon arose, and told the company that this man too must die in atonement for his brother's death. The poor lad was astounded at this, and turned toward the door to make his escape, but was stopped by two men who had orders to burn him. On the fourteenth of February, in the evening, they began with his feet, intending to roast him, at a slow fire, as far up as the waist, during the greater part of the night. After midnight, they were to let him rally his strength and sleep a little until daybreak, when they were to finish this fatal tragedy. In his torture, the poor man made the whole village resound with his cries and groans. He shed great tears, contrary to the usual custom, the victim commonly glorying to be burned limb by limb, and opening his lips only to sing; but, as this one had not expected death, he wept and cried in a way that touched even these Barbarians. One of Aharihon's relatives was so moved with pity, that he advised ending the sufferer's torments by plunging a knife into his breast—which would have been a deed of mercy, had the stab been mortal. However, they were induced to continue the burning without interruption, so that before day he ended both his sufferings and his life." Aharihon's career of death continued without interruption, and by 1663 he was able to boast that he had killed sixty men with his own hand and had burned fully eighty men over slow fire. He kept count by tattooing a mark on his thigh for each successive victim. He was known then as the Captain General of the Iroquois and was nicknamed Nero by the Frenchmen at Montreal because of his cruelty.

The French finally captured him near Montreal, but even in captivity his manner was impressive. "This man," commented Father Lalemant, "commonly has nine slaves with him, five boys and four girls. He is a captain of dignified appearance and imposing carriage, and of such equanimity and presence of mind that, upon seeing himself surrounded by armed men, he showed no more surprise than if he had been alone; and when asked whether he would like to accompany us to Quebec, he deigned only to answer coldly that that was not a question to ask him, since he was in our power. Accordingly he was made to come aboard our Vessel, where I took pleasure in studying his disposition as well as that of an Algonquin in our company, who bore the scalp of an Iroquois but recently slain by him in war. These two men, although hostile enough to eat each other, chatted and laughed on board that Vessel with great familiarity, it being very hard to decide which of the two was more skillful in masking his feelings. I had Nero placed near me at table, where he bore himself with a gravity, a self-control, and a propriety, which showed nothing of his Barbarian origin; but during the rest of the time he was constantly eating, so that he fasted only when he was at table."

But this voracious captain was not renowned among the Onondaga as a killer only. He was, on the contrary, also a trusted ambassador, dispatched on occasion to Montreal on missions of peace. He was, in a word, a noted man. He was a killer, but he was not an indiscriminate killer; he killed only those whom it was his right to kill, tortured only those whom he had the privilege of torturing, always as an expression of respect for his dead brother. And although his kinfolk sometimes felt he was a little extreme in his stern devotion to his brother's memory, they did not feel that he was any the less a fine man, or that they had a right to interfere with his impulses; they were willing to entrust the business of peace, as well as war, to his hand.

A century and a half later Mary Jemison, the captive white woman who lived for most of her life among the Seneca on the Genesee River, described her Indian husband in not dissimilar terms. "During the term of nearly fifty years that I lived with him," she recalled, "I received, according to Indian customs, all the kindness and attention that was my due as his wife.—Although war was his trade from his youth till old age and decrepitude stopt his career, he uniformly treated me with tenderness, and never offered an insult. . . . He was a man of tender feelings to his friends, ready and willing to assist them in distress, yet, as a warrior, his cruelties to his enemies perhaps were unparalleled. . . . In early life, Hiokatoo showed signs of thirst for blood, by attending only to the art of war, in the use of the tomahawk and scalping knife; and in practising cruelties upon every thing that chanced to fall into his hands, which was susceptible of pain. In that way he learned to use his implements of war effectually, and at the same time blunted all those fine feelings and tender sympathies that are naturally excited, by hearing or seeing, a fellow being in distress. He could inflict the most excruciating tortures upon his enemies, and prided himself upon his fortitude, in having performed the most barbarous ceremonies and tortures, without the least degree of pity or remorse. . . . In those battles he took a number of Indians prisoners, whom he killed by tying them to trees and then setting small Indian boys to shooting at them with arrows, till death finished the misery of the sufferers; a process that frequently took two days for its completion! . . . At Braddock's defeat he took two white prisoners, and burnt them alive in a fire of his own kindling. . . ."[6]

With this sort of man serving as an ego-ideal, held up by sanction and by praise to youthful eyes, it is not remarkable that young men were ambitious to begin the practice of war. All had seen captives tortured to death; all had known relatives lost in war whose death demanded revenge or replacement. The young men went out on practice missions as soon as they were big enough to handle firearms; "infantile bands, armed with hatchets and guns which they can hardly

(33)

carry, do not fail to spread fear and horror everywhere."[7] Even as late as the middle of the eighteenth century, Handsome Lake and his brothers and nephews were still busy at the old business of war for the sake of war. Cornplanter became a noted war-captain; Blacksnake, his nephew, was one of the official war-chiefs of the Seneca nation; and Handsome Lake himself took part in the scalping-party pattern as a young man. But Handsome Lake became a sachem and later a prophet, and he never gloried in the numbers of men he killed as his brother Cornplanter (somewhat guiltily) did. "While I was in the use of arms I killed seven persons and took three and saved their lives," said Cornplanter. And Blacksnake, in later life, told with relish of his exploits as a warrior. "We had a good fight there," he would say. "I have killed how many I could not tell, for I pay no attention to or kept [no] account of it, it was great many, for I never have it at all my Battles to think about kepting account what I'd killed at one time. . . ."[8]

The cultivation of the ideal of autonomous responsibility—and the suppression of its antinomy, dependency—began early in life. Iroquois children were carefully trained to think for themselves but to act for others. Parents were protective, permissive, and sparing of punishment; they encouraged children to play at imitating adult behavior but did not criticize or condemn fumbling early efforts; they maintained a cool detachment, both physically and verbally, avoiding the intense confrontations of love and anger between parent and child to which Europeans were accustomed. Children did not so much live in a child's world as grow up freely in the interstices of an adult culture. The gain was an early self-reliance and enjoyment of responsibility; the cost, perhaps, was a lifelong difficulty in handling feelings of dependency.

The Seneca mother gave birth to her child in the privacy of the woods, where she retired for a few hours when her time came, either alone or in the company of an older woman who served as midwife and, if the weather was cold, built and tended a fire. She had prepared for this event by eating sparingly and exercising freely, which were believed (probably with good reason) to make the child stronger and the birth easier. The newborn infant was washed in cold water, or even in snow, immediately after parturition and then wrapped in skins or a blanket. If the birth were a normal one, the mother walked back to the village with her infant a few hours afterwards to take up the duties of housewife. The event was treated as the consummation of a healthful process rather than as an illness. The infant spent much of its first nine months swaddled from chin to toe and lashed to a cradle-board. The child's feet rested against a footboard; a block of wood was placed between the heels of a girl to mold her feet to an inward turn. Over its head stretched a hoop, which could be draped with a thin cloth to keep away flies or to protect the child from the cold. The board and its wrappings were often lavishly decorated with silver trinkets and beadwork embroidery. The mother was able to carry the child in the board, suspended against her back, by a tumpline around her forehead; the board could be hung from the limb of a tree while she hoed corn; and it could be converted into a crib by suspending it on a rack of poles laid horizontally on forks stuck in the ground. The mother was solicitous of the child's comfort, nursed it whenever it cried, and loosened it from the board several times a day to change the moss that served as a diaper and to give it a chance to romp. The children, however, tended to cry when released from the board, and their tranquility could often be restored only by putting them back. Babies were seldom heard crying.

The mother's feeling for her children was intense; indeed, to one early observer it appeared that "Parental Tenderness" was carried to a "dangerous Indulgence."[9] Another early writer remarked, "The mothers love their children with an extreme passion, and although they do not reveal this in caresses, it is nevertheless real."[10] Mothers were quick to express resentment of any restraint or injury or insult offered to the child by an outsider. During the first few years the child stayed almost constantly with the mother, in the house, in the fields, or on the trail, playing and performing small tasks under her direction. The mother's chief concern during this time was to provide for the child and to protect it, to "harden" it by baths in cold water, but not to punish. Weaning was not normally attempted until the age of three or four, and such control as the child obtained over its excretory functions was achieved voluntarily, not as a result of consistent punishment for mistakes. Early sexual curiosity and experimentation were regarded as a natural childish way of behaving, out of which it would, in due time, grow. Grandparents might complain that small children got into everything, but the small child was free to romp, to pry into things, to demand what it wanted, and to assault its parents, without more hazard of punishment than the exasperated mother's occasionally blowing water in its face or dunking it in a convenient river.

The years between about eight or nine and the onset of puberty were a time of easy and gradual learning. At the beginning of this period the beginnings of the differentiation of the roles of boys and girls were laid down. The girls were kept around the house, under the guidance of their mothers, and assigned to the lighter household duties and to helping in the fields. Boys were allowed to roam in gangs, playing at war, hunting with bows and arrows and toy hatchets, and competing at races, wrestling, and lacrosse. The first successes at hunting were greeted with praise and boasts of future greatness. Sometimes these roaming gangs spent days at a time away from the village, sleeping in the bush, eating wild roots and fruits, and hunting such small game as could be brought down by bow and arrow, blowgun, or snare. These gangs developed into war parties after the boys reached puberty. Among themselves, both in gangs and among siblings of the same family, the children's playgroups were not constantly supervised by parents and teachers, and the children governed themselves in good harmony. Said one close observer, "Children of the same family show strong attachments to each other, and are less liable to quarrel in their youthful days than is generally the case with white children."[11]

The parents usually tried to maintain a calm moderation of behavior in dealing with their children, a lofty indifference alike to childish tantrums and seductive appeals for love. Hardihood, self-reliance, and independence of spirit were sedulously inculcated. When occasion presented itself, fathers, uncles, or other elder kinfolk instructed their sons in the techniques of travel, firemaking, the chase, war, and other essential arts of manhood, and the mothers correspondingly taught their daughters the way to hoe and plant the cornfields, how to butcher the meat, cook, braid corn, and other household tasks. But this instruction was presented, rather than enforced, as an opportunity rather than as a duty. On occasion the parent or other responsible adult talked to the child at length, "endeavoring," as a Quaker scribe gently put it, "to impress on its mind what it ought to do, and what to leave undone."[12] If exhortation seemed inadequate in its effect, the mentor might ridicule the child for doing wrong, or gravely point out the folly of a certain course of action, or even warn him that he courted the rage of offended supernatural beings. Obedience as such was no virtue, however, and blows, whippings, or restraints of any kind, such as restriction to quarters, were rarely imposed, the faults of the child being left to his own reason and conscience to correct as he grew mature. With delicate perception the adults noted that childish faults "cannot be very great, before reason arrives at some degree of maturity."[13]

Direct confrontation with the child was avoided, but when things got seriously out of hand, parents sometimes turned older children over to the gods for punishment. A troublesome child might be sent out into the dusk to meet Longnose, the legendary Seneca bogeyman. Longnose might even be impersonated in the flesh by a distraught parent. Longnose was a hungry cannibal who chased bad children when their parents were sleeping. He mimicked the child, crying loudly as he ran, but the parents would not wake up because Longnose had bewitched them. A child might be chased all night until he submitted and promised to behave. Theoretically, if a child remained stubborn, Longnose finally caught him and took him away in a huge pack-basket for a leisurely meal. And—although parents were not supposed to do this—an unusually stubborn infant *could* be threatened with punishment by the great False Faces themselves, who, when invoked for this purpose, might "poison" a child or "spoil his face." "I remember," recalled a Cayuga woman of her childhood, "how scared I was of the False-faces; I didn't know what they were. They are to scare away disease. They used to come into the house and up the stairs and I used to hide away under the covers. They even crawled under the bed and they made that awful sound. When I was bad my mother used to say the False-faces would get me. Once, I must have been only 4 or 5, because I was very little when I left Canada, but I remember it so well that when I think of it I can hear that cry now, and I was going along a road from my grandfather's; it was a straight road and I couldn't lose my way, but it was almost dark, and I had to pass through some timber and I heard that cry and that rattle. I ran like a flash of lightening and I can hear it yet."[14]

At puberty some of the boys retired to the woods under the stewardship of an old man, where they fasted, abstained from any sort of sexual activity (which they had been free to indulge, to the limit of their powers, before), covered themselves with dirt, and mortified the flesh in various ways, such as bathing in ice water and bruising and gashing the shinbones with rocks. Dreams experienced during such periods of self-trial were apt to be regarded as visitations from supernatural spirits who might grant *orenda,* or magical power, to the dreamer, and who would maintain a special sort of guardian-ship over him. The person's connection with this supernatural being was maintained through a charm—such as a knife, a queerly shaped stone, or a bit of bone—which was connected with the dream through some association significant to the dreamer. Unlike many other tribes, however, the Iroquois apparently did not require these guardian-spirit visions for pubescent youths. Many youths were said not to have had their first vision until just before their first war party. Fur-thermore, any man could have a significant dream or vision at any time. Girls too went through a mild puberty ritual, retiring into the woods at first menstruation and paying particular attention to their dreams. With the termination of the menstrual period the girl re-turned to the household; but hereafter, whenever she menstruated, she would have to live apart in a hut, avoiding people, and being care-ful not to step on a path, or to cook and serve anyone's food, or (especially) to touch medicines, which would immediately lose their potency if she handled them.[15]

The Europeans who observed this pattern of child experience were by no means unfavorably impressed although they were some-times amazed. They commented, however, almost to a man, from early Jesuit to latter-day Quaker, on a consequence that stood out dramatically as they compared this "savage" maturation with "civil-ized." "There is nothing," wrote the Jesuit chronicler of the Iroquois mission in 1657, "for which these peoples have a greater horror than restraint. The very children cannot endure it, and live as they please in the houses of their parents, without fear of reprimand or chastise-ment."[16] One hundred and fifty years later, the Quaker Halliday Jackson observed that "being indulged in most of their wishes, as they grow up, liberty, in its fullest extent, becomes their ruling passion."[17] The Iroquois themselves recognized the intensity of their children's resentment at parental interference. "Some Savages," re-ported Le Mercier of the Huron, "told us that one of the principal reasons why they showed so much indulgence toward their children, was that when the children saw themselves treated by their parents with some severity, they usually resorted to extreme measures and hanged themselves, or ate of a certain root they call *Audachienrra,* which is a very quick poison."[18] The same fear was recorded among the Iroquois, including the Seneca, in 1657. And while suicides by frustrated children were not actually frequent, there are nevertheless a number of recorded cases of suicide where parental interference was the avowed cause. And *mutatis mutandis,* there was another rationalization for a policy of permissiveness: that the child who was harshly disciplined might grow up, some day, to mistreat his parents in revenge.

This theory of child raising was not taken for granted by the Seneca; on the contrary, it was very explicitly recognized, discussed, and pondered. Handsome Lake himself, in later years, insisted that parents love and indulge their children.

· *Iroquois Polity: The Philosophy of Peace* ·

THE POLITICAL ORGANIZATION of the Iroquois—the system by which decisions were made about problems affecting village, tribe, or confederacy—had three levels. The town or village itself decided local issues like the use of nearby hunting lands, the relocation of houses and cornfields, movement to another site, the acceptance or rejection of visitors, and the raising of war parties. There was a village chiefs' council, numbering up to twenty men, formally organized with a chairman and one or more representatives for each clan. These chiefs were influential men and women, who might be League sachems, war-captains, warriors, or simply old men who were looked up to and consulted. The council generally met in the presence of the warriors and the women, and rarely diverged in its decisions from the popular consensus, or at least the majority view. This council met in the village's ceremonial longhouse, which usually was merely a large dwelling.

The tribes, or nations, had only an uncertain coherence in political matters, and readily split into factions, which might even remove geographically from one another and become permanent subdivisions. The Seneca, in particular, were divided into two groups: an eastern, pro-British group, and a western, pro-French group (the Geneseo Seneca). The Seneca national council met only occasionally, in the great council house at Caneadea or at another of the nation's towns as circumstances at the time might dictate. The membership of these tribal councils seems to have been simply the sum of all the chiefs of the village councils. Thus the Seneca tribal council might include as many as a hundred chiefs, and the membership changed as the composition of the village councils changed. The chairman, or speaker, of this council was elected by the council itself. The tribal council debated major issues of external policy such as war and peace, and sale of land; its recommendations, however, were contingent upon the willingness of the individual villages to carry them out, and in matters where agreement in the council was difficult, or an agreed-upon decision was expected to be unpopular, the whole nation might be presented with the problem at a mass meeting where anyone had the right to speak. The chiefs then waited for a consensus. Some of these tribal (i.e., village) chiefs and council speakers were chosen as perennial liaison men for dealings between colonial officials, like Sir William Johnson, and their village, factional, tribal, or even Six Nations constituencies. They were in this role sometimes referred to as "chiefs to do business," and most of the practical work of administration of policy and formulation and communication of issues was handled by these men rather than by the councils themselves. They were often better known to the whites than the hereditary, or sachem, chiefs. Still, the tribe was essentially not a political organization but a group of villages that spoke the same language.[19]

The only indigenous political structure that effectively coordinated communication and decision at a level above the individual village was the confederacy itself. In the Great Council of the Confederacy at Onondaga, voting representatives of each of the five original nations, together with nonvoting delegates from affiliated tribes like the Tuscarora, met annually in autumn, and at other times if called together by a member nation, to discuss crucial issues affecting the welfare of all the tribes: major wars and peacemakings and alliances; the sale of confederate territory; policy in matters of trade, religion, and relations with the whites; internal disputes that might threaten peace and good order. There were regular procedures for investiture of the sachems, and the strings and belts of wampum that were handed across the fire to emphasize the official nature of important statements were carefully preserved. One of the speaker's main responsibilities was to remember, word for word, what was said when each string or belt was handed across the fire. A well-trained speaker could relate with precision the transactions of the confederacy for a period of several generations into the past and could, moreover, present a diplomatic argument or a tribal council's decision with as much animation and eloquence as a European statesman addressing sovereign or parliament. The League also depended heavily upon "chiefs to do business" in the periods between meetings of its council.

Of the forty-nine sachems who sat around the great council fire at Onondaga, eight were Seneca. Each sachem had a special name, which was actually an official title, assumed when his clan matron appointed him and the council accepted the appointment. One of the Seneca titles was Ganeodiyo, or Handsome Lake, of the Turtle Clan. Although the tribes were unequal in numbers, no tribe had a greater voice in decision than any other, because the representatives of each tribe voted as a unit and decisions had to be unanimous. The Onondaga, whose principal town was usually the meeting place of the Great Council, were responsible for keeping the official wampum of the confederacy. The Seneca, the westernmost tribe, were known as the Keepers of the Western Door, because two of their sachems were appointed to inform the confederate council of embassies of peace or threats of war from the western nations and to keep a watchful eye over tributary tribes. These two chiefs had executive assistants whose formal duty it was to coordinate the normally small and individualistic war parties in the event of a major threat to the confederacy. In practice, however, military activities were organized by zealous and reputable warriors irrespective of title. The League was not an organization for more efficient warfare, and its contribution to military effort resided largely in its success in keeping domestic quarrels from becoming so bitter that they might prevent cooperation among villages and tribes. Although the fame of the Iroquois was based chiefly on their ruthless destruction of other nations, although much of the pride of each man resided in his personal accomplishments on the warpath, and although war was almost the constant condition of national existence, the Great League itself was in philosophy and in practice an inward-looking, harmony-maintaining body. Herein lay another paradox: The warlike Iroquois conceived the normal and desirable way of life to be a peaceful, quiet one and bent much energy toward the maintenance of peace among themselves and their near neighbors.

The League had originated many years earlier (about 1450) in a successful endeavor to revive an even more ancient, but less formally constructed, ethnic confederacy among the Iroquois. Ethnic confederacies were common among Indian tribes in the Northeast. Villages, bands, and tribes speaking similar languages, holding similar customs, and sharing a tradition of common origin usually combined into a loose union that at least minimized warfare among themselves. The Illinois Confederacy, the "Three Fires" of the Chippewa, Ottawa, and Potawatomi, the Wapenaki Confederacy, the Powhatan Confederates, the tripartite Miami—all the neighbors of the Iroquois were members of some confederation or other. But the Iroquois League was to them as ice is to water: a rigid crystalline form of a normally shapeless substance. The Great League, with its forty-nine chiefly titles representing most of the clans of the five tribes, its council fire at Onondaga, and its archives of wampum, was called Kanonsionni, the Longhouse, and the people of the Five Nations considered themselves, for many purposes, members of one family. "We bind ourselves together," had said the mythological founder, Dekanawidah, "by taking hold of each other's hands so firmly and forming a circle so strong that if a tree should fall upon it, it could not shake nor break it, so that our people and grandchildren shall remain in the circle in security, peace, and happiness." The chiefs were consecrated men, disqualified from taking part in war except as common warriors, and expected to have skins seven thumbs thick so as to remain untouched by gossip, envy, and criticism. "Be of strong mind, O chiefs!" they were charged. "Carry no anger and hold no grudges. Think not forever of yourselves, O chiefs, nor of your own generation. Think of continuing generations of our families, think of our grandchildren and of those yet unborn, whose faces are coming from beneath the ground."

The minimum purpose of the League was to maintain unity, strength, and good will among the Five Nations, so as to make them invulnerable to attack from without and to division from within. The native philosophers who rationalized the League in later years conceived also a maximum purpose: the conversion of all mankind, so that peace and happiness should be the lot of the peoples of the whole earth, and all nations should abide by the same law and be members of the same confederacy. "The white roots of the Great Tree of Peace will continue to grow," the founder allegedly announced, "advancing the Good Mind and Righteousness and Peace, moving into territories of peoples scattered far through the forest. And when a nation, guided by the Great White Roots, shall approach the Tree, you shall welcome her here and take her by the arm and seat her in the place of council. She will add a brace or leaning pole to the longhouse and will thus strengthen the edifice of Reason and Peace." But should a nation, after being invited three times to become a prop to the Iroquois Longhouse, persist in an obstinate refusal, it was supposedly incumbent upon the Five Nations to attack and conquer them, and thus bring the survivors into the circle by main force.

Thus the chiefs, tranquilly sitting about the fire at Onondaga, puffing on their long cane pipes, were easy in their minds about the forest wars. They could say that despite all the quarrels over beaver and boundaries, they themselves had always had in mind the extension of the Great Peace. Even with the French they had tried to live at peace. To the Jesuits, those cold-blooded, black-robed men of great courage but little tact, they had said, "If you love, as you say you do, our souls, love our bodies also, and let us be henceforth but one nation." They had restrained themselves, many times, from fully annihilating the French and their Algonquian allies at Montreal and Quebec and Three Rivers. "I heard the voice of my Forefathers massacred by the Algonquins. When they saw that my heart was capable of seeking revenge they called out to me in a loving voice: 'My grandson, my grandson, be good; do not get angry. Think no longer of us for there is no means of withdrawing us from death. Think of the living—that is of importance; save those that still live from the sword and fire that pursue them; one living man is better than many dead ones.'" And again and again they had proposed peace and union under the Great Tree. "Not only shall our customs be your customs, but we shall be so closely united that our chins shall be reclothed with hair, and with beards like yours." Again and again they had paddled up and down in canoes before a recalcitrant town while an old sachem cried in a loud voice: "Listen to me! I have come to treat for peace with all the nations in these parts . . . the land shall be beautiful, the river shall have no more waves, one may go everywhere without fear."

And the warriors, hidden in the bushes overlooking the stream, watched anxiously to see whether the foreigners made peace and agreed to share the fur trade with the Iroquois, so that they themselves might go home, or whether their deadly service would be needed after all. . . .[20]

· *Iroquois Warfare: The Strategy of Threat and Retaliation* ·

WHATEVER ITS PHILOSOPHICAL rationalization and economic consequences might be, the actual mechanism of Iroquois warfare was the traditional process of blood feud. A family, one of whose members had been killed by an alien (i.e., a person who was not one of the five or, after about 1722, Six Nations or their allies), was morally obligated to avenge the death by killing, or capturing and adopting, one or more members of the "enemy" tribe. Friends of the injured family could help in the satisfaction of the score, but the feud was fundamentally a personal matter between the injured family and the alien group. Such a feud could begin from various incidental circumstances: a chance encounter with a trespassing stranger; a drunken brawl; involvement in a military campaign initiated by a third party. Over a period of time, however, a sequence of mutually vengeful killings could occur, involving an increasing number of members of the two groups, until finally there were so many unsettled scores left on both sides that a state of chronic "war" could be said to exist, justifying an endless exchange of forays, some of them involving large numbers of vengeance-seeking warriors on both sides. Inasmuch as these forays were technically intended by the participants not to acquire territory nor to establish political sovereignty but to even the score in a feud, good tactics required minimal loss of life by the avenging party. A victory with heavy casualties was, in effect, a defeat, since the score then remained uneven.

This mechanism was partially controlled by political policy, particularly as expressed and maintained by the Great League. The League itself had been explicitly designed to prevent the proliferation of blood feuds within and among the various member nations; this purpose was clearly stated both in the Dekanawidah myth, which described the origin of the League, and in the rituals of condolence that were held whenever one of the forty-nine members of the council died. Indirectly, no doubt, the League's ethical position on intra-Iroquois blood feuds influenced Iroquois warfare by maintaining a climate of mutual confidence among the tribes. In this climate it was more feasible to organize large-scale military enterprises than in an atmosphere of mutual fear and suspicion. But it should not be supposed that Iroquois warfare was merely the military activity of the League. The League—and probably tribal and village councils also—functioned more as a restraining than as an initiating body. The League as an entity and its several chiefs could urge upon the warriors the wisdom of holding back their striking arms; and their influence was such that raids could be postponed or put off indefinitely while diplomats negotiated issues for the common good. Conversely, the League organization could deliberately sit silent while the war captains prepared their campaigns. Furthermore, the council organization served as an information center, receiving, discussing, filtering, and disseminating news and opinion that could influence the military passions of the warriors and the women. Thus, while the League was in itself not a war-making body, it could aim and time the unleashing of the war potential that, because of the wide ramification of the kinship-revenge motif, was always straining to burst into active hostilities. This process of control by restraining, directing, and timing the ever-ready mechanism of revenge operated most conspicuously in relations between the Iroquois and white groups, because the records of negotiations and of fighting are here more satisfactory; but the same process governed the relations of the Iroquois to other Indian tribes.

The major functions of Iroquois warfare—its consequences, both intended and unintended, for the Iroquois way of life and their situation in the world—were, in the early part of the century, threefold: to maintain an emotional equilibrium in individuals who were strongly motivated to avenge, or replace, murdered kinfolk, and thereby to maintain the social equilibrium of kinship units; to extend, or at least maintain, Iroquois political influence over other tribal groups, and thus to provide access by trade or hunting to land rich in peltries; and to perpetuate a political situation in which the threat of retaliation against either party could be used to play off the British and the French against one another. Territorial immunity, military support, trade advantages, and outright gifts of food, dry goods, and hardware could be extorted from both sides under the asserted or implied threat that the Iroquois and their allies would abandon their neutral role and would join the generous party in an attack on the stingy one if their wants were not satisfied.

The equilibrium-maintaining function of Iroquois warfare requires some amplification. Certainly the Iroquois were not unique among Indian tribes, or even primitive peoples generally, in the importance of kinship in establishing the individual's social rights and obligations and in defining his image in his own eyes and the eyes of others. Such discipline and security as the individual enjoyed tended to be provided by his family (and by "family" we mean not merely the immediate household but the various and widely ramifying connections of the kinship system). In such a setting an injury to an Iroquois Indian's relatives became doubly significant, not only because it disturbed the integrity of the group with which he was identified, but also because the affected individuals could not depend upon obtaining redress through police and courts. It was thus a matter of honor for kinfolk to protect one another and, if necessary, to avenge injuries. In the case of a killing, the most immediately affected parties might well be women—mother, sisters, and wife of the lost person—who could demand either the torture and death of the offender or the adoption of a captive to take the departed person's place. (In a fundamental sense, even the dead offender was adopted, since the scalp torn from the slain foe was often ritually adopted into the bereaved family, and the bodies of captives who had been tortured to death were sometimes eaten ceremonially.) While women could hold the initiative in demanding redress and could determine the fate of captives, men were responsible for risking their lives to bring back scalps or prisoners. Joining a war party thereby became a test of manhood, conducted under the watchful eyes of bereaved women, and failure to participate in the revenge process would prejudice the reluctant youth's standing in the eyes of his own family and the community generally.

The effectiveness of the League in partially blocking the free exercise of the revenge process among the five participating tribes may therefore have been partly responsible for the implacability and ferociousness of the Iroquois in pursuing external enemies; with the intrusion of political influence into the revenge motif locally, it became even more essential for warriors to validate their moral stature in the eyes of kinsmen and community by allowing no slackness in the settling of external scores. If this interpretation is sound, then the Iroquois reputation for pertinacity and ruthlessness in fighting with their external enemies may be regarded as an indirect consequence of the blocking of the blood feud among the participating members of the League. The *pax Iroquois* resulted in the displacement of revenge motivations outward, onto surrounding peoples, Indian and European alike.

But this displacement brought new difficulties in turn, perhaps more clearly recognized by the sachems of the League than by the warriors. The intensification of external warfare—augmented in the seventeenth century by the abrasive circumstances of competition in the fur trade—meant ever more costly raids and counter-raids, in what seems to have been a rising crescendo of violence. The strain on the Iroquois themselves was great: serious loss of manpower, the need to replenish the population by mass adoption of captives, and the development of something like a chronic combat fatigue, the symptoms of which—preoccupation with death and misfortune, persistent nightmares of captivity, of being burned alive, of attack by enemy warriors—were vividly described by the Jesuits. Paradoxically, the League of peace had become a facility for destruction. Thus the League, lest the revenge process get out of hand, perforce had to expand so as to embrace under its sheltering branches, which precluded the blood feud, ever more of the Iroquois' traditional enemies. Each accretion to the League required the warriors to go farther and farther away to settle a score, and thereby reduced the total frequency of raids and their cost in terms of lives and human suffering. By the middle of the eighteenth century a rough equilibrium had been established: The nearby Indian nations had been brought by various mixtures of conquest, threat, and diplomatic persuasion into some sort of affiliation with the League. While killings and counterkillings still occasionally occurred, they no longer threatened the survival of the tribes; and there was still sufficient opportunity, in the raid exchanges with the southern Indians, for the revenge motif to exercise the kinship devotions of the warriors and women.

The social interests of the League sachems, on the one hand, and the warriors and the women, on the other, conflicted. Warriors and women formed a bloc composed of complementary roles in the revenge process, each dependent on the other for validation and fulfillment of status. The sachems, however, *as sachems* had to view the revenge process as potentially destructive. Thus one repeatedly finds sachems, or their representatives in contact with Europeans, complaining that they could not control their young men, that the warriors were apt to heed the women rather than the chiefs. While such statements were certainly true, for reasons given above, the situation that they reflected was also fruitful in insuring the successful fulfillment of the third function of Iroquois warfare. The chiefs of the League, or of any particular tribe, could at any time say that the warriors and the women could no longer be restrained from striking a blow against some enemy to gain revenge for some recent or ancient injury. Thus, while the League as such, by the treaties of 1701, remained committed to neutrality between the French and the English, groups of warriors—acting according to the code of revenge—could, if offended, at any time assail either party. It was always possible, of course, for the British to seduce some Mohawk into service against the French, and the French to persuade some Geneseo Seneca to strike the British, but these breaches of contract served more as an ever-present reminder of the importance of keeping the League itself neutral than as an excuse for terminating the agreement. Thus, without more duplicity than was characteristic of either the British or the French themselves, the League chiefs were able to orchestrate the revenge mechanism of warfare into the contrapuntal melody of extorting political and material gifts from both the French and the English. The importance of this theme in Iroquois life from 1701 to 1755 can hardly be overestimated: It gave them territorial security, a relatively high material culture, a continued ascendancy over neighboring peoples, and an enormous sense of their own importance.[21]

3

THE RITUALS OF HOPE
AND THANKSGIVING

IN THE COURSE OF TRYING TO LIVE UP TO THE RIGOROUS IDEAL OF autonomy and responsibility, Iroquois men hunted, traded, fought, and negotiated at a high cost in loneliness and discomfort. They too on occasion yearned for someone's help to relieve pain and hardship, felt rage at insult and neglect, were jealous of others' success, were miserable when a loved one died. Even though their public behavior was stoic, they were underneath not nearly as insulated from one another, as self-sufficient and indifferent to human contact, as the overt fulfillment of the ideal of autonomy seemed to imply. Indeed, the severity of the ideal guaranteed an equal intensity of desire for its converse—dependency and lack of responsibility.

In general, Iroquois religion tended to be a means by which the disappointments and sacrifices entailed by living up to the ideal of autonomous responsibility could to some extent be compensated. Its rituals and beliefs were cathartic, satisfying the desperate needs for nurturance that could not be expressed, and might even be feared, in daily life. But the religion did its work in disguised, symbolic, and ceremonially insulated forms so that acting out normally disallowed wishes did not threaten self-respect. In the opinion of the Iroquois themselves, these rituals prevented both mental illness and social disorder.

The set of issues to which Iroquois religion addressed itself was unlike that to which contemporary European religions were oriented. European methods of social discipline in the main produced adults who were relatively tolerant of external restraint and whose typical problem was guilt, particularly over wishes for aggressive, dominant independence in matters of sex, politics, and human relations generally. The religious antihero of the Europeans was proud, independent Lucifer; of the Iroquois, it was the infantile, beggarly False Face. European religions provided a rich variety of ritual prescriptions for the management of guilt by confession, atonement, forgiveness, and absolution. Early Iroquois religion did not pay much attention to guilt of this kind because Iroquois people were not much bothered by it. But their religion did concern itself explicitly with cathartic ways of handling existential frustration. In general, these ways can be analytically separated into rituals of thanksgiving and hope and rituals of fear and mourning. The former—including particularly the communal thanksgiving festivals and the cult of dreams—worked to provide reassurance of continued protection and support from supernaturals and of ultimate impulse gratification, especially of de- sires for nurturance, within an indulgent earthly community. The latter—notably witchcraft, the masked medicine ceremonies, and the condolence rituals—attempted to cope with the consequences of loss: loss of love, loss of health, and loss of loved ones by death. Ultimately, of course, the two categories merge, for impulse gratifi- cation itself was believed to be prophylactic or even curative.

· *The Calendar of Thanksgiving* ·

IN THE EIGHTEENTH CENTURY, as now, most of the important com- munal ceremonies of thanksgiving were performed at fixed times through the year and were relevant to seasonal subsistence activities as well as to general themes of belief. Villages differed, then as now, in the number of such ceremonies and in the details of their execution. Among Handsome Lake's people, there were probably six: the Mid- winter Ceremony, in January or February, which marked the begin- ning of the Seneca year; Thanks-to-the-Maple, in late February or March, when the sap started to rise; the Corn Planting Festival, early in May or June; the Strawberry Festival, in June; the Green Corn Ceremony, late in August or September; and the Harvest Festival in October. The Midwinter Ceremony lasted nine days and the Green Corn four; the remainder were one-day affairs. The nucleus of all the ceremonies (with the possible exception of Thanks-to-the-Maple, about which little information has been recorded) was a morning-long ritual that constituted virtually the entire external form of the one-day ceremonies and occupied one day of Midwinter and of Green Corn. This archetypal ritual day began with the Faithkeepers notifying the people to assemble at the longhouse. When the people had gathered, a speaker opened the meeting by reporting any sickness in the village. Then he proceeded to give thanks to the pantheon in the standard Thanksgiving Prayer, starting with the spirit forces on earth and going on to more and more sacred beings: in the lower pantheon, the people (categorized as civil chiefs, religious chiefs, ordinary men and women, and children), the waters, the herbs, grasses, and other small plants, the saplings and bushes, the trees, the staple agricultural foods (corn, squash, and beans), the game animals, and the birds; in the middle pantheon, the thunderers (who made the rain), the winds, the sun, the moon, and the stars; and in the upper pantheon, the major deities and the Creator. Then the speaker announced the special purpose of the day's meeting, gave instruction concerning the forthcoming rituals, and announced the singers for the Feather Dance. The Faithkeepers, men and women, now performed the Feather Dance. Next he announced the names of the singers and dancers for the Women's Dance. The women danced, carrying ears of corn, while the male chorus described in song the life cycle of the corn. The speaker thanked the participants and announced the Great Feather Dance, which now included everyone who wished to join in. At morning's end the speaker concluded the proceedings by thanking on behalf of the chiefs all of the participants and announcing plans for the succeeding day (or, if the ceremony was over, for the next festival on the calendar). Everyone now left the longhouse and joined in a midday feast.

The theme of this basic ritual sequence was thankfulness and hope: thankfulness to the spirit beings for past benefits to the community and hope that they would continue to provide them. Paralleling this ritual address to the gods, there was a similar communication from the speaker to the human participants, who also had to be thanked for their help in order to ensure their continued interest in the communal ceremonies.

The Midwinter Ceremony began the ceremonial year. This ceremony regularly took place five days after the first new moon following the zenith of the Pleiades. This event, which occurs late in January or early in February, was observed by the two ritual Headmen, who had charge of the Faithkeepers. Midwinter was the longest festival of the annual calendar. Its main theme was a testimonial to the Creator, of thankfulness for the blessings and indulgences of the past year, and of supplication to Him to permit man to enjoy yet another spring.

On the first day of the festival there occurred the "boiling of the babies." This ceremony was the public naming of the babies who had been born since the Green Corn Ceremony. The "boiling" was not the fate of the babies even symbolically; what was boiled was the corn soup the participants ate after the naming ceremony.

The New Year began officially at dawn on the second day, when the Big Heads woke the occupants of the houses and notified them that the New Year had begun. The Big Heads were two men wearing shaggy bearskin coats and masks of cornhusks; they were not permitted to dress themselves and accordingly were fitted out by two women attendants. They received gifts of food and returned to the council house to reveal their dreams. If they did not attend, the Big Heads warned, the lazy dreamers would get their heads "stuck to the ceremonies." Having one's head stuck to the ceremonies was a miserable condition in which any dreamer who had failed to reveal his dream and to act out the ritual it indicated was obsessed by the desire that generated the dream. Later some False Face dancers went out to the houses, accompanied by female attendants, to stir the ashes again and to begin songs of thanksgiving. They returned and blew ashes on sick people. Finally, two Faithkeepers carrying paddles came to the houses to stir the ashes on the hearths visited earlier by the Big Heads and False Faces.

On the third day, called "ashes stirring," small groups of people carrying paddles made the rounds of houses in the village, again stirring up the ashes in the individual cabins. On their return to the council house, a singer sang the song of thanksgiving to the pantheon. After the thanksgiving, additional groups of persons walked from house to house, in response to dreams, asking that their dreams be guessed.

The fourth day was the day of the rituals of the secret medicine societies. A speaker and a singer, leading a party of men who danced the Great Feather Dance in the council house and in the circuit of private houses, exhorted the people to attend the rituals of the proper societies. The Great Feather dancers were followed by a party of women who danced the Women's Dance. Then the various medicine societies—the False Faces, the Buffalo Society, the Otter Society, and so on—performed brief curing rituals for those sick persons whose dreams indicated a need for their membership in a particular society and for those who needed a "booster" ritual on this anniversary of a previous cure. Men and women also on this day propounded their dream-riddles, and the guessers offered miniature talismans representing the tutelary revealed in the dream. That night bands of young people dressed up as False Faces roamed about the village, begging or, if rebuffed, stealing food.

On the fifth morning occurred the burning of the white dog. This dog, a spotless animal, had been strangled (its blood could not be shed) on the day of the Big Heads, and its body, garlanded with ribbons, beads, and metallic ornaments, hung on the wooden statue of Tarachiawagon, the Creator, before the longhouse. Now it was burned in the longhouse as an offering to the Creator, and the Thanksgiving Dance was performed, and people sang their personal chants. On this day also the medicine societies continued their curing rites in the longhouse, and, in the afternoon and evening, in private homes.

On the sixth day the Sacred Bowl Game was played briefly, a traveling team proceeding from house to house to contest with the occupants to make levies of food. In the afternoon again there were medicine society dances on behalf of the sick. The Buffalo Society dancers, for instance, butted their covered heads together and devoured corn mush; the leftovers were thrown out of the door for the "animals outside." In the Bear Dance, everyone ate a jam of preserved strawberries. The evening of this sixth day was the comedy hour of the festival. The evening started in the crowded council house with social dances and leftover medicine-society rituals. Then the False Face dancers—men dressed in ragged clothes, carrying huge turtle-shell rattles and wooden staves, and wearing grotesque wooden masks—burst into the council house, incoherently gobbling and cooing, rolling on the ground, and dancing the awkward, pompous False Face Dance in return for gifts of tobacco. The people laughed uproariously at their crude antics. After them came the Husk Faces. With them, the humor was more subtle. The Husk Faces, wearing round, popeyed, friendly looking masks made of braided cornhusks, arrived at the council house during a period of social dances. They announced their arrival by a great din of banging and scraping the bark walls of the council house with hoes and wooden shovels. Two heralds burst in, shoved the dancers aside, and seized some elderly gentleman as an interpreter. He was taken outside to interview their leader, who was supposedly a woman. He returned with his captors and delivered her "message," but part way through suffered from forgetfulness and excused himself, saying that he had to go outside once more to see the Great-Wet-Woman, whom, he said, he had not seen for a year. At last he came back and carried on an animated dialogue with himself, alternately as Great-Wet-Woman and her interpreter. The Husk Faces now revealed (as they did every year) that they were a race of supernatural agriculturists who lived on the western rim of the earth, whither they were now hurrying to cultivate their corn, which grew to vast heights, bearing prodigious ears, in fields filled with high stumps. Also their babies were crying and their women had to get home to tend them, so they could only stay and dance for a little while. Then the Husk Face women (actually men in women's dress) did the Women's Dance in honor of the "Three Sisters," corn, squash, and beans.

The seventh day followed the basic ritual sequence described above; the eighth focused on the singing of personal songs of thanksgiving. The ninth and last day was devoted to concluding the ceremonies. Adults who had changed their names were presented, new council-house officers were inaugurated, and there was a final performance of the Great Feather Dance. Personal chants of thanksgiving were held, and the sacred Bowl Game (symbolizing the struggle of the Good with the Evil Twin over control of the earth in the days of creation) was begun again. During the one or more days of the game's continuance, social dances were held in the evening, and the daylight hours were devoted to feasting and to the enactment of dream commands, lest those whose heads were still "stuck to the ceremonies" delay by their preoccupation the coming of spring.[1]

After the Midwinter Festival, toward the end of February, when the sap started to rise in the trees but before the ground had thawed and the ice and snow had run off the mountains, most of the people left the village to camp near family-owned groves of sugar maples. They spent several weeks in the woods, the women chiefly occupying themselves with sugar-making, while the men, in addition to helping in this process, hunted to support the camp and trapped the small fur-bearing animals, particularly the beaver, whose meat was regarded as a luxury and whose fur was a valuable article in trade. Everyone returned to the village before the spring thaw.

The sugar-maple season was also the occasion of the religious ceremony called Thanks-to-the-Maple. On the morning of the chosen day individual families returned thanks to the maple trees and burned tobacco as an invocation. Afterward there were social dances, and in the evening the people sang the songs of the Chanters for the Dead (the *ohgiwe* cycle). The Chanters for the Dead was a society, headed by a woman, which owned certain songs that, in addition to being sung at Thanks-to-the-Maple, were sung as occasion required throughout the year for persons (thereafter members) who were troubled by dreams of departed relatives or friends. At an *ohgiwe* ceremony the songs were sung to the accompaniment of a large water-drum; a diviner identified the troubling spirit, and a feast was held at which food was set aside for the restless ghost, to satisfy the needs that made him plague the sick man's dreams. These songs were supposed to have been revealed to a good hunter from a grave beneath a hard maple tree.

When the snow melted on the mountains, the ice became soft and crumbled over the lakes and streams, and small creeks swelled into brown frothing rivers, bearing the winter's watery debris down to the sea. This was the time when human life came almost to a standstill: Hunting, travel, even war were impossible because of the sogginess of the ground and the impassability of the fords; it was too early to plant, and the last year's store of dried corn was almost used up; clothes and cabins were worn and shabby, and the people were hungry, waiting for the renewal of warmth and sunshine and green things. They waited in their villages for the world's rebirth for which they had prayed at the Midwinter Festival a month or two before.

After the thaw, the pace of life accelerated. There was industrious fishing: men, women, and children armed with fish spears assaulted the cool creeks and lakes; weirs were emptied; nets of cord or brush were dragged up small streams. In April, when the passenger pigeons nested, the whole village took part in a hunt for squabs, knocking the young birds down from the trees and gathering them in baskets. Parties of women planted the corn in hillocks row by row, and other important plants—tobacco, squash, and beans in particular—were set at the same time, to grow in the carefully hoed and weeded gardens. Men and youths repaired old cabins or built new ones and busied themselves in the woods near the village, hunting for deer and small game. Toward the beginning of June small groups of women, with children and sometimes with menfolk, made picnic parties into the hills, picking wild strawberries and carrying them home in baskets of woven splints, to make into a syrupy tonic beverage and to dry and preserve for later seasons. These berry-picking excursions provided occasion for much merry and malicious gossip about who was seen with whom and about the supposed philanderings of certain men and the wantonness of certain women.

At the time of the planting of the corn, the Corn Planting Ceremony was held. One morning the Faithkeepers went about the village to the various houses, collecting corn, squash, beans, and other garden-vegetable seeds. These were taken to the longhouse and soaked. The Creator and all the spirit forces were thanked for their mercies in the past and asked for continued support. The Thunderers, "our grandfathers," were requested to water the crops, and "our older brother," the Sun, was implored not to burn them with too-fierce rays. And again in June, when the berry moon was five days old, the Faithkeepers called the people together for the Strawberry Festival. They thanked the spirit forces for permitting them to live to witness still another festival and for bringing the fruits, of which the strawberry is the first, to ripening; and they asked that the spirit forces permit all things to reach fruition. At some day during the spring, also, there was a great hubbub and to-do in the village. On the day of the exorcism of disease and witchcraft, two companies of men and women, boys and girls, wearing red and black wooden masks, marched through the village. They stopped at every house and rubbed turtle-shell or bark rattles over the cabins, brushed disease spirits out from under bunks, and collected tobacco, which was burned at the council house where the two companies, proceeding from opposite ends of the village, joined at last. There the Thunders and the Winds and the

False Faces themselves were implored to keep disaster, in the form of tornado or pestilence or witchcraft, away from the village.

Summertime in the Genesee Valley was a warm, dry season; the hills in the distance were soft in the misty air and a warm brownness mantled the earth. Thunderstorms and sudden showers from time to time broke over the villages, but the countryside was never watered well enough to achieve the lush greenness of regions farther south. The women were at their busiest in the summer, with the duties of agriculture added to the perennial chores of tending the children, cooking, making and mending clothing, and manufacturing pottery, baskets, and other housewares. By contrast, summer was of all the seasons the easiest for the men. There was casual hunting for small game near the villages and occasionally longer summer hunting and trading trips. There were, for the older or invalided men, various arts and crafts to be carried on now as in winter—the making of wampum, the carving of masks, ceremonial canes, and drumsticks, the fashioning of wooden spoons and ladles. Sometimes men went to war in the summer, but fall was preferred as the time for military adventure. Summer was, however, the best time of all for politics and diplomacy: for meetings of tribal councils, for councils of the Great Confederacy, for councils with representatives of other Indian nations, and for treaties with the whites. At such council and treaty occasions, not only the chiefs, speakers, and prominent warriors attended, but also (depending on the availability of food at the council site) hundreds of ordinary warriors, women, and children. The winter's catch of trade furs would be exchanged at forts and trading posts for hardware and dry goods. Summer was a time for visiting, for sociability, and for the renewal of friendships and alliances. During the summer there were no fixed religious festivals. If drought threatened the crops, the Thunder Rite was held: tobacco was burned, the game of hoop and javelin was played, the people danced, Elder Brother Sun was implored not to burn the corn, and the Grandfather Thunderers were requested to bring rain. A Condolence Council had to precede any formal treaty involving chiefs of the League if one of them had died during the winter or spring and his successor had not yet been installed.

Autumn was inaugurated by the Green Corn Festival, which among the Iroquois, as among the other tribes of the eastern woodlands, marked the middle of the year. When the corn was ready for eating, some time late in August or in early September, the community gathered at the council house to give thanks for the ripening of the crops for another year. The festival required four days. The first was for the naming of children born since the Midwinter Ceremony. The second was for the Great Feather Dance. The third was for the singing of personal chants (*adowe*), a performance of the Thanksgiving Dance including boastful recitations of war exploits, and the burning of a white dog as an offering to the Creator Tarachiawagon. And the fourth was for the Bowl Game, the sacred game of chance, which continued, if it was not decided on the morning of this fourth day, on as many succeeding mornings as were required for one moiety or the other to win all of the 102 beans. Although most sacred ceremonies ended at noon on each day, the afternoons and evenings were devoted to other rituals: social dances in the evenings, the Women's Rite (*towisas*) on the last afternoon, and the appearance of the False Faces. In form and content the Green Corn Ceremony was substantially the same as the first day and last three days of the Midwinter Festival, which was the longest ritual of all in the Iroquois calendar.

After the Green Corn came the time of harvesting. The winter was on its way now, and the surplus of vegetable stuffs had to be put away for later use. Corn and other vegetables were taken in from the fields; some corn was husked and hung up in braids to dry, and the rest was shelled and buried in baskets in bark-lined pits or stored on the ear in elevated cribs. Tobacco was hung for curing, beans were dried. In this work both men and women participated, for any failure to make maximum use of what the earth had yielded might mean hardship or even starvation later. When the harvest was in, and before the people moved out for the fall hunt, they devoted one day more to the Harvest Festival, thanking the Creator and His spirit forces for permitting them to reap a full harvest, and testifying to the happiness of the corn now that it had again been returned safely into storage to rest for the winter.

The late fall and winter was the prime season for the hunters and warriors. Some departed on the trails through the forest on forays against nearby tribes, like the Mahican, or on occasion against such distant peoples as the Cherokee and Catawba south of the Ohio River, and the Montagnais and Cree in Labrador and around Hudson's Bay, or even to the Illinois on the Mississippi River. Others, often taking with them wives and children, or sweethearts, traveled by canoe and afoot to favorite hunting grounds where beaver, otter, marten, elk, bear, deer, and other animals valuable for food and peltry might be found. Some moved to the region watered by the Ohio River, and northward about Lake Erie; others remained closer to home, along the Allegheny, and on the streams of western New York (although by 1700 these grounds were almost empty of the trade furs like beaver and otter). On occasion a large party of hunters would drive a herd of deer between converging lines of fire into corral or ambush, but most of the hunting was done individually. Some of the meat was cured by drying and smoking over fires and was briefly stored in underground pits. In the evenings the older people sat about the fires in the bark hunting lodges and told the sacred old legends and myths, which according to their belief should not be recounted in the summer lest the teller be assaulted by snakes.

By the end of January most of the hunting parties had returned to the village, and the reassembled community prepared for the celebration of the next New Year.[1]

· *Dreams and the Wishes of the Soul* ·

WHEN THE BLACK-ROBED Jesuit fathers began the preaching of the gospel to the Seneca nation in the year 1668, they quickly found that the Seneca were rigidly attached to Iroquoian religious traditions. Particularly obstinate were they in looking to their dreams for guidance in all the important affairs of life.

"The Iroquois have, properly speaking, only a single Divinity," wrote Father Fremin "—the dream. To it they render their submission, and follow all its orders with the utmost exactness. The Tsoanontouens [Seneca] are more attached to this superstition than any of the others; their religion in this respect becomes even a matter of scruple; whatever it be that they think they have done in their dreams, they believe themselves absolutely obliged to execute at the earliest moment. The other nations content themselves with observing those of their dreams which are the most important; but this people, which has the reputation of living more religiously than its neighbors, would think itself guilty of a great crime if it failed in its observance of a single dream. The people think only of that, they talk about nothing else, and all their cabins are filled with their dreams. They spare no pains, no industry, to show their attachment thereto, and their folly in this particular goes to such an excess as would be hard to imagine. He who has dreamed during the night that he was bathing, runs immediately, as soon as he rises, all naked, to several cabins, in each of which he has a kettleful of water thrown over his body, however cold the weather may be. Another who has dreamed that he was taken prisoner and burned alive, has himself bound and burned like a a captive on the next day, being persuaded that by thus satisfying his dream, this fidelity will avert from him the pain and infamy of captivity and death,—which, according to what he has learned from his Divinity, he is otherwise bound to suffer among his enemies. Some have been known to go as far as Quebec, travelling a hundred and fifty leagues, for the sake of getting a dog, that they had dreamed of buying there. . . ."

Father Fremin and his colleagues were appalled: Some Seneca might, any night, dream of their deaths! "What peril we are in every day," he continued, "among people who will murder us in cold blood if they have dreamed of doing so; and how slight needs to be a offense that a Barbarian has received from someone, to enable his heated imagination to represent to him in a dream that he takes revenge on the offender." It is small wonder that the Jesuits early attempted to disabuse the Seneca of their confidence in dreams, propounding various subtle questions, such as, "Does the soul leave the body during sleep?" and "Can infants in the womb dream?" either affirmative or negative answers to which would involve the recognition (according to the Jesuits) of logical contradictions in native theory.

But Jesuit logic did not discourage Seneca faith. The Quaker missionaries who reached the Seneca 130 years later found in them much the same "superstitious" respect to dreams that their unsuccessful predecessors had discovered. "They are superstitious in the extreme, with respect to dreams, and witchcraft," wrote Halliday Jackson, "and councils are often called, on the most trifling occurrences of this nature. To elucidate this—in the winter of 1799, while one of the Friends was engaged in instructing the children in school learning, a message came from a confederate tribe, eighty miles distant, stating that one of their little girls had dreamed that 'the devil was in all white people alike, and that they ought not to receive instruction from the Quakers, neither was it right for their children to learn to read and write.' In consequence of this circumstance, a council was called, the matter was deliberated on, and divers of them became so much alarmed, as to prevent their children from attending the school for some time."[2]

The Iroquois theory of dreams was basically psychoanalytic. Father Ragueneau in 1649 described the theory in language that might have been used by Freud himself. "In addition to the desires which we generally have that are free, or at least voluntary in us, [and] which arise from a previous knowledge of some goodness that we imagine to exist in the thing described, the Hurons [and, he might have added, the Seneca] believe that our souls have other desires, which are, as it were, inborn and concealed. These, they say, come from the depths of the soul, not through any knowledge, but by means of a certain blind transporting of the soul to certain objects; these transports might in the language of philosophy be called *Desideria innata*, to distinguish them from the former, which are called *Desideria elicita*.

"Now they believe that our soul makes these natural desires known by means of dreams, which are its language. Accordingly, when these desires are accomplished, it is satisfied; but on the contrary, if it be not granted what it desires, it becomes angry, and not only does not give its body the good and the happiness that it wished to procure for it, but often it also revolts against the body, causing various diseases, and even death. . . .

"In consequence of these erroneous [thought Father Ragueneau] ideas, most of the Hurons are very careful to note their dreams, and to provide the soul with what it has pictured to them during their sleep. If, for instance, they have seen a javelin in a dream, they try to get it; if they have dreamed that they gave a feast, they will give one on awakening, if they have the wherewithal; and so on with other things. And they call this *Ondinnonk*—a secret desire of the soul manifested by a dream."

But the Hurons recognized that the manifest content, or emptiness, of a dream, might conceal rather than reveal the soul's true wish. And so, "just as, although we did not always declare our thoughts and inclinations by means of speech, those who by means of supernatural vision could see into the depths of our hearts would not fail to have a knowledge of them—in the same manner, the Hurons believe that there are certain persons, more enlightened than the common, whose sight penetrates, as it were, into the depths of the soul. These see the

natural and hidden desires that it has, though the soul has declared
nothing by dreams, or though he who may have had the dreams has
completely forgotten them. It is thus that their medicine-men . . .
acquire credit, and make the most of their art by saying that a child
in the cradle, who has neither discernment nor knowledge, will have
an *Ondinnonk*—that is to say, a natural hidden desire for such or
such a thing; and that a sick person will have similar desires for various
things of which he has never had any knowledge, or anything approaching it. For, as we shall explain further on, the Hurons believe
that one of the most efficacious remedies for rapidly restoring health
is to grant the soul of the sick person these natural desires."

Disease or bodily infirmity could, according to Iroquois theory,
arise from three sources: from natural injuries, such as the wounds of
war or physical accident; from witchcraft, by which were projected
magically into a victim's body certain foreign articles such as balls
of hair, splinters of bone, clots of blood, bear's teeth, and the like;
and from "the mind of the patient himself, which desires something,
and will vex the body of the sick man until it possesses the thing
required. For they think that there are in every man certain inborn
desires, often unknown to themselves, upon which the happiness of
individuals depends. For the purpose of ascertaining desires and
innate appetites of this character, they summon soothsayers, who, as
they think, have a divinely-imparted power to look into the inmost
recesses of the mind. These men declare that whatever first occurs
to them, or something from which they suspect some gain is to be
derived, is desired by the sick person. Thereupon the parents, friends,
and relatives of the patient do not hesitate to procure and lavish upon
him whatever it may be, however expensive, a return of which is
never thereafter to be sought. . . ."

To the soul, the Huron, Seneca, and other Iroquoian peoples as-
cribed several faculties not unlike the faculties that European psychol-
ogists of the day (i.e., the theologians) recognized. The Huron
considered that the human body was inhabited by a single soul with
several functions, and depending on the function that was being
alluded to at the moment, a different name was used. There was a
name for the soul in its capacity to animate the body and give it life;
in its capacity to have knowledge; in its capacity to exercise judgment; in its capacity to wish or desire; and in its capacity to leave the

body, as it might during dreams or after death. The soul occupied all parts of the body, and so had head, arms, legs, trunk, and all the rest of the anatomy (in ethereal counterpart) of the corporeal body.

Intuitively, the Iroquois had achieved a great degree of psychological sophistication. They recognized conscious and unconscious parts of the mind. They knew the great force of unconscious desires, were aware that the frustration of these desires could cause mental and physical (psychosomatic) illness. They understand that these desires were expressed in symbolic form, by dreams, but that the individual could not always properly interpret these dreams himself. They had noted the distinction between the manifest and latent content of dreams, and employed what sounds like the technique of free association to uncover the latent meaning. And they considered that the best method for the relief of psychic and psychosomatic distresses was to give the repressed desire satisfaction, either directly or symbolically. It would be fair to say that the seventeenth- and eighteenth-century Iroquois' understanding of psychodynamics was greatly superior to that of the most enlightened Europeans of the time.

The dreams reported by the Jesuit fathers and in the ethnological literature up to the present time provide a measure of the range and types of manifest content, and to a degree of the latent content, of Iroquois dreams. Dreams involving overt sexuality were not rare, and since they were freely reported and often acted out in therapeutic orgies, they gave the fathers great concern. Normally the Iroquoian peoples were modest in dress, often rather shy in public contacts with the opposite sex, and although premarital affairs were freely permitted to the young people and divorce and remarriage were easy for adults, chastity and marital fidelity were publicly recognized ideals. The fulfillment of dream wishes, however, took priority over other proprieties.

In 1656, at Onondaga, three warriors came to the village during the Midwinter Ceremony. They had been absent for a year in an unsuccessful campaign against the Erie nation. One of the warriors "was as wasted, pale, and depressed, as if he had spoken with the Devil. He spat blood, and was so disfigured that one scarcely dared to look him in the face." This man, when he arrived, announced that he had a matter of great importance to communicate to the elders. When they had assembled, he told them that during the campaign he had seen Tarachiawagon, He-who-holds-up-the-sky, the Good Twin and Creator, in the guise of a little dwarf. Tarachiawagon had addressed the warrior thus:

"I am he who holds up the Sky, and the guardian of the earth; I preserve men, and give victories to warriors. I have made you masters of the earth and victors over so many Nations: I made you conquer the Hurons, the Tobacco Nation, the Ahondihronnons, Atiraguenrek, Atiaonrek, Takoulguehronnons and Gentaguetehronnons; in short, I have made you what you are: and if you wish me to continue my protection over you, hear my words, and execute my orders.

"First, you will find three Frenchmen in your village when you arrive there. Secondly, you will enter during the celebration of the Honnaouroria. Thirdly, after your arrival, let there be sacrificed to me ten dogs, ten porcelain beads from each cabin, a collar [belt of wampum] ten rows wide, four measures of sunflower seed, and as many of beans. And, as for thee, let two married women be given thee, to be at thy disposal for five days. If that be not executed item by item I will make thy Nation a prey to all sorts of disasters,—and, after it is all done, I will declare to thee my orders for the future."

The dreamer's demands were fulfilled.

The Jesuits noted also, among the Huron, a formal ritual of gratification for sexual wishes expressed in dreams. In 1639, among the Hurons, Father Le Jeune met an old man ("in the common opinion of the Savages, . . . one of the most respectable and virtuous men of the whole country") who was dying of an ulcer that had spread from his wrist to his shoulder and finally had begun to eat into his body. This man's last desires were "a number of dogs of a certain shape and color, with which to make a three day's feast; a quantity of flour for the same purpose; some dances, and like performances; but principally . . . the ceremony of the 'andacwander,' a mating of men with girls, which is made at the end of the feast. He specified that there should be 12 girls, and a thirteenth for himself."

During the dream-guessing rites at Midwinter and, on occasion of illness, at other times of the year, persons propounded riddles in a sacred game. Each person or a group announced his "own and special desire or 'Ondinonc'—according as he is able to get information and enlightenment by dreams—not openly, however, but through Riddles. For example, someone will say 'What I desire and what I am seeking is that which bears a lake within itself'; and by this is intended a pumpkin or calabash. Another will say, 'What I ask for is seen in my eyes—it will be marked with various colors'; and because the same Huron word that signifies 'eye' also signifies 'glass bead,' this is a clue to divine what he desires—namely, some kind of beads of this material, and of different colors. Another will intimate that he desires an Andacwandat feast—that is to say, many fornications and adulteries. His Riddle being guessed, there is no lack of persons to satisfy his desire."

Nightmares of torture and personal loss were apparently not uncommon among warriors. In 1642 a Huron man dreamed that non-Huron Iroquois had taken him and burned him as a captive. As soon as he awoke, a council was held. "The ill fortune of such a Dream," said the chiefs, "must be averted." At once twelve or thirteen fires were lighted in the cabin where captives were burned, and torturers seized firebrands. The dreamer was burned; "he shrieked like a madman. When he avoided one fire, he at once fell into another." Naked, he stumbled around the fires three times, singed by one torch after another, while his friends repeated compassionately, "courage, my Brother, it is thus that we have pity on thee." Finally he darted out of the ring, seized a dog held for him there, and paraded through the cabins with this dog on his shoulders, publicly offering it as a con-secrated victim to the demon of war, "begging him to accept this semblance instead of the reality of his Dream." The dog was finally killed with a club, roasted in the flames, and eaten at a public feast, "in the same manner as they usually eat their captives." In the period 1645–49 Father Francesco Bressani saw a Huron cut off one of his fingers with a seashell because he had dreamed that his enemies had captured him and were performing this amputation. In 1661–62 Father Lalemant describes three similar cases among the Five Nations. One man, in order to satisfy the dictates of his dream, had himself stripped naked by his friends, bound, dragged through the streets with the customary hooting, set upon the scaffold, and the fires lit. "But he was content with all these preliminaries and, after passing some hours in singing his death song, thanked the company, believing that after this imaginary capitivity he would never be actually a prisoner." Another man, having dreamed that his cabin was on fire, "could find no rest until he could see it actually burning." The chief's council in a body, "after mature deliberation on the matter," ceremoniously burned it down for him. A third man went to such extremes of realism, after a captivity nightmare, that he determined "that the fire should be actually applied to his legs, in the same way as to captives when their final torture is begun." The roasting was so cruel and prolonged that it took six months for him to recover from his burns.

Some dreams were violently aggressive. One Huron dreamed that he killed a French priest. "I killed a Frenchman; that is my dream. Which must be fulfilled at any cost," he yelled. He was only appeased by being given a French coat supposedly taken from the body of a dead Frenchman. A Cayuga man dreamed that he gave a feast of human flesh. He invited all the chief men of the Cayuga nation to his cabin to hear a matter of importance. "When they had assembled, he told them that he was ruined, as he had had a dream impossible of fulfillment; that his ruin would entail that of the whole Nation; and that a universal overthrow and destruction of the earth was to be expected. He enlarged at great length on the subject, and then asked them to guess his dream. All struck wide of the mark, until one man, suspecting the truth, said to him: 'Thou wishest to give a feast of human flesh. Here, take my brother; I place him in thy hands to be cut up on the spot, and put into the kettle.' All present were seized with fright, except the dreamer, who said that his dream required a woman." And a young girl was actually adorned with ornaments and, unaware of her fate, led to the dreamer-executioner. "He took her; they watched his actions, and pitied that innocent girl; but, when they thought him about to deal the death-blow, he cried out: 'I am satisfied; my dream requires nothing further.' " And during the Feast of Fools, the annual *Ononharoia* or "turning the brain upside down," when men and women ran madly from cabin to cabin, acting out their dreams in charades and demanding the dream be guessed and satisfied, many women and men alike dreamed of fighting natural enemies. Dreams in which hostility was directed at members of other nations were properly satisfied by acting them out both in pantomime and in real life; but bad dreams about members of the same community were acted out only in some symbolic form, which had a prophylactic effect. Thus, for instance, someone on the Cornplanter Seneca Reservation (during the nineteenth century) dreamed that a certain young woman was alone in a canoe in the middle of a stream without a paddle. The dreamer invited the young lady to a dream-guessing ceremony at his home. Various people gathered, and each one tried to guess what the dream was. Finally the dream was guessed. A miniature canoe with a paddle was thereupon presented to the girl. This ceremony was expected to forestall the dream-disaster from happening in real life.

Dreams in which the dreamer met a supernatural being who promised to be a friend and patron, and to give his protégé special powers and responsibilities, were very common. They were experienced often by boys at puberty, who deliberately sought such guardian spirits. One case was described in some detail by the Jesuits. At the age of fifteen or sixteen the youth retired alone into the woods, where he went sixteen days without food, drinking only water. Suddenly he heard a voice, which came from the sky, saying, "Take care of this man, and let him end his fast." At the same time he saw an old man "of rare beauty" descend from the sky. This man approached, gazed kindly at him, and said, "Have courage, I will take care of thy life. It is a fortunate thing for thee, to have taken me for thy master. None of these Demons who haunt these countries, shall have any power to harm thee. One day thou wilt see thy hair as white as mine. Thou wilt have four children; the first two and the last will be males, and the third will be a girl; after that, thy wife will hold the relation of a sister to thee." As he concluded speaking, the old man held out to him a piece of raw human flesh. The youth turned aside his head in horror. "Eat this," then said the old man, presenting him with a piece of bear's fat. When the lad had eaten it, the old man disappeared. On later occasions, however, the old man frequently reappeared with assurance of help. Most of the old man's predictions came true: the youth became a man, had four children, the third of whom was a girl; after the fourth, "a certain infirmity compelled him to . . . continence"; and as the eating of the bear's meat augured, the man became a noted hunter, gifted with a second sight for finding game. As an old man, looking back, he judged that "he would have had equal success in war had he eaten the piece of human flesh that he refused." This man in his last years became a Christian and was baptized. Dreams of supernatural protectors (or persecutors) also came often to sick persons, and from the identity of the spirit, the identity of the appropriate therapeutic ritual was deduced. Thus dreams of false faces call for the curing rituals of the Society of Faces; dreams of birds (in recent years, particularly of bloody or headless chickens) indicated that the Dew Eagle Ceremony was required. Sick persons often dreamed of someone (or a relative of the sick person dreamed), and the dream was interpreted to mean that the sick person "wants a friend." During the Eagle Society Ceremony, the sick person is given a "ceremonial friend"; thereafter the two treat one another as kinfolk, and the relationship of mutual helpfulness is life-long. If a boy's friend, for instance, is an older man, that man "must help the child to grow up to be a man. He must advise the boy, acting as his counselor. . . . When one is ill, they choose a friend for him from the other side (moiety). It is believed that the ceremony of making friends merges the relatives of the two principals into one kindred unit: the relatives of the man are linked with the relatives of the child. The older man must act as an example to his junior friend. The older man's conduct shall be observed by the younger boy who considers the older friend a model of behavior. The creator has ordained that these two be friends and it is hoped the younger one will grow up to be the fine man his older partner is supposed to be. Whatever he observes the older man doing, he shall do it. The old man bears the onus of the child's future. As a reward he will see the Creator when he dies. When the two meet on the road, the older person speaks first. 'Thanks you are well my friend?' The younger one answers, 'Truly thank you I am well my friend.' Every time he sees me, he calls me 'friend.' "[3]

The force of the unconscious desires of the individual, which are so compelling that "it would be cruelty, nay, murder, not to give a man the subject of his dream; for such a refusal might cause his death," sometimes was reinforced in native theory because the dream might be the vehicle for the expression of the desires and commands of those supernatural beings whom his wandering dream-soul had met. Some of these supernatural dreams have already been mentioned. Those involving powerful supernaturals like Tarachiawagon were apt to achieve great currency, and (if the chiefs considered the dream ominous) the whole nation might exert itself to fulfill the dreamer's demands; neglect invited national disaster. In the winter of 1640, during an epidemic of smallpox among the Huron, a young fisherman had a vision: a demon appeared to him under the form of a tall and handsome young man. "Fear not," said the being, "I am the master of the earth, whom you Hurons honor under the name of Iouskeha. I am the one whom the French wrongly call Jesus, but they do not know me. I have pity on your country, which I have taken under my protection; I come to teach you both the reasons and the remedies for your misfortune. It is the strangers who alone are the cause of it; they now travel two by two through the country, with the design of spreading the disease everywhere. They will not stop with that; after this smallpox which now depopulates your cabins, there will follow certain colics which in less than three days will carry off all those whom this disease may not have removed. You can prevent this misfortune; drive out from your village the two black gowns who are there." The demon continued with prescriptions for distributing medicinal waters to the sick; but after a few days, apparently, the popular disturbance subsided, and the priests were not expelled. In the winter of 1669–70 a woman at Oneida was visited in a dream by Tarachiawagon, who told her that the Andaste (southern enemies of the Five Nations) would attack and besiege the Oneida village in the spring, but that the Oneida would be victorious and they they would capture one of the most famous of the Andaste war-captains. In her dream she heard the voice of this man coming from the bottom of a kettle, uttering wailing cries like the cries of those who are being burned. This woman became for a time a prophet; every day people gathered at her house to hear her pronouncements, and she was believed absolutely in all she said. Prophetic dreams of this kind, of course, derived much of their impact from the conviction of the community that while some dreams expressed only the wishes of the dreamer's soul, others expressed the wishes of his personal guardian spirit or of various supernatural beings, particularly of Tarachiawagon, the Holder of the Heavens, the Master of Life, He who decided the fate of battles, the clemency of the seasons, the fruitfulness of the crops, and the success of the chase.

The effectiveness of the Iroquois dream-therapy was admitted, in some cases, even by the Jesuits, who had neither formal psychological insight nor religious sympathy for the primitive dream-theory. Father Le Jeune described the case of a woman who had gone to live with her husband in a strange village. One moonlit night during a feast she walked out from her cabin with one of her baby daughters in her arms. Suddenly she saw the moon dip down to earth and transform itself into a tall, beautiful woman, holding in her arms a little girl like her own. This moon-lady declared herself to be the "immortal seignior" of the Hurons and the several nations allied to them, and announced that it was her wish that from each of the half-dozen or so tribes she named, a present of that tribe's special product—from the Tobacco Nation, some tobacco, from the Neutrals, some robes of black squirrel fur, and so on—should be given to the dreamer. She declared that she enjoyed the feast then being given and wanted others like it to be held in all the other villages and tribes. "Besides," she said, "I love thee, and on that account I wish that thou shouldst henceforth be like me; and I am wholly of fire, I desire that thou be also at least of the color of fire," and so she ordained for her red cap, red plume, red belt, red leggings, red shoes, red all the rest.

The moon-lady then vanished and the mother returned to her cabin, where she collapsed "with a giddiness in the head and a contraction of the muscles." Thereafter she dreamt constantly of "goings and comings and outcries through her cabin."

It was decided by the chiefs that this was an important matter and that every effort should be made to give satisfaction to the sick woman: not only *her* wishes, but those of the moon-lady, were involved. She was dressed in red; the disease was diagnosed (from the symptom of giddiness) as demanding the Dream Feast or *Ononharoia* ("turning the brain upside down"); and messengers collected for her the articles she required. The Jesuits sounded a sour note, refusing to contribute the blue blanket she wanted from a "Frenchman," but the lady went through the five-day ritual, supported most of the way on the arms of sympathetic friends. She hobbled in her bare feet through over two hundred fires; she received hundreds of gifts; she propounded her last desire in dozens of cabins, relating her troubles "in a plaintive and languishing voice," and giving hints as to the content of her last desire, until it was finally guessed. Then there was a general rejoicing, a public council, a giving of thanks and congratulations, and a public crowning and completing of her last desire (which Father Le Jeune, exasperatingly, does not describe or even hint at).

An honest man, the father was compelled to admit that all this worked. "It is to be presumed that the true end of this act, and its catastrophe, will be nothing else but a Tragedy. The devil not being accustomed to behave otherwise. Nevertheless, this poor unhappy creature found herself much better after the feast than before, although she was not entirely free from, or cured of her trouble. This is ordinarily attributed by our Savages to the lack or failure of some detail, or to some imperfection in the ceremony. . . ."

Not all therapeutic dream-fulfillments ended in even a partial cure, of course, but this was not felt as any reflection on the principles of dream-therapy. The whole village vied to give the sick person his every wish, for any frustration was a threat to life. A dying man might be seen surrounded by literally thousands of scissors, awls, knives, bells, needles, kettles, blankets, coats, caps, wampum belts, beads, and whatever else the sick man's fancy, or the hopeful guesses of his friends, suggested. And if he died at last, "He dies," the people would say, "because his soul wished to eat the flesh of a dog, or of a man; because a certain hatchet that he wished for could not be procured; or because a fine pair of leggings that had been taken from him could not be found." And if, on the other hand, he survived, the gift of the last thing that he wished for during his illness was cherished for the rest of his life.

The material on Iroquois dreams can be divided into two major types of dreams or visions recognized by the society and separately institutionalized (although in many dreams the two types are blended). These two types may be called *symptomatic dreams* and *visitation dreams*.

A symptomatic dream expressed a wish of the dreamer's soul. This wish was interpreted either by the dreamer himself or by a clairvoyant, who for a fee diagnosed the wish by free association in reverie, by drinking a bowlful of herb teas while chanting to his guardian spirit, by consulting his guardian spirit in a dream or trance (sometimes going to sleep with a special herb under his head), by water scrying, and in later days by reading tea leaves and cards. Anyone, man or woman, could become a clairvoyant, and there were many in each community, some occupying roles of reputation—like famous doctors —and others of more humble pretensions helping their immediate families. These diagnoses served as signals for the execution of various more or less conventional patterns of acting out the wish, either literally or symbolically. Some of these acting-out patterns were prophylaxes against the fate implicit in the wish—for example, the symbolic or partial tortures and the abortive cannibal feasts. This sort of acting out seems to have been based on the idea that a wish, although irrational and destructive toward self or friends, was fateful, and that the only way of forestalling the realization of an evil-fated wish was to fulfill it symbolically. Others were curative of existing disorders, and prophylactic only in the sense of preventing ultimate death if the wish were too long frustrated. The acting-out patterns can also be classified according to whether the action required is mundane or sacred and ceremonial. Thus dreams of buying a dog, and then traveling a long distance to obtain the dog, involve no particular sacred ceremony revolving around the wish itself, nor would a dream of going on a war party require more than participation in the normal course of military enterprise. But most of the symptomatic dreams of mentally or physically sick people demanded a ceremonial action, often not only at the time of the dream, but periodically thereafter during the dreamer's whole life span. The annual festival at midwinter not merely permitted but required the guessing and fulfillment of the dreams of the whole community. There were probably several dozen special feasts, dances, or rites that might be called for at any time during the year by a sick dreamer: the *andacwander* rite, requiring sexual intercourse between partners who were not husband and wife; the *ohgiwe* ceremony, to relieve someone from persistent and troubling dreams about a dead relative or friend; the dream-guessing rite, in which the dreamer accumulated many gifts from unsuccessful guessers; the Striking Stick Dance, the Ghost Dance, and many other feasts, dances, and games. The repertoire could at any time be extended by a new rite, if the dreamer saw a new rite, or a nonsacred rite, in a dream, or if his clairvoyant divined that such a rite was called for; even ordinary "social" dances became curative when performed for someone at the instigation of his dream. Some rites were the property of "secret" medicine societies, membership in which was obtained by having received the ministrations of the society upon dream-diagnosis of its need. Visions of false faces called for the rituals of the False Face Society; visions of dwarf spirits indicated a need for the "dark dance" of the Little Water Society; dreams of bloody birds were properly diagnosed as wishes for membership in the Eagle Society; dreams of illness were evidence of need for the Medicine Men's Society Rite. The relationship of dreams to ritual was such that the repertoire of any community might differ from that of the next because of the accidents of dreams and visions, and from the annual calendar of community rituals any element might at any time be abstracted and performed for the benefit of an individual.

The symptomatic dreams described above displayed in their manifest content relatively humble and mundane matters: wanted objects, like dogs, hatchets, knives, clothing, etc.; familiar dances and rituals, and their ceremonial equipment; familiar animals, birds, and plants. The second category of dreams, however, showed powerful supernatural beings who, in the dream, usually spoke personally to the dreamer, giving him a message of importance for himself and often also for the whole community. Sometimes these were personality-transformation dreams, in which the longings, doubts, and conflicts of the dreamer were suddenly and radically resolved, the dreamer emerging from his vision with a new sense of dignity, a new capacity for playing a hitherto difficult role, and a new feeling of health and well-being. Such experiences were particularly common among boys at puberty. Retiring alone to the woods, fasting, and meditating in solitude, the youth after a week or two experienced a vision in which a supernatural being came to him, promised his aid and protection, and gave him a talisman. The guardian spirit, in a sense, took the place of the parents upon whom the boy had hitherto depended, and from whom he had now to emancipate himself emotionally if he were to become a whole man. Guardian spirits varied in character and power: Some gave clairvoyant powers, some gave unusual hunting luck and skill, some gave luck, courage, strength, and skill in war. Clairvoyants possessed particularly potent guardian spirits that enabled the shaman, simply by breathing on a sick man's body, to render it transparent. Prominent shamans claimed the power to foretell coming events, such as approaching epidemics, and other great public calamities. A few such men became known as prophets and were "apt to acquire great influence and their advice [was] usually followed without much question." This gift of prophecy was the endowment of a particularly good, and powerful, guardian spirit.[4]

In Iroquois theory a dream thus could reveal the wishes not only of the dreamer, but of the supernatural being who appeared in his dream. Frustration of the wishes of the supernatural was dangerous, for he might not merely abandon or directly cause the death of the dreamer, but bring about disaster to the whole society or even cause the end of the world. Hence dreams in which such powerful personages as Tarachiawagon (culture hero and favorite dream-figure) appeared and announced that they wanted something done (frequently for the dreamer's welfare) were matters of national moment. Clairvoyants were called upon; the chiefs met and discussed ways and means of satisfying the sometimes expensive or awkward demands of the dreamer (representing the powers above) or of averting the predicted catastrophe. Not infrequently this type of dream also bore elements of personality transformation for the dreamer, who in his identification with the gods assumed a new role as prophet, messiah, and public censor and adviser. Such prophets might make highly detailed recommendations about the storage of crops, the waging of war, diplomatic policy toward other tribes and toward the French or the English, measures to avert epidemics or famine. Rarely, however, did such prophets maintain a lasting influence; but on the rare occasions of their success, a prophet, basing his message on a visitation dream, might bring about a radical transformation of the Iroquois way of life.

The theory of dreams among the Iroquois was in evident accord with the theme of freedom in the culture as a whole. The intolerance of externally imposed restraints, the principle of individual independence and autonomy, the maintenance of an air of indifference to pain, hardship, and loneliness—all these were the negative expression, as it were, of the positive assertion that wishes must be satisfied, that frustration of desire is the root of all evil. But men are never equally aware and equally tolerant of all their desires; and dreams themselves, carefully examined, are perhaps the quickest portal to that shadowy region where the masked and banished wishes exist in limbo. What then, if anything, can we learn about the unconscious of the Iroquois Indians from scattered dreams recorded by the Jesuits and other casual observers?

The manifest content of Iroquois dreams was as various, probably, as the wishes of mankind: There were dreams of love and hate, pleasure and pain, of lost loved ones and longed-for guardians; inconsequential and absurd things happened, and incidental objects were transfixed by the arrow of desire; abhorrent actions and repulsive thoughts plagued the restless sleeper. Dreams as reported in the literature seem to have held a prevailing anxious tone, ranging from nightmare fantasies of torture to the nagging need to define the unconscious wish and satisfy it before some disaster occurs. The most dramatic and most frequently mentioned dreams seem to come from three groups of people: pubescent youths (who must renounce childhood's indulgences); warriors (who feared capture and torture); and the sick (who feared death). These were, perhaps, the stress points that generated desire. Adolescent conflict, dreams of battle, and the silent panic of the sick; these are things of which many men of many cultures, including our own, have experience.

The manifest content and the conscious rationale the Seneca gave to dreams themselves were mainly in the active voices, and such passivity as showed itself was laden with pain unless it occurred in visitation dreams, where a man might be passive in relation to a god. But the latent content, representative of the underlying wish, may be seen in the *acting-out*, which was so often passive or self-destructive. Dreams were not to brood over, to analyze, or to prompt lonely and independent actions; they were to be told, or at least hinted at, and it was for other people to be active. The community rallied round the dreamer with gifts and ritual. The dreamer was fed, he was danced over, he was rubbed with ashes, he was sung to, he was given valuable presents, he was accepted as a member of a medicine society. The man whose dream manifested a wish to attack and kill was satisfied by being *given* a coat; the man who dreamed of sleeping with a woman did not attempt to woo his mistress, he was *given* an available female by the chief's council. Only in the personality-transformation dreams of pubescent boys and adult prophets was passivity accepted in the dream, and these were the dreams of men *in extremis*.

This observation suggests that the typical Iroquois male, who as a matter of fact in his daily life was an exceedingly brave, generous, active, and independent spirit, nevertheless typically cherished some strong, if unconscious, wishes to be passive, to beg, to be cared for. This unallowable passive tendency, so threatening to a man's sense of self-esteem, could not appear easily even in a dream, and when it did, it was either experienced as an intolerably painful episode of torture, or was put in terms of a meeting with a supernatural protector. The Iroquois themselves unwittingly made the translation, however: An active manifest dream was fulfilled by a passive receiving action. The arrangement of the dream-guessing rite, indeed, raised this dependency to an exquisite degree: The dreamer could not even *ask* for his wish; like a baby, he must content himself with cryptic signs and symbols, until someone guessed what he wanted and gave it to him.

The culture of dreams may be regarded as a necessary escape valve in Iroquois life. Iroquois men were, in their daily affairs, brave, active, self-reliant, and autonomous; they cringed to no one and begged for nothing. But no man can balance forever on such a pinnacle of masculinity, where asking and being given are unknown. Iroquois men dreamed; and without shame they received the fruits of their dreams, and their souls were satisfied.[5]

4

THE RITUALS OF FEAR

AND MOURNING

THE INTENSE INTEREST OF THE INDIANS IN LOVE AND FRIENDSHIP WAS not always apparent to early observers, who were apt to be more impressed by the mask of stoicism. But numerous incidental comments confirm the existence of a tender side of Iroquois character. Far from being so autonomous emotionally that social slights were matters of indifference, behind the impassive façade the Iroquois were often agonizingly shy, sensitive, and vulnerable both to flattery and to insult. A visit from a great man delighted whole villages, for—as a successful negotiator said—"Indians have a great idea of personal importance."[1] Neophyte chiefs were warned that they had to develop a skin "seven thumbs thick" in order to endure the disappointments and malicious gossip in which a political life was bathed. Insulted persons silently nourished grudges for years and in secret sought the help of witches to punish their enemies. Elaborate rules of conversational etiquette, designed to preclude interruptions of speech and face-to-face criticism, worked to avert the too-frequent chafing of tender sensibilities. But neighbors feared neighbors, and kinsmen their relatives, who might nonetheless be responsible through witchcraft for all manner of misfortune. Death aroused the most violent reactions: severe anaclitic depressions or moods of paranoiac suspicion, which in native theory (and it was a theory based on exact intuition) could only be forestalled by replacing the lost object with an adopted substitute upon whom could be lavished, depending on the character of the mourner, either the most extreme love or the most vicious hate (tortured victims also were adopted), or in some cases both alternately. Descriptions of Seneca mourning behavior read like psychoanalytic essays on the dynamics of depressive states, and the paranoia of bereavement, which generated the blood feud and fears of witchcraft, was regarded by the Iroquois themselves as a continuing threat to the solidarity of the community.

· *The Importance of Love and Friendship* ·

THE SUPERFICIAL RESERVE between the sexes, the avoidance of public embraces, the apparent casualness of marriage unions, the cool acceptance of divorce, gave some early observers the idea that the Seneca were deficient in romantic feeling, or even in animal passion, and others that they were extraordinarily licentious. Neither impression was close to the truth: Avoidance at first, and disillusionment later, public reserve always, were inevitable, precisely because of the extraordinary height of emotional aspiration. The Seneca legendry was full of romantic tales of young men who braved incredible dangers to win their beautiful brides. The theme of sexual jealousy was recurrent in folklore. Love magic was almost a profession. Guy Johnson, the son-in-law of Sir William Johnson and his successor as Superintendent of Indian Affairs, summarized the matter as a kind of emotional dialectic between romantic enthusiasm and spartan reserve. "Although the Indians appear to be little attracted by personal beauty, yet they are no means defective in the Animal Passion for their Females or in Constitutional Vigour, but thro' Education and Habit they do not manifest them to Superficial Observers . . . the Indians being all Warriors whilst young, & valuing themselves on the Reputation, affect a Coldness of Character, however Amorous, there being no Reputation derived from the latter, by which, and the uncommon affection of Modesty in their Women, when sober, Strangers are easily deceived; besides which Indians, who naturally are very Jealous, assume a Seeming Indifference for the Sex in order to Satisfy their Doubts by rendering those whom they Suspect more ungarded in their Actions.—Therefore the Indians are by no means chaste, but being naturally of a cold Behaviour, rather than Disposition, they Spartan like, avoid the outward appearance of an Attention to that, which derogated from their Military Merit."[2] And Governor Black-snake in his old age described in nostalgic detail a romantic episode in his youth that illustrates this ideological conflict between love and duty. Blacksnake was traveling with his uncle Cornplanter to San-dusky, in the Ohio country, in order to negotiate with the Indians there. They hoped, by serving as diplomatic middlemen, to avert a war between the western Indians and the United States. Along the way they fell in with a band of displaced Osage Indians, and Black-snake "took a liken" to a young woman who was "the Handsomest that I ever See among my own people." Although they could not speak each other's language, Blacksnake managed to make his interest known, and she hers. Eventually he discovered that she had no hus-band. He wanted to marry her, but his uncle Cornplanter, the head of the Seneca party, said no. "I then said no more about it marriage," he recalled. "I have felt sorrow."[3]

The concept of "friend" also was vested with an extraordinary degree of interest. The guardian spirit was the "friend" par excellence; there was the ceremonial friend chosen in a dream, particularly in connection with the Dew Eagle Dance, whose comradeship was be-lieved to cure and prevent serious illness; and individual men (often warriors on the same expedition) not uncommonly entered into a compact of mutual loyalty and service. This bosom-friend relation-ship could be very close. Stone, in his biography of Joseph Brant, re-marked on Brant's "lamentations" when a white officer who was his friend was transferred to Jamaica. "Those unacquainted with Indian usages are not probably aware of the intimacy, or the importance attached to this relationship. The selected friend is, in fact, the coun-terpart of the one who chooses him, and the attachment often becomes romantic; they share each other's secrets, and are participants of each other's joys and sorrows."[4] But in friendship as in love, the exigencies of war and travel made such relationships insecure.

· *The Faces of the Gods* ·

THE PROMINENCE OF MASKS in the rituals and supernatural beliefs of the Iroquois Indians implies that they embodied an idea of peculiar importance. False Face dancers performed dramatic pantomime at the New Year's and Green Corn ceremonies; they drove out witches and disease in the spring and fall; and they cured illnesses at any time of the year. Cornhusk masks were worn by other ritual dancers at New Year's and Green Corn. Some of the more secretive medicine-societies employed special, rarely seen masks. Even the mythology dealt with beings who went by the name of False Faces and who possessed a curious dual character, compounded of strength and shyness.

The wooden False Face masks were by all odds the most conspicuous. These masks were not called false faces or masks by the Seneca themselves, but simply *gagosa* ("faces"), the same word that was used for the human face. They were somewhat larger than life size, twelve to eighteen inches from forehead to chin, and broad in proportion. Although no two masks were identical (as one old Seneca put it, there are as many types of faces as there are different people), they had with few exceptions certain common features: They were painted black, or red, or black and red; they had large, staring eyes made of pieces of copper or brass sheeting pierced for pupils; long, protuberant, and frequently bent noses extended from brow to lips; the mouths were open and dramatically distorted. The mouths were the bases of native classification. There were wide mouths, upturned at the corners in a sardonic leer, sometimes with huge teeth showing; mouths rounded into a wide funnel for blowing ashes, sometimes with tongue sticking out; mouths puckered as if whistling, the lips everted into two flat, spoonlike disks; mouths with straight, swollen, shelflike lips; mouths twisted at one corner to accompany the bent nose, as if the face had been twisted by paralysis. Each was crowned with long, flowing hair, anciently buffalo mane, more recently horse tails. The antiquity of these concepts is considerable. Archaeologists have dug up miniature stone replicas in prehistoric cemeteries and villages. Champlain first saw them among the Hurons in 1616; a Dutch traveler found them among the Mohawk and Oneida in 1634. Masks were not mentioned by observers among the Seneca before 1687, but there is no reason to suppose that they had not a similar antiquity there; the Seneca were less thoroughly missionized than the Hurons and the Mohawks. Probably the earliest wooden masks go back at least into the sixteenth century. Their origin is obscure, but they probably originated as individual icons, representations of personal guardian spirits revealed in dreams, and came to be institutionalized as their peculiar suitability to religious and psychotherapeutic practice led more and more persons to dream of them. Indeed, the legend of the origin of the Society of Faces, who own most of the wooden masks, has it that the Faces were indeed revealed to a lonely hunter in a dream; they taught him their songs and their rituals, and no doubt in his dream he discovered what they looked like.

The wooden masks were made to fulfill a dream. Whoever dreamed of a Face instructing him to make a mask was obligated either to make one himself or to employ a craftsman to make one. The mask-maker first carved the outlines of the face in the bark of a living basswood (or other soft wood) tree, and then released the living Face by notching the trunk above and below and splitting it away. The mask was completed carefully, its back hollowed out to receive a wearer's face, and finally "baptized" by being placed briefly in the fire at a council-house meeting, while the great False Face, of whom it was a living likeness and deputy, was supplicated by the burning of powdered Indian tobacco thrown onto the embers. Once thus baptized, a mask was alive and charged with a power that could do almost limitless good or ill. It must be carefully kept, when not in use, either hanging with face to the wall or neatly wrapped in a clean cloth and placed in a drawer, or box, or other safe storage place. A little bag of tobacco must be tied to the inside of the mask, because the Faces loved tobacco, and on occasion (if the mask fell or if the owner dreamed of it) a little tobacco must be burned as an offering; it must be fed "False Face pudding" on occasion, by smearing a thick gruel of parched cornmeal and maple sugar (the warpath diet) on its lips; and its face must be wiped with sunflower-seed oil to keep the "skin" soft and clear. Old masks developed a lustrous patina from repeated applications of the oil. Masks had names and personalities, even whims; they liked to be talked and sung to and caressed, to have their hair arranged and their foreheads stroked; they were addressed as "grandfather." If one were to be transferred to another party, or perhaps sold, the transaction must be explained, the owner's regret expressed, and assurances given that the new owner would continue to feed, anoint, and supply tobacco. A neglected mask might sweat or even cry; large tears could be seen rolling from its eyes. Such unhappy Faces might ultimately avenge themselves by bringing a fatal illness on the owner; but Faces were rarely mistreated. They were loved and indulged like children; childless owners were even known to request that favorite masks be buried with them.

Although the Faces thus normally lived a passive, happy life, they did have on occasion very important, if not onerous, duties to perform. Most of them belonged to, and all were at the disposal of, the members of the Society of Faces. The membership of this society included a large share of the community, for all those persons, old and young, male and female, who had ever been saved from the ravages of disease through the kindly interference of the Faces or who had ever dreamed of membership in their society were automatically members. The society had no clubhouse, and its leadership was informal: a pair of women, representing the moieties, who were generally responsible for the care and assignment of the masks to ritual duties, and some men who on ceremonial occasion led the expeditions of the Faces and from time to time instructed the membership in the origin legends associated with the masks and the beings whom they represented. Without the ministrations of the society, a Seneca community would (in theory) have faced extinction.

As we have seen, in the spring and in the fall the Company of Faces conducted a public exorcism of disease, tornadoes and high winds, malevolent witches, and ill luck of all kinds from the entire village. The Company of Faces divided into two groups, starting at opposite ends of the settlement. Preceded by heralds wearing masks of braided cornhusks and augmented by recruits as they went along, the Faces visited every house. Stripped to the waist, masked, bearing rattles, the young men shouted terrifying cries as they moved along. As they approached the house or any member of the society, the leader chanted:

> *A long voice, a long voice*
> *Yowige, yowige, yowige*

and when they returned to the council house whence they had started, he sang a song suggestive of an ancient song of thanksgiving to a guardian spirit:

> *It might happen, it might happen*
> *Hai ge hai*
> *From the mighty Shagodyoweh*

Hai ge hai
I shall derive good luck
Hai ge hai.

During their patrol the masked visitors crawled into each house on hands and knees, prowled through every compartment, swept under the beds, and peered into dark corners. They jostled the sick to their feet and played practical jokes on lazy people. The horseplay was high-spirited. "Once," comments a recent observer, "a leader was about to gather his company of exterminators and depart for another house when one turned up missing. They heard a most terrifying racket in the loft. They ascended to discover him violently shaking an old straw bedticking, from which bedbugs were fleeing by the score. This fellow, . . . possessed of an extraordinary sense of the ridiculous, was shaking his rattle and crying in the most orthodox manner."

At last the company assembled at the council-house, where the Faces rubbed their rattles on the windows, banged on the doors, and finally burst into the room and crawled toward the fire. Now the Faces had to be paid for their work; and they had to be paid quickly, lest they assault the stoves and scatter hot coals about the room. The speaker thanked all the spirit forces and burned tobacco (collected at the houses just visited), imploring the Faces to protect the people against epidemics and tornadoes.

Partake of this sacred tobacco, O mighty Shagodyoweh, you who live at the rim of the earth, who stand towering, you who travel everywhere on the earth caring for the people.

And you, too, whose faces are against the trees in the forests, whom we call the company of faces; you also receive tobacco.

And you Husk Faces partake of the tobacco. For you have been continually associated with the False Faces. You too have done your duty.

Partake of this tobacco together. Everyone here believes that you have chosen him for your society.

So now your mud-turtle rattle receives tobacco.

Here the Faces scraped their rattles on the floor in delight.

And now another thing receives tobacco, your staff, a tall pine with the branches lopped off at the top.

So presently you will stand up and help your grandchildren, since they have fulfilled your desires. Fittingly, they have set down a full kettle of mush for you. It is greased with bear fat. Now another thing is fulfilled: on top there are strops of fried meat as large as your feet.

At this news, the Faces rolled over in ecstasy on their backs and seized their feet, staring at them and trying to put them in their mouths.

Besides, a brimming kettle of hulled-corn soup rests here.
Now it is up to you. Arise and help your grandchildren. They have fulfilled everything that you requested should be done here for you to use. Arise and make medicine.

Now those sick persons who had dreamt of a False Face, or whose illness had been diagnosed by a clairvoyant as produced by the Faces, came forward and stood by the fire, or if they were not well enough for that, sat on the bench in the middle of the floor. The Faces swarmed over them, blowing ashes on their heads, rubbing ashes in their hair, manhandling them with roughly tender, kindly hands. Then they danced around the council house to the music of a turtle rattle and a singer. The Doorkeeper's Dance, which followed, was for the Great World Rim Being (Shagodyoweh). And finally all persons within the council house joined in a round dance. Dancing was compulsory, for those who resisted were said to become possessed by the Face, falling to the floor, crawling toward the fire, and shuffling the hot coals.

The Faces treated the sick again in public rituals in the council house at midwinter and at the Green Corn in late summer. Most of their curing rituals were not public at all, however, but private affairs, conducted in the home of the sick person by the Order of Common Faces. These ceremonies were performed, on a request being made to a leader, whenever they were needed in response to a patient's dream or the diagnosis of False Face Sickness made by a clairvoyant. In characteristic fashion, masked beings banged on the house with their rattles and rubbed their staves up and down the door frames, burst in howling and babbling incoherently, danced, blew ashes and laid on hands, received hot mush and tobacco, and departed.

But probably the most widely noticed occasions of the appearance of the Faces was on sixth night of the Midwinter Ceremony. At this time the Faces were known as Beggars and Thieves. Worn by little boys and youths, they had been going about from house to house begging for tobacco and stealing food if not given tobacco. On the sixth night they repaired to the council house to beg again for tobacco from the people congregated there. There were the usual rattling, bumping, and scraping noises outside the building; then the door banged open and in crawled a ragged company of men, dressed in ragged, patched, torn clothes, and wearing False Face masks. Some carried the big turtle rattles, some the smaller horn rattles, some staves with which they hammered incessantly on the resonant floor. A ripple of delighted laughter swept around the congregation, now and then interrupted by an exclamation of mock terror as a Face thrust its leering visage close to a pretty woman. A few pirouetted clumsily; one rolled around hugging its knees; a third walked up and down the rows of benches, peering hopefully into each face and cooing like a mourning dove. At last some young man handed over a handful of Indian tobacco; this is what the Face was waiting for, and he immediately began his dance, solo, with the tobacco-giver beating out the tempo with the sharp edge of the rattle on the scarred floor. Soon all the Faces had found kindred spirits with tobacco to exchange for a dance, and the floor was creaking under the clumsy feet of the capering Faces, until at last they all suddenly departed, their appetites for tobacco satiated.

The vast powers that the False Faces were able to control on man's behalf shared the uncanny quality known as $utgo^n$. Witches were $utgo^n$, as were disease, storm, and other evil or mysterious things. In witchcraft, perhaps, $utgo^n$ took its most dramatic form. Witches, both men and women, were universally feared, and people suspected of witchcraft were hated and avoided. The fear of inciting a witch or his client to take revenge may have dissuaded some from expressing hostility openly and from aggressive acts of insult, theft, mayhem, and murder. But the other side of the coin was the persistent fear that any accident, illness, or death in one's kin group was the work of a secret enemy. Witch fear thus served both to suppress overt acts of rudeness and aggression and to nourish an endemic suspicion of one's neighbors. Some witchcraft was performed out of the witch's or his clients' private malice against the victim, to make him sicken and perhaps die. Magical poisons could be blown on the intended victim, concocted from arcane matter like the decaying flesh and bones of corpses;

foreign objects could be magically projected into his body; a doll might be hidden near a longhouse against whose lineage revenge was sought; a peg representing an enemy might be driven into a tree to rot; or the witch could simply wish the victim to death. Professional witches were supposed by some to be leagued in a coven, membership in which had to be obtained by the sacrifice of a kinsman, and to be able to transform themselves into were-animals, such as owls, turkeys, dogs, and pigs. Some of the services of legitimate shamans or curers might also be classified as witchcraft, for such persons, although not lending themselves to murder, could use their arts to cure the sick, to confuse and terrify the enemy in war and opponents in sport, to induce abortions, and to control the sexual desires and capacities of persons in whom a client was interested, causing uncontrollable lust in one, impotence in another. The traffic in abortion- and love-magic was active although it was considered to verge on the unethical.

Protection against witchcraft was best secured from the benevolent protecting power (*orenda*) of a guardian spirit, whose influence could shield one against *utgo*[n] and could ensure good luck in the hunt, warfare, love, and other important interests. Circumspection in behavior could avert the jealousy and wrath that might prompt others to turn to witchcraft. Shamans used poultices, sucking, and massage of the affected part to remove introjected objects and poisons. And if all else failed, a known witch might be killed with public sanction and without fear of retaliation from his kin. Also, the False Faces worked to protect the whole community against witches, as we have seen.[5]

The central myth that explained and identified the power over witches and other evils possessed by these alternately comical and awful Faces was the creation myth, in which the prototype of all the Faces, the Great World Rim Dweller, is no other than the Evil Twin, the brother of the Creator. Thus the Faces are party to the inmost secrets of the cosmos. Although Handsome Lake himself did not leave any known document narrating the story of the creation and of the origin of the Faces, several of his contemporaries and descendants on the Allegany Reservation have done so, and we can be reasonably sure of what his own belief was concerning these matters. His own brother, Cornplanter, dictated to a white man through an interpreter a brief account of the Seneca cosmogony in 1821; and about 1843 either his nephew Governor Blacksnake or Brooks Redeye, the

Handsome Lake preacher at Allegany at that time, dictated a longer version of the creation myth. These, with other texts from Allegany and elsewhere, provide a complete and coherent story, which accounts for and identifies, among other things, the Faces.[6]

In the beginning, before there was any earth, there was a world above, in the sky. This sky world was all alive: the land was living and the waters were living and there was an abundance of delicious animals and fish and fruits. There were manlike beings there, too, who were never sick, or in pain, or too cold, or too hot, and who never had to work. There was no sun or moon or stars; instead, there was a great tree that shed light half the time and half the time kept dark, so that the sky-beings had a kind of night and day.

Now in this sky world there was a family with five sons, and the youngest son was preoccupied with his love for a young woman. He loved her so much that he became weak. So he told his parents to go to this young woman and tell her of his love and of his weakness, which was the consequence of prolonged passion, and to tell her also that if she would come and attend him and be his wife, he would become strong again. This they did, and she consented to become his wife; he soon became strong again. But not long after this he became sick once more with the same weakness; for several days he grew weaker and weaker, and all the while he complained of his weakness. At last he called his oldest brother and said, "I have been complaining of weakness for several days. Now I am willing to tell you the instructions I received in a dream during the last sleep I had. I dreamed that the youngest of my brothers said, 'The living tree, The-Tree-That-Is-Called-Tooth, must be plucked out by the roots, and by the hands of the four brothers; otherwise you will die.' Also in my dream the living tree said, 'There is another generation coming out of the living tree. It will sprout out of the ground beside that living tree which gives light and control over the land.' "

The four brothers understood what he said, but they did not know what to make of it. Finally they asked him, "If the living tree should be plucked out by the roots, what shall we do for light?" He answered, "There is a young tree growing beside the old tree, and this will give light forever. The first one will be done away with for the sake of the new creation of the world, and the other will grow on solid ground and will stand and live forever. This will come to pass."

So they went to the tree to see whether a new tree was growing, as

he said, or not; and they found that a young sapling was indeed growing on top of the ground. The youngest brother then said he would
go forward and take hold of the living tree and pull it down by hand,
as the dream dictated. But the oldest brother said again, "Why do you
think you will die if we do not pluck out the tree of light?" And the
sick man said, "It is a true dream that has power by itself. It must be
done; if not, I shall die for cause of disobedience."

And so at last the four brothers consented to pull the old tree
down. The oldest brother took hold of it first and pulled and worked
at it until he wore himself out; then the next younger brother took
hold, and so on, until the youngest of the four brothers at last pulled
the tree down to the ground. Then the whole tree, roots, trunk,
branches, and leaves, plunged through the hole.

The sick man got up at once and went to the falling tree, calling
his wife to come with him. When they came to the place where the
tree had stood, they saw only the hole in the plain. The man-being
stood at the edge of the pit and looking down saw a light. He called
to his wife, "Come and look. Sit close by me." So she did. Then he
blessed the tree that had fallen through the earth for the sake of the
new creation and he blessed the young tree that remained. While
they sat there and gazed at the light below, an air came up through
the hole in the earth, very tender, and they heard the sound of the
south wind, which is the air of life. And from this air she conceived
a child.

He said to her, "Do you see plainly the light below?" She answered, "Yes." "There shall be your new home, on a new-created
earth below, and you shall be the mother of the earth-beings," he
said. And he pushed her off the edge of the pit and she fell through
the hole in the sky.

She was not worried but rather contented. For a long time she
fell slowly through the hole in the sky-plain, but when at last she had
passed through, and looked back, she could see nothing; it looked
blue as far as her eye could see. Then she saw a white bird flying; the
bird noticed her and went away to notify other birds. Then it came
back and said, "Are you afraid, being cast away like this?" And she
said, "Yes," and she looked at the bird, and the bird turned into a man
and he said to her, "You shall be saved, and it shall be fulfilled according to the instructions from above. You shall be assisted. You shall
inhabit a place on the great waters below." Then he left, and another

one came and said to her, "You will see tens of thousands of the inhabitants of the air and the waters below. They are preparing to take care of you."

And, indeed, as she looked down to see where she was going, she saw a great multitude of fowl flying in the air and heard a loud sound amongst them, because they were talking to one another. When she came near them, they all assembled and flew up toward her. Then they stopped her fall a little distance above the water. Then they held a council to decide who would be strong enough to bear her upon his back. But all the fowls of the air and even the water birds excused themselves; they were not able to remain long on top of the water. Then they asked themselves whether any of the creatures that live below the surface of the waters might be able to hold her up forever. Everyone had something to say and someone to suggest. But in the end only the mud-turtle remained as a candidate. While all the other species excused themselves, the mud-turtle said, "I never tire out or die without my father's consent." So he swam up on top of the water, and then the birds let her down upon him, and she stood upon his back, and there she rested. And all the fowls lighted upon him to rest themselves too.

The turtle grew very fast. The water fowls flew in every direction and the water creatures dived under the water, all to find earth to put on the turtle's back. And when they came back, each one had a little bit of ground with him and laid it on the turtle's back. Soon the earth was large enough for her to walk about and exercise herself. Then the mud-turtle spoke once more and said, "I will stand forever under you, for you to live upon. And there will come a great race that will build upon this earth, for it was given to me to have the power to do this and it shall be fulfilled according to the dream from above. I shall stand under the earth until the Great Spirit calls for me." Now Mud-turtle is the foundation of the earth. And all the animals rejoiced upon the earth, where forever they might find rest, and they praised Mud-turtle, the foundation.

Not long after this the woman gave birth to the child who had been conceived in the world above. This child was a female, and the mother called it "daughter." Soon the daughter was able to talk with her mother, and soon after this she could stand up and walk around at her mother's side. Then she got to be big enough to walk out of the cabin, and she became very fond of going to the water. The mother always forbade the child's going to the water, but the child always replied, "I want to go to the water to catch the young fowls that are on the shore." Still the mother forbade the child; and still the child wanted to know why she was not allowed to go where she wanted. But the mother did not want to tell her what would happen if she went into the water. After a while the girl grew up to be a young woman and to have her monthly periods, and now she was even more desirous of playing in the water. But the mother still forbade it.

At last the young woman disobeyed her mother; she did go to the water, she did play with the water, she did go into the water. And soon afterward the mother discovered that her daughter was pregnant, and she knew that she had conceived by going into the water. The daughter was pregnant with twins, the Evil Twin Tawiskaron and his brother Tarachiawagon, the Good Spirit. The twins came into conflict even before they were born. Their mother heard them disputing in the womb over how to emerge. One of them said, "Let us go out the regular way and save the mother." And the other one said, "Let us go out the nearest and quickest way." But the first one said, "I will go out the right way to save the mother." And again the other one said, "I will go the nearest way and the cleanest way because I can see the light under her arm on the left side of her body."

The Good Twin was born in the right way. But the Evil Twin came out under his mother's arm. She immediately called the grandmother, for she knew that she was going to die. She gave directions on what to do, saying, "Mother, you must take my body and bury it under the ground. Lay my head against the wind, so that the sun will rise at my feet and go down toward my head and the moon likewise. And also build a fire at my head upon the grass every night till the ten days are up. After a while you will see two cornstalks growing from my breasts above the grave, and they will bear corn that will be good for seed. Keep it and plant it here, for generation after generation of my children will live here forever. One of my sons shall be called the Good Spirit, and he will place good things upon earth and will regulate it. And the other you shall call the Evil Spirit, and he will place all the evil things upon the earth." So the grandmother took the children and laid them aside, and then she took the dead body and buried it under the ground and laid the head toward the wind. Then she went to the children. They were in good health. And then it became dark and she went to sleep.

When she awoke it was light, and the twins were talking to one another and smiling happily because the night was passed. The Good Spirit said, "It is good. Let the sun be created and rise against the wind to shine and make light." And the sun did so, and it went down at the head of the wind and it became dark again. Then the Good Spirit said, "Let the moon be created and rise against the wind." And the moon rose and shone with the light of the night. And the Good Spirit was pleased at what he had done.

But the Evil Spirit made fun of it and contradicted his brother who was creating the world.

The Good Spirit formed man out of the dust of the ground and breathed into his nostrils the breath of life, and man became a living soul. The Good Spirit said, "Let the vegetables grow upon the land, and every kind of herb." But they did not grow because he had not yet made the rain and because there was not a woman to till the soil and to multiply the earth. So the Good Spirit made a woman, and he called the man and the woman together and said to the man, "That woman shall be your wife," and to the woman he said, "This man shall be your husband. And you shall enjoy yourselves upon the earth in order to multiply from generation to generation. And here are vegetables and herbs to sustain life from the fruits of the earth, which shall grow forever."

Thereafter the Good Spirit busied himself with completing the creation. He made rivers and streams, with double currents so that men would always paddle downstream; he scattered and improved the corn that grew from his mother's grave so that this corn was fatter, oilier, and easier to grow than any corn known today; he created the deer, elk, bear, beaver, and other game animals. But the Evil Spirit, his twin, always trailed after him, jealously undoing the good his brother made and, in his attempts to equal his creative elder twin, creating all manner of annoying and evil things, like bats, frogs, owls, worms, snakes, and carnivorous monsters. He changed the streams so that they flowed only one way, and broke them up with waterfalls, rapids, and whirlpools; he blighted the corn, so that ever after it grew smaller, was harder to raise and less tasty, and sighed mournfully in the wind; he made caves, and spread disease, storms, ice, and death. Once he even stole the sun, and he and his grandmother ran away with it to keep it for themselves, but the Good Spirit brought it back. Although the Good Spirit was not able to reverse all the damage his brother did, he was able to counteract most of it.

At last, one day, the great work was nearly completed, and the Good Spirit began a tour of inspection, walking westward around the earth. Far to the west, on the rocky rim of the world, he met his brother the Evil Spirit, who now was in the form of a giant. The Creator asked the stranger, as he had asked all the others, what he was doing. "Looking over my creation," said the giant. "It is *my* creation," said the Good Spirit. Finally they agreed to settle the dispute by a contest of magical power: each one would try to make the Rocky Mountains move. The Good Spirit said, "You try first." So the giant took a whole hickory tree as his cane and rubbed a snapping turtle across it. The mountains trembled but moved only a little way. Then the Good Spirit said, "Now it's my turn." He made the giant turn around with his back to the mountains, and while the giant's back was turned, he moved the mountains close up behind him. "Now turn around," he said. The giant turned and bashed his nose against the side of the mountain.

Then the giant said, "You are the Creator. I submit and beg to be allowed to live." The Good Spirit granted the request, on condition that he would help the people and take them as his grandchildren. So the bargain was made: If the people would wear masks representing the giant, and would burn tobacco for him and give him a little cornmush, he would give them power, through the masks, to handle hot coals without being burned, to withstand the cold without shivering, and to drive away disease, witches, and high winds.

So the Faces represented a being, the powerful giant Shagadyoweh, who dwelt on the rocky rim of the world and who was defeated by the Creator in a contest to decide who had created the world. The twisted nose of many of the masks was a memento of the event. But behind the bent-nosed giant stood, in shadowy file, other images who could be alternately (or simultaneously) invoked by the same masks: Tawiskaron, the Evil Twin; the sea-father of the twins; the Four Brothers (the "Mystery Masks") who control the winds; the Whirlwind Spirit; and He-Whose-Body-Is-Riven-in-Twain (the spirit, half Tawiskaron and half his good brother, who is half winter and half summer). And also represented by the masks were a whole legion of forest spirits, huge, shy, featureless heads who flitted from tree to tree on spindly legs, with their long hair snapping in the wind, and who sometimes visited lonely hunters, begging for food and tobacco.

Shy and querulous as these Forest Faces were, they were also powerful: the unexpected sight of them could cause paralysis, or nose-
bleed, or possession, but properly fed and placated, they brought
luck to the hunter. Logically, the same mask could hardly be an
embodiment of all these beings; but this was not a matter for logic.
The Faces were the faces of many gods.

On the various occasions when men wore the Faces the triangular
interaction among maskers, masks, and audience ran the gamut of
human feelings. The adult masker, wearing the Face and impersonat-
ing the Great World Rim Dweller or the Forest Faces, vented attitudes and feelings that were not permitted him in sober social life.
He might gurgle and coo like a baby, crawl on the floor, suck his
toes, and beg for things to eat. He might thump with sticks on walls
and windows, bang open doors, throw fire and ashes around, dance
uninhibitedly. He might throw people out of bed, smear them with
human excrement, upset the furniture, and frighten the timid with
wild cries. And at the same time he controlled mighty matters, having the power to cure incurable disease, avert deadly tornadoes, cast
out malevolent witches, and bring order to a whole community. The
Seneca, as masker, could recapture the fancied omnipotence of in-
fancy, doing the impossible with ease and the infantile with im-
punity, indeed even to the applause of spectators. The beings whom
he represented were the very prototype of the infant: ambitious
beyond their years, desirous of emulating their betters, mischievous
and destructive, quickly enraged at neglect or frustration, careless of
their parents' welfare, yet hopeful of forgiveness if their dreams of
stolen glory were discovered. And at the same time the omnipotent
infant was the omnipotent parent, able to cure disease, avert thunder,
and scare away evil people.

It is hardly to be wondered at, then, that not infrequently Seneca
men and women—normally so reserved, so self-sufficient, so hardy
and independent—were seized with an irresistible and terrifying urge
to be like the Faces. Some resisted it, refused to join the dance, tried
to get out of the council-house, but once touched by the doorkeeper
in a great "doctor" mask, they might fall to the floor in a fit. As far
back as 1616 Champlain saw women possessed, walking "on all fours
like beasts," and cured at length by the masked company who blew
ashes on them and pounded out raucous music with turtle rattles.
Sometimes people were obsessed by the idea of the masks: They

experienced repetitive nightmares in which they saw faces peering out of bushes in the twilight and heard the long drawn "Hoo-oo-oo!" Such disorders were specifically cured by the Society of Faces, which manhandled the victim, blew ashes, and inducted him into the society so that he too came to possess and recognize a Face, fed and anointed it, and wore it to cure others. The ministrations of the Faces also were helpful in a wide variety of difficulties, many of them, in the language of a later day, "psychosomatic" in large part, such as intractable aches and pains, paralyses and tics, and nosebleeds. Induction into the Society of Faces, identification with one or another of the legendary figures represented by the masks, and the acting out of infantile roles (modified by good taste, and in the name of socially desirable goals like the curing of disease, the averting of witchcraft, and the like) logically should, and indeed often did, produce a cure or at least give benefit.

The Faces of the gods, then, were really the faces of the Seneca themselves. They represented that strange and forgotten part of the self where repressed and disallowed desires of various sorts, often childish or infantile in form and content, normally subsisted in silent turmoil. Rage and fear, lust and hate, boundless ambition and abject passivity, cold cruelty and noble altruism, were all forever ready to emerge; and depending on time and place and person, they emerged in various ways. With unconscious wisdom the Society of Faces found a means of venting these emotions, of bleeding them off harmlessly, without too much frightening the patient. As with the cult of dreams, membership in the Society of Faces made it possible for the poised, independent, self-controlled, self-sacrificing Seneca to express what he did not allow himself to feel: a longing to be passive, to beg, to be an irresponsible, demanding, rowdy infant, and to compete with the Creator himself; and to express it all in the name of the public good.

· The Cult of Death ·

THE IROQUOIS were deeply affected by death. As they put it, the Being That Is Faceless, the Great Destroyer, roamed night and day with his club uplifted over the peoples' heads, waiting to strike down all men, and boasting, "It is I, I will destroy all things. . . ." But death could come in many forms: by violence, in war at the hands of an enemy, in peace at the hands of a drunken friend, by stealth at the wishing of a witch, by accident or disease. Death came to the mighty, the chiefs, upon whom the people leaned; death came to the weak and insignificant; death came to the proud captive. And what the people did in the face of death depended both upon who died and upon how he died.

"There is something peculiarly pathetic," wrote missionary Asher Wright, "in the attachment which these interesting people [the Seneca] cherish for their patriarchal sepulchres. The feeling of reverence for the graves of their ancestors is universal among them. Tis a national trait."

He described affecting instances. "Bury me by my grandmother," said a little boy of seven a few minutes before he died; "she used to be kind to me." And "Lay me by our mother," said a little orphan girl under the missionaries' care, when she knew she would not get well. An old woman of eighty, speaking of a planned tribal migration, lamented, "I am sorry for I had hoped to be laid by Mother in yonder graveyard." A chief complained also of the same removal: "We can not go to the west and leave the graves of our fathers to the care of strangers. The clods would lie heavily on our bosoms in that distant country should we do it." Wright spoke of seeing middle-aged men and women "weep like children" when the least allusion was made to dead loved ones, and he wrote of the solicitude with which the grave goods were placed beside the bodies: a chief's best clothes, guns, traps, and knives; almost the whole of an infant's wardrobe; even the poorest people would scrimp and borrow to buy for departed friends a respectable robe. Mothers often visited the graves of their children and noticed the least change in the appearance of the enshrouding earth; sometimes they identified the spot of an unmarked grave after years of absence.[7]

The death of a League chief, one of the forty-nine *royaner*, was symbolic of group calamity. When such a great chief died, it was as if the Great Faceless had kicked apart the burning brands and, exulting in destruction, stamped out the council fire with dancing feet. No business could be done; the people were (at least metaphorically) dismayed and appalled at the havoc. The universe itself seemed to be shaking.

The death of a chief was considered to be serious, not only because it formally interrupted council procedure, but also because grief was a principal cause of derangement. The death of a League chief, bereaving the entire moiety of the departed (i.e., roughly half of the Five Nations' population), was expected to produce catastrophic grief-symptoms in whole nations. It was a "calamity . . . hopeless and dreadful." The nations, personified as individuals, were thought of as lying alone in a darkened house, weeping and withdrawn from reality, unable to hear "the sounds made by mankind, nothing of what is taking place on earth," and unable to speak.

The description of the melancholia of bereavement is almost clinical in its detail and insight, as it is recited in the monotonous intonations of the Requickening Address of the Condolence Council. "The organs within the breast and the flesh-body are disordered and violently wrenched without ceasing, and so also is the mind. . . . Verily, now, the life forces of the sufferer always become weakened thereby. . . . The disorder now among the organs within [the] breast is such that nothing can be clearly discerned . . . when a direful thing befalls a person, that person is invariably covered with darkness, that person becomes blinded with thick darkness itself. It is always so that the person knows not any more what the day light is like on the earth, and his mind and life are weakened and depressed . . . the sky is lost to the senses of that person . . . such a person knows nothing about the movement of the sun [i.e., night and day and the passage of time are not noticed] . . . invariably the mind of that person is simply tossed and turned on the grave of him in whom he fondly trusted. . . . Verily, it is a direful thing for the mind of him who has suffered from a grievous calamity to become insane, [for] the powers causing insanity are immune from everything on this earth, and [insanity] has the power to end the days of man. . . ."

In order (theoretically) to prevent the consequences of extreme grief, when a League chief died a Condolence Council was held at an early opportunity and before the chiefs undertook any new business. At this council the mourners were cleansed of their despair, and a new chief was installed to replace the old. Little was said about the departed: It was the survivor, not the dead, who was the object of compassion.

The Condolence Council was "given" by the "clear-minded" moiety to the mourning moiety. The clear-minded ones came through the forest to the village of the dead chief, singing the *Hai Hai*, or Roll

Call of Founders of the League, as they walked along. It was a mournful song, recounting the glorious names of the original founding fathers, still preserved as titles of office, but lamenting that their work had grown old and that their successors were a weaker race. Then at the wood's edge, where the cleared fields began, the clear-minded and the mourners met and sat down together across a fire, to exchange greetings and the Three Rare Words of Requickening. The Three Rare Words were: Eyes, Ears, and Throat. The clear-minded, perceiving that the mourners' eyes were blinded with tears, their ears clogged and unable to hear, and their throats choked with sadness so that they could not speak and could breathe only with difficulty, wiped away the tears with the white fawn-skin of pity, cleaned out the ears, and removed the throttling obstructions from the throat. Then the mourners reciprocated, and the two parties marched in procession to the longhouse, where the Twelve Matters were dealt with, one by one, by the clear-minded on behalf of the mourners.

The Twelve Matters—each endorsed by a string of wampum passed across the fire—were the therapeutic or "requickening" ritual that delivered the melancholic mourner from the toils of his depression and paranoid suspicion. The first matter rearranged the wrenched internal organs by pouring in the water of pity. The second wiped clean the bloody husk-mat bed where the wretched one sat cross-legged. The third let daylight into the darkened house of grief. The fourth pointed out that the sky was still beautiful; the fifth that the sun still rose and set. The sixth leveled the rough ground over the grave and placed a little roof of wood and thatch over it, so that the heat of the sun and the wet of the rain would not disturb the corpse. The seventh reminded the mourners that if their kinsman had died by murder or witchcraft at the hand or instigation of another Iroquois, they were not to seek blood revenge but should accept the traditional twenty strings of wampum as were-gild. The eighth gathered together the scattered brands of the council fire and convened the council to do business again. The ninth exhorted the warriors and the women to be of strong heart, to help one another to do the work of life, and not to be listless and indifferent—for that mood of mind should properly prevail only when the earth is at last split asunder and the doom of all things impends. The tenth matter forbade the chiefs to neglect the mourning people lest their minds become insane from grief. The eleventh instructed the people of the

League, in case of another death, always to run with the Torch of Notification through all the villages of the League. The twelfth and final matter was the request of the clear-minded that the mourners point out the man who was their candidate to be the new chief.

After a return of condolences by the mourners to the clear-minded (who also were grieving, although less wretchedly) the new chief's face was shown. He was examined, and if the condoling moiety accepted him, the antlers of office were placed on his head, and he was charged to show henceforth the proper qualities of a chief: to have a skin seven thumbs thick, immune to malicious gossip and cantankerous criticisms; to act always in the best interests of the people, not only those living now, but also the generations to come; and to lead a good, clean personal life.

Then there was a feast for all in the longhouse, and finally an evening of dancing in which the chiefs "rubbed antlers" and the crowd of common people had a good time in a series of social dances. The clear-minded visitors were granted access to the mourners' women, with humorous appeals for self-restraint. "I now let escape from my hands our womenfolk. Accordingly you shall use them properly. Don't anyone treat them too roughly!" announced the master of ceremonies.

And he added, "So now another thing. Time may also be devoted to something else. Perhaps one of you may have had a dream. Then in that event let us amuse our minds with dreams."

And with clear minds the erstwhile mourners began life anew, feasting, dancing, flirting, and telling one another their dreams of the previous year.[8]

The origin of the Condolence Council was, according to Iroquois mythology, the result of an act of divine intervention in human affairs; in fact, it was the occasion of the founding of the Great League itself.

According to the Dekanawidah myth, there was a time when the five Iroquois tribes were not united in a league. They constantly warred and feuded among themselves, and were continually being warred upon by neighboring Algonquian tribes, so that no man, or woman, or child was safe. At last a man named Hiawatha, depressed by the death of his wife and family, fled into the forests, where he lived as a cannibal, waylaying and devouring luckless travelers. One day the god Dekanawidah, who had been born of a virgin and who had come across the lakes in a white stone canoe, found Hiawatha's cabin in the forest. Climbing on the roof, he gazed down through the smoke hole. Now at this moment Hiawatha, within, was staring into a pot of water, and he saw the face of the god reflected from its surface. He thought that it was the image of his own face that he saw, and he said to himself, "That is not the face of a cannibal." This was his moment of moral regeneration. Dekanawidah now entered the cabin and revealed himself and his mission to Hiawatha.

Dekanawidah's mission—and hereafter Hiawatha's, too—was to persuade the Iroquois to unite in a confederacy that would prohibit the usages of the blood feud among the five tribes, substituting in cases of homicide an obligatory payment of were-gild. Hiawatha now became Dekanawidah's spokesman, for the god had an impediment in his speech which prevented his ever addressing an audience (and some say he never was seen by any man but Hiawatha). Tribe by tribe, Hiawatha's eloquence persuaded the people and the chiefs to lay aside the blood feud and unite, until at last, having combed the snakes out of the shaman Atotarho's hair, he was able to bring sachems from all the tribes together into the great council at Onondaga.[9]

The deaths of ordinary people did not require such elaborate condolence procedures as those prescribed for dead chiefs, but burial and mourning rites were similarly calculated to relieve the mind of melancholy. The dead were buried in graves, frequently seated with knees drawn up under the chin, and surrounded by the goods they would need in the next world. The graves were lined with boards or bark. Because in Seneca belief the soul remained close to the body for some time after death and from time to time even re-entered it, a hole was cut in the tomb lining in order to give the soul easier access to the head. The funerals themselves were under the charge of the women, who during the procession to the cemetery near the village, and again on their return to the feast at the house of the deceased, wept and tore their hair and rolled on the ground. A woman was expected to abandon herself to despair if one of her near family died, casting herself onto the cold hearth over the grave, where ashes were thrown over her head and shoulders, to mix "with tears and drivel from the mouth and with blood oozing from many lacerations on the body." The female relatives and neighbors of the dead one, for nine more days, every morning gathered at the house of mourning to weep and lament. At last, on the evening of the tenth day after death there was held the "ten days' feast," at which the hungry soul of the departed was fed and sent on its way, and the mourners were constrained to dry up their tears and become clear-minded. The soul might, however, be reluctant to leave the neighborhood, and so occasionally for the next year food might be laid out for him. Furthermore, these haunting souls, frustrated in their longings for food and companionship, were apt to bother people in their dreams or even to plague survivors with sickness and misfortune. Such persecution by the spirits of the dead was countered by the *ohgiwe* ceremony: a night-time occasion, at which a feast is held for the ghost and the living together, and certain chants for the dead are sung. These *ohgiwe* songs were not to be profaned by being sung for no reason; if they were sung for amusement, some misfortune was bound to afflict the singer.[10]

For the dead were dangerous. The negative side of the passionate mourning for the lost loved one was an elaboration of gruesome fantasies about the cannibalistic appetites and sadistic humor of the dead. A particularly common legend was that of the vampire skeleton. Once upon a time, a man and his wife went out to hunt. The hunting ground was a two days' journey away, and on their way home, heavily laden with meat, they came to a cabin where the owner, a famous medicine man, was dead. Because it was already dark, the husband decided that they should spend the night there, in spite of the fact that the dead man's body lay on a shelf in a bark coffin. The husband gathered wood and lit a fire and then lay down to rest while his wife cooked meat and cornmeal cakes. After a while he fell asleep. The wife went about her work. Suddenly the woman heard a noise behind her, near where her husband lay; it was like the sound of someone chewing meat. She thought about the corpse on the shelf and remembered that the dead man was a witch, so she put more wood on the fire and made it blaze up, and then she looked again. She saw a stream of blood trickling out from the bunk. At once she knew that her husband had been killed by the dead man.

But she pretended that she did not notice. She said, as if speaking to her husband, "I must make a torch and bring some water." She made a torch of hickory bark, long enough to last until she could run home. Then she took the pail and went out; but as soon as she was outside the door, she dropped the pail and ran through the woods as fast as she could. She had gotten halfway home before the vampire realized that she had gone. He ran after her, whooping. She heard him behind her; the whooping came nearer and nearer. She was so scared she almost fell, but she ran on until her torch was almost out and at last reached a lodge in her village where people were dancing. She burst into the lodge and fainted.

When she revived, she told the story of what had happened to her and her husband. In the morning a party of men went to the cabin, where they found the bones of her husband, from which all the flesh had been eaten. The face and hands of the skeleton in the bark box were found to be bloody. Thereupon the chief said that it was not right to leave dead people that way. They took the bones of the vampire and buried them in a hole that they dug in the ground, and they brought the bones of the husband back to his village and buried them there also. And thereafter the dead were no longer placed on scaffolds or in shelves in bark lodges, but were buried in the ground.[11]

Beliefs about the life after death were various because any individual could, and many did, discover in a dream some new and different character for the heavenly world, and furthermore, by the eighteenth century Christian cosmology was widely known. In general, however, there was some sort of pleasant place to which, if his conduct during life was orderly and pleasing to the Good Spirit, a man would be admitted after death; and sometimes, but less commonly, there was also conceived to be a hellish place, governed by the Evil Spirit, where bad people went. An old man in a Huron village, for instance, a little while before he died, "fell into a swoon." When he came out of it, he said that he had just been to the other world, which was nothing like what the French had forecast to him (the Jesuits were accustomed to warn the heathen of the perils of hell). To the contrary, he had met several of his own departed family and other relatives, who welcomed him kindly and told him that they had been waiting for him for a long time and were preparing many "fire dances and feasts" in his honor. He was so confident of this dream's validity that in order to be able to present himself in the same magnificent dress and accouterments as his heavenly kinfolk, he had his whole face painted red, had brought and placed over him the finest articles he had, was given his plate and spoon—and thus he died. This man was reputed to have been one of the most respectable and virtuous men of the whole country, because he was peaceable, did no harm to anyone, and "greatly delighted in merrymaking and in giving feasts."[12] Other men after similar visions in illness reported that the village of souls was a mournful place like a natural village, but loud with the unceasing groans and complaints of the hapless dead. There was a story of a bridge made of a wobbly tree-trunk, which the souls of the dead must cross. This bridge was guarded by a dog, who jumped at some souls and made them fall, to drown in the torrent of rushing waters beneath.[13] Probably the conceptions of the next world corresponded with the preoccupations and wishes of the individual, as revealed to him in dreams, and only a loose framework of belief in a village of the dead, somewhere to the westward, united the opinions of the tribes.

The souls of the dead did not always rest in peace. Those who had been murdered by men of other nations could find no haven in the next world until their lust for vengeance had been appeased. Generally speaking, whatever economic or political considerations might be involved in the tensions that led to war, the actual formation of war parties was either inspired or rationalized by the obligation to avenge dead relatives. Women whose kinfolk had been killed would appear at public dances and feasts, weeping inconsolably; if this display did not succeed in arousing the warriors, the women might offer payments or accuse the lagging warriors of cowardice. Men might dream of their murdered kin and interpret the dream as the lost soul's desire for revenge; such a dream could compel the dreamer to organize a war party. Until the bereaved had "gotten even," until there had been retaliatory killings and tortures, it was as if the blood of the murdered one had not been wiped away and his corpse not covered. War-caused bereavement was a state of unavenged insult and shame (and, indeed, war parties might be organized to avenge mere verbal insults as well as killings). One might, indeed, regard the Iroquois war complex as being, psychologically, a part of the mourning process, an acting out of the paranoid resentments that were aroused by loss. But the social consequences of this propensity were momentous.

With some nations, usually distant, like the Catawba and Cherokee of the Carolinas, the Iroquois remained on terms of chronic warfare for generations. Neither side intended to exterminate or dispossess the other; the "war" consisted of occasional raids by revenge squads of ten to fifty men who at the most would burn a small camp, kill a few people, and bring back a dozen or so prisoners to be tortured or adopted. At any point in time, some family on either the Iroquois or the Catawba or Cherokee side had a score to settle, and young men seeking to validate their adult masculinity, led by the males of mourning families, sooner or later would take to the trail.

Such chronic wars, if they involved close neighbors, however, quickly reached a point of critical involvement. Separated by five hundred miles, the Seneca and the Cherokee were sufficiently insulated by distance for an equilibrium to be reached so that there was no cumulation of unavenged killings over the years. But with a neighboring tribe, physical proximity multiplied the opportunities for incidents, as well as for more diffuse economic and political tensions over such matters of competition as the fur trade. Thus feud-wars with neighboring tribes, like the Huron, the Erie, and the Susquehannocks, annually dragged more and more families into the revenge process and increased the opportunity and motivation for nonmourners to take part in a raid. Feud-wars with neighbors developed into total wars, which had eventually to be settled either by peacemaking diplomacy or by major campaigns involving hundreds of warriors. The process of involvement of a tribe in a war was like the building up of a nuclear explosion: as long as the two social masses were a long distance apart, their mutual bombardment by war parties remained in equilibrium without any cumulative increase in the rate of emission; but as the two masses were brought closer together, they stimulated each other to more and more activity, and when two sufficiently large masses were adjoining, the rate of mutual bombardment accelerated until the explosion of war occurred.

The common aim of all war parties was to bring back persons to replace the mourned-for dead. This could be done in three ways: by bringing back the scalp of a dead enemy (this scalp might even be put through an adoption ceremony); by bringing back a live prisoner (to be adopted, tortured, and killed); or by bringing back a live prisoner to be allowed to live and even to replace in a social role the one whose death had called for this "revenge." One death might be avenged several times over, in different ways; and the sentiments of the nearest (or loudest) mourner determined what disposition was to be made of a given case. In an earlier chapter was described the insatiable desire of Aharihon to kill and torture in honor of his departed brother. Other, less morbid, mourners were more humane: a woman who had lost her son might "cast her girdle" about a likely looking prisoner and adopt him as her son, a man might take a new brother, and henceforth these adopted kinfolk were regarded and treated almost as if they were the reincarnation of the dead. Whole villages might even be adopted; at times during the seventeenth century, when war casualties were heavy, as many as two thirds of the population of the Oneida nation were adoptees, and the other nations, including the Seneca, similarly depended heavily on adopted manpower. White prisoners thus adopted, as well as prisoners of other Indian tribes, apparently in many cases identified themselves thoroughly with their new roles and, in the case of white prisoners, objected vigorously to being repatriated when prisoners were exchanged. Many of the cases of reported mistreatment by returned "prisoners" (aside from deliberate torture) probably reflect either the adoptee's refusal to learn the language and accept normal native standards of living or the misfortune of being adopted by personally disagreeable relatives (a misfortune not unknown to adopted children in our own society).

Many prisoners were, however, consigned to torture, particularly during the seventeenth century; the manifest horror of the more civilized Europeans at the sight of tortures little different from those they deplored in their own societies was doubtless responsible in part for the lapsing of the torture complex during the eighteenth century. Torture was a ritual and followed a formal, predictable course, in which the victim and his tormentors were expected to play traditionally respectable roles. The victim (usually a man, occasionally a woman, rarely a child) was expected to show composure and hardihood; weaklings who were unable to perform the role, who broke down, wept, and cried for mercy, were sometimes dispatched in disgust with a quick hatchet-blow. While undoubtedly unconscious meanings, various according to the participant and spectator, attached to the torture ritual, many of the tormentors consciously were not anxious to see transports of agony and emotional collapse, but rather the reverse: they wanted to see a stouthearted man with unconquerable self-control, maintaining defiance and self-respect to the bitter end, and the torture was a test of these qualities. Since the victim was in many cases eaten afterward and had in some cases been previously adopted, he was in a very real sense being incorporated by a family and a community, and becoming a part of them, and a show of strength on his part was gratifying to those who identified with him.

The case of a Seneca man captured and burned by the Huron in 1637 illustrates the general pattern. A fifty-year-old warrior of some distinction, along with six other captives, was taken while he and twenty-five or thirty men were on a fishing expedition. The Huron council assigned him to Saouandaouascouay, a chief who had lost a nephew in a recent war. It was customary, "when some notable personage has lost one of his relatives in war, to give him a present of some captive taken from the enemy, to dry his tears and partly assuage his grief."

The prisoner, on delivery, was in bad shape as a result of mistreatment en route: one of his hands was badly bruised by a stone, and one finger had been torn off; the thumb and forefinger of the other had been half-amputated by a hatchet blow; the joints of his arms had been badly burned, and in one of them was a deep cut. The wounds were infected, stank intolerably, and were swarming with maggots; he could not lift food or drink to his lips. The villagers did everything possible to make him comfortable: he was fed solicitously, his wounds were gently cleaned and bandaged; he sang for them and they talked kindly to him. "My nephew!" announced Saouandaouascouay, "Thou hast good reason to sing, for no one is doing thee any harm; behold thyself now among thy kindred and friends." The Jesuits were impressed by the solicitude of the Hurons to the adopted captive. "To see the treatment they accorded him, you might have thought he was the brother and relative of all those who were talking to him." And so, as a matter of fact, he was.

But after a few days Saouandaouascouay changed his mind about keeping the prisoner in the family, and one morning gently explained the situation to "Joseph" (as the Jesuits had baptized him). "My nephew, thou must know that when I first received news that thou wert at my disposal, I was wonderfully pleased, fancying that he whom I lost in war had been, as it were, brought back to life, and was returning to his country. At the same time I resolved to give thee thy life, I was already thinking of preparing thee a place in my cabin, and thought that thou wouldst pass the rest of thy days pleasantly with me. But now that I see thee in this condition, thy fingers gone and thy hands half rotten, I change my mind, and I am sure that thou thyself wouldst now regret to live longer. I shall do thee a greater kindness to tell thee that thou must prepare to die; is it not so? It is [those who captured you] who have treated thee so ill, and who also cause thy death. Come then, my nephew, be of good courage; prepare thyself for this evening, and do not allow thyself to be cast down through fear of the tortures." Joseph, in a firm and confident voice, asked how he was to be tortured, and Saouandaouascouay said by fire. "That is well," said Joseph, "that is well." While this sad discussion was in progress, a sister of the dead man (and Joseph's adoptive sister) brought him some food. She was tender to him, her face was very sad, and her eyes were bathed in tears. "You would almost have said that he was her own son," observed Father Le Jeune, "and I do not know that this creature did not represent to her him whom she had lost."

At noon Joseph gave his farewell feast, "according to the custom of those who are about to die"; everyone in the village was welcome, and crowds came. Before the eating began, he strode through the middle of the cabin and announced in a loud and confident voice, "My brothers, I am going to die; amuse yourselves boldly around me —I fear neither tortures nor death." He danced and sang up and down the cabin, and after him some of the guests. The food was served, people ate, and then he was taken to the council house for the torture.

Soon after dark, eleven fires were lit down the length of the council house, and the people came, the old men seating themselves on the raised platforms and the young men crowded on the floor so tightly that there was barely room for passage. The young men, shouting with joy, armed themselves with firebrands and pieces of bark. There was a public announcement by a chief: the young men were to do their duty in this important business, which was viewed by the Sun and the God of War. They were to burn only his legs at first, "so that he might hold out until day break; also for that night they were not to go and amuse themselves in the woods."

The prisoner was brought in, amid a tumult of shouts, and forced to sit on a mat; his hands were bound; and he rose and walked around the cabin, singing and dancing. On his return to the mat, the chief took off his beaver robe and announced that it would go to a certain warrior; so and so was to have the privilege of cutting off his head; and the head, one arm, and the liver were to go to still another person, "to make a feast."

Now he began to run a circuit about the fires, again and again, while everyone tried to burn him as he passed; he shrieked like a lost soul; the whole cabin resounded with cries and yells. Some burned him, some seized his hands and snapped bones, others thrust sticks through his ears, still others bound his wrists with cords, pulling at each end with all their might, so as to cut flesh and crush bone. If he paused to catch his breath, he was forced to lie down upon hot ashes and burning coals. After making seven rounds, he collapsed on the coals and would not stir, and when a brand was applied to his loins, he fainted.

His fainting spell lasted for about an hour. The captains emptied the council house and would let no one molest him during this time; they gave him water; and at last he came to his senses again. Immediately he was commanded to sing; at first he was only able to sing in a broken and faltering voice, but he grew stronger and at last sang loudly enough for the young men outside to hear. Back into the council house they came, and the torture began again, more brutal than before, setting his feet on red-hot hatchets, burning the cords that bound him, hitting him on the head with clubs, repeatedly burning him, at first on the legs and then gradually up the body with firebrands and bark torches. Once he was forced to commit what the Jesuits called only a "shameful act."

Between the interruptions caused by his involuntary yells and groans, there was between Joseph and his tormentors a continuous interchange of jeering compliments, banter, and taunting inquiries about his welfare and comfort. Joseph never allowed himself to complain or to revile his tormentors. He was addressed, and he addressed them, with kinship terms. He was given food (roasted corn on the cob) and drink. On several occasions the priest was allowed to preach to the crowd, and the prisoner rested during these intervals. On occasion he addressed the crowd for some time, discussing the state of affairs in his own country, and describing the death of some Huron prisoners. "He did this as easily, and with a countenance as composed, as any one there present would have showed."

At dawn came the end. He was taken outside into the sunlight and made to mount a scaffold, where, tied to a post, he was burned continuously and cruelly from head to toe, and in every accessible body aperture, with hot hatchets and firebrands, until he was completely exhausted and hung motionless, scarcely breathing. At once a hand, a foot, and at the last his head were cut off and given to those to whom they had been allotted. A feast was made upon the rest of his body the same day.

Thus Joseph became a part of the Huron nation, and Saouanda-ouascouay was reunited with his nephew.[14]

II

THE DECLINE
OF THE
IROQUOIS

5

THE LAST WARS
IN THE FOREST

Handsome Lake was born at the end of the era of unques-
tioned power, respect, and prosperity for the Seneca nation.
His generation saw the delicate balance between the revenge mechanism of warfare and the political structure of the League shaken
and in the end destroyed. By the time he reached his forties, the
Seneca would be deprived of their military ardor, reduced to political
impotence, corrupted in their customs, disillusioned with their religion, stripped of their hunting land, and made to look depraved and
contemptible in the eyes of their white and Indian neighbors. During
his youth and early manhood, while he fought as a warrior in the
last of the forest wars, he watched his society and his culture slowly
crumble.

· The Play-off System ·

Ever since the latter half of the seventeenth century the British
and the French had been straining to contain one another's trading
empires in North America. French posts stretched in a great inland
arc from Quebec to New Orleans, by way of the St. Lawrence, the
Great Lakes, the Wabash, the Illinois, and the Mississippi. The British

settlements crowded the Atlantic coast from New England to Florida and extended inland up the Hudson, Delaware, Susquehanna, and Potomac rivers and many other smaller streams. Between the two lines of settlement was a territory of disputed political sovereignty: the so-called "Ohio country," including the land between Lake Erie and the Ohio River, bounded westward by the two Miami rivers in the present state of Ohio, and coastward by the Allegheny Mountains. To this region the Iroquois laid claim on the basis of ancient conquest, their continuing use of it for hunting, and the location on it of tribes politically dependent upon them. This claim both French and British recognized. Thus the Six Nations were able to use the Ohio country as the fulcrum in a game of playing off one side against the other that kept both the French and the British perennially off balance.

This successful system of aggressive neutrality had originated at the beginning of the eighteenth century. In the summer of 1701 the Iroquois confederacy, aware of the fruitlessness of a longer continuance of the beaver wars and desirous of avoiding further involvement in the skirmishes between the British and the French, made two treaties, almost simultaneously, at Albany and Montreal. These treaties together inaugurated a new era of Iroquois policy, which survived in principle until 1795: a policy of peace toward the "far Indians," of political manipulation of nearby tribes, and of armed neutrality between contending Europeans. This policy led to commercial profit and to the seizure of a balance of power between the French and the British. It was a policy that required of the Iroquois as much duplicity in diplomatic dealings with the Europeans as the Europeans practiced toward them; its success is measured by the fact that both the British and the French alternated constantly between the conviction that the Iroquois were on their own side and the conviction that they had turned to the enemy. In consequence, the basic policy of both French and British toward the Iroquois was to secure Iroquois neutrality by making political and economic concessions to them. Only secondarily, and occasionally, did either aspire to their full and exclusive alliance; and these aspirations were almost invariably dashed.

The maintenance of this balance of power, however, depended upon Iroquois capacity to make credible threats, or promises, of military action. The system did not require that both French and British be equally powerful in the area, but rather that the Iroquois should at any time be considered able, by shifting their weight, to make up the difference. Any actual or apparent rigidity (induced either by indecision or by insufficiency of resources) in Iroquois policy would threaten this system because it would permit one side or the other to anticipate decline to a point where it could no longer afford to pay the price for the necessary support. Such a point of critical imbalance could also be reached if, as a result of any outside circumstance, one side or the other thought that a power differential existed which no degree of shifting of Iroquois support could rectify.

This point of critical imbalance came in the 1740's, when the Iroquois gave the English too-extensive trading privileges in the Ohio country. In the Ohio Valley a lesion had over the years been slowly widening in the play-off system: the Iroquois hunters domiciled there, known locally as Mingoes, had increasingly turned, along with the Delaware, Wyandot, and other tribal groups in the region, to the English for trade. In 1744 they brought the Miami—hitherto prevailingly French in trade connection—to Lancaster, where an understanding was established between them and the English and an alliance worked out between them and the Six Nations. British tradeposts were built, with Iroquois sanction, on the Miami, Sandusky, and Cuyahoga Rivers, and George Croghan and other English traders and agents penetrated extensively into the Ohio. The Six Nations formalized their long-standing dominance over the Ohio area by appointing local "half-kings" and by allotting specific tracts to the dependent tribes.

This event compromised the ingenious policy of neutrality that the Iroquois had developed for coping with the European colonies on their flanks. The Six Nations probably did not expect the transactions to upset the French as much as they did. In fact, however, they impressed the French with the sense of a power deficit so extreme that in their opinion (and probably the opinion was correct) it exceeded the range of Iroquois capacity to redress it. The French, therefore, set out to destroy the play-off system itself. In 1749 Celoron made his celebrated voyage down the Ohio, burying his lead plates and claiming the land for King Louis. In 1752 French forces sacked the British-Miami trading post at Pickawillany and killed and ate the pro-English, pro-Iroquois Miami chief there, Old Britain. In 1754 French troops seized the post that the Ohio Company was constructing at the confluence of the Allegheny and the Monongahela and replaced it with Fort Duquesne. The British retaliated with Washington's move to the Great Meadows, and then with Braddock's expedition against Fort Duquesne, both of which failed catastrophically; and the French and Indian War was on.

The Six Nations, during this conflict, attempted to salvage the old play-off system, at first by preserving a measure of neutrality, and then by fighting on both sides—the Seneca, in particular, joining the war parties of pro-French Indians, while the Mohawk joined in British campaigns on other fronts. They explained their policy in a belt given to one of their dependent allies, a Delaware leader named Teedyuscung, who recited the policy in a treaty council. "You see," he said, "a Square in the Middle, meaning the Lands of the Indians, and at one End the Figure of a Man, indicating the English; and at the other End another, meaning the French; our Uncles [the Six Nations] told us [the Delaware], that both these coveted our Lands; but let us join together to defend our Lands against both, you shall be Partakers with us of our Lands." But the situation was largely out of their control, for now the British too were uninterested in maintaining the old play-off system, but wanted rather a firm alliance (in which they would be the dominant partner). The end of the war found the French expelled, British troops stationed at Fort Duquesne, Sandusky, Detroit, Venango, Le Boeuf, Presqu' Isle, Niagara, and Oswego in the Iroquois domain as well as in posts outside the Iroquois sphere of influence, and a new spirit of economy pervading Indian affairs. No longer were Iroquois promises bought with tons of hardware and dry goods; "presents" now were limited. The old free trade was likewise curtailed, there were fewer traders, and powder and lead were sold only at government factories by surly public servants. The introduction of rum into the Indian country was officially prohibited. In 1761, in order to block the Ohio Company's plans for settlement of the Ohio lands, Colonel Bouquet at Fort Pitt promised that no white homesteaders would be permitted west of the Alleghenies; but still, British troops were not going to leave the forts. The play-off system was out; a bargaining system was in.[1]

· Pontiac's Conspiracy ·

SENECA REACTION to the new dispensation was hostile. In 1761 a group of Seneca including Guyasuta, a maternal uncle of Handsome Lake, carried a red wampum belt from the Onondaga council to Detroit, and under the nose of the British commandant exhorted the Delaware and Shawnee of Ohio and the Ottawa, Huron, Chippewa, and Potawatomi of Detroit to join the Six Nations in a simultaneous surprise attack on the British posts at Detroit, Pittsburgh, Presqu' Isle, Venango, and Niagara. Although the Ohio Indians refused to join in the plot and revealed its content to the British commandant at Detroit, the scheme was revived in the spring of 1763. Two more Seneca war belts were sent out: one passed among the Delaware and the Shawnee on the Ohio and the Miami on the Wabash; the other went to the Detroit Indians.

The war began in due course. The Seneca plan was not followed in detail, but the Seneca proposal to drive the English out of the Iroquois and Ohio country was certainly an inspiration to the tribes who joined in that epidemic of frontier assaults that is now generally (and inaccurately) called the Conspiracy of Pontiac. Pontiac himself had not actually organized a pan-Indian uprising. That so many local assaults followed his own carefully prepared attempt to take Detroit is probably best explained as a concatenation of a number of factors: the prior circulation of the Seneca plan, which suggested the general movement as well as the specific actions; the subversive encouragements of the French, still holding out in Louisiana; the generally high level of resentment against the English, who occupied forts in Indian territory but would not open up a satisfactory trade; and the nativistic prophecies of the Delaware Prophet, a religious leader whose visions and preaching were in some respects like those of Handsome Lake a generation later. Pontiac's independent action was the spark that, falling on tinder, set the woods aflame.

The "conspiracy," which had for its aim the destruction of the British forts and garrisons and the removal of the English from the Indian country between the Allegheny Mountains and the Mississippi, was manned by the Ottawa, Chippewa, Potawatomi, Huron, Miami, Wea, Delaware, Shawnee, Mingo (Six Nations Indians resident in the Ohio country)—and by the Seneca. While the eastern members of the confederacy dallied with Sir William Johnson, lulling him and General Amherst into a false sense of security, the Seneca struck perhaps the severest blows of the war, destroying the forts at Venango, Le Boeuf, and Presqu' Isle and at Devil's Hole almost annihilating two British detachments on the newly cut road along the cliff above the whirlpool at Niagara Falls. Handsome Lake may have been involved in the taking of Fort Venango, for his uncle Guyasuta was present on the occasion and as we have seen war parties tended to recruit clan relatives. According to tradition, Handsome Lake definitely was one of the Seneca ambuscade at Devil's Hole. Another maternal uncle, Jugwesus, was also at Devil's Hole, as were some of the Venango party, and an adopted uncle, Gahnasqua, was the Seneca commander at the Hole. The ambush at Devil's Hole was a bloody piece of work. The Seneca war party, numbering upwards of five hundred men, first surprised a convoy of twenty-five horse- and ox-drawn wagons, escorted by an officer and thirty men, at that point on the trail to Fort Niagara where it wound along a narrow space between woods and chasm. A volley from cover stopped the column in confusion; then the Indians ran out from the trees and attacked with tomahawks before the suttlers and their escort could form an organized defense. Stampeding teams plunged over the precipice, drivers were tangled in the harness leather or knocked down by kicking, screaming animals. Unable to use their muskets, soldiers tried to fight hand-to-hand with their backs to the abyss. Only two men of this party escaped alive. Hearing the firing, two British companies, about eighty men in all, ran to the scene. They were met in a new ambush before they reached the Hole. They too were cut down by an initial volley and then overwhelmed by an immediate hand-to-hand assault in which muskets could not be used. Within minutes half of the relief force were dead. When the garrison from the fort finally arrived, the Indians were gone and five British officers and sixty-seven men lay dead on the trail, scalped and stripped of their clothing.

But the great scheme for burning the forts and driving British garrisons out of the Indian country was in the end a failure. Detroit, Fort Pitt, and Niagara held out; reinforcements arrived; the Indian food supplies ran low; and in the end the warriors laid down their hatchets and the councilors made peace. The Seneca settled their affairs with Sir William Johnson in July, giving up some leading offenders and ceding the portage route at Niagara to the Crown. Although the British prudently made few reprisals and exacted only minor indemnities, and although the Royal Proclamation of October 1763 had set a boundary between Indian and white territory that recognized the Indians as proprietors of their traditional lands, English colors flew still over the new garrisons in the heart of the Indian country.[2]

During the war it is probable that Handsome Lake heard indirectly of the Delaware Prophet's preachings, and he may even have been informed in some detail of the content of his doctrine. Although the prophet is not known to have made any converts among the Seneca, he did serve as the emotional catalyst of the movement. The Delaware Prophet of 1762–3 was one of the religious messiahs who about this time were beginning to appear among the disintegrating Indian communities on the frontier. This man, who lived on the Cuyahoga River near Lake Erie, had visions in which the Creator spoke to him. The Creator informed him of the peril of worldly misery and eternal damnation in which the Indians stood, and gave him a code of detailed instructions that, if followed, would enable the Indians to drive the white men out of their country, recapture the pristine happiness of the aboriginal state, and find the right road again to heaven. He, Neolin, "the Enlightened," was appointed to preach the tribes to repentence and to instruct them in the proper means of recovering the favor of the Creator.

The prophet's vision was reminiscent of the story of Moses and the Ten Commandments. He dreamed that he went in search of the Creator, and after several strange adventures—taking two false trails which led only to fountains of fire, finding at last a mountain of glass, meeting there a beautiful woman in white, disrobing, washing, and climbing the mountain using only his left hand and foot—he arrived in heaven. Here he found new wonders—a regularly built village, stockaded with a gate, and a handsome guide dressed in white, who guided him to the Master of Life. The Master of Life took him by the hand and gave him for a seat a hat bordered with gold, on which the prophet sat, rather hesitantly, to hear the Creator's words.

The Master of Life then addressed him at length, saying:

> I am the Master of Life, whom thou wishest to see, and to whom thou wishest to speak. Listen to that which I will tell thee for thyself and for all the Indians. I am the Maker of Heaven and earth, the trees, lakes, rivers, men, and all that thou seest or hast seen on the earth or in the heavens; and because I love you, you must do my will; you must also avoid that which I hate; I hate you to drink as you do, until you lose your reason; I wish you not to fight one

another; you take two wives, or run after other people's wives; you do wrong; I hate such conduct; you should have but one wife, and keep her until death. When you go to war, you juggle, you sing the medicine song, thinking you speak to me; you deceive yourselves; it is to the Manito that you speak; he is a wicked spirit who induces you to evil, and, for want of knowing me, you listen to him.

The land on which you are, I have made for you, not for others: wherefore do you suffer the whites to dwell upon your lands? Can you not do without them? I know that those whom you call the children of your great Father supply your wants. But, were you not wicked as you are, you would not need them. Before those whom you call your brothers had arrived, did not your bow and arrow maintain you? You needed neither gun, powder, nor any other object. The flesh of animals was your food, their skins your raiment. But when I saw you inclined to evil, I removed the animals into the depths of the forests, that you might depend on your brothers for your necessaries, for your clothing. Again become good and do my will, and I will send animals for your sustenance. I do now, however, forbid suffering among you your Father's children; I love them, they know me, they pray to me; I supply their own wants, and give them that which they bring to you. Not so with those who are come to trouble your possessions. Drive them away; wage war against them. I love them not. They know me not. They are my enemies, they are your brothers' enemies. Send them back to the lands I have made for them. Let them remain there.

Here is a written prayer which I give thee; learn it by heart, and teach it to all the Indians and children. It must be repeated morning and evening. Do all that I have told thee, and announce it to all the Indians as coming from the Master of Life. Let them drink but one draught [of liquor], or two at most, in one day. Let them have but one wife, and discontinue running after other people's wives and daughters. Let them not fight one another. Let them not sing the medicine song, for in singing the medicine song they speak to the evil spirit. Drive from your lands those dogs in red clothing; they are only an injury to you. When you want anything, apply to me, as your brothers [i.e., the Christian whites] do, and I will give to both. Do not sell to your brothers that which I have placed on the earth as food. In short, become good, and you shall want nothing. When you meet one another, bow, and give one another the hand of the heart [i.e., the left hand]. Above all, I command thee to repeat, morning and evening, the prayer which I have given thee.

Neolin remarked that he could not read, but the Master of Life told him that on his return upon earth he should give it to the chief of his village, who would be able to read it, and teach it to him, and also to all the Indians. The prophet promised to do as he was bidden and returned silently to his village, speaking to no one until he had presented to "the chief" the prayer and the laws that had been entrusted to his care by the Master of Life.

In response to a subsequent vision the prophet drew on a piece of deerskin parchment, about fifteen to eighteen inches square, a map of the soul's progress in this world and the next. This map he called the Great Book of Writing. Neolin traveled from town to town, preaching and holding the map before him while he preached, from time to time pointing with his finger to particular marks and spots on it, and giving explanations. He wept constantly while he preached.

The burden of his doctrine was that in the beginning the Creator had given the Indians a beautiful country in which to hunt, fish, and dwell (this was the outer border of the parchment). In ancient days, entry to the heavenly regions was easy and direct; but of late, the avenue to heaven has been stopped up by the white people. "Look here!" Neolin would say. "See what has been lost by neglect and disobedience; by being remiss in the expression of our gratitude to the Great Spirit, for what he has bestowed upon us; by neglecting to make him sufficient sacrifices; by looking upon a people of a different colour from our own, who had come across a great lake, as if they were a part of ourselves; by suffering them to sit down by our side, and looking at them with indifference, while they were not only taking our country from us, but this (pointing to the spot), this, our own avenue, leading into those beautiful regions which were destined for us." Instead of the old way, now the Indians were forced to find a new avenue to heaven; but this new one was hazardous, since the wayfarer must run a gauntlet of the sins and vices brought by the white people. Besides this, now there was a great gulf over which the soul had to leap, and many failed to cross and were seized by the evil spirit and carried off to his country, "where the ground was parched up by the heat for want of rain, no fruit came to perfection, the game was starved for want of pasture, and where the evil spirit, at his pleasure, transformed men into horses and dogs, to be ridden by him and follow him in his hunts and wherever he went." In the map of the heavenly regions, accordingly, the prophet drew a fat, well-fed deer or turkey, but a scrawny image in the Evil Spirit's.

"Such is the sad condition to which we are reduced," he would explain. "What is now to be done, and what remedy is to be applied? I will tell you, my friends. Hear what the Great Spirit has ordered me to tell you! You are to make sacrifices, in the manner that I shall direct; to put off entirely from yourselves the customs which you have adopted since the white people came among us; you are to return to that former happy state, in which we lived in peace and plenty, before these strangers came to disturb us, and above all, you must abstain from drinking their deadly *beson* [poisonous, bewitched "medicine," i.e., liquor], which they have forced upon us for the sake of increasing their gains and diminishing our numbers. Then will the Great Spirit give success to our arms; then he will give us strength to conquer our enemies, to drive them from hence, and recover the passage to the heavenly regions which they have taken from us." He made various other moral exhortations, too. In order to rid themselves of sin—the first necessity—the Indians were first to take emetics and to abstain from sexual intercourse. They were to quit the use of firearms; fire should be made by rubbing two sticks together, not by striking flint and steel, which was a white contamination. They were to learn to live again without trade with the whites, clothing and supporting themselves in the ancient way. In a word, they were to revive in a body their ancient customs and to live as they had before the white people discovered their country. And he prophesied (in 1762) that after a period of negotiation with the whites, there would be a war.

Actually, of course, despite his emphasis on a revival of the past, many of Neolin's recommendations were not traditional at all: he was advising the abandonment of many old cultural elements, such as "medicine songs," war rituals, polygyny; and he was introducing various quasi-European concepts, such as a high-god common to both whites and Indians, written prayers, and a written "Great Book." His code was a syncretism of native and white elements.

But nonetheless these teachings made a great sensation. The Prophet sold copies of his spiritual chart (he said it should be owned by every family) for one buckskin or two doeskins apiece. Copies were soon to be found far and wide, and disciples preached his doctrine in many villages. Indians traveled for miles to hear him speak. His suggestion of a cultural boycott was so effective that a Pittsburgh trader in 1762 wrote that the Delaware "mostly . . . have quit hunting any more than to supply nature in that way." And Pontiac himself became a convert to Neolin's doctrine and used it as supernatural sanction for his conspiracy.[3]

A similar doctrine, perhaps inspired by Neolin's, was preached by an unnamed Onondaga prophet, who about 1762 was told in a vision by the Great Spirit that "when He first made the World, He gave this large Island to the Indians for their Use; at the same time He gave other Parts of the World beyond the great Waters to the rest of his creating, and gave them different languages: That He now saw the white People squabbling, and fighting for these Lands which He gave the Indians; and that in every Assembly, and Company of Governors, and Great Men, He heard nothing scarce spoke, or talk'd of, but claiming, and wanting, large Possessions in our Country. This He said, was so contrary to his Intention, and what He expected wou'd be the Consequence at the time when the white People first came, like Children, among Us, that He was quite displeas'd, and would, altho their Numbers were ever so great, punish them if They did not desist."[4] With this revelation, too, Handsome Lake was no doubt acquainted.

· *A Dark and Bloody Ground* ·

HANDSOME LAKE, said his nephew Blacksnake in later years, was "much engaged in war prior to and during the American Revolution." Following the collapse of the Pontiac movement, in 1765 Handsome Lake betook himself with Giengwahtoh or Old Smoke, the famous Seneca war-captain of the Turtle Clan, and about one hundred other Seneca warriors, on an expedition against the Cherokee and Choctaw. This was a celebrated foray, remembered nearly a century later for the loot of scalps and other trophies with which the triumphant warriors returned. Giengwahtoh, a heavily built man over six feet tall, and sixty-some years of age, was then, or soon became, a principal civil chief of the Seneca. Handsome Lake was to see much of him during the Revolution.[5]

But although individual warriors might still find glory on the war-

paths that led south and west from the Seneca country into the Ohio
Valley during the thirteen years between the Conspiracy of Pontiac
and the American Revolution, that valley and its Indian residents were
rapidly being lost to the Iroquois. The Mingo and the dependent
Delaware, Shawnee, Huron, and other tribal remnants who lived
there under Iroquois hegemony had once turned confidently to the
Great Council at Onondaga for support and intercession with the
French and the English when they were threatened in their villages
and hunting grounds. But now British garrisons were in possession of
the soil and controlled the trade. And the Iroquois themselves, no
longer able safely to play off the French in Canada against the English,
could not risk a major war in which they would have to fight without
a European ally.

The immediate result of the impasse was the Treaty of Fort Stanwix in 1768, by which the Iroquois surrendered their own and their
tribal dependents' claims to the lands south of the Ohio and Susquehanna rivers. The Ohio lands in particular were then used for hunting
by, and occupied by villages of, Mingo, Shawnee, and other dependents of the Six Nations. The Iroquois, claiming to represent all the
occupants and users, negotiated the sale and kept all of the proceeds.
One of the principal negotiators was Guyasuta. By this stroke, the
Iroquois thought to get rid of a source of frontier friction between
the English and themselves, by opening up all of Kentucky and a large
area in western Pennsylvania and West Virginia to settlers. But the result was opposite to the intention, for they had sold off—in Kentucky
—the principal hunting grounds of their erstwhile allies and dependents, the Shawnee. And the Shawnee, suddenly dispossessed and un-
recompensed, secretly joined with the western Indians in a rival
western confederacy to resist white colonial expansion.

Iroquois diplomacy, after the Treaty of Fort Stanwix, had an impossible task to perform: to please, and retain the friendship and alliance of, both the Shawnee and the British. The British, taking a legalistic point of view, felt that they had bought the land from the true
owners, the Iroquois, who had acquired it by conquest; and now they
expected the owners to evict the old tenants to make way for Daniel
Boone and the rest of the settlers. But the old tenants, the Shawnee
and others, taking an equally legalistic viewpoint, pressed the Iroquois
to live up to the obligation to protect their interests, which the Iroquois had assumed when they invited them to live on Iroquois-owned

land. Iroquois credit with the British now depended upon their ability to control other tribes, and the Iroquois knew it; but Iroquois ability to control other tribes also depended on their ability to protect them from the British. Far from being able to play off two sides against one another, the Iroquois were now being squeezed. Iroquois negotiators trod a narrow course of equivocation in council, urging peace and restraint on all sides, but finding themselves unable to take decisive action either to chastise or to join the increasingly rebellious Shawnee warriors in their guerrilla warfare with the advancing settlers.[6]

Individual Iroquois warriors, however, and particularly among the Seneca, were clearly sympathetic to the western Indians. Chafing under the eyes of the British garrisons, they watched with sullen resentment the rowdy whites of the frontier crowding in upon their own borders. At last in 1774 many of them joined the Shawnee, Delaware, and Wyandot in the brief and bloody Lord Dunmore's War—a war that soured the temper of the tribes of the Ohio and almost irritated the Six Nations into a general attack on the English frontier. Lord Dunmore's War was symbolic of the deterioration in relations between the whites and the Indians, and for that matter, of the internal order of both white and native societies. The white colonial culture was breaking down as fast or faster, if for different reasons, than the Indian cultures, and one of the symptoms of its decay was an inability of colonial officials to deter individual invasions of Indian lands.

That brief orgy of irresponsibility, cruelty, and despair that was Lord Dunmore's War began in the spring when one Michael Cresap and a company of land jobbers were exploring some of the lands south of the Ohio, bought from the Six Nations at Fort Stanwix in 1768. Missing some of their horses one day, they blamed the Shawnee Indians still hunting in the territory for stealing them and impulsively slaughtered a peaceful hunting party camped by the river. Among the dead were some of the family of Captain John Logan, a Cayuga Indian born on the Susquehanna but emigrant to the Ohio, where he had a Shawnee wife. This was Logan, the Great Mingo, a son of Shickellamy, the famous old Iroquois half-king at Shamokin, and a staunch defender of the whites among his own people. A few days later, a small party of white men, unprovoked, invited a group of Indians across the Ohio to the Virginia side, on pretense of friendly parley. They made them drunk and then killed most of them, including a brother and a pregnant sister of Logan. This stroke wiped out all of

Logan's close relatives. Some more Indians from the other side tried to cross the river to save their fellows; these were shot down in their canoes.

Logan was obligated to avenge his family. Accordingly during the summer he and eight warriors annihilated a small settlement of white families who had located on Indian lands on the Muskingum. Men, women, and children were killed; Logan is said to have refused to countenance torture. As the summer wore on, other settlements were attacked, too. The smoldering frontier along the Ohio again burst into flame.

Seneca warriors from the Genesee joined the Ohio bands. The Seneca were exasperated by the peculiarly gruesome killing of Bald Eagle. Bald Eagle was a Seneca warrior who spoke English well and lived with the Delaware at Salt Lick Town. He was known as a "good hunter" and as "a very kind, good" man who gave no one any trouble. During the winter he had gone alone up the Monongahela to hunt, and on his return downstream in the spring he was shot by a white man. The murderer tore the scalp from the old man's head, propped the body upright in the canoe, and set it adrift. The corpse in the canoe was seen by many who thought it was Bald Eagle, alive, returning down the river with his peltry.

Lord Dunmore, Governor of Virginia, while recognizing the provocation to the Indians, felt obligated to call up militia to punish Logan's outrages. Several thousand "Long Knives" and Indians met in the Battle of Point Pleasant. The outnumbered Indians—Shawnee, Delaware, Mingo, Wyandot, Seneca, Cayuga, and others—were beaten in a bloody struggle. The Six Nations at Onondaga, despite the fact that many of their warriors were already in the field, at the last refused to give official sanction to the war. The Onondaga council was utilizing the occasion as a means of punishment of the refractory Shawnee, who objected to the Six Nations' sale of the hunting grounds in Kentucky, who had attempted to organize a competing confederacy, and who were now demanding aid from the Iroquois in a war into which their own refusal to accept Iroquois land cessions had plunged them. Cornstalk negotiated a peace with Lord Dunmore; and Logan, acquiescing, made the famous speech recorded by Thomas Jefferson:

I appeal to any white man to say if he ever entered Logan's cabin hungry, and he gave him not meat; if ever he came cold and naked, and he clothed him not. During the course of the last long and bloody war, Logan remained idle in his cabin, an advocate for peace. Such was my love for the whites, that my countrymen pointed, as they passed, and said, "Logan is the friend of the white men." I had even thought to have lived with you, but for the injuries of one man. Colonel Cresap, the last Spring, cold blood and unprovoked, murdered all the relations of Logan, not even sparing my women and children. There runs not a drop of my blood in the veins of any living creature. This called on me for revenge. I have sought it; I have killed many; I have fully glutted my vengeance. For my country, I rejoice at the beams of peace; but do not harbour a thought that mine is the joy of fear. Logan never felt fear. He will not turn on his heel to save his life. Who is there to mourn for Logan? Not one.

Logan, after the defeat at Point Pleasant and the negotiated peace, became melancholic and declared that life was a torment to him. Once in a drunken frolic he knocked his new wife down. Thinking that he had killed her, he fled to Detroit, while his wife, thus abandoned, returned to her own people. Along the trail Logan accidentally met a party of Indian men, women, and children, including his nephew Todkahdohs, "the Searcher," a Seneca who lived on the Allegheny and was a kinsman of Logan's wife. Logan, ridden with guilt, thought his nephew was pursuing him to take vengeance for having murdered his wife, and he recklessly announced that he was going to kill the whole party. As he dismounted, gun in hand, Todkahdohs cut him down with a shotgun blast.[7]

The old ways of honor now led, for many men, to dishonor, loneliness, and despair. The Six Nations had seduced their dependents and allies twice into lost campaigns, in 1763 and 1774, to drive out the whites, and had still preserved the semblance of their own neutrality. But the old way of playing both ends against the middle was becoming difficult and more dangerous. It was to become catastrophic as the American Revolution unfolded.

· *The Iroquois and the Revolution: The Neutrality Policy* ·

FRONTIER INCIDENTS like Lord Dunmore's War were the backwoods expression of a chronic, restless resentment of the Crown's authority that by 1775 had become epidemic in all social classes in the British colonies. While groups of stubborn frontiersmen, defiant of law, carried on the illicit trade in liquor and furs and settled their families on Indian lands west of the Proclamation Line, the provincial capitals were stirring with the other conspiracies to subvert the military establishments, the new taxes, and the new trade regulations that an English Parliament was imposing on an increasingly expensive empire. Since 1772 committees of correspondence had been generating opposition to British measures, and mobs had been terrorizing officials of the colonial administration; and in September 1774, while Dunmore's war and its train of negotiations were still in progress, colonial representatives met in the First Continental Congress to formulate grievances and to concert a boycott of British goods. In the spring of 1775 blood was shed at Lexington and Concord, and a Second Continental Congress met, in less temperate mood, to create an army. The tide of opinion was running rapidly to the left; conservative loyalists were already under persecution by local committees of patriots; by summer, the King's officers in America realized that they faced an armed rebellion.

The Continental Congress early considered what role the Iroquois, probably the most formidable single body of fighting men in the colony of New York, should play in the developing war. In July 1775, the Congress passed an act dividing the Indian country into three departments, with three commissioners for the northern department and one each for the others. The Continental policy, like that of the British in the years before the French were defeated, was to secure, if not the assistance, at least the neutrality of the Six Nations and their dependents. Continental Indian agents accordingly represented the struggle as a family quarrel among the white people, in which the natives had no interest. The Christian Stockbridge (Mahican), who had been enlisted as allies of the Congress after aiding the patriot cause around Boston in 1775, were moved to Oneida as propagandists of the Americans, to convince the Oneida of the justness of the colonists' cause and to deter them from joining the British in case of open conflict. Samuel Kirkland, the doughty old missionary to the Oneida, appealed to them for their neutrality. In consequence of these pressures, the Oneida, and the Tuscarora and Stockbridge who lived with them, early declared their intention to stand aside from the conflict.

The Mohawk also were quickly subjected to pressure. Kirkland sent them messages advising a neutral course. In May 1775, they were addressed by delegates from Albany who reassured them that the patriots really had no evil designs on loyalist Colonel Guy Johnson, Sir William's successor as Indian Superintendent, despite mutterings and threats by lively malcontents. Colonel Johnson thereupon departed for the western Iroquois nations, to advise them of the events of the hour. On his return Johnson found popular white sentiment in the Mohawk Valley congealing into the suspicion that he and his Mohawks would plot, spy, and if need be, take up arms against their rebel neighbors. He departed again for the Indian country, holding councils with the Six Nations in Oswego and Montreal. Report had it that in these councils he urged the warriors to war against the rebels, but actually he simply urged them—as the Congress was doing—to mind their own affairs quietly, avoid frontier incidents, and not to listen to evil birds. Taking him literally and maintaining the classic Iroquois neutrality policy, at Oswego the eastern tribes of the Iroquois agreed that they would permit neither British nor American troops to pass through their country.

In August 1775, the Continental commissioners met with the Iroquois at Albany, where they explained at length, and most pathetically, the moral justifications for the colonists' recourse to arms, and said again that this was a family quarrel between them and Old England, in which the Indians were not concerned. They did not want the Iroquois to take up the hatchet against the King's troops but rather urged them to remain at home, not joining either side and to keep the hatchet buried deep. The Six Nations replied, through Little Abraham, the notable Mohawk speaker, in clear language: "the determination of the Six Nations [is] not to take any part; but as it is a family affair, to sit still and see you fight it out."

But the Six Nations, by no means naive in this sort of diplomacy, set certain conditions upon the agreement to remain neutral. Specifically, the military activities of the Continentals should be confined to the coast. The free passage of Iroquois hunters from fort to fort, from trading post to trading post, within their wide country, was not to be interrupted (rumor had it that the road to Fort Stanwix was to be closed by Continental troops). Further, Sir John Johnson, an outspoken loyalist, was not to be disturbed, nor was the Reverend Mr. Stewart, the loyalist missionary among the Mohawk, although both of them were being threatened with reprisals by the patriots. The Six

Nations also made the satisfaction of their generations-old land claims against New York a part of their understanding of the agreement— an interpretation that was not so far-fetched as might appear, since the commissioners had made much of the renewal of the old covenant between the people of Albany and the Six Nations, which was celebrated on the occasion.

The suspicions so quietly expressed by Little Abraham were not ill-founded. Doubt of Albany people had been traditional among Iroquoians for a century, and for good reason; and now the reply of the commissioners was equivocal and therefore ominous. Congress would give no assurance that their territory would not be invaded. The missionary to the Mohawk was assured of his security (actually, he was forced to flee into Canada). An open trade was promised at Albany and Schenectady. And in answer to the request for settlement of ancient Mohawk land claims, the commissioners asserted that "the accusation is groundless," and anyway was a matter for the Albany people to discuss. To this Little Abraham replied evenly, "In case I was to answer that part of your speech, it might perhaps draw us into an argument." He went on briefly to advise the commissioners that Sir Guy's advice at the western and northern councils had been "not to take any part in this dispute, as it was a quarrel between brothers."

And "We are very glad," said Little Abraham, "that your language and Colonel Johnson's so well agree."[8]

Thus it appears that the settled policy of the Six Nations, in response to the official requests for their neutrality made both by Johnson and the Continental commissioners, was to wait and watch. Hotheads there were, like Joseph Brant, who argued for an early involvement on the British side; a few high-spirited warriors committed themselves to minor campaigns, some (primarily Oneida and Stockbridge) on the American side, some (primarily the Caughnawaga Mohawk in Canada) on the British. But in the main, at first, the Six Nations avoided military alliance. The neutrality was, however, conditional upon the contending parties refraining from encroaching upon their trade, their travel, or their land. The tribes had, in effect, implemented the classic play-off policy again; they would fight *against* whoever first invaded their territory, interfered with their trade and travel, injured their people, or demanded their alliance, and *for* whoever had not upset the *status quo*.

It was not easy for the Indians who lived near rebel communities to stay neutral. The Mohawk soon found it necessary to leave their homes. Colonel Johnson had left the Mohawk Valley in 1775 with a goodly number of Mohawk for his tour of councils. He had been previously threatened with seizure by a patriotic committee, and his response had been to fortify his house and assemble a private army of Mohawk defenders. He did not choose to return to New York, nor did many of the Mohawk who left for Ontario with him. The remaining Mohawk population of the valley gradually melted away. An epidemic swept through the villages shortly after the return of the ambassadors from Albany, and the Indian community at Schoharie was almost exterminated. Some of the survivors are reported to have conceived (possibly with the aid of the Reverend Mr. Stewart) the belief that the pestilence had been sent by the Great Spirit as punishment for not having declared for the King; in any case they too left the valley and followed their fellows westward. A few of these Mohawks from New York aided the British in the defense of St. Johns, Newfoundland, and Oswego; some Caughnawaga Mohawks, on the other hand, aided the temporarily successful Americans in the capture of Montreal and the abortive siege of Quebec. When the remaining Mohawk in the Mohawk Valley learned of the imprisonment by the Americans of two of their "debauched" brethren, however, they petitioned for their release and argued that it was after all the Americans who had spilled blood on the path of peace (by seizing Oswego), and that thereby the Americans had broken the Albany agreement.

The official policy of the Iroquois was still neutrality when, in the fall of 1775, a council was held at Pittsburgh between the Congressional commissioners and the Seneca, Wyandot, Shawnee, and Delaware. The commissioners wished to obtain from these western nations a firm commitment to neutrality. Guyasuta, the old Seneca half-king, speaking for the dependent nations, promised neutrality; and although the leader of a Delaware faction, White Eyes, defiantly announced the independence of the Delaware, the council as a whole agreed in an intention to remain neutral. Guyasuta promised to use his influence on the confederate council of the Six Nations to endorse the neutral policy. Handsome Lake's brother Cornplanter, and his young nephew Blacksnake, were present at this meeting; very likely Handsome Lake was there too. In July 1776, at Fort Pitt, another council was held, and Guyasuta again announced the policy that the Six Nations had formulated at Oswego and expressed at Albany: they would be neutral, but neither British nor Americans were to be permitted to pass through the territory of the Six Nations. "I am appointed," he said, "to take care of this country, that is of the nations on the other side of the Ohio, and I desire you will not think of an expedition against Detroit, for I will repeat, we will not suffer an army to pass through our country."

It was inevitable that the Americans would sooner or later break with the Six Nations, however, for they were revolutionaries attacking the established system and could not tolerate a neutrality that maintained the *status quo*. Patriotic fervor, indeed, sometimes verged on the paranoid, interpreting almost any sort of detachment or verbal disagreement as evidence of conspiracy. A loyalist Mohawk sachem, Peter Nickus, was wounded and then hacked to pieces by patriotic white swordsmen about 1775—the first war casualty in the valley. In 1775 the Americans had seized Oswego, in defiance of the Six Nations' warnings at Albany, and captured some Mohawk warriors. In 1776, on the basis of perjurous accusations, General Schuyler besieged and imprisoned Sir John Johnson (son of the old friend of the Mohawk, Sir William Johnson), after brushing aside Mohawk objections that the Albany treaty provided for his freedom and that this same treaty prohibited the "closing of the road" with armed men. The accusation on which Johnson's arrest was based was that he was secreting a small arsenal for a loyalist campaign against the patriots. Although this accusation was proven false, the arms not being found where the informer swore they were hidden, Johnson was not exonerated but was placed on "parole." A few months later General Schuyler, who suspected, no doubt sincerely but almost certainly mistakenly, that Johnson was attempting to persuade the Indians to massacre the patriots, sent men to seize and imprison him. Johnson, presumably considering this to be a violation by Schuyler of the parole agreement, thereupon gathered together his friends, and various official records and papers and in May 1776, fled through the forests to Canada. He was declared by the Continentals to have broken his parole, his estates were confiscated, and his wife, Lady Johnson, was seized and held as a hostage in Albany. Johnson thereafter became a militant antirevolutionary, a colonel commanding Indian and ranger detachments. Handsome Lake was to serve under him in several campaigns.

The Six Nations, who had in fact kept steadfastly neutral, took

Johnson's seizure and other events of that order as a sure sign that "the road was closed," in violation of the Albany agreement. More and more of the Mohawk slipped away from the Mohawk Valley; a few remained for a time, nervously guarding their homes and wondering how soon the patriots, now throwing off all restraints, would serve them ill. On May 20, 1776, some of the Mohawk, led by the firebrand Joseph Brant (who was acting without general Six Nations' sanction), fought against the Americans at the Battle of the Cedars, in which the American forces retreating from their invasion of Canada were disastrously beaten. Lurid, if false, atrocity stories were circulated concerning this affair, and Congress denounced the British for their outrageous use of Indian troops. At the same moment, however, and before news of the Cedars could have reached Philadelphia, Congress itself was preparing to use Indian troops. On May 25 Congress resolved that "it was highly expedient to engage the Indians in the service of the United Colonies," and authorized the Commander-in-Chief to recruit two thousand paid Indian auxiliaries. This resolution flatly contradicted the neutrality injunctions issued at Albany the year before, and news of it no doubt reinforced a growing Iroquois sense of the undependability of the Continental Congress. Indeed, this resolution was passed one day after an Iroquois deputation, then in Philadelphia, was exhorted to remain neutral. Few Indian warriors ever joined the American army, however, and most of those few were Oneida, Tuscarora, and Stockbridge, from the Reverend Mr. Kirkland's congregation.[9]

· *The Oswego Council* ·

THE FIRST STEP toward an official abandonment of the neutrality position by the warriors of most of the Six Nations and their allied tribes was taken at a grand but secret council at Niagara in September 1776. Most of the Seneca were there, including Handsome Lake and his brother Cornplanter, Red Jacket, Old Smoke, and Farmer's Brother. The Seneca, Cayuga, Onondaga, and Mohawk declared their adherence to the King's government, come what may; the "props" of the confederacy—Wyandot, Mississauga, Delaware, Nanticoke, and Conoy (all from Ohio) and the "Squawkies" (Fox domiciled in Seneca country)—joined in with the declaration; and a strong appeal was dispatched to the erring Oneida and Tuscarora to quit the Boston men and join their brethren. This action, although it was not yet a taking up of the hatchet, severed the chain of friendship with the Continentals and split the confederacy, for the Oneida and Tuscarora were now defined as a dissenting body.[10]

The actual decision to take up the hatchet, however, was postponed until 1777, when internal disagreement, American untrustworthiness, and British solicitation made the continuance of a policy of military neutrality impossible. The breakdown of the neutrality policy was assisted by an unexpected disaster. In January 1777, the council fire at Onondaga was extinguished: three sachems there, and eighty-seven others, perished in an epidemic, making political decisions impossible until the condolence ritual could be performed. This was at best difficult in midwinter, almost impossible in unsettled and divisive times, and so at this critical juncture there was no federal civil council; affairs of peace and war now rested with the warriors and the separate village and national councils.

The die was cast irrevocably by the warriors at a council with the British at Oswego in the early summer of 1777. At this fort and trading post on the south shore of Lake Ontario, hundreds of Seneca men, women, and children joined with the people of the other tribes of the confederacy (except the Oneida and Tuscarora) to hear the British agents at last make the formal request that the Six Nations take up the hatchet against the rebels. After plying the Indian delegates generously with food, rum, and gifts of clothing and hardware, the British commissioner outlined the origin of the rebellion: the Americans were described as being disobedient children who had violated the laws and challenged the government of their father and who therefore required "a Dressing and punishment." "Now here is your father," he went on (as Blacksnake later recalled the speech); "[he has] offered you to take his axe and Tomahawk to hold against American and here is the Buckenknife and Bowisknife that you will also take for to take the American lock and scalps and my father will pay much Each one scalps in money. . . ." He explained that the Americans were poor and had no regular government and would be easy to defeat. "First we will go from here to take all the forts Belonging to Americas. The Fort Stanwix we will take first and Wyoming &c. These two forts that Shall take will be Sufficients to Show our fathers strength. . . ."

Decision had now to be reached by the Indians whether or not to take up the hatchet. The chief warriors agreed to take the matter under consideration in private council that afternoon. (This was not a matter for deliberation by the sachem-chiefs from the confederate council, but by the warriors who were to do the fighting.) The warriors' council, however, came to no consensus. In the morning Joseph Brant rose first and spoke for taking up the hatchet, urging that neutrality could ultimately lead only to disaster: "if [we] shoul[d] lie down and sleep and we shoul[d] be liable to cut our throat by the Red coat man or by America. . . ." Red Jacket and Cornplanter, however, urged that this was a family quarrel among the white people, that the Indians did not really know what it was all about, and that interference might be a mistake. Brant called Cornplanter a coward, and the meeting broke up in some confusion. The people, warriors, and women divided into two parties, and there was heated discussion of the issues in private Indian councils. The Seneca generally supported Cornplanter's cautious view that it was better not to take sides in a civil war among white people. "Gi-en-gwah-toh & Co-ne-di-yeu [Handsome Lake] spoke strongly against it—thought they had better remain neutral," recalled Blacksnake; and so did Guyasuta and Red Jacket. But Brant and his Mohawks called all the pacifists cowards, and the Seneca warriors "can not Beared to be called coward," as Blacksnake put it. At last, by dint of this sort of moral exhortation and British openhandedness with rum and dry goods, and the display of a wampum belt purported to be the ancient convenant between the Six Nations and the Crown, the majority of the warriors agreed that they were after all obligated to defend their kind and indulgent father. A majority of the warriors passed a resolution to accept the King's hatchet, and "the mothers also consent to Regard to it. . . ." Cornplanter, taking his political defeat gracefully, accepted the decision and exhorted the warriors to unity. "Every Brave man Show himself Now hereafter for we will find an many Dangerous times during the action of the war, for we will see a many Brave man amongst the America Soldiers whicth we Shall meet, with their sharp adge tools, I therefore Say you must Stand like good Soldier against your own white Brother Because just as soon as he fined you out that you are against him he then will Show you his wit no mercy on you an us, I therefore Say Stand to your Post when is time come Before you

But agreed yourselves. . . ." The resolution became unanimous, and the next day Brant announced to the British commissioners that the Six Nations had taken up the hatchet against the Americans.[11]

· *The First Battles* ·

THE IMMEDIATE OUTCOME of the Oswego council was the enlistment of several hundred Iroquois warriors in Colonel Barry St. Leger's motley little army then assembling at Oswego. This task force was to sweep down the Mohawk Valley, while Burgoyne swept down the Hudson, to a triumphal meeting at Albany. The joint force then would proceed down the lower Hudson River to New York. But the campaign was hurriedly arranged. There was inadequate artillery; the troops were a miscellany of a few hundred each of loyalist guerrillas, Hessian mercenaries, Acadian militia, British regulars, and Indian volunteers; there was neither discipline nor training sufficient for execution. The force was stopped in its tracks by the moldy palisades of old Fort Stanwix (recently renamed, patriotically, Fort Schuyler) and its ill-trained garrison of some seven hundred and fifty men. The siege, the sanguinary battle at Oriskany nearby, and St. Leger's sudden withdrawal from the ground, not merely contributed to the failure of the grand strategy that was signaled by Burgoyne's later surrender; it also largely determined the nature of future Iroquois military tactics in the Revolutionary War.

The American fort, at the beginning of the summer, was not a very substantial obstacle to a British advance down the Mohawk River. Its surrounding ditch was filled with rubbish and debris; the outer pickets were rotten and falling down; the garrison had too small a supply of powder; the "bullets did not match the muskets"; they did not even have a flag! But at the end of June small parties of Indians, including a group of Seneca under Handsome Lake's venerable captain, Old Smoke, began sniping at the Americans and occasionally killing and scalping stragglers from the fort. This harassment stirred the patriots to rebuild their defenses. St. Leger's twelve-hundred-man force, arriving on August 3, found the fort in improved condition and a garrison prepared to defend itself. The patriot commander haughtily refused a summons to surrender, and the British forces encamped near the fort laid siege, and prepared to cut off any reinforcements.

The reinforcing provincial militia approached three days later, on August 6, and, somewhat against the advice of their aging commander, General Herkimer, at once impetuously hurled themselves into the midst of the ambush carefully prepared by Joseph Brant and his Indians and by Colonel Butler and Sir John Johnson and their New York loyalists. The American force of about nine hundred men, however, was too large to be annihilated in a few volleys. The skirmish turned into a bloody afternoon-long hand-to-hand contest with muskets, knives, bayonets, and tomahawks, which ended only when the Indians and British left the field to protect their encampments from a successful sortie from the fort. The American reinforcements retreated down the valley shortly thereafter, with their mortally wounded commander. From two to four hundred of Herkimer's men were killed, and several hundred others were wounded or captured, or fled at the first alarm. About one hundred of the Iroquois, and perhaps an equal number of the loyalists, also died. Both sides claimed the victory: the British, because they had inflicted such heavy losses and had prevented reinforcements from reaching the fort; the Americans, because their survivors remained (temporarily) on the field of battle.

The major blow, however, had fallen on the Indians. Thirty-six warriors of the Seneca alone, including several sachem-chiefs serving as common soldiers, were killed on the field or died later of wounds; many others were injured; and their encampment was sacked by the sortie from the fort. Others lost substantially in reputation: Red Jacket and three others fled at the sound of gunfire and went home to the Genesee. (Blacksnake recalled this as "cowardice" seventy-three years later, but said that because it was Red Jacket's first war experience, "nothing was done or said to him.") Since all of the Seneca leaders who had been at the Oswego council were present at the Oriskany battle, it may be presumed that Handsome Lake also was present.

A few days after the battle the British officers told the Seneca— and probably the other Indian allies as well—"to go home and see [their] families." Mary Jemison, then living along the Genesee, described the disillusioning return of the survivors, who had gone to Fort Stanwix expecting to look on peacefully smoking their pipes while the Americans surrendered to the British, and instead had borne the brunt of the heaviest fighting of the war to date. As Mary Jemison put it, "Our town exhibited a scene of real sorrow and distress, when our warriors returned and recounted their misfortunes, and

stated the real loss they had received in the engagement. The mourning was excessive, and was expressed by the most doleful yells, shrieks,
and howlings, and by inimitable gesticulations."

Two weeks after the battle the British themselves, failing further
reinforcements from Canada, unable to count any longer on their
shattered Indian allies, and alarmed by rumors (largely true) spread
by the "neutral" Oneida that a major American relief force under
General Arnold was advancing upon them, were forced to lift the
siege and to withdraw hastily across the lakes. Some embittered
Iroquois warriors who had remained with St. Leger plundered the
fleeing British and went home too in disgust.[12]

War was largely a summer and fall occupation among the Iroquois;
in winter, warriors became hunters and family men. As Blacksnake
explained, "We than Retreated for the winter ... we Replace ourselve,
at Near home for our hunting till Spring, Some of those which ware
family went on home But when we got Ready and hunt Deers & Bears
and Elks and others garms—for Provisions for the Next for to play
upon, and for our childrens and for the old folks, whicth we have to
provide for, all their wants, whicth we always maken preparation for
them before we leave them."[13] Thus the winter of 1777–8 was a
quiet one insofar as Indian warfare was concerned; Congress even took
heart to appeal again to the four hostile tribes (Seneca, Cayuga, Onondaga, and Mohawk) to join their alliance, claiming (optimistically)
that the Delaware, the Shawnee, and other western tribes were friends
of the United States. But the quietness of the frontier did not mean
peace: Brant's Indian emissaries and the three notorious Tories who
had escaped from their Pittsburgh prison—McKee, Elliot, and Simon
Girty—were busily recruiting warriors for next summer's campaign.
Rumor had it that Indians from twenty-two nations were going to
join Butler's Rangers in an attack on New York that would lay waste
all the settlements west of Schenectady. The white frontiers passed
the winter in fear.

War came again with the spring. The first attack of the season fell
on Springfield, a settlement at the head of Otsego Lake: the little fort
was burned, some of the men were killed and some captured, the
women and children were left unharmed.

This assault set the general style of the attacks by the organized
Iroquois raiding parties during the war: the first objective was the
seizure or destruction of property, and the expulsion of the rebel

inhabitants; if men resisted, or seemed prepared to resist, they were killed or captured; women and children were usually either left alone or taken as prisoners. There were no instances of torture (except for the case of some soldiers captured during Sullivan's Campaign) and no wholesale massacres, for the organized war-parties acted under instruction from British officers and were often accompanied by British officers, who firmly insisted on the Indians obeying the rules of civilized warfare. Brant, the Mohawk leader, was a college-trained man who consciously attempted to combine the idea of the English officer-gentleman and the Iroquois warrior-diplomat. Individual and isolated atrocities were committed, usually by independent bands of banditti who were bent solely on plunder, revenge, or sadistic enjoyment. But responsible British officers like Johnson and the Butlers, and Indian leaders like Old Smoke and Brant, wanted to prevent orgies of cruelty like those in which the Iroquois had indulged themselves in the seventeenth century. These were acculturated and, in some cases, like Brant's, "civilized" Indians, sensitive to the contempt of Europeans and anxious to acquit themselves with dignity in the eyes of a larger world.

While several additional raids were made under Brant's leadership during the summer on the settlements in the Mohawk Valley, chiefly destructive of property, the first major event of the 1778 fighting-season was the famous battle at Wyoming. Handsome Lake, as a "common warrior," participated in this battle, along with Blacksnake, Old Smoke, Farmer's Brother, and most of the other distinguished Allegany and Genesee Seneca. Following the plan announced at the Oswego council of the previous year, several hundred Tories under Johnson and Butler, and most of the Seneca warriors, were outfitted for the campaign at Niagara and early in July appeared before the Forty Fort, the rebel stronghold in the valley of Wyoming. On July 3, about 400 militia and regulars sallied forth from the fort and confronted the Indians and Tories. The two sides were arranged in a regular skirmish-line; the Indians managed to outflank the Americans, who fell back in disorder; the retreat became a rout, and 340 of the 400 were killed. The Seneca lost, according to Blacksnake, only five men. Next day the fort, under Colonel Denniston, surrendered. The settlements in the valley of Wyoming were thereafter burned and looted, and most of the inhabitants fled into the mountains. Although there was neither massacre nor torture of prisoners, the fleeing survivors spread lurid tales of atrocities; indeed, Wyoming became a symbol of Indian rapacity. Queen Esther, daughter of old Catherine Montour, was reputed to have tomahawked helpless prisoners with her own hand; the "monster Brant" (who was not even at Wyoming, being occupied with the relatively bloodless raids on the Mohawk Valley at the time) was accused of murder; tales of the slaughter of whole families by their black-sheep Tory sons made frontier blood run cold. The Seneca returned to Niagara with fifteen prisoners, whom they surrendered to the British; they received each a suit of clothes and some money, and went home, unaware that the military success of their mission was earning them an undeserved reputation for wanton savagery.

A year had now passed, during which Iroquois warriors had participated as brothers-in-arms with British troops in two major and strictly military engagements, at Oriskany and Wyoming. They had successfully raided and destroyed a number of small settlements in Pennsylvania and New York. Although as yet no retaliation had been offered by the rebels, the humiliating defeat at Wyoming, inflated in retrospect by atrocity stories, and the raids on frontier settlements in the Mohawk Valley were now beginning to spur action. Brant's summer camps for refugee Tories and refugee Mohawks, at Oquaga and Unadilla on the Susquehanna, were suspected of being the headquarters of the Iroquois raiders. Already in June he had been reported to be fortifying his post there, and the people from Cherry Valley nearby were sending out patrols and issuing challenges and threats to castrate Brant. After the Wyoming affair Congress resolved to speed its plans to chastise the Six Nations. A grandiose project for an expedition against Detroit was reduced to a program of building a string of pitifully undersupplied (and eventually abandoned) forts in the Ohio country, and the main attention was directed instead to the Susquehanna, on whose upper waters the Unadilla River lay. In September a task force of regulars and rangers from Schoharie assaulted the then-abandoned Indian towns at Oquaga and Unadilla and burned them to the ground, including in the fire the gristmill and sawmill, then the only mills of their kind on the upper Susquehanna. About the same time, some two hundred militia under colonels Hartley and Denniston drove up the Susquehanna from Wyoming, burning deserted Indian towns at Sheshequin, Tioga, and Queen Esther's Town. At Tioga, on hearing that Butler's force was nearby, they turned about and retreated toward Wyoming. They were forced to beat off an attack by Butler's Indians on their way down the river.

The consequence of these comparatively ineffectual threats was the hardening of Iroquois determination to protect their territory, which they conceived now to be in immediate danger of invasion and seizure by ruthless, land-hungry frontiersmen. Big Tree, the Seneca chief who had for a year held out against Seneca participation in the war and had continued to negotiate through the Oneida with the Americans, cast his lot with the warriors' party. In revenge for the attacks on Oquaga and Unadilla, the Iroquois attacked Cherry Valley, an old settlement founded in 1739. About one hundred of Captain Butler's rangers and perhaps two hundred Indians under Brant made up the party. Handsome Lake was one of them. (So also, for a time, was Red Jacket; but at the rendezvous he and three others turned back, complaining that the season was too far advanced for fighting. This was his second desertion.) As in the other attacks on settlements, the tactic was to immobilize the armed militia in their fort, capture a small number of men, women, and children, drive off the horses, cattle, and oxen, and take whatever movable plunder might be carried. The soldiers were kept busy in the fort answering sniping fire from the Tories, while the Indians killed people, burned barns, houses, and haystacks, drove off horses and cattle, and looted goods. A number of men, women, and children were killed in the fighting, and thirty or forty captives, mostly women and children, taken with the party on its departure. Most of these were released after a few miles' walk; others were held as hostages for the release of the wife and family of Walter Butler, who in turn were being held by the Americans as hostages for the return of Butler himself (although he was then under sentence of death). Eventually the exchange of the Cherry Valley prisoners for Walter Butler's family was arranged.

Cherry Valley was now added to Wyoming as the subject of atrocity stories; and this time the stories were more nearly true. At Cherry Valley some thirty-odd civilians, including women and children, Tory and rebel sympathizers alike, had been killed despite the efforts of Butler and Brant to maintain the disciplined behavior that had prevailed at Wyoming, where only men under arms lost their lives. In the course of an acrimonious correspondence with generals Schuyler and Clinton, Butler denied any widespread killing of women, children, and prisoners and explained the occasional killing of civilians as revenge for atrocities committed by Americans. But denials and excuses did not avail; the work of rumor made the atrocities even more enormous. The Iroquois were charged with ripping open and quartering the women and hanging their bodies on the trees, and with seizing infants from their mothers' breasts and knocking their brains out against posts. Such rumors as these had the twofold effect of sending the frontier settlements into panic and of building up in the frontier population a vindictive hatred for and contempt of the Iroquois that would later cost that people, and the British, dear.[14]

In the spring of 1779, after the winter's lull while the warriors hunted to feed their families, the Indian raids upon the frontier began again. Brant and his Mohawk and upper Susquehanna Indians burned settlements and cut to pieces pursuing militia, from the Mohawk River as far to the south as the Delaware River at the Minisinks. The Seneca and Cayuga captured Fort Freeland, near Sunbury on the Susquehanna, and looted and burned in the neighborhood; this series of raids locally was renowned for the fact that the Indians released all women and children and killed few men, although they took about thirty soldiers prisoner. Other miscellaneous bands made scattered attacks on small settlements and isolated farms all the way along the frontier from the Susquehanna to the Monongahela and the Allegheny about Pittsburgh.

Although the loss of life in these raids was relatively small, their effectiveness in destroying economic and military resources, in disorganizing the militia, and in reducing the local will to fight was very great. They were major blows to the American mobilization effort. In Brant's raid, for instance, on German Flats—one of the richest and most productive agricultural settlements in the Mohawk Valley—nearly 70 farms, including 63 houses, 57 barns, 3 gristmills, 2 sawmills, and crops in the field and furniture in the buildings were totally destroyed by fire, and 235 horses, 229 horned cattle, 269 sheep, and 93 oxen carried away. One hundred square miles of farmland were put to the torch while the several hundred inhabitants of the valley, cowering in their little forts—which were not even fired upon—watched in dismay. Only two white men were killed.

The raids by the Seneca and Cayuga on the towns along the Susquehanna were equally, if not more, disorganizing. After thirteen men were killed at the taking of Fort Freeland, the whole of the country was panic-stricken. A letter from Sunbury struck a note of hysteria: "The situation of Northumberland Country, beyond description distressing, not a single Inhabitant north of Northumberland Town. . . . I need not ask you what is to be done, Help Help; our whole Frontier laid open, and the Communication with Gen. Sullivan's army is cut off."[15] Local petitions were circulated for the recall of General Sullivan's army (whose mission was to force the Indian war-parties to withdraw to protect their families); court proceedings against the general were demanded; the forts were evacuated; the local militia refused even to leave their homes to defend the countryside. A lieutenant colonel of the militia reported to the president of Pennsylvania's revolutionary council that "Our Country is on ye Eve of Breaking up . . . there is nothing to be seen but Disolation, fire & smoak, as the inhabitants is Collected at particular places, the Enimy burns all their Houses that they have evacuated. . . ." Indeed, as the inhabitants themselves noted, it was like the French and Indian War of twenty years earlier all over again. Even the same desperate remedies were suggested: surveyor William Maclay reinvented Franklin's earlier (1755) suggestion of hunting down the Indians with dogs.[16]

· *Sullivan's Raid* ·

THE EFFECTIVENESS of the Iroquois and Troy raiders in laying waste a fifty- to one-hundred-mile belt of frontier land, from the Monongahela River to the Mohawk, thus was by now a matter of major concern to the Continental commanders. During the winter Washington had been laying plans for a blow against the hostile Indians; this campaign was to be the main American military effort of the year. In fact four American invasions of the Iroquois country took place during the summer of 1779.

The first move was a strike against the Onondaga, who had been attempting to straddle the issue of war, some of their men taking part in Iroquois forays and others, particularly the responsible chiefs, loudly proclaiming neutrality in various conferences at Albany. Three Onondaga villages were burned, twelve Indians were killed, thirty-three were taken prisoner, and considerable military equipment (including the cannon installed at the council-house) was taken or destroyed. (It is noteworthy that orders were issued by General

Clinton on the occasion of this campaign to emulate his notion of Iroquois treatment of prisoners: "Bad as the savages are, they never violate the chastity of any women, their prisoners. Although I have very little apprehension that any of the soldiers will so far forget their character as to attempt such a crime on the Indian women who may fall into their hands, yet it will be well to take measures to prevent such a stain upon our army."[17]) The immediate consequence was the alienation of the Onondaga, their commitment to the cause of British arms, and cries of outrage from the Seneca at seeing their neutralist brethren so treacherously attacked. Within the month three hundred Onondaga warriors—virtually the entire adult male population of the tribe—descended upon the little settlement of Cobleskill, east of Schoharie. Only two prisoners were taken; a fort was burned and twenty-two soldiers killed, and the whole settlement was burned and plundered.

The second, third, and fourth attacks, formulated and carried out in concert, were mounted by substantial armies under generals Clinton and Sullivan and Colonel Brodhead. Clinton with 1,500 men on 220 flatboats floated down the Unadilla River from Otsego Lake, on the crest of a flood formed by breaking a dam at the mouth of the lake, to join General Sullivan's army at Tioga. The flood ruined the Indian cornfields, and the army burned three Tuscarora villages below Oquaga and miscellaneous small Indian settlements still farther down on the Susquehanna. The passage downstream occupied Clinton's army from August 9 to 22. Sullivan took command of the combined army of about 3,000 men.

Sullivan's orders were to destroy totally the villages of the Iroquois, to take as many prisoners of all ages and both sexes as possible, and to cut a swath of terror to Niagara. A smaller force under Colonel Brodhead was simultaneously to move up the Allegheny River. Sullivan, a methodical New Hampshire lawyer, like effective anti-guerrilla fighters before and after him, was careful to maintain discipline, to bring up supplies and cannon, and to send out Indian (Oneida) spies and scouts to prevent ambuscade. Furthermore, he had the advantage of surprise: the British and the Iroquois were not expecting so massive an assault and had not assembled adequate forces for defense. The main battle, such as it was, was over almost before Sullivan's main march began: on August 29 a hastily assembled force of about 500 Indians under Brant and 250 Tory rangers under the

Cornplanter, by F. Bartoli (circa 1796). Courtesy of The New-York Historical Society, New York City

Red Jacket, by Robert W. Weir (1828). Courtesy of The New-York Historical Society, New York City

Joseph Brant, by George Catlin from the original by E. Ames

Henry Abeel (Cornplanter's son), by Charles B. King (circa 1828). Courtesy of the National Museum, Copenhagen

"The Chief Read Jaret" (probably Red Jacket), by Baroness Hyde de Neuville (1807). Courtesy of The New-York Historical Society, New York City

Charles and William Abeel (sons of Cornplanter), from a photograph taken prior to 1868. Courtesy of Warren County Historical Society, Pennsylvania

Peter, a Seneca from Tonawanda, by Baroness Hyde de Neuville (1807). Courtesy of The New-York Historical Society, New York City

the fair indian
of the buffalo tribe
drawn to canisteo y [...]
1808 —

"*The Fair Indian*" *of Canisteo (perhaps one of Mary Jamison's sons),
by Baroness Hyde de Neuville
(1808). Courtesy of The New-York
Historical Society, New York City*

*Seneca Woman and Child, by
Baroness Hyde de Neuville (1808).
Courtesy of The New-York His-
torical Society, New York City*

*Squah of Seneca tribe with his papou.
aout. 1808.*

*An Indian Family (probably Oneida), by Baroness Hyde de Neuville
(1807). Courtesy of The New-York Historical Society, New York City*

*"Mary, Squaw of the Oneida Tribe," by Baroness Hyde de Neuville
(1807). Courtesy of The New-York Historical Society, New York City*

an indian and his Squaw

"*An Indian and His Squaw*" (*probably Oneida*), *by Baroness Hyde de Neuville (1807). Courtesy of The New-York Historical Society, New York City*

First White Settler's Cottage at Angelica (near Allegany Seneca Reservation), by Baroness Hyde de Neuville (1808). Courtesy of The New-York Historical Society, New York City

Butlers and the Johnsons, without artillery, fighting from foxholes and behind thin breastworks screened with shrubbery, were badly beaten by Sullivan's army at the Indian village of Newtown on the Chemung River. Sullivan had artillery and sprayed the enemy with shrapnel; his men outnumbered their opponents three to one and turned their flank. The Indians and Tories, although they contested the field in hand-to-hand fighting, were forced into flight, and they did not re-form until they had passed the Genesee, where they prepared to resist Sullivan again. But the second battle never took place; Sullivan, traveling with only a few cannon and with his men on half-rations, stopped at the Genesee and then prudently retraced his steps to Tioga.

Although Sullivan's army did not inflict many military casualties, it succeeded in laying waste all of the surviving Indian towns on the Susquehanna River and its tributaries, all the main Cayuga settlements, and most of the Seneca towns. Sullivan proceeded about his work on precisely the same principles as did the Iroquois raiders, burning all houses and outbuildings, chopping down orchards, firing fields of ripe corn and other vegetables, and driving away the inhabitants. He captured few Indians, for the villagers fled before the army. The roster of destruction is a long one (and it earned Washington the name of Town Destroyer): three towns on the Chemung River; three towns on the Tioga River; all of the dozen or so Cayuga and Seneca towns on Cayuga and Seneca lakes; the half-dozen Seneca towns on the route westward to the Genesee River; and the complex of settlements at Geneseo itself. The army missed the towns on the upper and lower Genesee and several small settlements west of the Genesee Valley. Meanwhile Colonel Brodhead, with his force of four hundred men, was marching from Pittsburgh toward the Seneca settlements on the upper Allegheny. He burned the town at Jenuchshadago and the smaller settlements (already deserted) below it, but did not reach the large villages on the oxbow. The process was much the same again: one or two light skirmishes with Seneca warriors, much burning of houses and cornfields, no natives captured.

As a final fillip to the work of annihilation Sullivan even had a small detachment descend upon a small settlement of Mohawk who had remained at the lower "castle" in the Mohawk Valley. Surrounded by white neighbors, they had been at peace; but now they were taken prisoner, and their houses and farms turned over to white refugees. Although they were later released with apologies, it is not known that their farms were restored.

Thus, with the conclusion of the summer of 1779, the four pro-British Iroquois tribes were in as difficult a situation as were the white frontiers like the Mohawk Valley and the Susquehanna. The Mohawk, Onondaga, and Cayuga towns had all been destroyed or abandoned; the towns of their dependents on the upper Susquehanna and its tributaries had been obliterated; all but two of the larger Seneca towns had been razed. The Oneida towns, being regarded by the Americans as the homes of allies, had as yet not been touched; but because of the Oneida and Tuscarora service to the Americans both during Burgoyne's Campaign and later, the British and vengeful pro-British Iroquois now destroyed them in turn. Some time in the winter of 1779–80 a mixed force of Tories and Mohawks under Brant swept down on the Oneida settlement, burned the fort, the houses, and Kirkland's mission church, and drove the Oneida themselves to seek protection among the whites. They were, in fact, forced to take refuge at Schenectady until the close of the war.

Before the Revolution, the Six Nations and their dependents had lived largely in some thirty thriving villages scattered from the Mohawk River to Lake Erie and the Ohio country. Of all these towns, by the spring of 1780 only two survived undamaged. The others were in ashes or empty, moldering in rain and wind. A few people struggled to survive on the ruins of their old homes, but most were dispersed, some crowded into the undamaged settlements, many more camped in flimsy cabins on the banks of the Niagara River, where they had access to rations from the British garrison. Cold, hungry, racked by scurvy and dysentery, many dying, they waited for spring to replant, rebuild and gain revenge.[18]

· The Final Campaigns ·

ALTHOUGH THE AMERICAN RAIDS of 1779 were to have a secondary impact whose effects would be felt by the Iroquois for generations, their immediate consequence was not a taming but a stimulation of the warriors. The winter of 1779–80 was a quiet one: the unusually deep snows and bitter cold of that season, and the necessity of caring for the hundreds of displaced Indian families at Niagara, kept most of the warriors at home. But in the spring they were out again, in larger numbers than ever before. By July Guy Johnson at Niagara was able to write, "The Number of Men of the Six Nation Confederacy [exclusive of their people to the Southward] is about sixteen hundred, about twelve hundred of whom are Warriors, and of the latter, eight hundred and thirty are now on service agst the frontiers, and more in readiness to follow them, which far exceeds what has ever been out at one time without the army, few, or none remaining, but those necessary to assist in planting, and providing for their families. . . ."[19] The war parties, moreover, were on the move unusually early in the spring, some 390 having marched from Niagara in March. Others came down from Lake Champlain and Crown Point, and some (allies of the Iroquois) from Detroit and Sandusky.

The 1780 raids devastated settlements in a great arc from the Mohawk Valley south to the Catskills and the Delaware and Susquehanna rivers and west to the Ohio. Handsome Lake was one of three or four hundred Seneca warriors who took part in the raid in Canajoharie (where Cornplanter's father, John O'Bail, had his farm). They laid waste the south bank of the Mohawk for miles, burning fifty-three houses, fifty-three barns, a gristmill, two small forts, and a church. Some fifty or sixty prisoners were taken, including Cornplanter's aged father, the onetime Genesee peddler. The capture of Cornplanter's father was something of an embarrassment to his Seneca relatives. Cornplanter apologized for burning his house in ignorance of its owner's identity and offered as amends to take him to the Indian country, there to support him as long as he lived. When the old man demurred, a council was held, at which, according to Blacksnake, "it was agreed to let old O'Bail & most of the other prisoners go free—which was accordingly done, as a compliment to Cornplanter." After the burning of Canajoharie a smaller party of thirty Seneca, including Cornplanter, Blacksnake, Handsome Lake, and others, probably many of them kinsmen, drifted southward toward the Susquehanna, killing and plundering.

But the major campaign of the year 1780 was the notorious Schoharie Valley expedition, led by Sir John Johnson himself. Handsome Lake was a member of this expedition, too, along with Brant, Cornplanter, Red Jacket, Farmer's Brother, Old Smoke, Little Beard, Jack Berry, and the rest of his Seneca friends and kinfolk. This expedition was comparable in size and destructiveness to Sullivan's of the year before. Tory Rangers and Indians, converging from north, west, and south, met to make up an army of 1,500 men, well armed and even carrying mortars. This formidable force marched unopposed down the Schoharie Valley to its confluence with the Mohawk and then proceeded up the Mohawk, burning everything in its path. This raid, culminating three years of incendiary incursions, virtually wiped out all white settlement in the Mohawk Valley west of the environs of Schenectady. But Blacksnake's most vivid memory of the campaign was of hunger, and of gorging himself when they finally reached the first Schoharie settlement. "Cornplanter, Blacksnake, Connediyeu [Handsome Lake], & five others, making a party of 8, went into a house—found breakfast all set on the table ready to be eaten—& the people fled; the Indians helped themselves—didn't wait to sit down, says Blacksnake—snatched & devour'd what they wanted to satisfy the cravings of hunger—the first food they had tasted for two days."

The next two battle seasons, of 1781 and 1782, passed in much the same manner: raids into the Mohawk Valley, raids along the Hudson River itself, raids at Frankstown, Hannastown, and other places in New York, Pennsylvania, Virginia, Ohio, and Kentucky, burning and pillaging, generally leaving the garrisons bottled up in their little forts, skirmishing with the occasional parties of militia who blundered into their path or who pursued them too closely.

The effectiveness of the Iroquois frontier campaign cannot easily be exaggerated. Although the individual raids did not in themselves constitute major threats to the military forces of the colonies, in cumulation they produced economic impotence and paralyzed morale in a vast belt of settlements between the Mohawk and the Ohio. A thousand Iroquois warriors and five hundred Tory rangers were able to lay in waste nearly 50,000 square miles of colonial territory. Valley by valley, contemporary observers tell the story.

The valley of the Mohawk and its southern tributaries was the most severely damaged. From Fort Stanwix to the Hudson River, and south almost to the borders of Pennsylvania, that region was a shambles. Of a 2,500-man militia enrolled at the beginning of the war in Tryon County, by 1781 only 800 remained; of the rest, a third had been killed or captured, a third had deserted to the enemy, and a third had fled the country. There were in June 1783 said to be 300 widows and 2,000 orphaned children in Tryon County. The five

New York regiments had been reduced to two; Fort Stanwix was abandoned in 1781, and the other forts in the valley were difficult to supply because of Indian ambuscades on the supply trains; and the militia were insubordinate and deserting. Rebel leaders in the population, fearful lest invasion bring about a wholesale defection to the Crown, were witch-hunting for suspected Tories, removing suspects to concentration camps south of the river, expropriating their property, and burning their houses (spared by the Tory rangers).

The valley of the Susquehanna, in Pennsylvania, was in little better condition. As early as 1779 it was reported that "All the Houses along this River have been burnt and the Gardens & Fields the most fertile I ever beheld grown over with weeds and Bushes." By 1780 militia were refusing to stand to arms when summoned by their officers, rumors of Indians in the neighborhood were bringing all the settlers above Sunbury flooding down the river, and the local militia commander reported that "without some speedy assistance being Ordered here, I am afraid the County will break up intirely."[20]

The western parts of Pennsylvania were equally distraught. In 1780 a series of spring raids "drove the greatest part of the County on the north of Yohgeny River into Garrison." The officers of the Continental garrison at Fort Pitt—"reduced to about 300 Rank & file, many of which are unfit for the Service"—could not even buy food from the local civilians because their paper money was regarded as worthless. For five days in the fall of 1780 both officers and men at Fort Pitt—the entire garrison—were without bread. Efforts to impress cattle merely led the frontiersmen to take up arms against their own army. Rumor had it that half the population were Tory sympathizers.

A further effect of terror on the frontiersmen was to render them incapable of distinguishing between friendly and hostile Indians. Colonel Brodhead, after strenuous diplomacy unsweetened by gifts and unsanctioned by supplies, force, or kept promises, was able in the fall of 1780 to persuade a portion of the Delaware Indians at Coshocton on the Muskingum to take up the hatchet against the Seneca; but when he assembled one hundred of their warriors at Fort Pitt to help protect the neighborhood, he was forced to use soldiers from the garrison of Fort Pitt to protect the Indians. His diplomatic persuasions had been at last successful. "But as upwards of forty men from the neighborhood of Hannah's Town, have attempted to destroy them whilst they considered themselves under our Protection, it may not be an easy matter to call them out again. . . ." It was not easy; in fact, the Delaware now turned to the British. In 1781, in response to information that the Delaware had abandoned him, the enterprising Brodhead took his militiamen on the notorious "squaw campaign" to destroy the hostile Delaware towns on the Muskingum. Brodhead's troops refused to cross the Muskingum to fight the Delaware warriors, but burned the towns, destroyed the cattle, seized eighty thousand pounds' worth of plunder, and murdered almost all of their fifty prisoners—men, women, and children—before the troops reached Fort Pitt. One of them also managed to kill a Delaware chief as he stood talking over peace terms with Brodhead. The western militia next year slaughtered a band of ninety unarmed, pro-American, Christian (Moravian) Delaware at their settlement on the Muskingum, whither they had come from their bleak camps on the Sandusky to obtain food.

The revenge obtained by the Seneca and Delaware was substantial: the defeat of Crawford and Irvine on the Sandusky, and Crawford's celebrated torture; the devastation of Westmoreland County; the assault on Wheeling; and the defeat of the American militia at the Blue Licks in Kentucky.

Indeed, the war was still going well for the Iroquois warriors when the British had had enough. After the summer campaign of 1783 Blacksnake and other Seneca visiting at Fort George were told that Washington had surrendered. The news of the imminent British capitulation finally filtered through the screen of official denials to the few warriors at Fort George and to the three thousand men, women, and children at Niagara; but it was slowly that the Iroquois came to believe that the rebels had actually defeated the Great Father and that a peace was being made between them in which Iroquois interests were not mentioned.[21]

⮐ 6 ⮐

THE COLLAPSE
OF THE CONFEDERACY

THE IROQUOIS DID NOT REGARD THEMSELVES AS A CONQUERED PEOPLE in 1784, and their warriors were prepared to continue fighting. But since the Americans were not openly threatening an attempt at territorial conquest and since their own ally and source of supplies, Great Britain, had made a peace with the Americans, it seemed sensible to end the bloodshed. And so the Iroquois and their allies among the tribes to the westward entered into the preliminary negotiations for a treaty at Fort Stanwix in the naive expectation that it would be an honorable peace, a laying down of hatchets by the warriors of both sides.

But the realities of politics had placed the Iroquois in an unstable position. It would be thirteen years before their position was redefined; and during those thirteen years they would lose over the council table the lands and the political sovereignty that white armies had been unable to seize by force. That they retained anything, even their reservations, after those thirteen years, was determined solely by the opinion of the members of the Continental Congress, despite the belligerent public language of American negotiators, that complete military expropriation would cost more in blood and money than the new country was willing to pay.[1]

During these years of disastrous negotiation Handsome Lake, as one of the chiefs of the confederacy, was in all likelihood present at most of the sequence of councils and helped to preside over the collapse of the confederacy.

· Federal and State Indian Policies and the "Conquest Theory" Treaties ·

ALTHOUGH THE AMERICANS in 1784 had no stomach for an Indian war, they still wanted the Indian lands. Both the states and the Continental Congress had come out of the war with heavy debts and poor credit; the troops had been paid, when funds were available, in a rapidly depreciating currency, and many had not been paid in full or at all; and the new government was faced with further outlays that demanded both public credit and a reasonably stable currency. The solution to these problems lay in the public lands. Public land could be used to stabilize an unstable currency by exchanging it for that currency; public land could be donated to officers and soldiers in lieu of back pay; public land could be sold to meet the debts and expenses of government. Thus from the standpoint of rational legislators and administrators the acquisition of Indian lands appeared to be an absolute necessity in order to finance both the war and the peace. But the pressure to acquire Indian lands was augmented by two other forces: the greed of land speculators, who saw the possibility of vast profits to be made from the sale, to thousands of individual settlers and entrepreneurs, of virgin timber and agricultural land, of waterways, mill sites, trading locations, harbors, town sites, and so on; and the vengeful hatred of the frontiersmen, who had lost so heavily in goods, in kinsmen, and in self-respect from the successful Indian forays.

The conflict of these interests led immediately to a scramble for advantage in Indian land purchase among the states and the Congress (now functioning only under the feeble Articles of Confederation). The Articles provided that the Congress had the sole right to regulate "Indian" affairs—that is, affairs with Indians "not members of any of the States, provided that the legislative right of any State, within its own limits be not infringed or violated."[2] The determination of the boundaries of the several states and the disposition of their overlapping claims, arising from the vague language of the British charters, at once assumed critical importance, because Indian lands within state boundaries would be public lands of the state, not of the nation. Thus Massachusetts and New York fell at once into dispute over the sovereignty and ownership of the lands of the Iroquois; Pennsylvania quarreled with New York over their mutual boundary through Iroquois territory; Virginia and Pennsylvania continued their long argument over the ownership of the Ohio Valley, to parts of which the Iroquois still claimed sovereignty; and so on *ad nauseam*. These various states'-rights assertions conflicted with the similar interests of the Congress itself. The matter, in the areas involving the Iroquois, was eventually settled by reserving to the United States the sovereignty over public lands south of the Great Lakes and west of the present state boundaries of New York and Pennsylvania, and by various specific accommodations, which need not be examined in detail, among Pennsylvania, New York, Massachusetts, and the United States about their respective rights to tracts east of that line.

The method by which the land was to be acquired was diplomacy. And that diplomacy was based on an impromptu legal theory: that the United States had not only won a war with Great Britain but had also conquered Britain's Indian allies and that therefore the Treaty of Paris of 1783 gave the United States and its several member states not only political sovereignty over, but also ownership of the soil of, all Indian territory south of the Great Lakes and the St. Lawrence River and east of the Mississippi River. Treaties of peace, of course, were still to be made with the Indian tribes, who had not been mentioned in the Treaty of Paris, but these treaties were to be considered as unilateral actions by which the United States "gave" peace to already conquered tribes and "gave" them such tracts of land as it, or its member states, might out of humanitarian motives wish to allot from the public lands. If the Indians were unwilling to surrender on these terms, the war would (theoretically) be continued until they were either annihilated or expelled.[3]

The Treaty of Fort Stanwix of 1784 was ostensibly to have been the peace treaty with the whole Iroquoian confederacy, led by the Six Nations and including the Delaware, Shawnee, Wyandot, Chippewa, and other western allies and dependents. But as a settlement of differences it was a failure. The Americans refused to recognize the

Iroquoian confederacy; negotiations were held at gunpoint; hostages were unexpectedly demanded and taken by the United States for the deliberate purpose of coercion of the Indian delegates; the tone of the Continental commissioners was insulting, arbitrary, and demanding; and two Indians given up by the Seneca to be punished according to white law were lynched by a mob shortly after the treaty. Some of the Indian delegates, including Brant, left in disgust before the peace treaty was signed. There was real question as to whether it could be considered legally valid from the Indian standpoint, even as a peace treaty, let alone as a cession of land. As Brant remarked before his departure, "we are sent in order to make peace and . . . we are not authorized to stipulate any particular cession of land." Yet by this treaty the Six Nations, under the threat of continued war, made peace and "yielded" to the United States their lands west of New York and Pennsylvania and received a reservation in New York. And on the same occasion, although in a much more amicable transaction, the Seneca sold to Pennsylvania their lands in Pennsylvania west of the line of 1768.

Two years later the Six Nations publicly repudiated the treaty, asserting that they were sovereigns of their own soil and "equally free as you or any nation under the sun." At a meeting of the League council the actions of the delegates and the language of the treaty were reviewed by the chiefs, and it was decided that the treaty was unacceptable. Rather than give up their right to the soil, they would continue the war. Furthermore, as an Iroquois speaker observed in denying the validity of the sale, "it is not the Six Nations only that reproach those Chiefs that have given up that country. The Chippewas and all these Nations who live on those Lands Westward, call to us and ask us, Brothers of our Fathers, where is the Place you have reserved for us to lie down upon?" But despite their protests the Iroquois were unwilling to renew hostilities, and the Fort Stanwix treaty was tacitly allowed to stand by default.[4]

The United States now proceeded to coerce "representatives" of the occupants of the Ohio lands into making peace under the conquest theory. In 1785 a similar treaty was held at Fort McIntosh by the U.S. commissioners and a group of the Wyandot, Delaware, Ottawa, and Chippewa of Ohio, who in return for peace received a reservation between the Maumee and the Cuyahoga, south of Lake

Erie to a line between the site of Pickawillany and the Tuscarawas-Cuyahoga portage. This treaty also was repudiated by the tribes concerned, on the grounds that the Indian signers were unauthorized and drunk. But on the strength of it the Northwest Territory was organized. In 1786 a third treaty was held, with the Shawnee, at Fort Finney at the mouth of the Great Miami. This "allotted" to the Shawnee a tract adjoining the Wyandot-Delaware reservation. It too was soon repudiated. By these treaties, all held under the conquest theory, the United States asserted that it had completed the title to the lands in Ohio and western Pennsylvania that had been acquired in 1783 from Great Britain. The Indian residents, on reservations, were to remain on sufferance.[5]

Soon the citizens of New York and Massachusetts, hungry for soil, were gnawing at the Iroquois homelands. The few Mohawk remaining in the valley of the Mohawk River had been driven off during the war; but west of the Old Line of Property of 1768 lay the lands of the five other tribes—the Oneida and Tuscarora, and the Onondaga, Cayuga, and Seneca. The Oneida and Tuscarora in 1785 sold the first parcel of land; by 1789 New York State had purchased all of the Oneida, Onondaga, and Cayuga lands, except for small reservations.[6] Almost all of the Seneca lands, however, lay west of longitude 77° W. —the so-called "preemption line." West of this line Massachusetts had the right to assert or acquire title to the land although New York retained political sovereignty. Fear of Iroquois military resistance meant that the land could not be settled without at least the forms of a real-estate transaction. A scheme was conceived by various New York politicians and financiers to subvert the constitutions of both New York and Massachusetts by acquiring in 1787 a private 999-year "lease" of *all* remaining lands of the Six Nations west of the 1768 Line of Property, including the Seneca lands. The Iroquois repudiated the fraudulent agreement[7] and the conspiracy of "Livingston's Lease" was quashed by the New York State legislature, which threatened to use force to keep out Livingston's settlers. The grand scheme died in a last feeble, failing effort by Livingston to establish a secessionist state west of the Genesee River.[8] Thereafter, in 1788, a land company acting under the Massachusetts right and advised in Indian affairs by the missionary Samuel Kirkland (who had also acted for Livingston) bought a third of the Seneca territory for $5,000 and an annuity to the tribe of $500 per annum.[9] This "Phelps and Gorham" purchase, as it was called, brought white settlements up to, and in places beyond, the ancient Seneca citadels on the Genesee River.

· *The Rise of the Western Confederacy* ·

To ADD TO THE DISCOMFITURE of the Iroquois, their allies and tributaries in the Ohio country were deciding that the Six Nations could no longer be depended upon to protect them in war or even be trusted to represent them in peaceful negotiations. The old Iroquois confederacy had already begun to crumble; by the close of 1784 it was no longer an effective organization. As we have seen, the western Indians had had some experience with independent action in organizing their parts of the conspiracy of Pontiac in 1763, although the initial stimulus had been provided by the Iroquois. After the failure of this effort to drive out the British, the Iroquois had left the western Indians to their fate, selling their lands out from under them at Fort Stanwix in 1768 and refusing to support them officially in Lord Dunmore's War. From about 1770 on, therefore, the Shawnee, Delaware, Wyandot, Ottawa, Potawatomie, Chippewa, Miami, Cherokee, and other western Indians had been organizing their own confederacy overlapping the Iroquois-centered confederacy. The disappointing performance of their Iroquois representatives at Fort Stanwix in 1784 spurred these western Indians to complete the separation of their confederacy from that of the Six Nations.

The Northwest Territory of the United States was still in 1784 inhabited by dozens of Indian tribes, some of them ancient dependents of the Six Nations and others ancient enemies, and all of them contemptuous of American pretensions to empire. Within the Ohio country, where Iroquois influence had been most weighty, were the Delaware, the Miami, the Wyandot, the Shawnee, and a few Ottawa. These tribes had observed from afar the humiliation visited upon their "uncles" the Six Nations in 1784 and had experienced at first hand the arrogance of the American commissioners at Fort McIntosh and Fort Finney, where paper cessions of land had been extorted from incompetent negotiators under the guise of the "conquest" theory. Their reaction, unlike that of the more vulnerable New York Iroquois, was not dismay but resolute determination to fight for their property.

The first general meeting of the new western confederacy was held at Detroit in the fall of 1785. It was intended to forestall a piecemeal buying-off of individual tribes whose lands had been weakly deeded away by the Iroquois in 1784. The confederacy promptly issued a demand that the United States recognize its existence and treat with it rather than with the individual tribes.[10] By next fall, however, the Americans had concluded the two treaties with the Ohio tribes and claimed to own the whole country, apart from the reservations. The confederacy now, in the fall of 1786, formulated a four-point policy, denying the validity of the conquest theory and declaring that the three treaties of Fort Stanwix, Fort McIntosh, and Fort Finney were invalid, that the Ohio River was the boundary between the Indians and the United States, and that a new treaty between the western confederacy and the United States was required.[11]

But the United States, hoping to exploit the tenuous political advantage it believed itself to have secured at the three treaties of 1784, 1785, and 1786, ignored the new confederacy. A series of laws was being enacted, culminating in the Northwest Ordinance of 1787, by which most of Ohio was opened to settlement. Extensive tracts of land were granted to military personnel in lieu of pay or in gratitude for extraordinary services during the Revolution. Companies like the Ohio Land Company, the John Cleves Symmes Associates, and the Scioto Land Company bought up land on speculation, hoping to sell it to waiting settlers. It was as much to protect the interests of the land companies as to safeguard the rights of the still-resident Indians that stringent regulations prohibited entry into the territory without license. Some squatters crossing the river had since as early as 1781 been following the frontier tradition of making deals with local Indian families and preempting land to be purchased officially only years later. Others did not even bother to purchase privately, but simply occupied desirable tracts and defended them with guns.

The western confederates responded with violence to these incursions. An ugly border warfare, ever renewed by outrages and atrocities committed both by whites and Indians, contained the initial beachheads of settlement within narrow limits north of the Ohio River. The United States was unable to wage either war or peace to expand these beachheads. Federal control of frontier territories was, at the time, largely nominal: the Articles of Confederation made concerted action difficult in the face of the pressures from an unpaid soldiery, from the land companies, from squatters, from secessionist adventurers, from states' righters in the Congress. The Indians, on the other hand, presented a tolerably united front. The western confederacy had high morale and had the moral encouragement of some of the Iroquois and of the British, still ensconced in their old lakeside forts, who reassured them that the conquest theory, so pompously announced at the earlier treaties, was an empty bluff and that the Indians had only to hold their ground in order to secure their rights. The British agents do not seem to have promised the Indians outright military support, but undoubtedly many Indians, including Joseph Brant, hoped and half believed that such help would be forth-coming in the event of crisis. It was obviously in the British interest to see the western confederates maintain a buffer zone between the aggressive United States to the south and the Canadian provinces to the north, a buffer state, indeed, that could continue to supply British traders with peltries. The Indians were also encouraged by past military successes, for they had defeated George Rogers Clark and his band of land-hungry Virginians in their efforts to seize the Ohio country and had virtually paralyzed American arms north of the Ohio River during the Revolution.[12]

· *The Treaty of Fort Harmar* ·

By 1787 THE UNITED STATES was becoming aware that it could not depend on the treaties of Fort Stanwix, Fort McIntosh, and Fort Finney to ensure the peaceful occupation of the Ohio country. Further and more liberal negotiation would be required, perhaps based not on the conquest theory at all, but on an admission of Indian ownership of the soil. Plans were accordingly laid to convene a general council with the Indians. At this council an acceptable, but even larger, cession of the lands required would be obtained by a new combination of over-the-table concession and under-the-table sub-version.

But communication was slow and chronically distorted by "evil birds" who scrambled messages; and to make the task of organization still more difficult, the United States presented many faces to the Indians. American policy was uncoordinated: while official minds moved toward conciliation, land companies sent in surveyors, settlers built cabins, and mounted frontier militia ravaged Indian settlements. As a confederate spokesman observed sadly, the white governments had their problems, too, and yet these problems of civil order among the whites only made war the more likely:

> If the great men of the United States have the like principal or desposition as the Big knifes [i.e., frontiersmen, not merely Virginians] had, My nation and other Indians in the East would been long ago anihilated. But they are not so, Especially since they have their liberty—they begin with new things, and now they endeavour to lift us up the Indians from the ground, that we may stand and walk ourselves. . . . [But] the United States, could not govern the hostile Big knifes, and . . . the Big knifes, will always have war with the Indians. The Big knifes are independent, and if we have peace with them, they would make slaves of us.
>
> . . . The reason the Big knives are so bad, is this because they have run away from their own country of different States, because they were very mischivous, such as theives and robbers, and murderers and their laws are so strict these people could not live there without being often punished; therefore they run off in this contry and become lawless. They have lived such a distance from the United States, that in these several years the Law could not reached them because they would run into the woods. . . . But at length the people of the United States settle among them.[13]

The confederacy even modified its policy to allow minor relinquishments of land west of the Ohio River to accommodate some existing settlements and to encourage, by making a few concessions, a more reasonable attitude on the part of the United States. [14]

There is no doubt that the western confederacy was an effective political entity; and eventually, both in council and in the field, the United States recognized its authority. But American policy in preparing for the treaty of Fort Harmar was weak because it was motivated by fear: fear of conceding too much and fear of conceding too little. If too much were conceded, the United States would lose what little color of right it still had to the Ohio lands. If too little were conceded, a cruel and costly Indian war was inevitable. A compromise solution was embodied in the instructions to General St. Clair, the governor of the Northwest Territory, the principal American negotiator. He was to go only so far in concession as to recognize, by making some payment for the lands, the unsatisfactory nature of the three treaties about which the Indians were now complaining, and to answer the confederacy's request for a peace treaty by proposing a general council. But he was to seek a compensating advantage by confirming, and even if possible enlarging, the previous cessions, by sowing seeds of discord within the confederacy and by avoiding any formal question of the earlier treaties' validity. Meanwhile, in January, 1788, the western confederacy was summoning its members, including the Six Nations, to a final meeting. The confederacy was also tiring of half measures. Since no reply had been received from the United States, the decisions made in 1786 would have to be implemented by the members. "Decisive measures" would be the subject of this council. There was still some disposition to compromise. When the American invitation to a treaty was received, the confederates were not informed of its land cession aspects. But they were suspicious nonetheless. At a summer's council in 1788 there was disagreement over whether the confederacy should go to the treaty at all. The Wabash and Miami Indians at last unceremoniously refused to attend. Shawnee attacks on surveyors and supply trains in the neighborhood of the falls of the Muskingum forced the Americans to remove the treaty grounds from that site to the mouth of the river, where negotiations might be held under the protective guns of Fort Harmar. In the fall the compromise-minded Joseph Brant and his Mohawks decided at the last moment not to attend, disgusted by the discovery that the Americans were assembling militia and were still sending surveyors across the river.[15]

The council at Fort Harmar, when it was finally held in January 1789, was a fiasco. Of the confederates, only Detroit-area Indians appeared—a few straggling Wyandot, Delaware, Ottawa, Pota-watomi, and Chippewa, together with some misplaced Sac refugees (the Sac tribe itself lived far away, on both sides of the Mississippi). According to well-informed observers, of all the Indian signatories only four were chiefs of any sort: two Potawatomi, one Delaware, and one Chippewa; and none of these were "great chiefs" qualified to transact important business.[16] This rump council in effect confirmed the earlier treaties of Fort McIntosh and Fort Finney. Certain "sachems and warriors of the Six Nations," headed by Cornplanter, also transacted two treaties, one with the United States, renewing the cessions of land previously made at Fort Stanwix; and another with

Pennsylvania, ceding to the state the Erie Triangle but reserving to the Six Nations the Seneca-occupied lands east of the Conewango Creek and Chautauqua Lake (which Cornplanter and white officials alike mistakenly believed to be west of the line sold earlier).[17] The quality of the negotiations may be judged from Indian agent George Morgan's remark that "Few of the natives attended and none were fully represented; here the treaty was negotiated and speeches and explanations to the Indians made by our superintendent in the French language through a Canadian interpreter who had to guess at his meaning for he can neither write nor speak the language so as to make himself understood in any matter of that importance . . . he could find no other medium."[18]

· *The War for the Northwest Territory* ·

THE IMMEDIATE AFTERMATH of Fort Harmar was a series of diplomatic and military catastrophes for the United States. The United States at first cherished the rosy delusion that with the Six Nations, Delaware, and Wyandot pacified, it remained only to conclude a peace with the Wabash and Illinois Indians or, if they refused a peace, to chastise them into good behavior.[19] Accordingly Governor St. Clair was ordered to send emissaries to invite them to a treaty. These emissaries brought back disquieting word that not merely the "lawless banditti" who had refused to attend at Fort Harmar, but the "pacified" Delaware and Wyandot also, denied its validity and doubted the sincerity of the American intentions. At another council of the western confederacy to be held in the fall, it was rumored, the treaty of Fort Harmar was to be publicly condemned, and the hostiles were sending out war belts among the tribes, including the Iroquois, proposing a common war with British support to drive out the Americans.[20] Depredations along the frontiers were continuous, the hostiles raiding on both sides of the Ohio (by now, as Brant complained, they were "so much addicted to horse-stealing that . . . that kind of business is their best harvest")[21] and the frontiersmen and militia retaliating with massive mounted forays that indiscriminately burned the hastily emptied villages of both hostile and friendly Indians. These exchanges culminated, however, in a series of pitched battles. In 1790 the Americans lost about 190 and the Indians about 120 casualties in an engagement on the Maumee. And in 1791 a serious defeat was inflicted on an American army. Sickly General St. Clair—an officer of minimal foresight even in health— allowed his combined force of regulars and militiamen to be surrounded and ambushed in Indian country. The surviving militiamen and camp followers fled all the way to Pittsburgh; the regulars, who stood their ground, suffered some 600 fatal casualties, amounting to about two thirds of the entire regular army of the United States.[22]

While human relations deteriorate on frontiers, wisdom accumulates in capitals. In 1789 Henry Knox, as secretary of war, formulated a new and more rational federal policy, which under the newly adopted constitution could be executed with less interference from the states. It was essentially a return to the old British policy that an inexperienced revolutionary bureaucracy had temporarily forgotten. It was recognized that in order to secure possession of the Indian lands for settlement in the future, two means were available: war and negotiation. War would be prohibitively expensive to a nation which could summon for any campaign no more than a few hundred trained men, and might end in the United States actually losing the Northwest Territory. Furthermore, war without prior negotiation would be unjust. Hence a policy of negotiation was, for the time being, the only proper one. Such a policy would have to be based on a reversal of the conquest theory; it must be explicitly recognized that the Indians "possess the right to the soil." Good relations between the Indians and the white citizens of the United States could be expected to develop *pari passu* with the civilization of the Indians, which, in accordance with the currently popular doctrine of progress, was inevitable as a stage in the general "process of society, from the barbarous ages to its present degree of development." Knox suggested the importance of introducing "a love for exclusive property" as the fundament of such a march toward civilization. He also recommended the appointment of missionaries of excellent moral character to live among the Indians, and the establishment of well-stocked and well-equipped model farms.[23] Knox's formulation of federal policy was endorsed by George Washington; and one of its first practical consequences, as we shall see, was the establishment of the Quaker mission to the Allegany Seneca Indians.

But there were difficulties in the "conciliatory" policy recommended by Secretary Knox. One of these was, of course, the intransigence of the western Indians, many of whom refused to abandon their demand that the Ohio River be a permanent boundary between the races. Another was the continued presence of armed British garrisons in several forts in the Indian country. At Niagara and Detroit, in particular, British agents continued to supply Indians with hunting equipment and political advice. This advice, as understood by Joseph Brant, was in fact to make some territorial concessions for the sake of preserving peace and the bulk of their lands. But in American eyes, a British lion lay crouched in the forests of Canada, panting from past exertions but waiting only for an opportune moment to spring forth to recover the Crown's lost colonies. Thus Indian resistance was interpreted as part of a British conspiracy to destroy the new nation in its hour of birth. In such an atmosphere "conciliation" sounded to many ears like "appeasement" of united empire loyalism. And finally, to frontiersmen the platitudes of the enlightenment about the inevitability of progress and the natural equality of all men were meaningless. The frontiersmen were interested in freedom for profitable and safe exploitation of Indian land, and this goal was easier to rationalize by a doctrine of manifest destiny than by "impractical" theories about the perfectability of mankind. A conciliation policy was unenforceable on the frontiers, which instead demanded and eventually got (in 1792) a militia act and which supported the preparations for St. Clair's and Wayne's campaigns even while peace negotiations were underway.[24]

The Indians had their own troubles in developing coherent policy. By 1789 the western confederacy had split into two factions: the hostiles (Shawnee, Miami, Wea, Piankeshaw, Kickapoo of the Wabash, and various renegade Cherokee); and the moderates (Brant's faction of the Six Nations, the Wyandot, the Delaware, and the Ottawa, Chippewa, and Potawatomi in the area). The intransigent Shawnee after 1789 were the acknowledged leaders of the confederacy. The chiefs of the Six Nations in New York at first sympathized with the moderates under Brant; but the apparent profits of the play-off policy enticed them too, in 1792, into the arms of the United States. The gradual defection of the New York Iroquois put Brant into the uncomfortable position of being a moderator between extremists as well as the proponent of his own moderate policy. He played this dual role with dignity, resisting threats and refusing bribes and blandishments. The United States once offered him 1,000 guineas down and double his British military pension and, when he refused that, preemption rights to land worth £20,000 plus an annuity of $1,500 per annum, which he also refused, merely to "use my endeavours to bring about a peace." Steadily he insisted that the rational and honorable solution was a general settlement in which the United States would retain only the lands east of the Muskingum and south of a line from the Muskingum-Cuyahoga portage to Venango. But Brant's policy, although the United States would have eventually agreed to it, did not please the Shawnee, who, rashly confident after the victory over St. Clair, abandoned hope of peace in 1793. The end was inevitable: the Battle of Fallen Timbers in 1794 and the Treaty of Greeneville in 1795, by which the Indians made peace and accepted the political sovereignty of the United States and by which the United States officially recognized the Indian right to the soil. The western confederacy became a cipher (although meetings continued for years at Brownstown), and American garrisons sealed off the New York Iroquois from their western and northern brethren.[25]

· The Splitting of the Iroquois Confederacy ·

THE WAR FOR THE NORTHWEST TERRITORY was the rock on which the Six Nations finally foundered. Brant and his Mohawks since 1784 had been established in Canada, and the British Crown eventually granted them a reservation at Grand River. For a time Brant hoped to draw the remainder of his people from New York into Canada. And as the successive land cessions dispossessed more and more of the Oneida, Tuscarora, Onondaga, Cayuga, and Seneca, many of the refugees did move into Ontario, most of them to Grand River. But others re-settled in New York, especially at Buffalo Creek, and the chiefs there refused to move their council fire again.

Brant's Iroquois, as we have seen, allied themselves with the western confederates, within whose councils Brant took a relatively moderate position, advising the Indians to resist but to offer to con-cede land already occupied by settlers in return for a recognition by the United States of Indian rights to the soil. The Iroquois in New York, however, did not identify themselves with the British and the moderate wing of the western confederacy, but rather with the United States. They favored much the same way of resolving the conflict that Brant was urging on his allies, to be sure, but their apparent identification with American interests made the rift with Brant's group and with the western Indians a deeply emotional one.

It was not that the New York Iroquois liked the frontier Americans. Among the warriors there was hatred and contempt for white men and strong sympathy for the plight of their red brothers in the west, who were fighting desperately for survival against the invasion of a horde of coldhearted surveyors and settlers. On their own frontiers, too, rowdy white men stole, cheated, and murdered luckless Indians whenever opportunity offered; they knew that for every acre sold, a hundred became uninhabitable. Within Cornplanter's own connection, for instance, a nephew and the husband of his wife's sister were killed by white frontiersmen while out hunting.[26] Surveyors were already marking off the boundary lines of the Phelps and Gorham purchase and of the State of Pennsylvania; another quantity of land would be lost when the Erie Triangle was surveyed. Threats and rumors that the Iroquois, including the Allegheny Seneca, were about to take the warpath, both in New York and Pennsylvania and in Ohio, rumbled continuously through the woods during the period of the western troubles.

The tragedy of the situation for Cornplanter's band was the bitter and open contempt that was visited upon them by the western Indians, who saw them as degenerating from stalwart warriors to conniving cowards. The first snarls of contumely came in 1789, when the embattled Shawnee called upon the Seneca "to go to War to secure them a Bed to lie upon."[27] When the western Indians learned that Cornplanter planned a unilateral conference with Washington in Philadelphia, "the Shawanese brought a Virginia scalp and insisted on our seizing the scalp, or they would treat us the same way as the Big Knife."[28] By 1791 the threats of the western Indians had become so ominous that the Delaware from the Allegany River and the Mississauga from Conneaut, on Lake Erie, both on the borders of the Cornplanter band, were frightened off and had to be assigned new places to live, the Delaware at Cattaraugus and the Mississauga at Buffalo Creek.[29] Both of these bands eventually emigrated to the Grand River.[30] And at the council with the western confederacy at Buffalo Creek that winter, the hostiles declared that they were determined to reduce Fort Franklin and to "shake the Cornplanter by the head & sweep this [Allegheny] River from end to end."[31] Such threats as these for a time threw Cornplanter's band and the whites in his neighborhood into an alliance of necessity. If Cornplanter's people were unable to reach Pittsburgh, they would be cut off from supply; therefore in self-defense they had to protect white settlements and garrisons in French Creek Valley by providing intelligence, scouts, and even war parties against the hostile Indians.

But in 1791 Cornplanter began to gain some support from the chiefs at Buffalo Creek. Although the chiefs were still reluctant to lend themselves to a pro-American policy, Cornplanter achieved a political triumph by requesting, as chief of the warriors of the confederacy, that the women be consulted in an issue so grave as war. The matrons favored peace in the west and a "friendly" attitude toward the Americans. This alliance of warriors and women forced the chiefs to accept the Cornplanter policy and, perhaps against better judgment, they agreed to accompany American officers on a peace mission to the western Indians.[32]

The mission to the west in 1792 was the nadir of Iroquois diplomacy. To begin with, there were two missions, both carrying messages from the United States, one headed by the Oneida Captain Hendrick, which reached the Maumee in July, two months before the confederate nations assembled, and another headed by Cornplanter, Red Jacket, Farmer's Brother, and various other chiefs from Buffalo Creek. Under the great council elm at the Maumee, Hendrick was hooted and laughed at as he spoke. Red Jacket, the Six Nations' speaker, praised the United States as a strong, honest "new father" and advised the western Indians to accept their new father's proposals: i.e., to make peace and to accept the lines established at Fort Harmar in 1789. But the Shawnee, as titular heads of the western confederacy, threw the document containing the American offer into the fire and called the Six Nations of New York "very coward Red men." The conference concluded with the Six Nations of New York being assigned the role of mere intermediaries between the western Indians and the United States in the arrangement of the never-to-be-consummated council of 1793. Cornplanter's party felt fortunate to get away without a fight and on the return trip were in such haste to make their escape that they subsisted on dried venison and stopped only to sleep.[33]

Next year, in 1793, the year when Wayne began organizing the slow campaign that would end the Indian resistance, Cornplanter and a few comrades more brave than wise undertook a final peace mission westward. They set out late in the spring, before the formal correspondence between the commissioners at Niagara and the confederates at Miami had begun, but not before General Wayne began active preparations for the invasion of the Indian country. Cornplanter complained of this duplicity to no avail; plans for the invasion continued; bids were taken in Philadelphia for military rations to be supplied at the Maumee Rapids—the seat of the confederacy! When his party reached the western encampments on the Sandusky River, they were (according to a Seneca legend that was still current a hundred years later on the Cornplanter grant) seized, held prisoner, and threatened with death. The western confederacy refused to meet the American commissioners. Released at last, the Indian emissaries were offered food; Cornplanter and a few others, fearful of being poisoned, refused to eat and fasted all the way home. During this homeward trip a number of men died—poisoned, according to Seneca belief.[34]

This disaster concluded the relations of Cornplanter's band with the western Indians; and with the battles and treaties of the following year the rest of the New York Iroquois in effect resigned from that grandly designed confederacy which their forefathers had built up on the foundation of their own League. An era had ended; and Handsome Lake and his fellow chiefs of the League might well chant in the condolence ceremony the mournful lines:

Hail my grandsires! Now hearken while your grandchildren cry mournfully to you—because the Great League which you established has grown old. . . .

The final repudiation of the Iroquois by most of their erstwhile allies and dependents in 1794 was accompanied by the further growth of dissension among the Iroquois themselves. The war of the Revolution had brought the Oneida to blows with their confederate brethren. Now the war for the Northwest Territory set Seneca against Seneca, and Seneca against Mohawk, in a civil discord whose wounds gaped wider with the years. Despite the peaceful policy of both Cornplanter's faction and the chiefs' faction during the years of warfare in Ohio, many individual Iroquois took up arms and fought against the Americans. Some of Brant's Mohawks, a few of the New York Indians, and probably numerous "Mingo," who before the wars had lived among the Delaware and Miami, fought effectively in the campaigns against Harmar, St. Clair, and Wayne. At the end of the wars many of these people remained in the Ohio country, living on the Sandusky and Miami, later drifting westward to Oklahoma, and in some instances emigrating as far as the Rocky Mountains. Others who did not emigrate retaliated, by threats, killings, and kidnappings, on their white neighbors along the Allegheny and the Genesee. Probably many of these incidents were perpetrated in obligatory revenge by Indians whose kinfolk had been killed by white frontier hoodlums.[35]

These disgruntled Iroquois, unwilling to accept the "official" policy of friendliness toward the United States, were contemptuous of Cornplanter, and as the situation deteriorated, some of them became his declared enemies. It is said that sometime after the Fort Harmar treaty an unsuccessful effort was made by some Seneca to break him of his war chieftaincy; he was defended against his critics by, among others, Big Tree.[36] The Seneca criticism of his policies continued, however, and gradually focused on his cession of the Presqu' Isle (Erie Triangle) area in 1789 and 1791. In point of fact, these "cessions" of Cornplanter's were merely quit-claims in favor of Pennsylvania to part of the lands already ceded at Fort Stanwix; they represented not a new loss of territory, but actually a gain, since the United States simultaneously was dropping *its* claims to Seneca lands along the Lake Erie shore east and north of the Erie Triangle. But these intricacies were not understood by the Seneca, nor at that time were the boundaries of the Triangle clearly known. Thus, between 1792 and 1794 Pennsylvania's efforts to survey and settle the Triangle were met with violent Seneca opposition.

After Pennsylvania began to occupy the area with surveyors, troops and settlers in the spring of 1794, attacks were planned on the forts at Venango, Presqu' Isle, and Le Boeuf, and finally a small settlement on French Creek was assaulted and the settlers forced to flee to Fort Le Boeuf.[37] Cornplanter was probably forced by political necessity to assume an antiwhite posture. He proclaimed that his "sale" of Presqu' Isle had been only a conditional cession anyway, not binding on other Seneca without their consent, and since that consent had not been given, the intruders must be removed. If they were not removed, he announced, there would be war. At a council on the Allegheny he struck the war post, bragged about his past exploits in combat, and offered Adlum, the surveyor, a pair of moccasins to wear in the field against the Indians when war came. In all this the bare bones of the play-off policy showed through: this last gesture so encouraged the British at Niagara that when he returned thence to the Allegheny in June, 1794, he came loaded down with presents; and in the fall, at Canandaigua, in order to settle the Presqu' Isle and other matters, the Americans loaded him and the rest of the Six Nations with still more presents and increased annuities, earmarked for the "civilization" of the Six Nations.[38]

The pulling and hauling of the New York Iroquois, their frantic maneuvers to please the Americans without losing their allies in the west, their internal disputes over cessions and presents, was complicated by another issue. This was the subject of the adoption of white customs. As yet it was not a prominent issue, but the division of opinion was already evident. It came to the surface in 1791, when Brant was in Philadelphia and Red Jacket at Newtown Point were almost simultaneously announcing diametrically opposite accultura- tion policies. Brant and Cornplanter wanted the Indians to give up liquor and to plow, to erect flour- and sawmills, to build frame houses, to spin and weave, to read and write.[39] Red Jacket declared that it would be a matter of "great time" before the Indians gave up their beloved ancient customs and became educated and civilized.[40] This division of opinion was destined to recur in the following years.

Brant and his Canadian settlers on the Grand River were sorely disillusioned by all of these examples of what they chose to regard as Seneca avarice and deceit. As early as 1788 Brant observed in disgust, "As for the Five Nations, most of them have sold themselves to the Devil—I mean to the Yankeys. Whatever they do after this is must be for the Yankeys—not for the Indians or the English. We mean to speak to them once more . . . and will show our example of getting together ourselves; also, we shall know who is for the Yankeys and who is not."[41] Although Brant and his people never ceased to speak to the New York Iroquois, the division between the two groups be- came sharper with the years, and by the end of the wars in 1794 relations were strained. Brant refused to attend the treaty at Canan- daigua in 1794, where the New York Iroquois settled their differences with the United States, and instead made a separate settlement of Mohawk land claims in New York in 1797.[42] The past defection of the New York Iroquois and the intermediate role that Brant had been forced to play alienated the western Indians even from him and virtually ended his influenec with the dissolving remnants of the western confederacy. His further efforts to bring the New York Indians into Canada failed. And within a few years, in 1803, the New York chiefs deposed Brant and the few members of the League council who resided in Canada, and replaced them by New York residents. Although the Grand River Indians refused to abide by this action, its consequence was a separation of the two groups into politically autonomous entities whose relations were inter- rather than intratribal. There were henceforth to be two council fires, one at Onondaga in central New York (after its removal from Buffalo Creek) and one at Ohsweken, on the Grand River in Canada.[43]

· *The Establishment of the Cornplanter Seneca* ·

WHILE BRANT'S PEOPLE were moving northward from Buffalo Creek into Canada and the refugees from the ceded lands were settling at Buffalo Creek, Cornplanter and his band of Seneca were establishing themselves in a cluster of little towns along the Allegheny River above and below the Pennsylvania boundary.

Cornplanter's band was composed of families displaced by Brodhead's sacking of the Allegheny River towns and by Sullivan's burning of the Genesee towns in 1779. Thus some of them had been Allegheny residents before the war and were now coming home. Among these old settlers the most prominent was Cornplanter himself. Some of the newcomers were relatives of his: Guyasuta, the old viceroy, whose sister was Cornplanter's mother, had lived in many places, but most recently on Cattaraugus Creek,[44] and Handsome Lake, his half brother, who had lived at Canawaugus on the Genesee. This repopulation of the upper Allegheny probably commenced shortly after the invasion of 1779 but took many years to complete; the new population probably did not become substantial until 1784 or 1785.[45] By 1792 the Seneca in and around Cornplanter's settlement on the Allegheny numbered about 350 souls, which was a sizable proportion of the approximately 1,800 Seneca of that day.[46] By 1792 one of the main villages was "Cornplanter's Town," also known as Jenuchshadago or Burnt House, on the west side of the Allegheny River just below the state line on the site of one of the towns burned by

Brodhead. Until they were moved north to Cattaraugus about 1792, a group of about 150 Delaware dependents of the Seneca lived at Hickory Town, some thirty or forty miles downriver.[47] Upriver from Cornplanter's Town were a substantial settlement at Genesinghuhta and a smaller one at Ichsua. Westward were small groups at Kiantone, on one of the tributaries of the Conewango, at Cussawago, on the upper waters of French Creek, and at Conneaut, on Lake Erie. These and a miscellany of one-or-two-family settlements scattered along the main streams tended to consolidate as time went on, their residents moving to the larger settlements at Cornplanter's Town and Genesinguhta or to other large Seneca villages at Cattaraugus, Tonawanda, and Buffalo Creek.[48]

But the Allegany Seneca were in a vulnerable location. Their position liberated them from the pressures associated with nearness to Brant's faction at Grand River, the British garrison at Fort Niagara, and the neutralist chiefs at Buffalo Creek. But it also placed them in a location where they were dependent on the American traders at Pittsburgh and under the watchful eye of American soldiers at Fort Franklin. This fort, garrisoned by regular troops, was constructed in 1787 along the Allegheny at the mouth of French Creek, the traditional southern limit of the Seneca tribal territory. Fort Franklin guarded the white settlements springing up in the neighborhood of the Indian towns and stood athwart the hunters' access to the traders in Pittsburgh, upon whom much of the Seneca livelihood depended. Fort Niagara and its British traders and troops, upon whom the Iroquois at Buffalo Creek could call for supplies and, in case of need, asylum, was a difficult hundred miles to the north. And anyway, of all the Iroquois, the Allegany Seneca—late of Geneseo, perpetrators of the Devil's Hole massacre, holdouts against taking up the British hatchet in 1777, traditionally less devoted to British interests than the eastern band—had least assurance of British support if they were attacked by Americans. Nor could they depend in either negotiation or in armed combat on the united support of the Six Nations, for Brant's followers were now streaming into Canada, and the chiefs of of the confederacy at Buffalo Creek, including the eastern Seneca, were seemingly unable to agree on a common positive program. Thus, both economically and militarily the Allegany Seneca were an orphaned band, dependent upon their enemies for economic support and bereft of the military backing of their allies and confederates.

This situation, and the growing conviction of Cornplanter that only by a rapprochment with the United States could the Seneca survive, probably led Cornplanter's band into adopting its leading role in the effort to end the war for the Northwest Territory.

Cornplanter, a vigorous war-captain and eloquent council-speaker, was attempting to find the best way out of a difficult situation for himself and his band. He saw no advantage in refusals to compromise and was not given to rigid adherence to the language of past rhetoric. As one of the leading war-captains of the Iroquois in the late war he had been a principal speaker at the treaty at Fort Stanwix because war captains were responsible for the public ceremony of laying down the hatchet. Although he had initially demanded that the Americans respect the existing boundaries of the Six Nations, he had not made the speech accepting the American ultimatum (this dubious honor fell to the Oneida Good Peter) and had only promised to lay the dictated treaty, in which lands were ceded, before the confederate chiefs' council for approval or disapproval, his name stood on the document. Thus Cornplanter personally received much of the blame when the chiefs' refusal to ratify the treaty was blandly ignored by the United States and when Cornplanter's protestations in 1786 resulted only in promises to make minor boundary adjustments. Feeling against the speakers at Fort Stanwix rose high. The fact that the terms had never been proposed by him, were not personally agreeable to him, and could not be accepted or rejected by him alone did not cancel the fact that he was there at the time of the catastrophe.

It is impossible to know in detail how Cornplanter analyzed the situation in which he and his band found themselves; but some inferences are possible from his behavior. During the next several years, from the time of his return from New York until the treaty at Fort Harmar in 1789, he played a passive and unobtrusive role, avoiding any challenge to the Americans. When surveyors came up to Fort Franklin to lay out the donation lands, it was not Cornplanter, among the Indians who were hunting in the vicinity, but two other "chiefs" who halted the surveyors and politely warned them to proceed no farther. In 1787 Cornplanter failed to accompany a delegation of Seneca, including his nephew Blacksnake, who visited Albany to protest the extension of New York's sovereignty at the Niagara strip and on the borders of Pennsylvania. In 1787 he signed Livingston's infamous lease and, according to report, used his influence, in return for a substantial bribe, to persuade other "chiefs" to sign it. In 1788 he signed the deed of Phelps and Gorham's purchase, by which the eastern half of the Seneca lands was alienated. Seneca hearts despaired after the Phelps and Gorham purchase; one chief is said to have declared that he would fight rather than give up his homeland, another to have asked to be "put out of his pain," and a third to have prepared to eat the "fatal root." Cornplanter's life was threatened for this betrayal.[49] And all the while, despite the glowering of the warriors, surveyors from Pennsylvania and New York quietly proceeded to mark out the state boundaries and to lay out towns and farms in the midst of the Allegany Seneca hunting grounds. It would seem that Cornplanter had decided that the New York Iroquois would have to get along with the Americans and make the best of a bad bargain.

Of all the participants in the ill-fated treaty at Fort Harmar, only Cornplanter and his delegation of Allegany Seneca (who constituted virtually the bulk of the "Six Nations" present) derived any advantage. He and his associates confirmed the language of the Fort Stanwix land agreement (it was the Senate of the United States that refused to confirm the proceedings) and concluded the sale of the Erie Triangle to Pennsylvania (recovering in the process part of the lands lost at Fort Stanwix).[50] For all this his people received a bundle of motheaten blankets, the concession of lands on the Conewango, and in all likelihood various goods and monies at the treaty ground (which may have been a substantial trove, for nearly two hundred Allegany Seneca were present). Cornplanter himself achieved more personal rewards. At the treaty ground he was promised by a land company a tract of 640 acres in Marietta itself; the deed to this tract was, however, according to Indian tradition, stolen from him in some frontier town on the way home when the Indians were drunk. And the grateful Commonwealth of Pennsylvania assembly, in order to reward him for his services and "to fix his attachment to the state," gave to Cornplanter in fee simple 1,500 acres of land "in this tract or country on Lake Erie." This land was surveyed under Cornplanter's direction in three tracts along the Allegheny River in 1795, and a patent was issued in 1796. Two of the tracts, "The Gift" at Oil City and "Richland" at West Hickory (the latter including the site of the Delaware town abandoned about 1792), he sold: Richland in 1795 to General John Wilkins, who established a farm there; and "The Gift" in 1818 to two partners whose failure to complete the title has left the ownership of

"The Gift" unclear to this day. The third tract, encompassing about 750 acres, included the site of the old Seneca town of Jenuchshadago and two nearby islands in the river.[51]

· *American Concessions to the New York Iroquois* ·

THE NEW YORK INDIANS, however, under the leadership of Cornplanter, Red Jacket, and Farmer's Brother, were also able to salvage something more general than presents and private land-grants from the debacle. During a series of at least seven major conferences with American officials between 1790 and 1794, the Iroquois spokesmen demanded—and received—promises of correction of abuses in the context of not too subtle, but also not too sincere, warnings of defection to the enemy. Thus Cornplanter in 1790 on the occasion of an address to the Congress of the United States observed quietly that: "When last Spring they [the western Indians] called upon us to go to War to secure them a Bed to lie upon, the Senecas entreated them to be Quiet until we had spoken to you. . . ."[52] And the chiefs on the Genesee in the same year took occasion to remind Pennsylvania, apropos of the murder of two Seneca hunters on Pine Creek, that this was the latest outrage in a series of eleven killings of Seneca by Pennsylvanians. The bereaved families wanted vengeance or reparations:

> Brothers, you must not think hard if we speak rash, as it comes from a wounded heart, as you have struck the hatchet in our head and we can't be reconciled until you come & pull it out; We are sorry to tell you, you have killed Eleven of us since peace. . . .
>
> Brothers, it is our great brother, your Governor, who must come to see us, as we will never bury the hatchet until our great brother himself comes & brightens the chain of friendship, as it is very rusty—Brothers, you must bring the property of your brothers you have murdered, and all the property of the murderers, as it will be great satisfaction to the families of the deceased. Brothers, the Sooner you meet us the better, for our young Warriors are very uneasy, and it may prevent great trouble. . . .[53]

These muted threats, coupled with offers to polish the chain of friendship, had great effect in thrusting together in amicable conference the leading dignitaries of both societies. George Washington, Henry

Knox, Timothy Pickering, and dozens of other American officials met Cornplanter, Red Jacket, Blacksnake, Joseph Brant, Farmer's Brother, Handsome Lake, and hundreds of Iroquois warriors and matrons in a series of negotiations. The history of these negotiations —the climax of a political generation during which "Indian Affairs" was the major public business of an entire nation—would make a fascinating volume; and some day a student of the period will tell the story in all the dramatic detail that it deserves. Here, however, we can only outline and summarize the course and significance of these events. Each of these conferences was preceded and followed by the long journeys, private councils, secret visits, exchange of letters, and so forth that made diplomacy an almost continuous theme in the daily lives of the Indian participants. Handsome Lake's half brother and his nephew, Blacksnake, were principal actors in the matter, and Handsome Lake himself probably attended the last and most impressive council of the series: the Treaty of Canandaigua in 1794.[54] Although his name was not recorded at other conferences, it is likely that he was intimately acquainted with the course of events.

At one time or another during these meetings thirteen demands were made upon the United States by the Indian speakers, who were usually Cornplanter and Red Jacket (for Joseph Brant, having retired to Canadian soil, could act only occasionally, and then chiefly as an intermediary). These demands concerned:

1. *The Treaty of Fort Stanwix.* The Six Nations denied the validity of the cessions of land extorted at Fort Stanwix in 1784. Their speakers claimed that the cessions had been made under duress by unauthorized representatives who had given up more land than the Six Nations would have willingly relinquished under any circumstances. The United States was requested to annul this treaty and to negotiate a new cession acceptable to the Six Nations, and particularly to the Seneca, who had been most directly injured.[55]

2. *The Phelps and Gorham Purchase.* The Six Nations claimed they had been cheated by Phelps and Gorham. These "land-jobbers" had initially revealed their bad intentions by trying to move the treaty site from the proper council-fire at Buffalo Creek to Canandaigua, had insisted on a larger tract of land than the Indians had intended to sell, had held the talks late at night, and had misled the Indians into thinking the conveyance was a lease, not a purchase. The final blow was altering the text of the papers of

cession so as to reduce the cash payment from $10,000, as promised, to $5,250. The annuity of only $500 per year amounted to about a shilling apiece when it was paid; and in order to collect the annuity, the Seneca each year had to spend the annuity itself, and all their silver ornaments besides, to buy bread in Canandaigua.[56]

3. *The Erie Triangle.* The Erie Triangle, including the lake port of Presqu' Isle, had technically been a part of the lands ceded at Fort Stanwix. Before the United States sold the land to Pennsylvania in 1792 in order to provide the commonweath with a port on Lake Erie, the commonwealth "quieted the claims" of the Seneca at Fort Harmar in 1789. Since the Triangle had not been surveyed, the Seneca believed that it would engross lands on which some of their people had villages, and they resisted surveying and settlement in the area until 1794, despite a second quit-claim Cornplanter made in 1790 upon receiving assurances that Half Town. Big Tree, and his own people would not be disturbed.[57]

4. *Other Land Grievances.* Miscellaneous other grievances over lands still rankled: e.g., fears that Livingston's lease might be upheld by legislature and courts; complaints that lands in Virginia and Pennsylvania still had not been paid for by white occupants.[58]

5. *The Conquest Theory.* Fortified by advice from British agents, the Six Nations denied the correctness in international law of the American assertion that Britain had ceded to the United States the right of soil in Indian lands. Britain, the Six Nations argued, had acquired only political sovereignty and consequently could relinquish only that.[59]

6. *Frontier Outrages.* After the peace of 1784 (which was the feature of the Fort Stanwix treaty to which the Iroquois did not object) Indian and white were, theoretically, to live amicably side by side. But the Indians were subjected to continuous outrages by frontiersmen and town dwellers alike whenever they met whites. By 1790, when the notorious Pine Creek murders were committed, at least eleven Seneca and an unknown number of others from different tribes had been killed, including two kinsmen of Cornplanter's. There were also thefts of horses, hunting gear, and personal effects, frequently from murder victims, and even more commonly attacks that did not end in fatalities: e.g., Cornplanter's party was fired on on its return from Fort Harmar, the chief Big Tree was shot in the leg in Philadelphia in 1790 during the state visit, and an assassin tried to kill Brant in New York in 1792. In 1794 occurred the famous "Brady's Beaver Blockhouse" affair, in

which a hunting party of nine—five men, a woman, and three children—were attacked and robbed by a band of twenty-seven white hunters. Four of the Indians were killed, one was wounded, and the survivors lost their horses and gear.[60]

7. *Unilateral Justice.* When whites suffered outrages at Indian hands, white courts convicted the Indian culprits (if they were found) and punished them; but little or no attention was paid to preventing or punishing informal retaliation by frontiersmen, which was not always discriminating in its object. White men guilty of crimes against Indians were either not apprehended or not tried, or if tried were neither convicted nor punished. Indians were prohibited from seeking personal vengeance, which was defined by whites as "war" or "massacre" (as in the celebrated case of Logan in 1772).[61]

8. *Security of Land Tenure.* The loss of hunting grounds and the general depletion of game in the Northeast had made it plain to the Six Nations that they would have to turn even more heavily to farming (including both crops and livestock) for subsistence. But such an investment of labor, material, and social organization required that the Six Nations receive assurances that further arbitrary seizures of land, like those first extorted at Fort Stanwix and still being imposed on the western Indians, would not be made either by the states or by the federal government.[62]

9. *Private Land Grants.* Land was the currency of Indian bargaining. Thus Indians, like Cornplanter and Big Tree, sought to obtain as "rewards" for their concessions land titles guaranteed by the whites; and they sought also to pay their faithful white friends, like interpreter and trader Joseph Nicholson, in grants by white governments from ceded lands.[63]

10. *Traders, Agents, and Whiskey.* Far from desiring unrestricted trade and occasional official communication, the Six Nations wanted traders to be licensed, in order that unscrupulous whiskey-sellers and other undesirables could be excluded from the Indian country; and they wanted a system of official, recognized Indian agents close to their borders with whom they could conveniently communicate as needed.[64]

11. *Technical Assistance.* The Six Nations generally recognized that the great changes taking place in their relations to the land and to the white society required that they invest heavily in new cultural equipment: the implements of plow agriculture, of animal husbandry, of spinning and weaving, of lumber milling, etc.; and in

the knowledge and skills necessary to use this equipment efficiently and to have confident intercourse with white men. Cornplanter in particular requested capital goods, rather than a dole of food and clothing in hard times, and schoolteachers, resident farmers, and missionaries to teach them.[65]

12. *Illegitimate Half-breeds.* The offspring of temporary unions of white men and Indian women were frequently abandoned by their fathers. They were a burden to an Indian community. Six Nations spokesmen requested that they be adopted by white society or, at least, that the white society contribute to their support and education.[66]

13. *The Western Indians.* No doubt prompted both by sympathy with their ancient dependents, allies, and kinfolk and by the needs of policy, the Six Nations' spokesmen—principally Joseph Brant— urged that the United States be moderate in its demands on the western Indians who were objecting to a set of treaties precisely comparable to the Treaty of Fort Stanwix; to Iroquois eyes, these objections were valid.[67]

The response of the State of New York, the Commonwealth of Pennsylvania, and the United States of America to these requests was, at least officially, friendly and in the main favorable. Why this should be so, despite the bitter, unquenched hatred of Indians by a large proportion of the people of the frontiers, is easily understood. Those elements of the population who hated Indians most were at this time least effectively represented in the seats of government, not only in Indian affairs, but in various economic and political issues as well. This was the period, the reader will recall, of the Articles of Confederation, of the Whiskey Rebellion, and of various secessionist movements inspired or directed by such figures as Aaron Burr, George Morgan, Philip Livingston, and other ambitious and sometimes disaffected men of wealth. The Federalists were, by and large, eighteenth-century intellectuals who sought to direct the interests of natural man into the channels of natural law; they preferred order to anarchy, commerce to virtuous isolation, and negotiation to war; they tried to pursue in all affairs a policy of enlightened self-interest. From the Six Nations they hoped to secure at least neutrality and at best their services as intermediaries. Their major fear was that the Six Nations would go over wholly to the enemy (the British and the western Indians). And the Six Nations, both through their demands in council and by their violence on the frontiers (for Iroquois warriors did their share of murder, kidnapping, mayhem, and theft) conscientiously kept alive this fear. Thus, irrespective of frontier passion, it was self-evidently to the interest of the United States to take such measures as would most effectively secure the neutrality, and eventually the allegiance, of a neighboring Indian people. And therefore a number of significant concessions were made:

1. *The Conquest Theory*. It was Indian insistence, expressed both by the Six Nations and by the western Indians, that caused the United States to reverse its interpretation of the Treaty of Paris and, between 1787 and 1793, publicly to declare that the Indian tribes had the right of soil to the lands that they occupied within the territorial limits of the United States. Although the United States maintained political sovereignty, it recognized the right of an Indian tribe to continue to occupy its lands forever if it so pleased. Specifically, it secured the Six Nations from arbitrary expropriations of lands by individuals, states, or the federal establishment, within the boundaries established at Fort Stanwix in 1784.[68]

2. *Specific Concessions on Land Grievances*. Although the validity of the Fort Stanwix cessions was upheld against Six Nations objection, several actions by various parties—individuals, states, and the federal government—had the effect of minimizing the hardships it imposed. These actions included: a promise of federal protection of Indian land rights (including supervision of any cessions); grants to individual Indians (specifically, to Cornplanter and Big Tree); assurances that Half Town and his people would not be disturbed in their villages (and the line of the Erie Triangle, as eventually run, did indeed leave them undisturbed); nullification of Livingston's lease; and postponement of plans for the settlement of Presqu' Isle and for the purchase of Seneca lands in western New York.[69]

3. *A Technical Assistance Program*. Acting on the principles that Indians were as capable of civilization as white men and that civilized Indians would be friendly neighbors, the federal government and various private agencies responded enthusiastically to Seneca and Oneida requests for technical assistance. Washington in 1790 promised to secure federal funds to support educational and capital investment programs. In 1792 Six Nations annuities were increased (to \$1,500) for this purpose. In 1794 at Canandaigua annuities

were raised to $4,500, and benefits worth $10,000 were granted, for civilizing the Six Nations. Later missionary teachers were being sent to the Cornplanter Seneca and to the Oneida, a smith was established on the Genesee to work for Indians only, and Cornplanter's sons were brought to Philadelphia for education. A regular Indian agent for the Iroquois was appointed in 1792; he distributed annuities and managed various other matters.[70]

4. *Equal Justice.* An improvement was made in the handling of civil and criminal complaints by the Six Nations. The murderers of Indians were brought to trial, Indian victims or their families were indemnified for their losses, and access to the courts of white men was promised by Washington himself.[71]

These concessions were far from being mere verbal assurances; they became the basis of a new, if somewhat demoralizing, Indian way of life—the reservation system. From the United States standpoint, they were worth the cost, for the Iroquois never did turn to the aid of the western Indians, even during the anxious summer of 1794. From the Six Nations standpoint, they established Cornplanter and his people firmly on lands that their descendants occupy to this very day and made it possible for the Iroquois generally to remain one of the few Indian peoples east of the Mississippi who still live in territory that was theirs before Columbus. Furthermore, the concessions included the abandonment of the conquest theory—and this change in the Indian policy of the United States affected the future of the continent. And they gave the Six Nations a head start in the process of technical acculturation so that their villages were for a time somewhat more civilized settlements than those of the frontier whites that surrounded them.

But these were advantages slow to mature, and they had been purchased at a fearful price: the collapse of the confederacy. For while these favors were being secured by a temporary coalition of factions pursuing the ancient play-off policy, the choice of the play-off policy rather than of war at the side of the western Indians was making certain the conquest of those western Indians; and on their continued independence the play-off policy itself depended. When the western Indians were defeated in 1794, and Jay's treaty in the same year soothed the mutual fears of Canada and the United States, there were no more bargains to be made. The Six Nations had at last been outflanked. No more respect could be extorted from the United States; the confederacy itself, whose white roots of peace once undergirded half a continent, was like a great pine dying on a flood-torn hillside.

· *The Treaty of Big Tree* ·

THE SLOW PROCESS of political disintegration, which had begun with the failure of the neutrality policy in the 1750's and had culminated in the disastrous treaties of the 1780's and 1790's, left the Iroquois with a shrunken homeland, a reduced standard of living, and a demoralized society. The Seneca alone had preserved a major part of their tribal territory for themselves and other Iroquois refugees; but within a few years this too would be gone, and the reservation system, in squalor exceeded only by the surrounding frontier settlements, would impose a new way of life.

In 1797, at the Treaty of Big Tree, the Seneca administered the *coup de grâce* to themselves: they sold their lands. With the exception of a few reservations, all of the Iroquois territory in New York east of the Genesee River had already been sold. The Mohawks had gone from the valley of their name, and only a few still clung to a marginal settlement along the St. Lawrence River at St. Regis, opposite Caughnawaga; the Oneida, Onondaga, and Cayuga occupied only their tiny reservations (and the Oneida and Cayuga would soon lose these entirely); the Seneca had given up everything east of the Genesee. But west of the Genesee there remained a substantial region in which stood many of the old Seneca towns and hunting grounds and, at Buffalo Creek, whole villages of Seneca, Cayuga, Onondaga, and Tuscarora. This last vestige of ancient glory they now proceeded to sell.

The legal right to purchase these western lands was held by Robert Morris of Philadelphia, a financier of the American Revolution who now hoped to make a fortune out of speculation in frontier real estate. Morris quickly sold his preemption right to the Holland Land Company, a coalition of Dutch bankers who were in a better position than Morris to finance the actual opening of the territory to settlement (an expensive process involving long-term administration, surveys, and even the construction of roads and buildings). A condition of his receiving payment, however, was that he negotiate the purchase of these Seneca lands from their Indian owners. At first this seemed like an easy task. But Morris was delayed in the project by the war in the Northwest Territory. When in 1795 peaceful conditions were restored, he was hampered by the financial depression of that year. His creditors hounded him. He became increasingly desperate to quiet the Seneca title, for only by doing so could he claim credit from the Dutch bankers and thereby stave off bankruptcy and debtor's prison. As he told his son, "I must have it."[72]

Morris had to move fast. Against the advice of his friend Washington (who had in earlier years speculated in the very Ohio lands that had been finally secured only after thirty years of warfare) he applied for the appointment of a federal commissioner, who was now required by law to oversee any purchases of land from Indians. Morris was a gambler: "I can never do things in the small," he declared, "I must be either *a man or a mouse.*" With a commissioner appointed, he hastened to seduce the Seneca into selling. The old reliable Cornplanter was brought to Philadelphia, wined and dined, and persuaded to agree that "it will promote the happiness of his Nation to sell at least a part of their lands and place the purchase money in the Public funds so as to derive an annual income therefrom." But by the time appointed for the treaty at Big Tree on the Genesee River in the summer of 1797, Robert Morris was a prisoner in his own mansion, unable even to answer the door lest he be arrested and jailed for debt. His son Thomas therefore conducted the actual preparations for the treaty, laying in stores of food, clothing, hardware, powder, and whiskey—the latter calculated at twenty-five gallons a day for thirty days. The whiskey, however, was not to be provided at once, but paraded before the thirsty Indians with the promise that it would be given them when the sale was made. Special presents of clothing were prepared for the women, and funds for bribery of the men were set aside at the outset. Red Jacket, Farmer's Brother, and Little Billy were offered life annuities of sixty dollars. Little Billy, a widely respected war chief, was a good target for bribery. Almost blind, he lived in poverty with his mother; he had a few years before been very ill, and he and his mother had been "stripped by doctors and conjurers, in order to effect his cure." The canny Red Jacket demanded a bond for the annuity at once, but the equally canny Morris refused.[73]

Seneca anxiety mounted. The year before Red Jacket had requested that the Congress issue no license to Morris to purchase Seneca lands, saying of the corpulent banker, "We are much disturbed in our dreams about the great Eater with a big Belly endeavouring to devour our lands. We are afraid of him, believe him to be a conjurer, and that he will be too cunning and hard for us. . . ." The Seneca sachems—probably including Handsome Lake, who was present—were at the outset of the conference officially and publicly opposed to any cession. Red Jacket, the official speaker for the chiefs, after a drunken spree at the start of the conference declaimed nobly against the proposal that the Seneca sell their sacred homeland: they were respected, he claimed, by the western tribes only because they owned lands on which lesser peoples could take refuge; they had no desire to become ignoble broom- and basket-makers like the Oneida. And when Thomas Morris refused even to consider the Indian offer to sell one township six miles square at a dollar an acre near the Pennsylvania line, Red Jacket leaped to his feet and shouted, "We have now reached the point, to which I wanted to bring you. You told us when we first met, that we were free, either to sell or retain our lands; and that our refusal to sell, would not disturb the friendship that has existed between us. I now tell you that we will not part with them; here is my hand. I now cover up this Council fire!" The Indians whooped and yelled and upbraided Thomas Morris for having tried to cheat them.

But bribery had done its work too well; a deliberate plot to subvert the decision of the chiefs had been in the making for months. In May Cornplanter informed Thomas Morris through one of his sons that he had called "a general Meeting of all the Warriors and Chiefs of Warriors at which no sachem was to be present, that his Intention was to induce the Warriors to insist upon a division of the property and to sell their proportion of it."[74] Red Jacket, who by day as professional orator was rejecting Morris's offers, at night sent messages to Morris saying that his negative speeches were made only to please some of his people and were not his own sentiments, and that if Morris persevered he would gain his purpose. Before Red Jacket covered the fire, Cornplanter asserted publicly that the warriors did not agree with the chiefs. On the day after Red Jacket covered the fire, the commissioners were called to a council of the warriors. There Cornplanter (who had been bribed) announced that this meeting was to smooth over the difficulties of yesterday. Little Billy (also bribed) apologized for Red Jacket's speech. Farmer's Brother (also bribed) declared that since Morris, not Red Jacket, had lit the council fire, only he and not Red Jacket could extinguish it. Furthermore, he said, "It is an ancient custom that when a difference arises among us that it should be referred to the Warriors as being the greatest number. We the sachems have therefore referred this business to the Warriors & head women and hope they will give an answer that will be satisfactory to all parties." The same day, Morris made his offer to the chief women, declaring that the $100,000 he offered for the Seneca territory would particularly alleviate the distresses of the women and children: they would be able to hire white men to plough their fields, and buy good clothes and liquor.[75] He handed out baubles and trinkets. He appealed to the women's resentment of their neglect by men: "I . . . informed them of the offers that had been made to their Sachems; I told them that the money that would proceed from the sale of their lands, would relieve the women from all the hardships that they then endured, that, now they had to till the earth, and provide, by their labour, food for themselves and their children; that, when those children were without clothing, and shivering with cold, they alone, were witness to their sufferings, that their Sachems would always supply their own wants, that they fed on the game they killed, and provided clothing for themselves, by exchanging the skins of the animals they had killed, for such clothing, that therefore the Sachems were indifferent about exchanging for their lands money enough, every year, to lessen the labour of the women, and enable them to procure for themselves and their children, the food and clothing so necessary for their comfort."[76] The Seneca women capitulated to this verbal assault and declared themselves ready to sell. For several days thereafter, little knots of women and warriors might be seen arguing and discussing the matter. The warriors wanted reservations around the villages. Morris agreed. Handsome Lake insisted on adding to the list of reserves a tract at Oil Spring, just north of the Allegany Reservation. This "spring" was a natural flow of petroleum, which the Seneca used to gather and use for a liniment to treat rheumatic pains and old ulcers. Handsome Lake's interest in the place may have arisen from his practice as shaman. In addition to the reservations, private concessions were made to individual signers:

Cash grants

Red Jacket	$600
Cornplanter	300
Hotbread and other sachems	1,000

Annuities

Cornplanter	$250
Red Jacket	100
Farmer's Brother	100
Young King	100
Little Billy	100
Pollard	50
Little Billy's mother	10

The nation as a whole received the sum of $100,000, to be invested in bank stock for the use of the Seneca; the "crop of money" amounted annually, for more than fifteen hundred Seneca residents in New York State, to less than four dollars per person. The deed was signed on the evening of September 16, 1797, by some fifty Seneca, including Cornplanter and Handsome Lake.[77] Handsome Lake's name stood third on the list of signatures.[78]

Thus the embers of the old confederacy guttered out in a welter of liquor, bribery, and high-pressure salesmanship. The name of the Great League still remained; but its people were now separated, one from another, on tiny reservations boxed in by white men and whitemen's fences. For the Seneca in New York there remained only their eleven reserves surrounding the main villages, whose total land area amounted to 311 square miles, or about 200,000 acres:

1. *Canawaugus*, on the Genesee River, 2 square miles;
2. *Big Tree*, on the Genesee River, 2 square miles;
3. *Little Beard's Town*, on the Genesee River, 2 square miles;
4. *Squawky Hill*, on the Genesee River, 2 square miles;
5. *Gardeau*, on the Genesee River, 2 square miles;
6. *Oil Spring*, on Cuba Lake, 1 square mile;
7. *Caneadea*, on the Genesee River, 16 square miles;
8. *Buffalo Creek*, on Lake Erie; and
9. *Tonawanda*, on Tonawanda Creek, together 200 square miles;
10. *Cattaraugus*, on Lake Erie, 42 square miles; and
11. *Allegany*, on the Allegheny River, adjacent to Cornplanter's private tract, 42 square miles.[79]

SLUMS IN THE

WILDERNESS

THE RESERVATION SYSTEM THEORETICALLY ESTABLISHED SMALL asylums where Indians who had lost their hunting grounds could remain peacefully apart from surrounding white communities until they became civilized. It actually resulted, however, in the creation of slums in the wilderness, where no traditional Indian culture could long survive and where only the least useful aspects of white culture could easily penetrate. The Iroquois, even those of the relatively prosperous Cornplanter band, had lost much to the ravages of war, hunger, pestilence, and disease. But more damaging to the spirit, perhaps, than these objective losses was a loss of confidence in their own way of life, a lessening of respect for themselves, which resulted from their confrontation with the white man's civilization. Facing now at close range this vast and intricate machine, they experienced the dilemma that all underdeveloped societies suffer: how to imitate superior alien customs while reasserting the integrity of the ancient way of life.

· *Cornplanter's Town* ·

LIKE THE OTHER RESERVATIONS Cornplanter's Town was a slum in the wilderness. But in a way it was a unique slum. It was a kind of mountain fortress, a shabby Shangri-la hidden from alien eyes in the forests of the Allegheny Mountains where by tradition no white man could enter. Here, insulated from alien presence, Indian and white alike, the Allegany band of Seneca could maintain a greater measure of autonomy than the Iroquois living near Buffalo and Niagara and along the Genesee.

Most of the members of the Allegany band were in 1798 living in the old town of Jenuchshadego, or Burnt House, within the grant; the smaller towns upriver in the reservation proper, and on the smaller tributaries, were nearly deserted. The grant was, in effect, a sheltered sliver of fertile bottom-land, bounded on the east by the river itself, a hundred and fifty yards wide and up to six feet deep, and on the west by steep, ravine-cut, green cliffs that climbed five hundred feet to a razor-backed ridge. The cliffs swept in to within a few feet of the river above and below the grant, effectively sealing it off from unwanted horsemen and foot travelers. The principal way of access to the grant was an awkard Indian trail that cut north across the razor-back hills, up and down the ravines, from the mouth of Conewango Creek. From Cornplanter's Town the trail proceeded up the west bank of the Allegheny River to the Indian towns in the reservation at Genesinguhta and Ichsua. Pinched in between cliffs and water, or scaling steep ravine slopes, this path was often blocked by snow and mud and rock slides in the winter and in the spring and summer by swamps, fallen trees, and underbrush. Here was one of the few areas in the craggy, forested Allegheny mountain country where an Indian town and its cornfields could be maintained.

There were in 1798 only three or four whites permanently residing within fifty miles of the grant (although dozens of migrants on their way west, land prospectors, and surveyors passed through the region every summer). Fifteen miles down the river at Warren, at the mouth of the Conewango, was the Holland Land Company's local storehouse, to which supplies were brought upriver for the surveyors, the two or three hardy settlers who had bought land in the area, and the local Indians who bought goods and whiskey on credit. The storekeeper had arrived in 1796; he was joined in 1798 by two brothers-in-law. In 1800 their parents, wives, and children arrived to increase the settlement to a size of about fifteen or twenty. Warren, the best of the upper-river town sites, was nevertheless discouraging to early settlers. In the miasma-conscious nineteenth century it had the reputation of being a place "where the health-destroying clouds . . . bank upon the ground in the valleys at nightfall, and remain until eight or nine o'clock each morning for seven months in the year."[1] But it was a site easy to clear and map, for it was an old Indian town; furthermore, in the winter of 1795 a severe storm had blown down much of the timber, and a forest fire a few years later burned up the windfall. Settlement proceeded slowly in Warren County, and in 1806, ten years later, there were still only about two hundred taxable settlers, In that year also the county had seven sawmills, two gristmills, 169 cows, 75 horses, and 53 pairs of oxen. Lots in the town itself moved slowly too; in the same year there were only the company store-house, four dwelling houses, and a licensed tavern (also used as a school) run by the local magistrate (a temperate man, it is said, who died as a result of being bitten on the thumb in the course of keeping law and order). Some lots in town were sold as investments to Alle-gany Seneca Indians (including three to Handsome Lake).

Outside of Warren, there was no other white town within fifty miles of the grant. Sixty miles west of Warren was Meadville; King's Settlement, a Quaker family village, was just being established on the headwaters of the Allegheny, to the east. To the north, in New York State, there was nothing within a hundred miles; by the year 1800 there would still be only twelve taxable white persons in the whole of the Holland Company purchase. A substantial influx of settlers, emigrants, riverboatmen, and loggers would not be seen for another decade in the remote corner of the Allegheny Mountains where the Cornplanter band had taken refuge.[2]

The town lay between the bank of the river and a bend of a little stream—Cornplanter Run—that ran down from the cliffs. The run was a lonely and mysterious spot, associated with ghosts and snakes. On its banks and in the adjoining groves of pine and hardwood grew all kinds of medicinal plants. In such richness did the run supply a shaman's pharmacopoeia of medicinal teas and poultices that the Indian doctors of this band were widely famed as herbalists. On a summer day's excursion the doctor could find white boneset (for colds), purple boneset (a diuretic), *cicuta maculata* (a liniment—and also a poison for suicide), angelica (for pneumonia), mint (for colds and bilious attacks), elder (for heart disease), plantain (for stomach trouble), wire grass (for warriors and ball players to use as a muscle tonic, an emetic, and a liniment), white pine and wild cherry (for cough syrup), *Prenanthese altissima* (for rattlesnake bite), aspen (for worms), sumac (for measles and sore throat), Christmas fern (for consumption), and many others. Handsome Lake was an herbalist and no doubt collected plants along the edges of the run. Up the river above the narrows was another mysterious spot: a narrow, deep ravine extending straight up the hill, "the place where the snake slid down the cliffs." Local mythology had it that here the Thunderer discovered a giant horned serpent two or three hundred feet long. He threw bolt after bolt of lightning at it and forced it to escape by sliding down the hill, gouging out the ravine in its way. Then it slithered down the river and dug the deep bottom at the eddy. In the smooth backwater of this eddy, just opposite the town, the Indians now collected fish in organized drives.

In the uninhabited, pine-forested hills around the valley the men and boys hunted for bear, deer, elk, and turkey. There was little small game. Hunters traveled on foot and in the winter used snow-shoes. Farther down the river, most easily reachable by canoe, were the maple groves where the Indians brought their big kettles and camped in the spring to make sugar. Still farther down the river was the place for spearing fish in the rough water at the mouth of Kinzua Creek. Behind the peaks lining the river was the best hunting country, well known by the hunters and trappers, who knew the location of every salt lick. Northward, on both sides of the Allegheny, pine-forested hunting grounds stretched as far as the divide between the waters of the Genesee and Allegheny. But for the past ten years game had been noticeably scarce, the fur trade was limited, and meat was becoming a rarity.[3]

The town itself consisted of about forty houses scattered in an irregular line in the meadow thirty yards or so from the water's edge. In the middle of the village stood the famous statue of Tarachiawagon, the ritual center of the community, where the ceremony of burning the white dog was performed. Nearby stood Cornplanter's house, a pair of cabins joined by a long roofed porch, close to the medicine spring where Handsome Lake drew water—always in the direction of its natural flow—for the preparation of teas, emetics, and liniments. Cornplanter's house served on occasion as the council-house. The burial ground lay between the houses and the bank of the river.

The population of the town was about four hundred persons; thus each house was occupied, on the average, by five to fifteen people. It

is difficult now to establish the rules governing residence. Cornplanter's town had been the home of Cornplanter's wife, and in this
very loose sense he was living matrilocally; but the composition of his
own household suggests that a combination of matrilineal and affinal
kinship ties, health, and economic and political power determined the
actual choice of residence. Living in Cornplanter's house at this time
were fourteen people or more, including at least two households:
Cornplanter's and his brother Handsome Lake's. Cornplanter and his
wife had five daughters and at least one son living with them. This son
was retarded and was known as "the idiot." From time to time daughters brought husbands to stay there. Two other sons, Henry and
Charles, also lived in the settlement. Henry was the only Seneca who
could speak English. He had lived in Philadelphia and New York as
a youth, in the period 1791 to 1796, and had boarded with Christian
families and gone to school. He could read and write English and
could speak it well enough for broken conversation but not well
enough to serve as a professional interpreter. Handsome Lake, a
daughter, her husband, her children, and perhaps his other daughter
lived in the second half of the house. Other close male kinfolk of
Cornplanter and Handsome Lake occupied several of the other houses:
their nephew Blacksnake, and Blacksnake's sister, the matron of the
Wolf Clan and leading woman of the community; until his recent
death Cornplanter's uncle, the ancient Guyasuta, who had a sister and
six sons; Handsome Lake's own son; his grandson, James (Jemmy
Johnson); the old war chief Canawayendo; Captain Decker, another
nephew of Guyasuta. These other kinsmen of the two brothers, with
their wives, children, and assorted relatives, many of them members
of the Wolf Clan, probably occupied another half-dozen of the houses
and made up, together with the Cornplanter–Handsome-Lake household, a good twenty per cent of the village's population. The names
of many of the other distinguished men of the Allegany community,
men of middle and old age, the chiefs and noted warriors who would
sit on the platform at the council, have been recorded; each of these
men probably was associated with a separate household, and in many
cases their patrilineal descendants still live on the Allegany Reserve:
Wundungohteh, who later moved to Cattaraugus, the chief who
temporarily replaced Cornplanter a few years later; Bucktooth; Captain Crow; Peter Crouse, a white man who had been captured and
adopted as a boy and now was married and a father; two white men

married to Indian women, Elijah Matthews and Nicholas Demuth, who served the community as interpreters; Chief Half Town, who practiced the dreaming of gifts of rum and pork on unwary white visitors; Captain John Logan, the matrilineal nephew of Logan the Great Mingo; Captain Hudson; Redeye; Chief New Arrow; Chief Skendashowa; the Black Chief, husband of one of Sir William Johnson's daughters who was one of the leading women, and by her the father of ten children; Broken Tree, frequently employed as a messenger between the town and the white settlements lower down the river. These twenty or so men were elite members of the community, although not all of them were residents of the town itself. They regularly participated as chiefs and chief warriors in council meetings and carried the burden of community relationships with whites and other Indian groups, as speakers, messengers, and interpreters. They were all veterans of the wars in the forest, all husbands and fathers, most of them heavy drinkers on occasion, and all hunters and traders who traveled up and down the river, and into the mountains, to help support their women and children. In many of their households there were also younger men, common hunters and warriors who either because of youth and inexperience or lack of the capacity for responsible leadership were not numbered among the elite.[4]

The houses were not large. Cornplanter's, the biggest, was a full 64 feet long by 16 feet wide and consisted of two apartments, one 24 and the other 30 feet in length, separated by a roofed 10-foot porch that served as an entryway and a place to store wood and pound corn in the big wooden mortar. The other houses were one-room structures about 16 feet square with attached woodshed. They were nearly all built of logs, sometimes chinked with moss, with sharply peaked roofs of chestnut or hemlock bark, sheets of which could be seen lying about pressing flat under their own weight. (A few small cabins sheathed entirely with bark stood in the village, but this older type of construction was usually reserved for the temporary camps at the maple groves.) A single door at one end opened into each house. There were no windows, but the smoke hole in the center served as a skylight. The floor was earth. The fire burned constantly in the center of the room on the floor below the smoke hole. On either side of the room ranged two tiers of bunks four feet wide, one a foot off the ground and spread with deerskins on which people slept, and the other at a five-foot level, which served to store brass kettles, wooden bowls and ladles, blankets, deerskins, the leather sack of bear's oil, guns, traps, clothing, ornaments, and baskets of corn and other vegetables. At a height of six feet from eave to eave ran rafters, and between the two center rafters a pole was laid, from which a large kettle hung over the fire by withes and wooden hooks. Enormous quantities of firewood were required for heating and cooking in this cool mountain climate, where frosts were expected from September to May. The task of collecting the firewood belonged to the women and girls of the house. They spent much of their time in the summer hauling wood from distances up to half a mile, carrying it in large bales on the back supported by a belt around the forehead, splitting it into short, narrow lengths, and storing it all neatly in a pile or shed next to the house. Trash and garbage was simply thrown out of the door into a pile near the house, where it rotted and fed swarms of flies. There were no outhouses or public latrines; people relieved themselves in the privacy of woods or brush away from the houses. There was no soap, and lice infested hair and clothing.

The economy of the village depended upon the women, who owned it collectively. All land was "national" land; users had private rights to its produce only. An area of about two hundred acres surrounding the houses had been fenced in to protect it from the deer, bear, wolves, and other hungry animals. Within the fence the ground had been fairly well-cleared of trees and brush, although bushes and patches of grass remained. The women of each household, from old women to little girls, sick or well, all took part in the cultivation of the fields. One old gray-haired woman whose feet had been frozen was a notable sight in the village, for every day in the summer she hobbled on her knees about the meadow doing her household tasks—carrying wood, making the fire, fetching water from the river, and hoeing the corn in her field two hundred yards from her house. The garden plots were small, interspersed among the bushes, and the total area under actual cultivation was only about sixty acres. Each household, on an average, gardened less than a couple of acres. The females of individual households worked the plots in parties of four or five; each household kept its own garden produce. They raised corn, squash, pumpkins, cucumbers, beans, melons, potatoes, and tobacco, cultivating the individual corn hills, each up to a foot high, with the hoe throughout the growing season and supporting the beans on sticks. The men regarded the gardening strictly as women's work and did not participate in it in any way except to split the rails for the community fence. Men did however build and repair the houses. Except for dogs, there were few domestic animals: in all of the Allegany band, a total of three horses, fourteen cows, one yoke of oxen, and twelve hogs. The cattle and hogs supplied some fresh meat and so also did the hunt, which was the male's contribution to the food quest; but the hunt now procured only a small supply of venison, bear's meat, wildfowl, and fish. Both meat and vegetable foods, including blackberries, strawberries, and whortleberries, were whenever possible dried and preserved for the winter and spring. Dried corn was pounded in huge wooden mortars by triads of women using heavy pestles up to four feet long. The meals served in the households were generally soups made of corn and all available vegetables with small chunks of meat thrown in if any was to be had. It was served in wooden bowls and supped with wooden ladles. Like the other food, it was unsalted. Corn dumplings, dipped in bear's oil or sweetened with maple sugar and dried berries, were a special delicacy. For traveling, hominy cakes were made of pounded meal-corn mixed with beans and maple sugar.

Physically the Allegany Seneca were a mixture of Indian types with white parentage visible in a few. Skin colors ranged from light tan through copper to dark brown; faces from the round-faced, flat-nosed, to the narrow, hollow-cheeked, aquiline-nosed Mongoloid types. Except for moccasins they clothed themselves entirely in brightly colored cloth. The basic garments for both men and women were tight blue or scarlet leggings, worn below the knee by women and up the thigh by the men; a breechcloth supported by a belt and hanging down fore and aft; and a ruffled calico shirt reaching to the hips. The women also wore a loose blue skirt made of a couple of yards of cloth looped over a string tied around the waist. In cold weather this basic wardrobe was amplified by waistcoats, jackets, and overcoats of blanket cloth, by blankets loosely draped around the shoulders, and by a loose hood of blanket cloth for a cap. The men still pulled out all the hair on the head except for the scalp lock on the crown; the women tied their long black hair in a pony tail and liberally oiled it with bear fat. The men frequently wore nose- and earbobs and rings of silver, and some chose singular ear ornaments, such as silver crosses, a pair of padlocks hanging from one ear, or a watch. The clothing of both sexes was liberally decorated with silver brooches, and the women decorated their garments with needlework of beads and porcupine quills. On occasions of ceremony this dress was still further elaborated by special head-ornaments of feathers and animal tails. In general, both clothes and hands were dirty by white standards, for people seldom bathed and made no soap.

The people of Cornplanter's Town were trying to survive by the old ways, with such modification as the press of need and opportunity dictated. The physical modifications were obvious: their dress was cloth and ornamented with metal; their houses were sometimes made of log rather than bark (an innovation made practical by the steel hatchet) and were too small in most cases to house whole lineages; they used steel knives, brass kettles, and guns; they buried their dead in pine coffins. Socially, too, there had been changes: the confederacy was no longer a sheltering tree, and Cornplanter—eloquent speaker, successful war-captain, and adroit politician—had become a local leader more powerful than tradition would have allowed. He had acquired personal capital from the whites, which he administered somewhat arbitrarily on behalf of the band: the land of the grant, a sawmill up the river, and credit enough to pay in cash for such favors as the release of jailed Indians in Pittsburgh. But the old town council system still remained, with the twenty or thirty chiefs and captains, the half dozen or so leading women, and the common warriors and women all lobbying with each other over public issues according to old principles. The women still claimed to own the land and had the right to urge or restrain the warriors in war matters independently of the chiefs' policies; a great man like Cornplanter, if he became too arrogant, might be deposed or even assassinated by his own relatives in the public interest.

And the ancient religion still brought the people together for the annual calendar of ceremonies and prompted the crisis rituals on occasions of death, illness, or danger. The religious center of Cornplanter's Town was still the huge painted wooden statue of a man standing on a pedestal carved from the same block, near the council-house. This statue represented Tarachiawagon, the Good Twin and Creator of the Indian way of life. At Green Corn and New Year's the statue was lavishly decorated with skins, handkerchiefs, ribbons, and feathers, and the white dog was hung on it, strangled and waiting to be burned. The drummers sat on a deerskin at the foot of the statue, and up to two hundred men, women, and children moved round it in a large circle in the Worship Dance. The ritual speaker still thanked the spirit forces and exhorted the people to live virtuously. The members of the Society of Faces still ministered with rough kindness to the sick and cavorted for the entertainment of the people in the council house. The people still burned tobacco to the Thunderer in time of drought and for good luck kindled their new fires with splints of wood from a lightning-riven tree and saved stone bolts believed to have been slung to earth by the Thunderer in his hunting of snakes. The souls of the dead were still fed at the death feasts.

On the surface, then, the old way of life seemed to be intact. The several hundred survivors of the wars, the epidemics, the famines who now made up the Allegany band of Seneca were able to maintain the ancient marriage customs, the old religious rituals, the traditional economy from year to year with only marginal change. But although they were protected from intrusion, their situation was now a precarious one even by their own spartan standards. The population was small and isolated both politically and geographically. The game was becoming scarce, and this meant little meat and also little hardware and dry goods. The river from which they took their cooking and drinking water periodically flooded the banks of sandy loam on which the fields were laid and washed away not only the year's supply but the seed corn for next year (the circumstance which had brought all the people together at Cornplanter's Town in 1798). Sometimes, in spring flood, the river washed out whole stretches of bank, eating at fields and the cemetery. In the winter and spring, the trails by which they could reach refuge with other Iroquois to the north were made almost impassable by snow, swamps, and fallen timber. In the summer, the lightning-struck forests burned for days around them until the whole village was obscured by smoke.

And the people liked to drink. They preferred not to drink alone but in large convivial groups. In the spring, hunters took their peltries to Warren, got drunk by scores, and brought more liquor home with them; at other seasons, they were able to get credit for liquor from the Holland Company factor. Raftsmen taking logs from Cornplanter's sawmill downstream to the white towns as far south as Pittsburgh spent their money on whiskey. Bringing liquor back to the grant, returning travelers sold the whiskey at retail and buyers threw all-night parties where, plied with liquor, groups spent whole nights singing, dancing, drumming, and quarreling. Women could be seen after such routs, lying in stupor beside the paths to their homes. And in the late morning the sodden households woke sometimes to find a member dead, or cut in a brawl, or frozen in the snow outside.[5]

· Depopulation ·

THE DEMOGRAPHIC CONDITION of the Iroquois of New York and Pennsylvania had deteriorated continuously during the twenty years from the beginning of the American Revolution to the Treaty of Big Tree. The net effect was to reduce the Iroquois population approximately by half.

Despite the fact that they were still able to wage an effective guerrilla war at the end of the Revolution, casualties were severe. Approximately two hundred warriors were killed in the fighting, about two or three per cent of the total population and ten per cent of the able-bodied adult males.[6] These men were not merely professional soldiers but also husbands, sons, and fathers whose labor as hunters and traders was important to the survival of nearly two hundred households. Relatively few adult male captives were taken and adopted to replace them. A small number of women and children were doubtless also lost during the fighting and perhaps as many as fifty men, women, and children by murders, both at the hands of whites and of drunken Indians, in the ten years after the war. Nevertheless, by 1788, when Samuel Kirkland made his household census of the New York Indians, the proportions of adult males and females were nearly equal. Among the Seneca, Kirkland then counted 423 females to 409 adult males.[7] These figures suggest that there was no very significant underproportion of males resulting from combat losses.

Even more damaging than direct combat casualties were the economic losses resulting from Sullivan's, Van Schaick's, and Brodhead's famous raids in 1779. The American armies, waging total war, systematically destroyed all the Indian settlements that they reached. Houses were burned, apple and peach orchards chopped down, caches of corn, squash, cucumbers, beans, and tobacco and dry fields of ripe corn, hay, and other vegetables were put to the torch. Five hundred Indian dwellings in two dozen settlements were reduced to ashes; nearly a million bushels of corn were incinerated.[8] Some of the refugees, after the armies had gone, returned to their burned-out villages along the Allegheny and Genesee. But the winter of 1779–80 brought a new catastrophe: cold. That winter was the most severe within living memory. New York Harbor froze over solidly enough for cannon to be wheeled across it. Snow covered western New York five feet deep; vast numbers of deer and other animals died of starvation, and their carcasses were found under the snow in the spring. The Indians who had returned to the burned villages were unable to secure even enough food "to keep a child one day from perishing from hunger." Another famine winter occurred in 1887–8.[9]

And still another apocalyptic horseman was riding in the sky: pestilence. About two thousand Iroquois refugees were settled after 1779 in a line of "poorly constructed wigwams" for eight miles along the road leading to Fort Niagara; according to Blacksnake many died from "salt food and exposure," and according to another Indian report three hundred died of dysentery.[10] In 1794 the Seneca and Oneida parties who visited the western Indians brought back with them an epidemic of dysentery and spread it on the reservations. Forty Oneida died; and six months later Cornplanter reported that he and Guyasuta were still sick and that now the disease had become very bad among his people as well. In 1795 an epidemic of measles killed a number of Oneida and probably of the other tribes.[11] An epidemic of smallpox had cut down the Onondaga in the winter of 1776–7, when some ninety persons had died in their principal village.[12] In the winter of 1781–2 smallpox struck again, this time among the wretched and panic-stricken survivors on the Genesee. According to an eyewitness, "The Indians appealed to the commandant of Niagara who sent English surgeons, the sick were separated from the well, huts were prepared outside the village to serve as hospitals, and as soon as symptoms appeared the individuals were sent to these rude retreats. Few persons on the upper Genesee escaped the contagion. Many died and were immediately buried. Only those who had recovered from the plague could be prevailed upon to care for the sick and the reckless indifference of some of these unwilling attendants was such that several persons were buried alive when it appeared probable they could not recover."[13] It may be presumed that the epidemic was not confined to the Genesee but spread, that same winter or later, among the rest of the susceptible Iroquois in their shabby, hungry camps at Niagara.

One cumulative consequence of the multiple disaster—combat and invasion, hunger and cold, and disease and pestilence—was a substantial reduction of the total population of the Iroquois. As early as 1779, a few months after Sullivan's raid, their British agent at Niagara observed somberly that "their number is now reduced to 2,628."[14] While this number is unduly low, it is evident that the population was declining. By 1794 no more than about 4,000 Iroquois remained: some 3,500 in New York and about 500 in Canada.[15] This figure contrasts sadly with Sir William Johnson's estimate of nearly 2,000 warriors in 1763—a figure that implies a total population of between 8,000 and 10,000 souls and that was probably close to the correct figure at the beginning of the Revolutionary War.[16] Evidently the losses through combat, murder, starvation, exposure, and disease had in the twenty years following the onset of the war cut the population of the Six Nations approximately in half.

· Loss of Confidence ·

MORE DAMAGING TO THE IROQUOIS than the actual loss of population was their declining confidence in their ability to survive as a people. A pessimistic view was maintained both tacitly and publicly by many American whites, despite official plans to "civilize" the "savages," and it reinforced in Indian thinking the somber evidence of recent experience. Benjamin Lincoln, Revolutionary War hero, one of the commissioners to the abortive treaty of 1793, and a person with whom the Iroquois had done business on several occasions, wrote piously that ". . . to people fully this earth was in the original plan of the benevolent Deity. I am confident that sooner or later there will be a full accomplishment of the original system; and that no men will be suffered to live by hunting on lands capable of improvement. So that if the savages cannot be civilized and quit their present pursuits, they will, in consequence of their stubbornness, dwindle and moulder away, from causes perhaps imperceptible to us, until the whole race shall have become extinct, or they shall have reached those climes about the great lakes, where, from the rocks and the mountainous state, the footsteps of the husbandman will not be seen."[17] The depression produced by such attitudes was vividly expressed in 1794 by an Allegany Indian named John Logan. A man of about fifty, he lived by himself in a bark camp near the American fort on French Creek. Logan was widely known as the man who had killed his uncle Logan, the Great Mingo. But when surveyor John Adlum encountered him unexpectedly, he was "astonished to see the tears rolling down his manly cheeks very copiously." When Adlum, through an interpreter, asked why he looked so sorrowful and whether there was anything he could do, Logan explained that it was "a disease of the mind." He was worrrying about the prospect of a frontier war in which the Iroquois would be inevitably destroyed. And almost echoing Lincoln and the other "savagist" white philosophers of Indian doom, he declared, "It appears to me that the great Spirit is determined on our destruction—Perhaps it is to answer some great and now incomprehensible purpose, for the better And whatever his will is I will bear it like a man."[18]

Not only did whites and Indians doubt the survival of the Iroquois: The moral value of their culture was persistently attacked. In 1784, for instance, in order to press the diplomatic attack more effectively, the federal representatives adopted a conscious policy of destroying Iroquois self-esteem, corrupting their leaders, and subverting their political system. James Duane, who had been lately a delegate to the Continental Congress and a member of its Committee on Indian Affairs, in advance of the treaty advised the Governor of New York to break down Iroquois morale at Fort Stanwix by every device of psychological warfare available to his commissioners. "They assume a perfect equality," he wrote; this attitude was to be broken by constantly treating them as inferiors, as a dependent minority group. It had been the custom of New York, Pennsylvania, and Crown commissioners for a hundred years to follow Indian usage in councils. Now these rituals were to be abandoned. "Instead of conforming to Indian political behavior We should force them to adopt ours—dispense with belts, etc." Their very existence as a political unit was to be denied: "I would never suffer the word 'Nation' or 'Six Nations,' or 'Confederates,' or 'Council Fire at Onondago' or any other form which would revive or seem to confirm their former ideas of independence, to escape . . . they are used to be called Brethren, Sachems & Warriors of the Six Nations. I hope it will never be repeated. It is sufficient to make them sensible that they are spoken to without complimenting twenty or thirty Mohawks as a nation, and a few more Tuscaroras & Onondagas as distinct nations . . . they should rather be taught . . . that the public opinion of their importance has long since ceased." Spies and provocateurs were sent among them to bribe compliance and sow dissension: "If you find that any Jealousy of, or Envy to, Brant, prevails; you will try to discover who are most jealous or envious of him, and promote it as much as You prudently can. . . ."[19]

This policy was put into effect at Fort Stanwix, where the initial Indian speakers were cut short in their delivery, informed that Great Britain had given their lands to the United States, and ordered peremptorily to sign articles of submission and cession. American spokesmen pointed their fingers at the Indians to emphasize each instruction: ". . . it made the Indians stare. The speech was delivered . . . in a language by no means accommodating or flattering; quite unlike what they used to receive." The credentials and authority of the chief Indian spokesman—a Mohawk warrior authorized to make peace on behalf of the Six Nations and all their allies and confederates, including the Ottawa, Chippewa, Huron, Potawatomi, Mississauga, Miami, Delaware, Shawnee, Cherokee, Choctaw, and Creek—were impugned, and the very existence of such a confederacy was denied (although its reality was assured enough).[20] And behind the whole proceeding lay a pose of withering contempt on the part of the white delegates, many of whom were slaveowners and only too ready to regard the Indians as lesser breeds. Washington, himself a slaveowner, about this time compared "the savage" to "the wolf" as "both being animals of prey though they differ in shape."[21] And Washington, like many another American official, had before the Revolution become an investor in abortive schemes to acquire the same Indian lands whose final relinquishment was a prime object of the treaties at forts Stanwix, McIntosh, and Finney.[22]

The Iroquois were at this moment ill-equipped to rebut, to their own satisfaction, these assaults upon their self-respect by any coordinated movement toward reform. But various individuals and groups were taking public positions that were relevant to the renaissance when, under Handsome Lake's guidance, it did develop. Against the intensification of race prejudice, some spoke for a pan-Indian resistance. When the western confederacy met in 1786, for instance, the proposal was made that *all* the nations "of our colour" unite and be of one mind. There it was urged, "Let us then have a just sense of our own value and if after that the great spirit wills that other colours should subdue us let it be so."[23] Cornplanter and others vehemently denied the popular stories of Indian atrocities and accused the whites of being more cruel than the Indians. Thus individual men of eloquence were able to reject the challenges to self-respect and to cast them back upon their enemies in the destructive dialogue of identity. But most of the time, for many of the Iroquois, the doubts remained: Were they going to survive? Were they worthy to survive?

· Social Pathology: Alcohol, Violence, Witch Fear, Disunity ·

THE MOST CONSPICUOUS social pathology was a great increase in the frequency of drunkenness. In earlier days, indeed, Iroquois Indians had been accustomed on occasion to drink heavily (witness Zeisberger's graphic account of a Seneca orgy in 1750). But these had been brief and periodic sprees in which whole towns indulged. Chronic individual alcoholism had long been known among the Delaware, who had lost their lands two generations earlier;[24] but until now it had been rare among the Iroquois. Now, added to the periodic drunken saturnalia, drinking became a serious social problem. Many of the most distinguished men among the Six Nations became notorious drunkards, including Red Jacket, Hendrick Aupaumut, Young King, Logan (the Great Mingo), Skenandoa, and Handsome Lake. The few leaders, like Cornplanter and Brant, who generally avoided over-indulgence were by that very fact made notable.[25]

Contemporary descriptions by white men of Iroquois drinking behavior are seldom written in a tone of amusement. Thus a surveyor noted at the Tonawanda reservation in March, 1801, "Some drunken Indians here; but this is hardly worth recording, as these people are seldom sober when whiskey can be had in sufficient quantity to make them otherwise."[26] The schoolteacher at Oneida in June 1793 (just after the annuity monies were paid, and also not long after his house burned down), wrote desperately to the Indian agent, "Since the Indians received their money this place has been almost a little Hell on earth. Wish you at least to write orders that no one white man in the place shall either sell rum or lend it to the Indians on any pretence whatsoever."[27] At Newtown Treaty in 1791 drunken warriors boasting of their exploits at the Full Moon Ceremony had to be prevented from killing one another by Fish Carrier, the Cayuga chief. One of the luminaries at that occasion was the Oneida Peter Otsequette, otherwise known as French Peter. He had been taken to

France as a youth by Lafayette and had lived there for seven years. He learned French perfectly and could recite Corneille and Racine. But "He had not been many months restored to his nation, and yet he would drink raw Rum out of a brass kettle, take as much delight in yelling and in whooping as any Indian, and in fact become as vile a drunkard as the worst of them." (He died a year later on a visit to Philadelphia and was buried with military honors at a public ceremony attended by the clergy of all denominations, the secretary of war, and a detachment of light infantry. His wife was consoled with a "present" and the return of his black silk handkerchief, leggings, black cloth mantle, and breechcloth.)[28] And the Treaty of Big Tree in 1797 saw one whole day lost to demon rum, when "Red Jacket & many of the Indians . . . from intoxication fell to fighting in groups, pulling Hair biting like dogs were ever they could get hold. . . ."[29] The prevailing mood of drunken Indians was an explosive, indiscriminate hostility that vented itself in fighting even within the family. Young Isaac Brant, the drunken ne'er-do-well son of Joseph Brant, attacked his father with a knife at an inn and suffered in return a scalp wound from which he eventually died.[30] Two drunken brothers from the Allegany band quarreled during a hunting excursion, and the elder killed the younger.[31] Mary Jemison's son Thomas in his drunken fits threatened to kill his mother for having raised a witch (for so he regarded his brother John) and was at last killed by this same brother. John later killed another brother and finally was killed himself by two Indians from Squawky Hill in the course of a drunken brawl.[32] Drunken persons, "aged women, in particular . . . were often seen lying beside the paths, overcome by [liquor]." Additional evils flowed from the drinking: skins and furs that might otherwise have been used or traded for meat and vegetables, dry goods and hardware, were spent on whiskey, which Indian women brought up to the villages and there retailed among the Indians themselves.[33] In 1796 the agent to the Iroquois wrote a discouraging report to the secretary of war: "The Indians of the Six Nations . . . have become given to indolence, drunkeness and thefts, and have taken to killing each other, there have been five murders among themselves within Six months—they have recd their payments and immediately expended it for liquor & in the course of a frollick have killed one or two. . . ."[34]

When sober, the Iroquois tended to be depressed and even suicidal. A sympathetic missionary at Buffalo Creek summarized this aspect of the problem: "Indians, as has been observed, bear suffering with great fortitude, but at the end of this fortitude is desperation. Suicides are frequent among the Senecas. I apprehend this despondency is the principal cause of their intemperance. Most of the children and youth have an aversion to spirituous liquor, and rarely taste it until some trouble overtakes them. Their circumstances are peculiarly calculated to depress their spirits, especially these contiguous to white settlements. Their ancient manner of subsistence is broken up, and when they appear willing and desirous to turn their attention to agriculture, their ignorance, the inveteracy of their old habits, the disadvantages under which they labor, soon discourage them; though they struggle hard little is realized to their benefit, beside the continual dread they live in of losing their possessions. If they build they do not know who will inhabit."[35] An unusually strong tendency for the humiliated Iroquois to commit suicide during this period is not easy to document with specific cases. One instance, however, was the suicide of Big Tree, who stabbed himself to death in Wayne's camp during the winter of 1793–94. Apparently he had felt publicly dishonored: He had been pro-American during the Revolution, had been an associate of Cornplanter's thereafter, had urged the western Indians to accept the American terms, and at the last was reputed to have become melancholic and deranged.[36]

Suspicions of witchcraft, to which disappointed Iroquois had always been vulnerable, was another expression of the fundamental demoralization of Iroquois society. The literature of the period is rife with witchcraft accusations: Cornplanter charging that his party was "poisoned" on the Maumee; Mary Jemison revealing that not only was she called a witch, but that her murderous, and eventually murdered, son John was called a witch by the first brother, whom he killed; a woman suspected of witchcraft being burned to death on the Genesee flats in 1798; and Mary Jemison, enlarging on the subject of witchcraft, noting that the Indians believed witches to be, next to the author of evil, "the greatest scourge to their people . . . more or less who had been charged with being witches, had been executed in almost every year since she has lived on the Genesee"—which was in 1798 no less than thirty-five years![37]

Many of the Indians blamed the whites for all this. The white people had once seemed a noble, virtuous, honest people; but they had brought the Indians five things: "a flask of rum, a pack of playing cards, a handful of coins, a violin, and a decayed leg bone." And the Evil Spirit had laughed and said: "These cards will make them gamble away their wealth and idle their time; this money will make them dishonest and covetous and they will forget their old laws; this fiddle will make them dance with their arms about their wives and bring about a time of tattling and idle gossip; this rum will turn their minds to foolishness and they will barter their country for baubles; then will this secret poison eat the life from their blood and crumble their bones."[38]

· *Paths to Salvation* ·

IN RESPONSE TO THE DILEMMA of civilization two points of view developed among the Iroquois, one advocating the assimilation of white culture and the other the preservation of Indian ways. We may call their proponents, for want of better terms, the progressives and the conservatives.

The progressives are better known to us today because their spokesmen were either literate, like Brant, and left written record of their policies, or else were at least in frequent contact with sympathetic white men. Cornplanter among the Allegany Seneca, the Mohawk Brant at Grand River, Captain Hendrick at Oneida, Sturgeon among the Oneida: these men, and their associates, favored extensive adoption of white customs. The two most successful of the reformers were Brant and Cornplanter; and of the two, the more radical was Brant.

Joseph Brant was a devout Episcopalian, and his acculturation policy was Episcopalian, too. This was hardly remarkable, for resident missionaries from England had been converting and educating Mohawk Indians in the Christian religion for two hundred years. A good proportion of the migrants to Canada were already baptized Christians, literate enough to read in Mohawk the New Testament and the Book of Common Prayer; and many, like Brant, spoke English well. On his trip to England in 1786 Brant had collected funds for an Episcopal church, and a church was built as soon as he reached home, with Brant himself hanging the bell in the steeple. It was a substantial building, sixty feet in length and forty-five in breadth, built of squared logs boarded on the outside and painted, with pews, pulpit, reading desk, communion table, and even a small organ. Literate Indian curates and schoolteachers supervised the flock between visits from peripatetic missionary clergymen like their old pastor John Stuart from the Mohawk Valley. But Brant's plan went beyond evangelism. Recognizing that the reservation was too small for hunting but larger than necessary for the agricultural support of the population, he proposed that lands be held in severalty and that the men take up farming on a white model. Parts of the excess reservation land could be sold off to whites and the proceeds invested in capital equipment, like plows, livestock, and a flour mill; other parts could be leased out in order to gain an annual tribal income. Brant also spoke out strongly against the evils of strong drink. But Brant was outdistancing the people he wished to lead, with his literary tastes and European dress and his plans to learn Greek in order to prepare a Mohawk translation from the original Scriptures. Before he died (in 1807) he was to see the development of a conservative faction that went so far as to attempt to impeach him for his efforts to allot lands in severalty to Indians and to sell or lease parts of the reservation to white people.[39]

Cornplanter's progressive policy was not based on a Christian rationale, for neither Cornplanter nor any of his band (with the possible exception of a few white captives who had been adopted into Indian families) was a professing Christian. Cornplanter had much respect for the members of the Society of Friends whom he had met on several occasions at Philadelphia and at Canandaigua; but this respect was based on personal liking rather than religious admiration. His policy, nevertheless, had much in common with Brant's. As we saw earlier, he was anxious to establish a secure tenure for Seneca landholdings as a basis for economic reorganization involving male agriculture with plow and cattle. In his several eloquent appeals to Washington during the winter of 1790–91 he observed: "The Game which the Great Spirit sent into our Country for us to eat is going from among us. We thought that he intended that we should till the ground with the Plow, as the White People do, and we talked to one another about it. . . . We ask you to teach us to plow and to grind Corn; to assist us in building Saw Mills, and supply us with Broad Axes, Saws, Augers, and other Tools, so as that we may make our Houses more comfortable and more durable; that you will send Smiths among us, and above all that you will teach our Children to

read and write, and our Women to spin and weave. . . . We hope that
our Nation will determine to spill all the Rum which shall hereafter
be brought to our Towns."[40] And again like Brant, Cornplanter
favored the idea of selling a part of the Seneca lands in return for an
investment of tribal funds, which by guaranteeing an annuity in cash
would ensure a continuing income usable for capital improvements
and for emergencies like legal expenses.[41] Furthermore, Cornplanter
was ready to discard ancient and revered customs if they seemed to
impede the Indians in dealing with the whites, on one occasion even
proposing that the rule of unanimity in consensus and the traditional
female veto over warfare should be treated as mere "superstitions"
and disregarded.[42] About 1792 he arranged for the Quakers to educate two of his sons in Philadelphia.[43] In 1795 he was writing to in-
quire about his son, saying that he wished "to hear from my son and
what progress he is making in his learning, and as soon as he is learned
enough I want him at home to manage my [sawmill] business for
me." Cornplanter put great importance on his sawmill, which he
built "in order to support my family by it," and his correspondence
included negotiations for the sale of boards as early as 1795. This was
five years before the white men got around to constructing the first
sawmill on that part of the Allegheny that was a generation later to
become a great lumber route![44]

The most prominent expositor of the conservative position at
this time was Red Jacket. Red Jacket was a professional council-
speaker, and thus not all of his public utterances were consistently
conservative, for he was, when he spoke on behalf of a council,
obliged to represent that council's views, conservative or progressive.
But being resident at Buffalo Creek and commonly chosen as speaker
for the Seneca sachems there, he was frequently the man who put
into words the conservative policies of the council. His personal attitude toward the whites does not seem originally to have been so much
nativistic as competitive. He regarded Colonel Pickering—the Indian
expert whom Washington had sent to Newtown Point in 1791 and
later chose to be superintendent of Indian affairs, who had organized
the Treaty at Canandaigua in 1794, and who became Postmaster
General and eventually Secretary of War—as his opposite number
among the whites and delighted in vexing him with superior rhetoric.
When he learned that Pickering had become the Secretary of War,
Red Jacket remarked sadly, "Ah, we began our public career about

the same time; he knew how to read and write, I did not, and he has got ahead of me; but if I had known how to read and write, I would have been ahead of him."[45] But Red Jacket's response to this frustration of a natural equality of talent was, paradoxically, an increasingly bitter defense of the old Seneca ways. At Newtown Point in 1791 he declared in regard to the "civilizing" of the Indians by teaching them to read and write and so forth that "it would be a matter of great time before they would give up their ancient customs."[46] In 1800 to a missionary who visited Buffalo Creek he declared that he and Farmer's Brother "cannot see that learning would be of any service to us; but we will leave it to others who come after us, to judge for themselves." Farmer's Brother in support of this view observed that some years ago he had sent one of his grandsons to Philadelphia to be educated. But on a visit to that city he found his grandson successively in a tavern, in a gambling den, in a brothel, and dancing.[47] Red Jacket's nativism found its most eloquent expression in 1805 in his celebrated reply to the Reverend Mr. Cram, who came to Buffalo Creek to tell the Six Nations that there was but one true religion—his own. After reviewing the traditional Indian history of inter-racial relations (at first you were weak, and we were kind; now we are weak, and you are merciless), he declared the official chiefs' policy:

> Brother, our seats were once large, and yours were very small; you have now become a great people, and we have scarcely a place left to spread our blankets; you have got our country, but are not satisfied; you want to force your religion upon us.

> Brother, continue to listen. You say that you are sent to instruct us how to worship the Great Spirit agreeably to his mind, and if we do not take hold of the religion which you white people teach, we shall be unhappy hereafter; you say that you are right, and we are lost; how do we know this to be true? We understand that your religion is written in a book; if it was intended for us as well as you, why has not the Great Spirit given it to us, and not only to us, but why did he not give to our forefathers the knowledge of that book, with the means of understanding it rightly? We only know what you tell us about it; how shall we know when to believe, being so often deceived by the white people?

> Brother, you say there is but one way to worship and serve the Great Spirit; if there is but one religion, why do you white people

differ so much about it? why not all agree, as you can all read the book?

Brother, we do not understand these things; we are told that your religion was given to your forefathers, and has been handed down from father to son. We also have a religion which was given to our forefathers, and has been handed down to us their children. We worship that way. It teacheth us to be thankful for all the favors we receive; to love each other, and to be united; we never quarrel about religion.

Brother, the Great Spirit has made us all; but he has made a great difference between his white and red children; he has given us a different complexion, and different customs; to you he has given the arts; to these he has not opened our eyes; we know these things to be true. Since he has made so great a difference between us in other things, why may we not conclude that he has given us a different religion according to our understanding; the Great Spirit does right; he knows what is best for his children: we are satisfied.

Brother, we do not wish to destroy your religion, or take it from you; we only want to enjoy our own.

Brother, you say you have not come to get our land or our money, but to enlighten our minds. I will now tell you that I have been at your meetings, and saw you collecting money from the meeting. I cannot tell what this money was intended for, but suppose it was for your minister, and if we should conform to your way of thinking, perhaps you may want some from us.

Brother, we are told that you have been preaching to white people in this place: these people are our neighbors, we are acquainted with them: we will wait a little while and see what effect your preaching has upon them. If we find it does them good, makes them honest, and less disposed to cheat Indians, we will then consider again what you have said.[48]

And as we shall see, Red Jacket's cultural nativism became more and more uncompromising as the years went by.

It is evident, then, that the ground was well stocked with the nutrients of factional strife between progressives and conservatives. Beyond agreement on a generalized sense of cultural inferiority and of the need for separateness from the wicked among the white people, the Six Nations were divided. Each little reservation had its own progressive and conservative faction. These factions worked against one another, as we have seen, both in political maneuvering at crucial council meetings and at treaties with the whites. And at times the struggle became violent. In 1787, for instance, the Onondaga war-captain named Sturgeon was murdered by a fellow tribesman. It was reported that two motives combined to make the murder: Jealousy of Sturgeon's despotic pretensions to leadership, and resentment of his progressive policies. Sturgeon "began to adopt the Dress and customs of the United States, and introduced them into his own Family—this gave great umbrage." He also planned to send his son to Baltimore to receive an English education. The friends of the murderer paid were-gild to the amount of £375 in order to save his life.[49]

In a world as confusing as this, it might be expected that other solutions would be offered, less rational than those formulated by the avowed progressives and conservatives. Minor prophets began to emerge, their words bursting like bubbles over a boiling cauldron. The best-known of these was a Mohawk at Grand River, a young man of "unblemished character" and of "a sedate and reflecting mind." In the fall of 1798 he fell into a trance for a day or more. During this time he dreamed that he had an interview with the great Tarachiawagon himself. Tarachiawagon complained grievously of "the base and ungrateful neglect of the Five Nations [the Seneca excepted] in withholding the homage due to him and the offering he was wont to receive from their fathers, as an acknowledgement for his guardianship. Many were the evils which had come upon them in consequence of this neglect. Sickness, epidemic disorders, losses in war, unfruitful seasons, scanty crops—unpleasant days." The popular response at Grand River was enthusiastic, and even Joseph Brant agreed to allow the renewal of the sacrifice to Tarachiawagon, provided it did not take on an anti-Christian tone. The sacrifice was the white dog ritual, which had fallen into disuse among all the Iroquois except the Seneca (among the Oneida, it had not been celebrated for thirty years).

News of the revival of the white dog ceremony at Grand River traveled fast. It reached the Oneida in New York in the spring of 1799. Blacksmith, the only surviving pagan priest and a son of Good Peter (one of the unlucky envoys to the Western Indians), celebrated the white dog ritual and was joined by a large number of the community. Blacksmith, after the eating of the white dog, delivered a little sermon warning the communicants not to drink any rum for ten days or they would pollute the rest of the ceremony. He also discussed the relation between the white dog sacrament and the Christian Mass, saying that eating the flesh of the roasted dog "was a transaction equally sacred and solemn, with that, which the Christians call the Lord's feast. The only difference is in the elements, the Christians use bread and wine, we use flesh and blood." Again the following May the white dog was sacrificed to the accompaniment of sermons against drinking. This time liquor was prohibited to communicants for four days before the ritual; abstinence for ten days thereafter was strongly recommended; they expected "a full blessing, a rich and ripe harvest next fall." And he spoke kindly of Christianity, exhorting "with great earnestness the whole of his disciples to exercise candour and gentleness towards their brethren, the Christians; never to tantalize or insult them for the path they had chosen. Lastly, he told them that as the religious rites of their ancestors did not require them to meet every Sunday, as the Christians do, they were at liberty, whoever so minded, to attend the Sabbath worship of the Christians and learn what good they could there."

Poor pastor Kirkland feared that the Oneida would unanimously accept the new paganism, whose potency for evil, he believed, was only magnified by the uncommon "solemnity and order" of its religious festivals and by the civility, sobriety, and philanthropy of its votaries, who drank not one twentieth as much as the Christian Indians and who included a number of apostates from his own congregation.[50]

· The Ragged Conquerors ·

DURING THE LAST FEW YEARS of the eighteenth century and the first decade of the nineteenth, the Seneca reservations were being gradually encircled by a peculiarly dilapidated and discouraged brand of European culture brought by hopeful speculators, by hungry farmers fleeing the cold and rocky hillsides of New England, and by hard-drinking Scotch-Irish weavers driven from Ulster by high taxes and the new weaving machines. The men came with golden dreams, but the dreams quickly faded. Villages were built and abandoned, roads were cleared and then grew up in brush, and the clearings were taken again by the forest. These pioneers were almost a lost legion, more primitive in material standard of living, and perhaps socially as well, than the Indians on their reservations. Even as late as 1814 there were not many more white men in Warren and Cattaraugus counties (in the center of which lay Cornplanter's tract and the Allegany Reserve) than Seneca Indians. The small, isolated farmer, up to his ears in debt to some land company, scratched the soil with a hoe, planted an acre or so of corn and potatoes, shot a few deer, and then sat back helplessly to watch his horses and cattle run away and flood, frost, windstorm, and drought ruin his crop. Dietary deficiency diseases were common: goiters plagued the settlers about Pittsburgh, rickets and jaundice were common, complexions were pasty; fleas infested the cabins, flies bred in the refuse about the yard, mosquitoes spread an endemic malaria; skin diseases, respiratory diseases, cholera, and typhoid epidemics came and went with the seasons. Witches were blamed for illness by whites as well as Indians; the bloodletting, purgatives, and emetics of the few professional doctors were probably inferior to the folk remedies, many of them herbal recipes learned from the native inhabitants. There were almost no schools; a school-teacher, when hired, was "hired at the lowest wages, and generally one who could get no other employment." A general spirit of apathy inhibited the construction of public works; "they built no bridges, and would leave a tree accidentally fallen across the road, to lie there until it rotted." In 1816 a traveler in the region "south and west of Meadville" (i.e., in the white settlements most nearly adjacent to Cornplanter's lands) recognized the area as blighted. "An almost total want of energy prevails. Many small farms, which had been cleared some years ago, including fruit trees of handsome growth, are completely deserted; and the solitary buildings, or the burnt spots where they stood, fill the passenger with melancholy reflections. Even the improvements of former years, now occupied, are retrogressive. The chief part of the remaining inhabitants reminded us of exiles; and if they escape the ravages of famine, they must be nearly estranged to the common comforts of civilized life. . . . [The] road, indeed, only deserves the name of a track. It is little used and less repaired. . . . To increase the measure of disaster, provisions of every kind are scarce. . . ."[51]

Thus, although a Seneca Indian might still not see a white man more often than once or twice a week, after 1797 he was no longer able simply to withdraw into his own country and there, sheltered behind a wall of forests, ignore these contemptuous, quarrelsome, pushing people. For now the reservations were little islands in a slowly rising sea of white men—islands, indeed, lying so low in the flood that they were constantly awash. And, as the Indians could readily observe, many of the frontier whites were as demoralized as the natives on their reservations. There was little to emulate, even in technology, in the most immediately accessible examples of white culture.

The reasons for the difficulties of the early white settlers in the Seneca country were partly technological and partly administrative. The central technological problem seems to have been that the available cereal grains, particularly wheat, were not yet adapted to the short, cool summers and harsh winters of the regions chosen for initial settlement. The importation of non-adapted cereal strains, together with the inadequacy of the roads and an insufficiency of agricultural equipment, made the establishment of a substantial family farm a precarious enterprise. The administrative problems grew from an inefficient and often corrupt mingling of governmental and financial interests in the development of the region. The pyramid of debt, from government down to the individual settler, in effect reduced the philosophy of settlement from a capital investment program to a vast real estate promotional scheme. Because the disorganized character of the surrounding white settlements encouraged a somewhat negative Seneca response to white civilization, it is worth examining in some detail the process by which the white communities too were being made into wilderness slums.

The exploitation of the area was not conducted on an impromptu plan. It was organized and reorganized, by government first and by land companies second, each taking opportunity to lay down conditions and to take its profit. By the time the common "pioneer" himself arrived, the land had been explored, bought from the Indians, garrisoned, pacified, partially surveyed, mapped, and picked over by land companies, public officials, and private speculators seeking the most probable localities for quick profit.

Three separate regions in New York and Pennsylvania, each with its own set of Indian communities and its own topographical and climatic features, were chosen for initial development. The regions were the lush and gently rolling lower valley of the Genesee River, the flat, cold, and forested shorelands bordering on lakes Erie and Ontario and hinging on the so-called "Niagara frontier," and the mountainous and heavily forested upper Allegheny. On the Genesee were the little Seneca reserves, from Canawaugus on the north to Caneadea on the south, strung like pearls on a string, and soon to be snatched away forever. On or near the lake shore were the Cattaraugus, Buffalo Creek, Tuscarora, and Tonawanda reservations. And southward on the Allegheny was Cornplanter's band. The Genesee was the most immediate target of exploitation, for Sullivan's army and the early settlers of the Phelps and Gorham purchase had brought home bright tales of its hardwood-forested uplands, proud in oak, ash, and elm, its fertile meadows, its rich supplies of limestone. Especially famous were the Genesee flats, where the Seneca themselves had for many years concentrated their villages and where the soil was "a black, vegetable mould [overlying] a deep stratum, formed by the finer particles of loam, washed from the hills surrounding the headwaters of its tributaries, and floated down and deposited, by the river. . . ." The Genesee headwaters, however, were a harsher, colder land of steep hills, shale soil, and conifer forests.[52] Similarly severe was the Allegheny country to the south and west. But in both these regions were many fertile bottom-lands and many stands of fine hardwood and pine timber; and the Allegheny, besides, was a navigable stream and therefore a potential artery of commerce and travel. The Niagara frontier was a strategic site for commerce, being situated at the crossroads of the lake traffic and of the international ferry.

Pennsylvania's problems came immediately to the surface. By act of March 12, 1783 (while the country was still in a fervor of patriotic gratitude), the state reserved most of the land west of the Allegheny for the reimbursement of the long-unpaid officers and men of the Pennsylvania line. This action was taken before the Iroquois title was quieted at Fort Standix. The southern part of this reserved tract, the "depreciation lands," were to be sold for the now depreciated currency with which the Continental troops had been paid, thus at once rewarding the soldiers and stabilizing the currency; while the northern part of the tract, the "donation lands," were to be given away by lottery to officers and men according to rank and service. When few veterans took advantage of their opportunities to settle the wilderness parts of the state, an "actual settlement act" was passed, in the spring of 1792, opening the territory for sale. Any enterprising homesteader, veteran or not, could now acquire land: he could either pay for and have his four hundred acres of land surveyed first, then improve and settle, and finally complete title, or he could settle and improve first, and have his four hundred acres surveyed and complete title last.

There was a loophole in this law, however, that made it appeal to the enterprising speculator: he could buy for a few shillings apiece hundreds of warrants taken up by hundreds of straw men. Government officials leaped to share the spoils of one of the most profitable land grabs in the state's history. On the day the act was passed, the Surveyor General picked up eight hundred acres at a likely mill and town site on Beaver River; practical surveyors, who had explored the western lands and knew the best locations, snapped up large tracts and then resold them to Dutch bankers who, in order to avoid the law prohibiting aliens from holding lands, assigned the warrants to cooperative citizens; and the Comptroller General of the commonwealth became the president of the board of managers of the Pennsylvania Population Company, whose members included General Irvine, the surveyor and manorial neighbor of Cornplanter, George Mead, another neighbor at Cussawago on French Creek, Aaron Burr, and various other prominent men. Between 1792 and 1794, when the assembly plugged the loophole by prohibiting warrants except on the basis of prior settlement and improvement, the Pennsylvania Population Company acquired in the neighborhood of 450,000 acres, engrossing nearly the whole of the Lake Erie region west of the upper Allegheny, and the Holland Land Company engrossed about 1,000,000 acres there and to the east of the river. These two companies and a few private speculators thus managed to seize a middleman's title to nearly the whole of northwestern Pennsylvania.[53]

The consequences of speculative investment in the Pennsylvania public lands were in the long run disastrous for the region. Although the land companies cut timber, opened roads, laid out towns, built houses to be sold or even given to settlers, erected gristmills and sawmills, and opened stores where food and hardware could be bought on extended credit, they failed. They were unable, in part because of the roughness of the land and in part because of the independence of the frontiersmen, who did not like to owe money to eastern financiers, to improve and settle their lands within the legal limit of two years after the ending of the Indian Wars. The assembly, after 1799 dominated by western delegates who favored the small farmer, declared the land company claims void and encouraged independent settlement and improvement. The land companies brought suit, shots were fired, the commonwealth became embroiled in a state's rights controversy in the United States Supreme Court. The companies continued to organize settlement, but for years no settler knew whether his title was good. In the opinion of one historian of the period, "The uncertainty of title which so long prevailed in western Pennsylvania . . . seriously delayed the full and natural development of that region since the intelligent and most desirable type of settler passed by it to Ohio and northwestern New York where his title would be good."[54]

In western New York, in contrast to their situation in Pennsylvania, the land companies—particularly the Holland Land Company— were in control from the first. Land companies, not the state, had purchased the land directly from the Indians; land companies conducted the surveys of the reservations, of the towns, of the country estates. Land companies sold or leased the lands to the farmers. The Holland Land Company did not maintain so elaborate an organization as the Pennsylvania Population Company, finding it less necessary to improve the land in order to sell tracts in the fertile northern valley of the Genesee, where old Indian towns, clear fields and meadows, and well-worn trails made the task of development less severe, or in the city of Buffalo, which the Company laid out into lots. In the Phelps and Gorham purchase, however, attempts were even made to draw settlers by building good roads, hotels, and racecourses.[55] And again, as in Pennsylvania, the land companies were able to make use of public officials. General Israel Chapin, Sr., for instance, the federal Indian agent from 1792 until shortly before his death in 1796, was an old army friend of Oliver Phelps, the purchaser of the Seneca lands east of the Genesee. Both men were from Massachusetts. After the purchase in 1788, Chapin became the paid agent for the Phelps and Gorham Land Company and its business partner in land dealings in the new purchase. Phelps was attentive to Washington's tastes (ordering for instance a yoke of beef for his table) and it was very likely on Phelps's and Gorham's recommendation, directly or indirectly, that Chapin, and later his son, became an Indian agent. (Robert Morris, the Pennsylvania financier, also used his influence later to secure Chapin's son's appointment to that post.) Even after his appointment as Indian agent, Chapin was still on

Phelps's payroll, taking instructions in such duties as the care of the financier's horses and receiving promises of proper reward. A similarly equivocal relationship is apparent in the arrangement of the treaty at Big Tree, which we have already discussed: the United States commissioner, by law appointed to supervise that transaction in order to ensure fair and honorable dealings to the Indians, was none other than Jeremiah Wadsworth, perhaps the largest land speculator in the Genesee Valley. The white negotiators stayed in the house of William Wadsworth, Jeremiah's cousin and the agent in charge of selling off the elder Wadsworth's Genesee lands. Israel Chapin, Jr., was of course present as Indian agent (and it was Chapin who had notified the secretary of war, after Thomas Morris had promised bribes to the Seneca chiefs at Buffalo Creek, that the Seneca had offered to sell a part of their lands to Robert Morris). And Commissioner Wadsworth himself advised Thomas Morris on the strategy by which the Seneca were to be brought to terms, threatening that if young Morris didn't take his advice, he would leave the grounds and go home.[56]

And in New York, again as in Pennsylvania, but more slowly, agrarian discontent developed as farmers began to resent their lingering obligations to impersonal absentee landlords. Eventually rumors circulated that titles procured from the land companies were worthless, farmers refused to pay for their lands, law suits multiplied, there was gunfire. In New York, however, when the mobs formed, the government supported the land companies by calling out the militia. But nonetheless, by 1835 only about half of the Big Tree purchase had been sold off.[57]

Frequently one great company, rather than waiting for years to dispose of its land lot by lot, would sell it off to lesser companies in parcels of tens or hundreds of thousands of acres, and these companies in turn would sell to still smaller companies and to private speculators, so that by the time the theoretically intended ultimate purchaser, the small emigrant farmer, was reached, the price of the land had increased beyond his capacity to pay.[58] Actual settlement, surprisingly hesitant everywhere, was very slow in the southern Genesee and the upper Allegheny country, which remained virtually a wilderness while regions far to the westward were becoming agriculturally prosperous and even urbanized. A few taverns, some land company storehouses, and a half a dozen small and isolated settlements, whose nucleus usually was an extended family consisting of a father, his sons, and their wives and children,[59] were scattered here and there in the Allegheny country after 1794; but it was fully twenty years before settlement in substantial numbers, or even extensive lumbering, began. The watershed of the upper Allegheny and the upper Genesee was a backwater. In 1801 three Quaker visitors to the Allegany Seneca remarked, "It is not probable these Indians will have any white settlers near them soon. In all directions excepting south, we believe none are nearer than sixty miles and very few so near, and south of them there is about twenty miles of barren ridges not inviting to settlers."[60]

The land companies were placed in a desperate situation by the failure of settlers to take up the lands. Various remedial schemes were attempted: long-term credit was offered, in some cases up to fifteen years, in others indefinitely, provided taxes were paid; high-pressure advertising was circulated by the public press in handbills and at town meetings in depressed areas farther east; the transport of whole groups to planned communities was offered; great manorial estates were created (particularly by the Wadsworths on the Genesee) on which lands could be leased by tenant farmers. But none of these schemes was fully successful along the Allegheny. The cold, windy climate and the soil conspired against the raising of wheat at most locations (except those already preempted by the Seneca); the spring floods wrecked the mills, and the cutting of the timber lowered the water level and stranded them; great towns failed to materialize at strategic harbors, fords, and highway intersections. The early settlers who had enough money moved quickly on to better land in the west; the poor, trapped by debt and despair, clung to their cabins in the woods until they starved or became sick; the wise avoided the region entirely. Hundreds of thousands of acres in the central and southern portions of the tracts remained largely unsettled for generations.[61]

Thus the difficulties of the early settlers in the Seneca country were not merely the first-year sufferings of pioneers in a new land. To the inevitable hardships and disappointments of frontier life had been added the misery of irredeemable poverty. It is not surprising, therefore, that across this dark and barren country a wave of religious enthusiasm began to swell, stretching in a wide arc from the hillsides of New England, across the lonely marches of the land company tracts, down into the back country of the south. New sects sprang up;

and old denominations, their members congregating in great camp meetings, poured their sorrows into the first Great Revival.

The most lurid events of the revival occurred outside the immediate environs of the upper Allegheny region, however. In the Genesee Valley and about the Finger Lakes, where the settlers were New England Congregationalists, the wave struck in 1799–1800; the waters of faith did not flood until 1802 in western Pennsylvania south and west of Pittsburgh, where Lutherans and Presbyterians predominated. The upper Allegheny was a mission area late to be served by the joint efforts of the Presbyterians and Congregationalists, who had divided the region between them as far as church organization was concerned but who cooperated in missionary enterprise. Not until 1801 was the Presbytery of Erie organized to serve the needs of the people who lived north and west of the Ohio and the Allegheny. The first missionary is said to have reached Cattaraugus County in 1810. Thus, in religion as in economy, the Allegheny was a depressed area.[62]

But throughout the adjacent regions, in the period 1798 to 1802, and of course later, white men in hundreds communed with God. These orgies of communion laid the seed, especially in the "burned-over district" of western New York, for that territory's traditional hospitality to sectarianism, spiritualism, and millennarianism. For this was to be the country of Joseph Smith and the golden tablets of Mormon; of Jemina Wilkinson, the reincarnation of Christ; of the Millerites and the end of the world; of the Shakers at Sodus Bay; and of many other exotic flowers of religious enthusiasm that grew in the hearts of dour and drunken men. It was in these times that the camp meeting was invented, where hundreds of persons of all ages would gather over a period of several days to worship and experience religious ecstasy. Self-appointed evangelists rode the circuits of the forest, striving to save sinners from hell.

Events at these camp meetings generally followed a predictable course. An evangelistic preacher would speak vividly of hellfire and damnation. Hundreds of people were quickly seized with hysterical symptoms. A contemporary observer described the scene: "when a person begins to be affected, he generally sinks down in the place where he stood, and is for a few minutes overwhelmed in tears; he then makes a weeping noise—some person near lays hold of him— he shrieks aloud—and discovers a desire to be on his back—in this he is indulged—and a friend sits down and supports the head of the person in his lap. Every tear now leaves his eye and he shouts aloud for about 20 minutes. Meanwhile the features of his face are calm and regular. His voice becomes more and more feeble for about 20 minutes more. By this time he is speechless and motionless, and lies quiet perhaps an hour. During this time his pulse is rather lower than the usual state,—the extremities are cold, the skin fresh and clear, the features of the face full, the eyes closed, but not so closed as in sleep. Speech and motion return in the same gradual manner; the features become more full than before. Pleasure paints the countenance as peace comes to the soul, and when faith is obtained the person rises up, and with most heavenly countenance shouts—'Glory to God.' This ecstasy abates in about a quarter of an hour and the person is generally led away by a friend to his tent. Calm, mild, sedate pleasure marks the countenance for several days; and those who have been often exercised in this pleasing manner, show sweet mixture of love and joy which no tongue or pen can describe." Some victims suffered from "the jerks," in which the whole body was seized with violent contortions. Some danced for hours, others ran, some turned cartwheels endlessly. In Kentucky groups of people ran about on all fours, barking, snarling, and baring their teeth like dogs.

· *The Friendly People* ·

IN THE LAST YEARS of the eighteenth century the official policy of the United States was to confine the Indian tribes to small reservations around their villages and there to promote their civilization. It was not until years later that the removal policy, rationalized by the popular theory that Indians were savages incapable of civilization, came into official sway in the hands of the frontier politicians like Andrew Jackson and his secretary of war, Lewis Cass.

The policy of civilizing the Indian natives was embedded in a solid matrix of treaties. For the Iroquois the controlling treaties were, of course, Fort Stanwix (1784), Fort Harmar (1789), Canandaigua (1794), the Treaty of Greenville (1795), and Big Tree (1797). These agreements recognized the political sovereignty of the United States over the Indian tribes, defined the legal boundaries of the Indian communities, specified the annuity payments, and guaranteed to the

Indians certain services and immunities and to the United States certain privileges. The Iroquois boundaries we have already discussed. Their annuities amounted to: $4,500 per annum forever, payable to all the New York Iroquois by the United States under the Treaty of Canandaigua; about $8,000 paid by the State of New York to the Oneida, Onondaga, and Cayuga for lands purchased; the interest from $100,000 per annum forever, payable to the Seneca under the Treaty of Big Tree; special annuities for the Oneida and their associates who had been loyal to the United States during the Revolution; and the personal annuities of Cornplanter, Red Jacket, Farmer's Brother, and other chiefs and captains. Services guaranteed to the Indians included a superintendent (and his agents) appointed by the president of the United States, authorized to disburse annuities and to transmit Indian requests and complaints to the federal establishment. Indians were free to pass the border between the United States and Canada without such hindrance as customs duties on personal baggage. The United States reserved the right to build certain roads, to pass freely through Indian lands, and to make free use of rivers, harbors, and emergency landing places.[63] Supporting and carrying into effect these treaties were various acts of Congress and administrative regulations. Trade with the Indians was controlled by a system of licenses with heavy penalties for infractions. Land sales were to be made only at public treaties held "under the Authority of the United States." Equal protection of the criminal law was extended over both Indians and whites, even in Indian territory.[64]

The civilization policy was implicit in the eighteenth century's doctrine of progress, which regarded it as natural that, as Secretary of War Henry Knox put it in 1789, every people should pursue the same path in "the process of society from the barbarous ages to its present degree of perfection." Knox in his early formulations suggested that it was important to introduce "a love for exclusive property" as "a happy commencement of the business" of civilizing the Indians. Knox also recommended the appointment of missionaries as resident teachers of both the academic and domestic arts, and the provision of model farms, livestock, and other capital goods. His plan was endorsed by Washington and other prominent figures.[65] A few years later Timothy Pickering also offered a "plan" to Washington for introducing the arts of husbandry among the Indians instead of taking away a few Indian youths for education among white men.[66] This practice, common among the French and the British, was now almost universally regarded as bad by the Americans because the return of the native to his village so frequently produced only "the most bitter mortification. He is neither a white man nor an Indian" and met with disdain in both societies. Such a marginal man "will take refuge from their contempt in the inebriating draught; and when this becomes habitual, he will be guarded from no vice, and secure from no crime. His downward progress will be rapid, and his death premature."[67] Washington was so well impressed by Pickering's plan that he offered him the post of Superintendent of the Six Nations; and Pickering did later become secretary of state and the negotiator of the Canandaigua Treaty. The Federalists' thinking in these matters was doubtless also stimulated by the exchange of views between Cornplanter and Washington in 1790 and 1791. Cornplanter, it will be recalled, had asked for a technical aid program, and Washington in reply had promised that the United States would teach the Indians how to keep domestic animals and to till ("the only Business which will add to your Numbers and Happiness") by sending "one or two sober Men to reside in your Nation," to maintain model farms and to serve as schoolmasters.[68]

This initial federal effort to "civilize" the Indians was not confined to the Iroquois; it extended to the southern Indians (e.g., the Creeks), who were encouraged by their agent Benjamin Hawkins to plow, fence, spin, weave, and raise cattle and hogs.[69] The funds came from federal annuities intended for "purchasing for them clothing, domestic animals, and implements of husbandry, and for encouraging useful artificers to reside in their villages."[70] But in the Iroquois case the federal program was not notably successful: a large proportion of the very limited funds went for consumer goods (food, ornaments, powder and lead, dry goods, and miscellaneous household hardware). Each of the Iroquois villages was in 1792 to be given one set of carpenter's tools. A schoolmaster was to be supplied the Oneida and a smith installed with them and one on the Genesee.[71] But even with the supplemental funds afforded by other treaties, as at Canandaigua in 1794, the amounts of money and of enthusiastic personnel were too small to make a successful program. The federal establishment therefore turned to religious denominations for assistance, for here were groups of American citizens already dedicated to the improvement, either spiritual or temporal, and sometimes both, of their Indian brethren.

The one organization that responded with an active interest in the Seneca was the Philadelphia Yearly Meeting of the Society of Friends. The Pennsylvania Quakers had for a hundred years, since the founding of the commonwealth, advocated a policy of peace and friendship toward the American Indians, and during the French and Indian Wars had exerted themselves (not always wisely) to see justice done the Delaware, whose hostility they laid to past iniquities (committed, as they argued, by the Quakers' political competitors) in land transactions.[72] The Friends had received Cornplanter and his associates with warm professions of love on their visits to Philadelphia after the Revolution, and members of the Society's "Meeting for Sufferings" had attended the treaty at Newtown in 1791, the negotiations at Sandusky in 1793, and the Canandaigua Treaty in 1794 as observers interested in guarding the interests of the natives. In November 1795 a "committee . . . for the civilization & real welfare of the Indian natives" was appointed by the Philadelphia Yearly Meeting. This Indian committee immediately consulted with Timothy Pickering, the secretary of state, and (probably with his advice) formulated a plan of action. Pickering then in February 1796, wrote officially to the Six Nations, describing and recommending the Quaker plan to introduce plow agriculture and animal husbandry among them. He also wrote to Jasper Parrish, their erstwhile captive and trusted interpreter, and to Israel Chapin, Jr., their agent, asking that they support "the plan" by recommending it heartily to the Indians when their advice was asked. He pointed out that the Friends had no ulterior motive beyond "the happiness of their fellowmen." They did not intend to proselytize nor to teach "peculiar doctrines"; nor did they or the agents whom they would employ expect any economic gain for themselves and would in fact expect to operate at a loss, since the money would be raised by themselves and not by the government. Their plan, in essence, was simply "to introduce among them . . . the most necessary arts of civil life . . . useful practices: to instruct the Indians in husbandry & the plain mechanical arts & manufactures directly connected with it. This is the beginning of the right end, and if so much can be accomplished, their further improvement will follow, of course."[73]

"The plan" went forward with remarkable dispatch. In April a letter was received from the Stockbridge Indians, signed by Hendrick Aupaumut, in response to the Quaker offer of aid. The Stockbridge (a band of Mahican domiciled with the Oneida) had conferred and "were willing to unite in endeavours towards their improvement." They asked for a number of tools and other necessaries. In June 1796, seven Quakers set out for the Oneida and Stockbridge, preceded by a shipment of tools. In June also the Onondaga replied to the Quaker offer of farmers, teachers, blacksmiths, and carpenters with an enthusiastic note of acceptance.[74] Three months later the committee sent a shipment of tools to Benjamin Hawkins to aid him in his program with the Creeks, and shortly thereafter tools were being sent to the Cherokee, Chickasaw, Shawnee, Wyandot, Delaware, Potawatomi, Ottawa, Chippewa, and Miami to the west, the Cherokee, Chickasaw, and Choctaw to the south, and the Onondaga, Cayuga, and Oneida to the north. By the beginning of 1797 the Indian committee had inaugurated technical aid to a large proportion of the Indians of the eastern United States.

In March 1797, the committee voted "to assist and encourage any suitable friends who may feel their mind drawn to go into this country . . . of the Seneca Nation of Indians . . . for the purpose of instructing them." A year later, in March 1798, three young men—Halliday Jackson, Joel Swayne, and Henry Simmons (who had already lived among the Oneida and Stockbridge)—volunteered to "spend some time" among the Seneca. And in May 1798, the Seneca mission, including the three young volunteers and two older friends, John Pierce and Joshua Sharpless, set out on their trip to the Allegany Seneca. In 1799 the Seneca mission was expanded to include the Cattaraugus band. And a year later still, in 1800, the Oneida having learned sufficiently in the mechanical arts to justify the experiment, the Oneida mission was closed in order to "make tryall" of Indian abilities to proceed alone. Thereafter the Seneca mission, with headquarters on the Allegheny River, was the focus of the Philadelphia Yearly Meeting's efforts to civilize the Indians.[75]

The five Quakers reached Cornplanter's village of Jenuchshadago ("Burnt House") on May 17, 1798. They found that a large part of the Allegany Seneca, about four hundred hungry people in all, were now settled here, many of them having in the last year or two deserted the upper settlement at Genesinguhta nine miles up stream,

apparently as a result of severe floods that destroyed their corn. The
visitors from Philadelphia had come at a time poorly calculated to
yield them the most favorable image of the Seneca. Their first contact
was with a band of drunken Indians at the land company store at
Warren. This was the season when the men could not hunt or fish
and when last year's food was almost exhausted; thus they saw no
more than a few pounds of venison in weeks and were unable to buy
meat at all. Cornplanter explained that last year's spring flood and
early frost had damaged their corn harvest and left them now in near
famine. The women were now very busy planting the fields, "while
the men were standing in companies sporting themselves with their
bows and arrows and other trifling amusements."

The Quakers first explained to the Seneca the purpose of their
visit. At a public council convened the day after their arrival, Cornplanter introduced them to his people and apologized for their poverty and the primitiveness of their houses. The Quakers read the
letters from the Philadelphia Yearly Meeting and from General
Wilkinson at Pittsburgh, which served as their credentials. (Cornplanter's educated son Henry, fresh from school in Philadelphia,
served on this occasion and henceforth as their faithful, if not too
skillful, interpreter.) Then they got down to business, advising the
Indians that they had left loving families and comfortable houses
solely for the sake of improving the lot of the natives. They were
come among them to teach "the works of the handy workman"[76]
and not to secure any profit to themselves. The Indians were exhorted
to "stillness & quietude and an attention to the Good Spirit in their
own hearts." Finally, the Quakers, who were sophisticated in the
theory of cultural progress, adroitly insinuated that the changes in
way of life that they were urging on the Seneca were changes that
their own ancestors had had to make in times past. They advised
them to "guard against discouragements that might present in their
looking forward towards a change in their manner of living, for we
did not doubt but there might be many difficulties in their way, and
their progress might be slow; yet there are accounts among the
writings of the white people of a people who lived beyond the great
waters in another island, who many years ago lived much like they
do now, yet were by industry and care become very good farmers
and mechanics of all kinds and from that people many of those fine
leggings with the other striped and nice clothing they had on, came."

They told the Indians that plow-irons, hoes, axes, shovels, spades, and various carpenter's, mason's, and cooper's tools were on their way in a boat from Pittsburgh, and that the Quakers while they stayed would lend them out, and when they left would leave them with the Indians. And they concluded by stating their faith that the mission was pleasing in the sight of Him "whose regard is toward all the workmanship of his hands."

Cornplanter responded next day. After apologizing for the in-adequacies of his son as an interpreter, he went on to give the views of the council, which had deliberated over the Quaker message:

Brothers, We take great pains to settle the proposals you made to us but we differ in opinions and we must take great pains to have everything complete—

Brothers, We suppose the reasons you came here was to help poor Indians some way or other, and you wish the chiefs to tell their Warriors not to go on so bad as they have done, and you wish us to take up work like the white people.

Now Brothers some of our sober Men will take up work & do as you say, & if they do well then your young Men will stay longer; but some others will not mind what you say—

Brothers, We can't say a Word against you, it is the best way to call Quakers

Brothers, you never wished our lands, you never wished any part of our lands, therefore we are determined to try to learn your ways & these younger Men may stay here two years to try, by that time we shall know whether Morris will leave us any Land & whether he will pay us our money; for last Summer we sold our Land & we dont know yet whether we shall get what we reserved, or whether we shall get our Money; but by that time we shall know & then if they like it, & we like it your young Men may stay longer

Brothers, If your young Men stay here we want them to learn our children to read & write.

Brothers—Two of you are going home again, if they hear anything about our Land or our Money they must write to these young Men here & they must tell us, if we are like to be cheated.

Brothers—This is all I got to say at present.

The next day was "First Day" (Sunday), and the Friends held their own religious meeting. Several sober Indian men, including

Cornplanter, sat with them during their meditations, and Cornplanter, who was extremely anxious to make a good impression, again apologized to the Friends, this time because the Indians did not keep the Sabbath: "We are ignorant, & can't read & write, besides we are poor & have work & our Men are often out ahunting. . . ."

On Monday the twenty-first Cornplanter and the Friends paddled up the Allegheny to Genesinguhta, the abandoned town on the reservation proper, in order to seek out a suitable place for the Quakers to live and build their demonstration farm. The neighborhood of Jenuchshadago, while more convenient to the population, was disqualified because it was on the Grant. Quaker improvements there, such as the house and barn, would after they left have legally belonged to Cornplanter personally rather than to the Seneca tribe. The site they chose consisted of about 150 acres of fertile flats, now much grown over with brush and covered with fallen timber; only three or four Indian families still remained. The Friends bought the cabin of an old Indian woman and her daughter for twenty dollars and moved in two days later with assurances to Cornplanter that they were not buying the land and would vacate it eventually, leaving the improvements to the Indians. The cabin that they secured was a typical Seneca house made of unchinked logs, twenty feet long by fourteen wide, with a shed before the door and a bark roof. Two rows of bunks and shelves extended along the sides; deerskins with the hair on served as mattresses. No boundaries were stated for the Quaker tract; Cornplanter told them that they were free to go anywhere and to hunt, fish, and cut timber at will. By the end of the week the Friends were physically established.

On Monday, May 28, the Quakers at their own request met the Indians in a second council at Cornplanter's. This time, their planting done, the women were present, including five or six of the important "respectable old women." After expressing their gratification that they and the Indians "seem to agree like Brothers, having but one mind in everything we do," the Friends expressed the hope that "some of your sober young men will settle by ours, and fence off Lots, as they see our Young Men fence off theirs; and our young Men will be willing to instruct & assist them a little about working their lots." If the community raised substantial quantities of corn and wheat this summer, the Quakers would supply half the money to build a gristmill, and the Indians could supply the other half out of their annuities. The Quakers also announced a four-year plan of individual cash awards to encourage men and women to learn the "works of the handy workman":

> Brothers, We will give to every Indian Man, living on this river, who shall raise 25 Bushel of Wheat or Rye in one year, on his own land, not worked by white people, the sum of two Dollars.
>
> 2. For every 50 Bushel of Indian Corn raised by any one Indian Man, in like manner aforesaid the sum of two Dollars.
>
> 3. For every 50 Bushel of Potatoes raised by any one Indian Man, in like manner aforesaid, the sum of two Dollars.
>
> 4. For every 2 Tons of Hay raised as aforesaid, and put into a stack or Barn, not being mown or drawn in by white people, the sum of two Dollars.
>
> 5. For every 12 yards of linen Cloth, made by any Indian woman, out of flax raised on her own, or her husbands land, & spun in her own house, the sum of two Dollars to be paid to the Woman.
>
> 6. For every 12 yards of woolen Cloth, or linsey made by any Indian woman, out of the wool of her own, or her husband's sheep, & Spun in her own house the sum of two Dollars, to be paid to the Woman.

A little added pressure toward sobriety was applied by denying an award to any person who had been "intoxicated with strong drink" at any time during the preceding six months.

The overt reaction of the town council was divided. Some, "particularly the women," appeared, in the Quaker phrase, "solid"—that is to say, gravely thoughtful and seriously concerned. But by far the larger number seemed to regard the proposals with levity. They retired to hold a private discussion; on their return an hour later Cornplanter spoke the group sentiments. These sentiments were, in effect, a very conditional agreement to the Quaker suggestions. The Friends themselves were personally acceptable. They had come a long way to help the poor Indians, who had been cheated out of their lands, "to become as white people." But although the consensus was that "we will try to learn your way," the community was not confident of success. For one thing they weren't sure their annuity monies would yield the required four hundred dollars for the gristmill, an essential ingredient in the plan. Furthermore, there were "some bad people" and some irresponsible young warriors among the Seneca, and indeed a certain generalized bitterness over being cheated out of their lands, which distracted their attention, "makes us bad, and our minds uneasy" and unable to "think upon the good Spirit" as they might if they were "rich people & had plenty of everything." The fact that Cornplanter had allowed the Seneca to be cheated out of their lands now made many of the young men scornful of his advice to adopt white customs: "some of my warriors wont mind what I say to them, but will have their own way, because they know I have been often cheated by the white people. If I had never been cheated, then my warriors would believe me, & mind what I say to them, but now they wont mind." And finally, the lack of tools, such as hoes and axes, and the ever-present need for the men to continue to hunt and therefore to conserve part of their money for repairing and replacing the guns, would slow down the process.

The Quakers responded to these reluctant excuses with the firm statement of two rational principles: first, that it was simply "unreasonable" (i.e., inefficient) to "suffer their women to work all day in the fields & woods with the hoes & axes, whilst the Men & Boys were at the same time playing with their bows & arrows"; and second, that the Good Spirit had endowed the Seneca with faculties and opportunities precisely equal to those of their white brethren. Thus "the great disparity, which they so frequently spoke of between them & the white people, with regard to plenty & poverty was the natural result of the different plans pursued in the obtaining the blessings of this life, and that, as their ground was equally good, with that possessed by the white people, it would also be equally productive, if the same Industry & methods of farming were pursued."[77]

A few days later the boat from Pittsburgh arrived, carrying the long-awaited hundred and twenty pounds of bacon and the plows, saws, and other equipment, and the Quakers were able to begin the demonstration farm. The older guides and mentors, Joshua Sharpless and John Pierce, departed on June 7. The three young Friends hurriedly plowed and fenced several fields, in the hope, although the season for planting corn was nearly past, to get in some kind of crop for subsistence during the winter. They were constantly visited by Indians "in great Numbers" from the lower settlement at Jenuchshadago and from the upper settlement at Cold Spring. Again the women, as they had been at the councils, seemed particularly interested. The Indians were visibly impressed at the ease with which the plow, in comparison with the hoe, prepared the ground for seed. A lively barter developed, the natives supplying the Quakers with venison, fish, strawberries, and other foods, and the Friends distributing needles, thread, scissors, combs, spectacles, and bandanna handkerchiefs. A number of Indians borrowed the carpenter's tools and even some few the farming equipment. The Quakers instructed the men in the use of the woodworking utensils. "Several of them constructed in the course of the summer, much better houses than they had been accustomed to, and manifested a considerable share of ingenuity in the use of carpenter's tools." Nor were all the men abashed by farm work. While the white men were in the fields, "the Indians would frequently come about them and sometimes take hold of their tools and work a little—some of the lads were pleased with driving the horses." Early in the fall the Friends completed their own house and stable. The house was "a comfortable two Story hewed House 18 feet by 22 Covered with White pine Shingles & Cellared underneath, with a chimney composed of Stone & clay." It was larger than any of the Indian dwellings, and when they moved in, on October 6, "the Heathen flocked about us" and expressed great admiration for the dwelling.

That winter Henry Simmons, the one of the three who had had previous experience in establishing an Indian school at Oneida, moved into the village at Jenuchshadago and set up a school for Indian children, as Cornplanter had asked. The school was only a partial success: at one time or another "nearly twenty children attended, and made some progress in learning to spell and read; but as their parents had little control over them, they were very irregular in their attendance, and no great progress in learning was made."

In general, it would seem, the responses of the Allegany Seneca was friendly. Nowhere do the diaries of the Friends record an instance of hostility, verbal or physical; the only negative reactions would seem to have been the somewhat defensive "levity" and "indifference" reported at councils. There seems to have been very determined support from the community's elite: Cornplanter and his family, who not only provided official backing but practical assistance (Cornplanter's wife sold the Friends milk and butter); the teetotaler chief who lived near them at Genesinguhta; and the clan matrons. The women, in general, seem to have taken their message to heart most deeply; only a few men tried their hand at carpentry and farm work. The annual cycle of village activities proceeded undisturbed; the men went out on summer hunts in July and August, then the women harvested their corn and other vegetable products, and in December, after the first snows, nearly the whole population went off to the hunting grounds. "Game was now plentiful. Some of their best hunters killed near one hundred deer, and some even more than that number; taking off the skins and leaving much of the meat scattered about in the woods." The women as usual packed the venison on their backs, through snow and ice, across hill and dale from where it was killed to the camps. And the ritual cycle continued unchanged as well. The False Faces had made their rounds in the spring when they arrived; the Green Corn was celebrated late in the summer, and Midwinter about the end of January.

Perhaps the most significant change was the reduction of drinking. Whiskey had been constantly available at Cornplanter's mill from the millwright who sold it to obtain food and other necessities from the Indians. But Jackson remarked, "The use of whiskey and other strong drink . . . considerably decreased among the Indians, in the course of the . . . year [1798], and many of their chiefs seemed desirous of preventing its introduction in the village."[78] It was a good augury for the coming year.

· *The Cruel Spring* ·

CORNPLANTER'S TOWN had been peaceful and prosperous during the fall and winter of 1798; but, paradoxically, the success of the winter hunt turned the village into a little hell on earth in the following spring. Handsome Lake contributed to this denouement. Late in the fall, after the Harvest Festival, Handsome Lake with a party of hunters and their families had left the village and drifted down the Allegheny to hunt. They set up their first camp at the mouth of the Conewango Creek, near Warren, where the Holland Company had its store. Then they hunted on down the Allegheny, moving camp southward from time to time as the weather and the game demanded, probably returning to the village for the Midwinter Festival, but going back to their growing cache of skins and dried meat. Probably about the middle of April the men left their wives and children and went on to Pittsburgh, where they bartered the skins, furs, and fresh and dried meat for various goods, including several barrels of whiskey. Then they lashed their canoes together into a raft and began the long journey northward to Cornplanter's village. The men in the middle canoes, where the whiskey was stored, were free to drink, and they yelled and sang "like demented people." They picked up their wives and children at the rendezvous and pressed on, homeward bound, in roistering good spirits, and oblivious to the tensions that were developing in the village during their absence.[79]

While Handsome Lake and his fellow hunters were on their excursion down the river, tensions were building up rapidly at Cornplanter's Town, where Henry Simmons since November had been teaching Indian children to read and write English. (The other two Friends were busy at the farm, making and mending tools for the summer's work.) Simmons' presence precipitated a crystallization of opinion among both the conservatives and the progressives. He was teaching in the house of Cornplanter, where community meetings were held and where the major religious rituals were celebrated. And before his very door stood the wooden statue of Tarachiawagon, the Good Spirit, the symbol of the traditional way of life. His school was daily a challenge to the village to take sides for or against the white man's customs and ideas.

The dissatisfaction of the conservatives grew, and at last one Sunday morning in the beginning of February young Simmons was put to the test. A dozen chiefs and warriors demanded that Simmons tell them "how the World and things there in were Created at first." Simmons knew that this was a trial on whose outcome the success of the mission might rise or fall and "immediately apply'd [his] Heart with fervent breathings to the Lord for His Aid and support." Then he launched into an account of the Christian cosmogony, as revealed by "a certain good Book, Called the Holy Scriptures," which came miraculously close to recapitulating the Seneca cosmogony. He told "of the World being made (and of all the living creatures both in Water and on Land) by the great Spirit, and also the first man & Woman whom the great Spirit created of the dust of the Earth, and breathed into them the breath of Life, and they became living Souls, who had two Sons, one of them was a good Man, and the other Wicked who killed his brother, because he was more righteous than himself." Here Seneca listeners may well have been reminded of their own myths of the primordial Good Twin (Tarachiawagon)

(229)

and Evil Twin (Tawiskaron), whose contests for power (translated into the present by the Great World Rim Dweller, whom the False Faces personified, and the still immanent Tarachiawagon, whose statue stood in the village) formed the moral structure of their universe. Simmons then went on to ask them "if they did not see it so now a days; that wicked people envy'd good ones, and at times were ready to take their lives." This too must have struck an answering chord, for "wicked people"—i.e., witches—were indeed believed to be precisely those persons who in a communal society would kill for spite. But Simmon's remark had a further implication: it pinned the label of wickedness on precisely those who opposed, out of jealousy for his prominence and wealth, Cornplanter himself, the chief proponent of white civilization and its Quaker representatives. Then Simmons went on to point out that every person experienced the presence of the good spirit, "pricking at there Hearts, and telling them not to do so . . . when they thought of doing something which they ought not to do." When Cornplanter and others of the chiefs owned that it was so, he told them that "it is the Devil that urges us to do it" and the great spirit "that tells us not to do so." Finally, he pointed out that "there would be an advantage to their Children, in learning to read, as the great Spirit pleased to enlighten their understandings and make them Sensible of this good Book; as well as many other benefits which will be likely to attend their Children, thus being Educated."

The results were gratifying. His inquisitors told Simmons, after some consultation, that they all approved of what he had said and suggested that he mention it to the rest of the people, "as there was some of them, who were averse to their Children being educated." And after this meeting the school "was much Larger than before," counting now between twenty and thirty pupils, several of them grown men, "and some of them anxious to learn, though many of them very tedious."

A week later another trial was imposed on Simmons: a runner arrived in haste from Buffalo Creek, saying "that one of their little Girls had Dreamed, the Devil was in all white people alike, and that the Quakers were doing no good among them, but otherwise, and it was not right for their Children to learn to read and write." The little community of Jenuchshadago held a council on this dream ("many of them put great confidence in their Dreams"), and a number of the people were frightened. Cornplanter, however, made fun of the story, saying that "he did not believe it, and had got very tir'd of hearing so much noise about their Dreams," and urged Simmons not to be discouraged. Simmons promptly and publicly branded the report as the whispering of bad white people and the work of the Devil. But the Devil, after all, was powerless against the plans of the Great Spirit. He therefore denounced such dreams as "nonsensical" and declared that he would "continue teaching them that would come." "The School was a little smaller for one day. But afterward was Larger than it had been at all."

Simmons was a forthright and sincere man who, when on the subject of religion, was apt to speak both bluntly and with passion. Two weeks later he became thoroughly exasperated with the "Danceing Frolicks" that were carried on to the din of tortoise-shell rattles almost every other night. These parties were the occasion of social dances at which "Men and Boys" danced and shouted "in such agitation" on account of a forthcoming dance that he could scarcely teach them anything next day. Simmons burst unannounced into Cornplanter's house and announced to the chief and his astonished family and friends that these frolics were "the Devils works" and that before he would suffer such doings in *his* house, he would "burn it to Ashes & live in a cave." Next day, when Simmons went to teach school, he found that the schoolroom was occupied by a formal council, to which, at last, and "in much fear," Simmons was summoned. But the apprehensive Simmons was much relieved to discover that he had won again! Cornplanter informed him that they had been counciling on the subject of these frolics, and had concluded (although they did not all see alike) to quit them, "for some of them thought it must be wicked, because they had Learned it of white people, as well as that of drinking Rum and Whisky & getting Drunk, which they knew was Evil." But the dances at their religious ceremonies they intended to continue.

Then they asked Simmons some questions on race relations: first, whether he "thought it was right for Indians & White people, to mix in marrying"; and second, whether "Indians & White people, went together to the same place after Death." To the first question, Simmons said, "It might be right for some to marry so, but thought it would not be right for me." The Indians then told him "of one of their Women who had a child by a White Man who then resided at

Pittsburgh, and never came to see any thing about his Child they thought the Great Spirit intended that every Man should take care & maintain his own Children." To the second question, Simmons declared "there was but two places, a place for the Good, and a place for the Bad, of all Nations of People," and when asked "whether all would be of one Language, When there," he answered "yes." "They seemed satisfied." Simmons then stood up and made a long speech denouncing "the Evil of many customs prevailing among them particularly that of Dancing, & Shouting, in such an hideous manner." He broke down in tears in the course of his peroration.

To support Simmons in his evangelical role there now emerged an unexpected ally—a young Seneca man who had had, a few nights before when out in the woods hunting, a prophetic dream. This dream he recounted to the council:

He thought an Indian Struck him twice with a Knife, when he fell, and thought he must Die, but soon appear'd to asscend upwards, some distance along a narrow path, in which appeared many tracks of People all going up some barefoot and some not; at length he came to a house, and the Door opened, for him to go in, which he did, where he beheld the beautifulest Man sitting that ever he saw in his Life; Who invited him to sit down, which he endeavoured to do, but could not, and tried to stop, & to talk. So passed on, out at a Door opposite to the one he came in at, when out, he heard a great noise and after travilling some distance he came to another building, which had an uncommon Larg Door, Like a Barn Door, in which a man met him, who looked very dismal, he Mouth appear'd to move in different shapes, from one side of his Face to the other, this person conducted him in, where he beheld numbers like Indians who seemed to be Drunken & very noisy, and looked very Distressed, some of whom he knew, who had been Dead several years.

Amongst them was one very old white headed Woman, whom they told him was dying, and when she went, the World would go too. There appeared to be a fire place on the ground, although he could not discern any thing but smoke & Ashes, of which their hair on their heads were Covered, He soon found he could sit and talk fast enough in this House, which he could not do in the other.

The person who conducted him in, who appear'd to be their officinator, gave him some stuff to Drink, Like melted Pewter, which he told him he could not take, but he insisted he should, by telling him he could Drink Wiskey & get Drunk, and that was no worse to take than it, he then took it, which he thouht burnt him very much, He then took a chain & bound round him, he asked him what that was for, he told him to prevent him from going after Women & other Men's Wives, He then told him to go strike a Woman, who was sitting there, which he attempted to do, but could not for his arms were off, He told him the reason of his loosing his arms, was because he had often been guilty of striking his Wife, And if he would entirely quit that practice, he should have his arms made whole again, and if he forsook all other Evil practices which he had been guilty of, he should have a Home in the first House which he enter'd. He was then bid to go home, when he awoke he found himself Crying, & could not tell his Dream for some time after, for Crying, for he knew it was true, And confest in the Council that he had been guilty of all those actions above mentioned.

And he added that "he intended to try to do better than he had done, and intended to learn to read."

Simmons, who in this case was willing to endorse dreaming, declared that it was his opinion that "his Dream was true," and pointed out to the Council that the old gray-haired woman in the dream was "the Mother of Wickedness who was Dying from among them, and when she was dead, the Worldly Spirit would go too." Cornplanter added piously, "The Devil would Die, if they tryed to do good."

And thus matters stood in the spring of 1799. Cornplanter and his family and a growing number of other Indians ranged themselves behind the Quakers, promising to send "a number of Boys, & some girls" to school, where Simmons should "do by them, as I would by my own Son, . . . to learn them to work, and correct them as they deserved." This group dominated the councils. But there remained a stubborn band who refused to see and think as Cornplanter did, who believed that the Quakers were up to no good, and who resented his high-handed interference with the traditional Seneca way.[80]

Handsome Lake's band of drunken hunters burst into this arena of tense and sober social consideration about the middle of May. They were probably unaware of the changed atmosphere. Cornplanter and his friends had been babbling for years about farming, and education, and temperance, but most of them had not been taking it seriously. All that they had seen was last summer three young men building a model farm nine miles north of the village. Handsome Lake's later memory of the time was lurid:

> Now that the party is home the men revel in strong drink and are very quarrelsome. Because of this the families become frightened and move away for safety. So from many places in the bushlands camp fires send up their smoke.
>
> Now the drunken men run yelling through the village and there is no one there except the drunken men. Now they are beastlike and run about without clothing and all have weapons to injure those whom they meet.
>
> Now there are no doors in the houses for they have all been kicked off. So, also, there are no fires in the village and have not been for many days. Now the men full of strong drink have trodden in the fireplaces. They alone track there and there are no fires and their footprints are in all the fireplaces.
>
> Now the Dogs yelp and cry in all the houses for they are hungry.[81]

And Simmons' contemporary diary confirms Handsome Lake's account:

> About the middle of the same [May], the Indians returned from Pittsburgh, with a quantity of Wisky, which caused much Drunkenness amongst them which lasted for several weeks and was the means of some of their deaths. One old Woman perrished out of doors in the night season with a bottle at her side; numbers of them going about the village from morning till evening and from evening until morning, in a noisy distracted condition sometimes fighting each other, and entering into the houses in a detestable manner, ready to pull others out of their Beds, even in the very house where I lodged myself, in the dead of the night also.

Simmons was not one to permit such a situation to prolong itself. He summoned his colleagues and the Seneca community, where (feeling himself to be "divinely favoured to communicate some pertinent & juditious Counsel to them on various Subjects, to the furtherance of Civilization and their future well being") he spoke out vehemently against "the great Evil of Strong Drink and of the many abominations it wrought in the Earth." The Seneca council deliberated for several days before delivering its answer through Cornplanter's mouth. But the answer, when it came, was a declaration of national reform:

They had made enquiry and conversed with each other about us, and said they could not find any fault with us, but found we were just and upright in all our ways of proceedings amongst them Etc. and that the fault and bad conduct lay on their own side, and wished us to be easy in our minds, for they would take our advice and try to learn to do better, they had concluded with a resolution not to suffer any more Wisky to be brought amongst them to sell, and had then Chosen two young men as petty Chiefs, to have some oversight of their people in the promotion of good among them, and that they intended to take up Work, and do as we said, would assist their Wives & Women on the Labour of the Field etc.

The village now began more seriously to undertake the work of reform, which had for so long been advocated by Cornplanter and others. The Indians who were settled near to the Friends' farm at Genesinguhta early in the spring set to work splitting rails and fencing in parcels of land. The Friends plowed a number of these lots for these enterprising Indian men. Other Indian males, unburdened with family responsibilities, hired themselves out to the Friends, "and seemed capable of doing as much in a day as the generality of white people." Meanwhile, at Jenuchshadago, the Indians had as early as March offered to assist the Friends in building a more commodious and convenient school, and in June the work of construction was well started at a site about half a mile from Cornplanter's house.[82]

Handsome Lake, however, did not participate in any of these activities. After the abrupt termination of the carousal in the middle of May, when the whiskey ran out and the council announced the temperance policy, he became sick and took to his bed in the cabin of his daughter and son-in-law. It may be that he was suffering from delirium tremens induced by the long carousal and by the inadequate nutrition that so often accompanies prolonged drinking (a particularly likely thing, since this was the hungry season anyway, with little to subsist upon but dried corn and traders' flour). Handsome Lake's mind was filled with thoughts of death. The spring performance of the Corn Planting Ceremony, and its attendant Death Feast, was conducted late in May, and the dead person whose soul was the subject of concern was none other than Cornplanter's daughter, who had died about February after a lingering six months' illness. Handsome Lake, whenever he could commandeer a bottle, sang the sacred songs to the dead, the *ohgiwe* cycle—a group of songs properly never sung except at the Feast of the Dead.

Witch fear began to preoccupy the village. It was suspected that Cornplanter's daughter had died by witchcraft at the hand of an old woman who had a reputation for poisoning the families of her enemies. Now she was said to be threatening the life of a baby just recently born into Cornplanter's household. This old woman even Simmons "took . . . to be a bad Woman." When Cornplanter heard of her threats, he ordered three of his sons to kill her. On June 13 they found her working in a field and in full view of the community stabbed her to death and buried her. A drunken Indian the same day had to be physically restrained by Simmons and another Indian from beating his wife "in a cruel manner" with his fists. The village was now considerably upset, and a chiefs' council was held to deliberate the slaying of the witch. The decision was that justice had been done and that in order to put away evil from the people, "those of familiar Spirits" must be driven out of the land.[83]

III

THE
RENAISSANCE
OF THE
IROQUOIS

8

PREACHING TO

REPENTANCE:

The First, or Apocalyptic, Gospel

W HEN THE MISERY OF POVERTY AND HUMILIATION IS COMBINED
with a hope of moral and material salvation, the resulting
mixture is explosive. Along the Allegheny, where the Quakers were
busily stirring these ingredients, an emotional explosion did occur, and
the sparks that ignited it were the prophetic visions of Handsome
Lake. Beginning with his first vision in June 1799, and continuing for
years thereafter, Cornplanter's brother articulated the dilemmas in
which the Iroquois were trapped and prescribed both religious and
secular solutions. His first preoccupation, expressed in his visions and
teachings from 1799 to 1801, was with apocalyptic themes: sin, damnation, and the destruction of the world. He condemned in particular
the drinking of whiskey and the practice of witchcraft and magic,
and urged his people to confess their sins, abandon their evil ways,
and achieve salvation before it was too late.

· *The First Vision of Handsome Lake* ·

IN THE SPRING OF 1799 Handsome Lake lay on his bunk, bound in
sickness by "some strong power," and pondered the cause of his illness and the disturbed state of his people. He feared that he would

soon die. Part of the time he was depressed and melancholy and thought that he must appear "evil and loathsome" in the eyes of the Creator. At other times, when he had whiskey, he would get drunk and in defiance of custom sing sacred songs. Then in remorse he would resolve never to touch alcohol again. At night, he would pray to see another day; with the dawn, he would feel gratitude to see the sunshine and hear the singing of the birds, and in proper Iroquois fashion would give thanks to the Creator. He brooded over the witches who had killed his niece. He was, in fact, suffering from the classic Iroquois bereavement syndrome compacted of depression, bitterness, and suspicion.

And then, on the morning of June 15, when the Strawberry Festival was due to be held, Handsome Lake had the first of the visions. Henry Simmons and Cornplanter were about half a mile from Cornplanter's cabin, Cornplanter directing some men in building him a new house, and Simmons and Joel Swayne busy constructing the schoolhouse, when a runner came to say that Handsome Lake was dying. This was not entirely unexpected news, for he had been "on the decline of Life for several years." Cornplanter left at once and found a number of people, including his nephew Blacksnake, assembled at Handsome Lake's cabin. The old man's daughter reported that they had been sitting outside the house in the shed, cleaning beans for the planting. The sick man had been within, alone. Suddenly through the open door they heard him exclaim, "*Niio!*"—"So be it!" Then they heard him rising in his bed, and heard him walking across the floor toward the door. Then the daughter saw her father, who was "but yellow skin and dried bones," coming out of doors. He tottered, and she rose quickly and caught him as he fell. They thought he was dead or dying, and so the husband ran off to fetch first Blacksnake and then Cornplanter, Handsome Lake's closest male relatives.

Blacksnake was the first to arrive. He asked, "Is he dead?" but no one answered, so he examined the body as it lay in the shed. There was no perceptible breathing or heartbeat, and the body was cool to the touch, so he went next door and got the neighbors to help him carry the body into the house, where they straightened it out. But in handling the body Blacksnake discovered a "warm spot" on the chest. Cornplanter, when he arrived, also found the spot of warmth. After about half an hour breathing began again, and then the pulse recovered, the "warm spot" spread, and at last, after two hours,

Handsome Lake's eyes opened and his lips began to move as if he wanted to speak. Blacksnake asked, "My uncle, are you feeling well?" And Handsome Lake answered, "Yes, I believe myself well."[1]

Then, after a pause, he began to describe his vision, which, as recorded at the time by the Quakers and remembered in oral tradition, was as follows. Handsome Lake heard his name called and left the house. Outside he saw three middle-aged men dressed in fine ceremonial clothes, with red paint on their faces and feathers in their bonnets, carrying bows and arrows in one hand and huckleberry bushes in the other. Handsome Lake collapsed from weakness, but the angels caught him and let him down gently. They told him they were sent by the Creator to visit Handsome Lake, whose constant thankfulness had earned him the right to help from his sickness.

After instructing him in the choice of medicine men (the appointed herbalists were his sister and her husband), he was told to join his kinfolk next day at the Strawberry Festival and report what the Creator had to say about how things should be on earth. He was to say that the Strawberry Festival should always be held and all the people must drink the berry juice. If he did not preach the message, he, like another reluctant prophet, would be buried in a hot, smoking place in the hollow between two hills visible across the river to the southeast. The message was contained in four "words" that summarized the evil practices of men about which the Creator was sad and angry. The four evil words are whiskey, witchcraft, love magic, and abortion-and-sterility medicine. People who are guilty of doing these things must admit their wrongdoing, repent, and never sin again, and a ritual was prescribed by which moderate sinners were to confess privately to Handsome Lake. The relatively innocent could confess in public; the most wicked of all were to confess alone to the Creator. The angels referred with approval to the recent execution of the witch but said a male witch still lived in the village. Handsome Lake himself they charged only with sometimes getting drunk and singing sacred songs while intoxicated; suffering, however, excused him. After threatening him that he must not drink even in private ("for the great Spirit knew not only what people was always doing but even their very thoughts"), the messengers left with the promise to return.

At the end of his narration Handsome Lake requested his brother Cornplanter "to Call his People in Council, and tell them what he had said to him, and if they had any Dried Berries amongst them, he wishes all in the Council might take if it was but one apiece." It was accordingly done, the same day, and "a large[r] number of them assembled with shorter notice than ever I had seen them before, men Women & children." Cornplanter related his brother's visions (for Handsome Lake was too weak to address the company), and Simmons and Swayne were present at Cornplanter's request and heard the vision recited through their interpreter, Henry. Simmons recorded the vision in his diary.

The relating of this vision produced a profound effect on its audience. Simmons, ever ready to empathize spiritually with others, observed that many of the Indians appeared to be "Solid and weighty in Spirit," and he "felt the love of God flowing powerfully amongst us." He was so moved that he was impelled to speak to the council. His message evidently was laudatory of the words of Handsome Lake, for it was well accepted and the prophet's sister came over after the meeting ended and thanked Simmons for what he had said to them.[2]

This was the beginning of the new religion.

· The Sky Journey ·

HANDSOME LAKE REMAINED in a generally poor state of health after the first revelation. He told Cornplanter that the three angels had said there was a fourth angel who had not been with them on their first visit but whom he would see subsequently. On the night of August 7 he dreamed that the fourth angel ("who appear'd like the Great Spirit") manifested himself and declared that he was now come to take him along, if he were willing, out of pity for his sufferings. Handsome Lake gave the angel no answer, but in the morning when he awoke he put on his best clothes and sent for Cornplanter. Cornplanter stayed with him through the day. About evening he fainted away briefly. On recovering his senses, he told Cornplanter that he must go, but not forever, for his people wanted him. He told his brother not to dress him for burial or to move him even if he appeared to be dead. After a little while he said that he was now going, but would return, and expected to see his son who had been dead several years and his brother's daughter who had been dead about seven months. And then he fell into a trance that lasted, he claimed later, about seven hours. His arms and legs were cold, his body warm, his breathing imperceptible.[3] During the trance Handsome Lake had the vision of the sky journey. Led by a guide who carried a bow and arrow and was dressed in sky-blue clothes, he traversed heaven and hell and was told the moral plan of the cosmos. This second vision would become the core of the new religion's theology.[4]

The course of the sky journey can be reconstructed from Henry Simmons' account, which was written down on August 10, two days later, probably from Handsome Lake's own lips (he "had then much recover'd of his sickness"), and from Parker's version of the later Code.[5] It began with Handsome Lake, the guide, and the other three messengers standing together on earth. "Suddenly as they looked, a road [the Milky Way]slowly descended from the south sky and came to where they were standing. Now thereupon he saw the . . . tracks of the human race going in one direction. The footprints [the individual stars] were all different sizes from small to great. Now moreover a more brilliant light than the light of earth appeared." This road, which they soon were treading themselves, was the path by which human souls ascended into the afterworld. On it could be observed, in various situations, many different types of people striving heavenward, and from its vantage point a vast panorama of the human scene could be observed below.

The vision took the form of a series of discrete visual scenes, upon each of which the guide made a moral commentary, rather like a lecturer running through a set of colored slides. The tour thus merely provided a rationale for the presentation of loosely connected thoughts. The tour began with a miscellany of images. They saw a fat woman, unable to stand; she represented the sin of stinginess and preoccupation with material things. They saw a large group of people divided into three sections, one large, one middle-sized, and one small; they represented, respectively, the unrepentant, the lukewarm, and the true believers in Handsome Lake's message. They saw a jail, and within it a pair of handcuffs, a whip, and a hangman's rope; this represented the false belief of some that the laws of the white man were better than the teachings of *Gaiwiio*. They saw a church with a spire and a path leading in, but no door or window ("the house was hot") and heard a great noise of wailing and crying; this illustrated the point that it was difficult for Indians to accept the confining discipline of Christianity. They saw two great drops of liquid hanging in the eastern sky, one red and one yellow, threatening to drop and spread death over the earth; they represented the danger from which Handsome Lake and the angels were trying to save mankind. Similarly they saw a large white object revolving in the sky near the setting sun; it regulated the air on the earth, and it too was under the control of the messengers of *Gaiwiio*. They met George Washington, sitting on the veranda of a house with his dog, halfway to heaven; he was the good white man, who at the Canandaigua Treaty told the friendless Iroquois to live happily in their own villages as long as the sun shines and the waters run, "for they are an independent people." They met Jesus, bearing nail scars on his hands and feet, and on his breast a bloody spear-wound. Jesus reported that his people had slain him in their pride and that he would not return to help them "until the earth passes away." He asked Handsome Lake how the Indians received his teachings. When Handsome Lake said that half his people believed in him, Jesus declared, "You are more successful than I for some believe in you but none in me. I am inclined to believe that in the end it will be so with you. Now it is rumored that you are but a talker with spirits. Now it is true that I am a spirit and the one of him who was murdered. Now tell your people that they will become lost when they follow the ways of the white man."

The second phase of the journey was a set of encounters at the fork in the sky road where human souls were directed, by judges stationed there, onto the narrow road that led to heaven or the wide road that led to hell. They saw that it was mostly children who were directed to heaven. They saw a repentant woman directed heavenward, and the messengers explained that each human being was given three chances to repent and follow *Gaiwiio* and that even a deathbed repentance was efficacious. And they saw a man's breast with a bullet hole in it hanging by the road as a sign to the unrepentant to turn left onto the wide, rough road to hell.

The third phase of the journey was a tour of the domain of the Punisher. In this Indian inferno were kept under eternal torture the souls of those who had committed great sins and failed to repent. Here Handsome Lake learned, in more vivid detail than in his first vision, the nature and punishment of evil. The Punisher was a protean monster of continually changing shape who occasionally took the form of the Christian devil with horns, tail, and cloven hoofs. He ruled a vast iron lodge, longer than the eye could reach, which they first viewed from a distance through a magnifying crystal. As they approached, they felt heat radiating from the lodge and nearly suffocated in the blasts of hot wind. Within were firepits and the damned, vainly stretching out their hands for help and shrieking ceaselessly in pain. The Punisher delighted in devising sadistic torments to fit the crimes of his prisoners: the drunkard was forced to swallow molten metal; the witch was alternately plunged into a boiling cauldron and chilled on the floor by its side; the wanton woman, who had been used to attract men with love powders, was forced to expose herself naked, gaunt, with rotting flesh and serpents writhing in her body hair; the wifebeater was forced to strike a red-hot image of a woman; a quarrelsome couple were compelled to dispute till their eyes bulged from their heads, their tongues protruded, and flames shot from their genitals; a promiscuous woman was made to fornicate with red-hot penes, white, red, and black; a violin player sawed away on his own arm with a glowing iron bar; card-players handled red-hot iron cards.

Having seen the tortures of the damned, the prophet and his guide now turned back to the fork in the great sky-road and began their journey again, this time up the narrow road that led to the lands of the Creator. They hurried along, smelling the flowers and admiring the delicious fruits by the side of the road and the birds flying in the air. They refreshed themselves at a spring whose clear water, once placed in a bottle, could not be exhausted. Handsome Lake met his dog, whom he had sacrificed at the white dog ceremony last New Year; it was still decorated as for the ritual, and when it saw Handsome Lake, it wagged its tail and sprang upon him. Shortly after this Handsome Lake met his own son and infant grandson and his niece, Cornplanter's daughter, still great with child. They, like the guide, were dressed in clear blue raiments. They all embraced, and then Cornplanter's daughter expressed her sorrow that her father and her brother Henry so often argued and became angry at each other, "her brother thinking he knew more than his father, and would not take his advice, but must have his own way, which was very wrong." And she told Handsome Lake to carry this message and bid the brothers to cease disagreeing with their father.

The allusion to the controversy between Cornplanter and his son Henry implied more than a domestic squabble between an unruly youth and an aging patriarch. Henry, the Philadelphia-educated son, was an extreme protagonist of "civilization" who went even farther than his father in advocacy of the white-man's technology and re-garded "native" customs, including the ancient religious traditions, with outspoken contempt. He was a rash and angry young man who proposed to find salvation by simply abandoning Seneca culture for white. And so now the guide launched gradually into an extended lecture on the things that the prophet, and the Indians generally, must do and must not do in order to achieve personal salvation from torture in the house of the Punisher above and collective salvation from physical annihilation on the earth below. The guide first told Cornplanter's daughter to stop "and said it was true what She said about her brother abusing his Father, for he ought to obey him, as long as he lives." Next Handsome Lake's son spoke, regretting that his father had suffered so much and that his other son then living had taken so little care of him and had even avoided him in his worst ill-ness for fear of having some trouble. The guide, agreeing, declared, "every Son ought to do good for their father."

The guide now went on to lecture Handsome Lake. He praised him for reporting his vision to the people, repeated the warnings against alcohol and witchcraft, and deplored the human tendency to confuse dreams inspired by the Great Spirit with those instilled by the Devil. He advised Handsome Lake that the dispute among the Allegany Indians over letting the Quakers instruct them in white ways was bad; everyone should agree, one way or the other. And he warned again that even though many people denied it, the Great Spirit "sees & knows all things and nothing is hid from Him!" And he threatened that unless the people mended their ways, thought more about the Great Spirit, and immediately conducted the white dog ceremony, a "great sickness" would come upon the village. Handsome Lake himself was advised that if his people took care of him and gave him medicine, he might soon be well. He was not to expect to see the angels again until his death, which would come when the hair on his head was half gray. Then, if he had done "right and good as long as he lived," he would be escorted to heaven by the angels once more, this time to stay.

The guide and the prophet took up their journey again but went only a short way before they stopped and the guide said, "We have arrived at the point where you must return. Here there is a house prepared for your eternal abode but should you now enter a room you could never go back to the earth-world." And so they parted, Handsome Lake returning to his people in the little village on the banks of the Allegheny River.[6]

On his recovery the prophet recited to his brother the events of the vision, and Cornplanter at once summoned a council to meet next morning. Henry Simmons, who was invited to attend, heard them discuss Handsome Lake's second vision. Simmons was asked whether he "believed it to be true"—for if the vision were "true," it bore major implications for Seneca behavior. Simmons's reply was encouraging. He told them that white people, too, including Quakers, sometimes had visions of heaven and hell and that he believed they were true revelations. Since Indians and whites were "all of one flesh & Blood made by the Great Spirit," he saw no reason why Handsome Lake's vision should not be valid, although, "perhaps, as there was so much of it, the man might not have recollected so as to tell it exact as he seen or heard it."

The Indians were pleased with Simmons's reaction, which confirmed their own, and in the afternoon of the same day they celebrated the Worship Dance, which the guide had recommended so strongly as a prophylaxis against the great sickness that threatened to end the world. They "prepar'd a White Dog to eat, and burnt his Skin to ashes During which time it was burning a number of them Circled around the Fire, Singing, Shouting & dancing greatly; after which they all partook of their Delicious dish, of Dog Meat Etc."

Next day Simmons went to Cornplanter's house "in order to make a note of the Sick Man Saying," and while there "the old Chief" (probably Cornplanter) fell into conversation with Simmons. Cornplanter felt obliged to advise Simmons of how his thinking now stood on acculturation as a result of his brother's visions: "The old Chief said he liked some ways of the white people very well, and some ways of the Indians also, and he thought it would take some length of time, to lead them out of all their own Customs, & as to their Worship Dance which they hold twice a year, they intended to keep it up, as they could not read, they knew of no other way of Worshiping the great Spirit, if they declined that they would have no manner of Worship at all. further said it was the white people who kill'd our Saviour how he had heard about our Savior I know not, but it seems he had." Simmons was quick to retort that it was the Jews who killed Christ, and perhaps the Indians were descendants of the Jews, in view of the similarity between some of their customs and those of the ancient people of Israel. But be that as it may, "we were all still, Crucifying & Killing Him, while we were doing Wickedly." Cornplanter meekly replied that "that was very true, very true."[7]

· The Third Vision ·

THE NEXT VISION of Handsome Lake took place six months later, on February 5, 1800. Since his health was now improving notably, the prophet related this vision himself in a council on March 2. The burden of this third revelation was that the Great Spirit was still troubled over the condition of the Indians. The three angels asked Handsome Lake whether the Indians had given up witchcraft and whiskey, and Handsome Lake said he did not know. They deplored the fact that the whites had taken away so much of their land and were so arrogantly sure that the mind of the Great Spirit was in their books. Handsome Lake was advised to have his revelations "written in a Book" so that the Indians could remember them always. The children were to be raised in the teachings of *Gaiwiio*. Cornplanter should visit all the towns of the Six Nations and try to bring unity among the chiefs. The people were to "keep up their Old form of worship . . . and must never quit it," particularly the Midwinter Ceremony, and the ritual leader known as "the Minister" must not despair or turn to drink. Handsome Lake was advised to devote half his life to his family and half to his mission.

By the time of this third vision Handsome Lake had gained the strong support of the one woman and the two men who were probably the most necessary adherents: his half sister Gayantgogwus, who, with her husband, was "the best of the medicine people"[8] and a power in the community, appearing at councils and speaking on behalf of the women; his brother Cornplanter, the political leader of the community; and the Minister. The three angels had appointed Gayantgogwus to make the medicines that cured the prophet. Cornplanter's role in publicizing the visions, in summoning councils to have them discussed, and in attesting loudly to their validity has already been noticed. The role of the Minister is more obscure to us now but was probably no less significant. It would appear from Henry Simmons's account that among the Allegany Seneca (and perhaps in other Iroquois communities as well) there was an individual who functioned as a part-time priest. No doubt he was the senior of the two male Headmen. In May, 1799, at the Worship Dance held at seed planting time, this Minister functioned as a master of ceremonies and moral adviser: "After they had taken two heats at dance, their minister (who was a very lusty Indian) said it was enough, and thanked them, and shortly after addressed them with a long speech by way of advice, after which they concluded the business with eating. . . ." Again in August, at the Green Corn Company, this same religious functionary played a prominent role in the Worship Dance: "At certain intervals, of their dances, some of the fore rank of men made Speeches to the company, by way of Preaching, especially one who was particularly called their Minister." And at the end of Green Corn, after the Bowl Game was concluded, the Minister led the salutation of the sun: "They were then closing the Scene which was done by Shooting Guns, about 50 men stood in a Longitude direction opposite their Wooden Image & shot twice or thrice up towards the Sun, their Minister Shot first, and so on."[9] It is tempting to suspect that this Minister was none other than that later disciple of the prophet, Joiise, who followed Handsome Lake in his hegira to Tonawanda and who was celebrated in the Code, after his death, as the "faithful and good" man with "commanding voice" who called the people together for the Great Feather Dance.[10] And to this man, as to Cornplanter, Handsome Lake's revelation of the Creator's concern for and about his human creatures came as a deeply felt reassurance.

· *The Apocalyptic Gospel* ·

WITH THE ANNOUNCEMENT of the third vision in the spring of 1800, Handsome Lake's first gospel had been essentially completed. This first gospel was apocalyptic and contained three major, interrelated themes: the imminence of world destruction; the definition of sin; and the prescription for salvation.

World destruction fantasies were pervasive. In addition to the threat of the great drops of fire and of the veil-over-all, Handsome Lake formulated other images of cosmic catastrophe. Although some of these additional prognostications are contained in sections of the Code that cannot be identified with revelations occurring on specific dates, we shall include them here because of their consonance with the predominant theme of this phase of the prophet's teaching. It is also possible that some of these apocalyptic fantasies were revealed during the journey over the great sky-road. They added up to a vivid account of how the world would end after a period of three generations. Signs of the coming apocalypse would be disagreements among the civil chiefs, among the Faithkeepers, and even among the Headmen. False prophets would arise. Crops would fail, and an inexplicable plague would kill many people. Witch women would boldly perform their spells in broad daylight and boast openly of how many they had slain. The poisonous creatures from the underworld would be released to seize and kill those who did not believe in *Gaiwiio*. The true believers would be spared the final catastrophe, simply lying down to sleep and being taken up to heaven by the Creator. At the last, the Creator would suspend all the powers of nature, and the earth would be enveloped in flames; the wicked would perish in the fire. Some other contemporary accounts of the prophet's teaching also emphasize the end-of-the-world theme. Thus an anonymous correspondent of the *Evangelical Intelligencer* in 1807 reported:

This prophet says, he has repeated visions, in which he sees three spirits or angels, who make communications to him. Sometimes in dreams or visions, he pretends to have seen devils flying, and hovering over their new town, Canadesago, seeking some place to light, but could find none, because the people were now orderly, temperate, and industrious; he saw them then fly to Buffalo Creek, and light among the whisky casks. Sometimes, he says, he has seen idle, drunken Indians, clothed in rags and filth, in old worn out canoes, on lakes at a distance from shore, clouds gathering in thick and black, with awful thunder, lightning and tempest. . . . He has stated to the Indians, that great judgments would follow them, if they disobeyed the commands of the Great Spirit, such as floods, droughts, &c. . . . He is deeply impressed with the opinion that judgments are coming on the nations, unless they reform.[11]

The second theme was sin. It is noteworthy that in most of these forecasts of universal disaster and individual damnnation it was specified that only the sinful and unrepentant would suffer. The all-encompassing sin, of course, was refusal to believe in and follow *Gaiwiio*, the gospel, which Handsome Lake was revealing. Belief in *Gaiwiio* was important, however, not because of the efficacy of pure faith, but because of its exclusive power to dissuade men and women from committing the great sins: witchcraft, love magic, abortion, drunkenness, and the various other evil practices specified in his description of hell. The listing of these sins constituted the second theme of the apocalyptic gospel. The definition of sin, of course, also constituted the groundwork for the second, or social, gospel.

The third theme of the early *Gaiwiio* was salvation. Men and women could preserve themselves from personal damnation and perhaps even delay the destruction of the world if they but believed in and followed the practices recommended by Handsome Lake. This meant, of course, first of all, confession and promise to sin no more by witches, purveyors of love magic, and abortionists; second, strict temperance; and third, the performance of correct ritual, pleasing to the Creator. Except for solitary confession, only public communal ritual, performed in the course of the great ceremonies of the annual calendar devoted to the Good Spirit, was permissible. And to these traditional observances he gave general sanction. Four rites were singled out as having particular virtue: the Worship Dance, which included the burning of the white dog; the Thanksgiving Ceremony, including the Great Feather Dance; the *adowe*, or individual sacred songs of thanksgiving; and the Bowl Game. Furthermore, the old organization of the Headmen and Headwomen, a man and a woman from each moiety, and of the Faithkeepers was endorsed and the people urged to obey these religious leaders.

Handsome Lake was thus not introducing a radically new religion; he was endorsing and reviving the old. He fully supported the ancient calendar of ceremonies, and his pantheon was isomorphic with the old, for the Creator of Handsome Lake's revelation was simply the ancient culture-hero Tarachiawagon, whose wooden effigy stood outside the council house; the Punisher was but Tawiskaron, the culture-hero's Evil Twin; and the four angels were in all likelihood the Four Winds of ancient belief. These deities were, of course, now revealed to have unsuspected powers and sentiments, but the revelation of these qualities and desires and the propriety of using new names in reference to old divinities was not upsetting to a people who were prepared for such progressive revelation by the customary usages of name change and by their theory of dreams. The idea of a cosmic struggle between the Good Twin and the Evil Twin had in the old mythology been relegated to the origin myth. Now it was

made a salient issue in contemporary life, with the two beings contesting for power over the minds of men on earth and ruling the
dead in heaven and hell. The principal cosmological innovation was,
in fact, the notion of heaven and hell itself. This had not hitherto
been a general belief among the Seneca, and some of his hearers
questioned the conception. Handsome Lake had this to say to them:

> Now it is said that your fathers of old never reached the true lands
> of our Creator nor did they ever enter the House of the tormentor,
> Ganos ge'. It is said that in some matters they did the will of the
> Creator and that in others they did not. They did both good and
> bad and none was either good or bad. They are therefore in a
> place separate and unknown to us, we think, enjoying themselves.

But Handsome Lake did propose several major ritual changes. One
of these had to do with the old medicine societies. Each of these hon-
ored a different animal spirit and called upon the power ("medicine")
of its tutelary to cure disease, chase witches, and divert natural catastrophes like tornado and drought. Their members often met in secret
and sometimes livened their proceedings with alcohol. Their membership was restricted to those who had been treated by the society.
Handsome Lake wished these secret medicine-societies to disband,
particularly the Society of Faces, whose wooden masks were made in
the image of the very being who in his theology was the Creator's
archenemy, the Punisher. Furthermore, secret meetings gave off to
his nostrils an odor of witchery, a taint of evil use of nature's powers.
And in the uncontrolled performance of these privately owned
rituals ardent spirits—the Punisher's principal weapon against virtue
—were freely employed. And so he commanded that all the medicine-
societies disband. But the people objected to the banning of the
medicine-societies and attributed the prevalence of illness to their
discontinuance, and eventually Handsome Lake compromised, sanctioning the rituals of the medicine-societies if strong drink was not
used. Furthermore, the societies should hold their feasts only on one
of the "great days" of the annual calendar, under the supervision of
the Faithkeepers, in public where all the people could see and
benefit.

A second major ritual change was the introduction of confession
as a major sacrament. The prophet believed although the earth-

world was full of sin, if all men would but repent "the earth would become as new again." He repeatedly emphasized the possibility of individual salvation through repentance even up to the point of death. In the old days, forcing a witch to confess under threat of death had been a traditional means of ending her power; but coupled with the notion of repentance as a condition of salvation and as the symbol of the acceptance of *Gaiwiio*, it gradually became a customary act even for those whose sins were less heinous. When the "Six Nations meetings" were devised after the prophet's death, a regular occasion for public confession was provided for every one.

The third major ritual change that Handsome Lake proposed—probably with little effect—was the elimination of anniversary mourning ceremonies. The prophet felt that too much attention was being paid to death and that the traditional ten days of mourning, followed by the funeral ceremony, was enough. Protracted grief merely added to the sorrows of the dead.

In all of these proposed ritual innovations it is noteworthy that Handsome Lake was minimizing the traditional ceremonial opportunities for cathartic relief of the unsatisfied wishes of the soul. He disapproved of the False Faces and of other old and new medicine-societies that had been formed in response to dreams; he deplored the indulgence of romantic fancies by the use of love magic; he grimly opposed any use of alcohol; he wished to do away with prolonged mourning. He demanded the repression of desire rather than its ritual satisfaction and offered in place of human beings the more abstract images of the Creator and the Punisher, of heaven and hell, and of the prophet as the objects of strivings for dependency.

His own role in the pantheon Handsome Lake cast at first in modest terms: he was merely a preacher, a messenger of the messengers. But within the year, as we shall see, his role as leader of the new religion was to become dictatorial and even grandiose; and on one occasion at least he presented himself as divine. This arrogation of personal supernatural power was based on revelation, too. In the fall of 1800 he was persuaded by the messengers that he was clairvoyant, able to see down into the earth as deep as the elm's root, and that it was his personal responsibility not merely to preach the gospel but also "to judge the earth and cure diseases." It was no mean responsibility, for as a shaman, with the messengers as his tutelaries, he had the power to diagnose witchcraft. And apocalyptic fears led him to use this power to launch the great witch hunt and to assume, for a short time, the unprecedented role of dictator of the Iroquois.

· *The Great Witch Hunt* ·

IROQUOIS SHAMANS practiced divination by several techniques. One was to drink a bowl of tea made from various roots and herbs while chanting an invocation to their guardian spirits. Then, by breathing on the sick person's head, chest, and body, the shaman could render it transparent and thus directly locate and identify the malady.[12] A second method was to interpret the dreams of the patient, for in the patient's dream, either manifestly or concealed in symbols, was often expressed the identity of the supernatural being or of the witch controlling the illness. A third method—known also among northern Algonquian hunters—was for the diviner to hide his head under a blanket until in dream or reverie the nature and cause of the illness was revealed. This was Handsome Lake's own method, and it was described as follows by a contemporary observer: "Sometimes sick persons send a shirt or some other article of clothing, to the prophet that he may prescribe a cure. In such a case, he takes two handfuls of tobacco, puts their ends to the fire on the hearth, lies down and covers himself with a blanket, after he has arisen he prescribes for the disease."[13] In many cases the diviner recommended the services of the appropriate medicine-society and the performance of the proper ritual (e.g., the Eagle Dance). In cases in which a witch was at fault several courses of action were open. One was to treat the "poison" itself. Witches were able magically to project into the body of their victim various irritating objects—splinters of wood or bone, a ball of hair, a worm, and so on. If the diviner or a colleague was able to extract this malefic article by putting fire ashes on the afflicted part and "drawing" it out into the poultice, he could then burn it or cast it back into the witch's body, injuring or destroying her. Or the witch could be attacked directly (even after the death of the victim) for purposes of revenge and for the protection of the rest of the community. If the witch could be brought to confess and to repent, by threats or physical torture or by such magical devices as burning the living heart of a blackbird, the witch's power would be broken. And as a last resort, the witch could be killed. Witches were believed to be jealous and hypersensitive persons who were likely to revenge themselves on people who offended them, not by poisoning the enemy himself, but by attacking his children and relatives. Thus the cure or death of a bewitched person did not imply an end of the matter; the real target of the witch's spite was, presumptively, still living, and he and all his kinfolk were still in danger.[14]

Handsome Lake professed reluctance to practice as a diviner. As soon as he announced that the angels had promised to make him a clairvoyant, his brother Cornplanter came running with tobacco for an offering and said, "Why, having the assurance of powers, do you not commence now. Come prophesy! My daughter is very sick." But Handsome Lake refused, claiming that final permission to use his powers had not yet been granted. Again Cornplanter made his request, more earnestly than before. This time when Handsome Lake refused, people began to say that Handsome Lake "would not respond to the cry of a brother and had no hearing for the voice of a brother." A third time Cornplanter came, asking that Handsome Lake use his clairvoyant power, and with him "the people," urging that, in the terms of his own vision, "Have we not something to say to you as well as the messengers of the Creator?" The reluctant diviner then was forced to admit that he did have an obligation to the people, and he promised, despite the lack of complete authorization from the angels, to do what he could. He went into a deep sleep (using the dream method of divination), and when he awoke he reported that in his vision he had learned that *ohgiwe* should be sung for the sick woman.

But Handsome Lake's niece—a young unmarried woman who had recently born a daughter—did not improve in health. By October she was gravely ill. The failure of *ohgiwe* to cure her was explained as the result of an incorrect performance of the ritual. Handsome Lake claimed that not only Jiiwi's illness but an epidemic of unnamed disorders was being abetted by the Seneca refusal to close the secret societies.

Other Seneca argued that the epidemic was the result of Handsome Lake's own interference with the traditional medical rituals. The mysterious illness of the young woman dragged on. Handsome Lake was persuaded to examine her; after examining her, he gave it as "his opinion" that she was "bewitched by several of those Muncy [Delaware] Indians combined together for that purpose," and that "the principle Muncy Chief" was one of the witches.[15] It seems that a young chief named Silver Heels (another account gives his name as John Logan) lived at the Delaware settlement at Cattaraugus. This was the small band of about thirty cabins, containing one hundred and sixty souls, who had moved here from their old village at West Hickory on the Allegheny about 1791. In the fall of 1799 Silver Heels had come down to Cornplanter's settlement to ask permission, as was the annual custom, for Delaware hunters to use the winter hunting grounds on the Allegheny, and as usual the Allegany Seneca had agreed. During his week's visit he stayed at Cornplanter's house, and he and Cornplanter's daughter Jiiwi slept together. Then the hunting party left, and the young chief with it. When the hunters returned, probably during the Midwinter festival period, the Delaware chief and the Cornplanter girl resumed their relationship. After a while the Delaware hunters went home to Cattaraugus. Cornplanter's daughter was pregnant; she gave birth; and then she became ill. Rumors began to circulate that a Delaware witch had poisoned the girl to save young Silver Heels the trouble of taking her as wife.[16]

The accusation against the Delaware was rendered plausible not only by the circumstances of the case but by the reputation that the Delaware held among the Iroquois for witchcraft. There had been trouble of this kind before: Back in 1749, on the Susquehanna, the granddaughter of the Cayuga viceroy Shickellamy had died, and then Shickellamy himself. Shickellamy's daughter-in-law and his sons accused a Delaware "conjuror," and next year a Delaware shaman was killed for "conjuring" several Indians to death.[17] Cornplanter's people, placing full reliance on Handsome Lake's judgment (he "is esteemed by us for his sobriety and knowledge in many things superior to any of our nation"), sent several messages to the Delaware, entreating them "to remove the cause of the woman's illness that peace and harmony might again resume its place between us." At last one of the principal persons accused came to Cornplanter's village. He was unable to effect a cure. Cornplanter's people therefore held him prisoner, a hostage for the woman's life. By about January it appeared that poor Jiiwi would not long survive.

A terrible dilemma now presented itself. The prophet had declared the illness to be a case of Delaware witchcraft. The Delaware denied the charge even though they had provided the services of one of their medicine men in an effort to help the sick woman. If the woman died, and if the Seneca in retaliation killed the hostage, war between the Seneca and the Delaware would be inevitable. Yet if they failed to take revenge, the authority of Handsome Lake and the sanctity of tradition would be violated. A council was held at Jenuch-shadago to deliberate the matter, with both chiefs and warriors present and the Cattaraugus Seneca represented by two principal chiefs. The council could not agree on whether or not the hostage's life should be forfeited if the woman died. Handsome Lake's advocates demanded death; others refused to sanction such an act and questioned Handsome Lake's wisdom. The council did agree, however, to ask for advice from the white people.

The Quaker missionaries at Genesinguhta were not eager to give advice. Sophisticated Quakers had long since given up their fore-fathers' beliefs in witchcraft and magic and censured any of their own members who fell prey to such ignorant superstitions. But they were hardly in a position to intervene in a local dispute or dissuade the Seneca from a belief that had just been emphasized by a prophet whose other preachings, such as temperance, they endorsed. Pre-occupied by the "frequent meetings, councils, dances &c," the people did not send their children to classes and the grammar school had to be closed down for want of pupils. The Friends were forced to be careful and guarded in their actions. "The subject has afforded us much exercise from time to time," they eventually reported, "but so intricately situated as to require much caution had we interfered . . . the distempered state of their minds through the enthusiasm and artful contrivance of their director exceedingly obstructed any counsel or advice being profitably received. The difficulty originated from an apprehension of injuries sustained by witchcraft are not uncommon for these poor Natives to be annoyed with."[18]

At last a desperate letter[19] imploring advice was dispatched to the nearest substantial white settlement, that of David Mead and his fellow pioneers at Cussawago, on the upper waters of French Creek. The chiefs did not know what to do if the woman died. Should they take life for life, "as it has been our custom"? Or should they spare the prisoner? They were sure that Handsome Lake, "The man we confide in that professes to search into these things tells us the truth as far as he sees." They were satisfied that he was "fully capable of explaining how they [i.e., witch's spells] were contrived and executed and tell us of many of those dark inventions which is the presant cause of our trouble." But still, some of the council did not believe that they should execute the prisoner if the woman died or that other persons accused of witchcraft by Handsome Lake should be subject to the same punishment. These liberal chiefs questioned explicitly whether the use or efficacy of witchcraft could be proven by the methods employed by Handsome Lake.[20]

The settlers at Meadville held a council of their own and hastened to reply to Cornplanter and his people, advising them not to kill the suspected witch even if Cornplanter's daughter died, but taking care not to cast aspersions on Handsome Lake's good intentions. David Mead then proceeded in haste to Lancaster to deliver Cornplanter's letter to the Governor of Pennsylvania. Word also was sent to the Indian superintendent at Canandaigua that the Seneca were threatening war against the Delaware unless they discontinued their witchcraft, and this news was duly reported to the office of the Secretary of War in Washington.[21]

By April the Delaware at Cattaraugus had heard of the Cussawago settlement's efforts to intervene in the matter, and wrote on their own account to David Mead and his friends, requesting aid and blaming the trouble all on Handsome Lake. "The Accation of this great dispute is on account of Cornplanters Brother who says he has conversed with God the Great Spirit—We are accused of witchcraft which our people is entirely strangers to and puts no belief in. Also our Brothers the White people we think is of the Same Oppanion." This letter too was discussed at a council at Cussawago and then was sent posthaste to the Governor at Lancaster. The Delaware at Cattaraugus also appealed to their fellow tribesmen in Ohio, and as a result "a number of Indians of the Muncy and other tribes to the amount of about two hundred, are collected in New Connecticut near the line of Pennsylvania, that they, have left their families behind and are prepared for war, waiting to join their Brethren in case the existing dispute should not be amicably settled."

By May the Quakers in Philadelphia had learned from the Governor of Pennsylvania of the threatening conflict and prepared a message to both the Seneca and the Muncy, advising them both to hold back from bloodshed and denying that there was any such power as witchcraft. In a companion letter to the Muncy, also enjoining peace, the Friends observed that the Bad Spirit had been at work "among some of the Seneca nation" and that they had written to the Cornplanter Indians "to take the dust out of their eyes" so that they could distinguish between the promptings of the Good and the Bad Spirit.

Although Cornplanter's daughter clung unexpectedly to life, the controversy generated by her illness was transformed by Handsome Lake into a wider problem. A general council of the Seneca was convened at Buffalo Creek in June 1801, at which delegates from all Seneca villages, including those in Canada, for three days discussed both the Delaware witchcraft case and the issue of witchcraft in general. Handsome Lake had by now articulated the general thesis (already implicit in Iroquois culture) "that most of their bodily afflictions and disorders arose from witchcraft," that he was authorized by the Creator "to tell the Individuals who are afflicting these disorders on other Individuals," and "that the Whiskey is the great Engine which the bad Spirit uses to introduce Witchcraft and many other evils amongst Indians."[22] At the council at Buffalo Creek he accused "sundry old women & men of the Delaware Nation, and some few among [his] own nation" of the sin of witchcraft. The council deliberated, it is said, for three days on the question of punishment and at last determined "that those persons accused of Witchcraft should be threatened with Death, in case they persisted in bewitching the People."[23] One of those whom he accused was none other than his nephew Red Jacket, the speaker of the Seneca nation.

The confrontation between Handsome Lake and Red Jacket was precipitated by an argument over land. One of the issues brought to discussion at the Buffalo Creek council in June 1801, was the proposed sale of a strip of land along the Niagara River (the Black Rock corridor), which, as a favorite fishing place of the Seneca, had been left unsold in 1797 but was now desired by the white people for the security of their road to Niagara Falls from the head of navigation on Lake Erie.[24] Many Seneca objected not only to the idea of a sale to New York, but even to the present situation, which allowed the whites to maintain a fort at Black Rock to protect the road through their territory and to encroach by the road on their fishing ground.[25] And of those who objected, Handsome Lake was foremost, basing his opposition on the grounds of a special revelation he had received from the four angels.[26] Red Jacket (possibly representing the council) favored the sale. According to later report Handsome Lake publicly denounced Red Jacket "at a great council of Indians, held at Buffalo Creek, and [Red Jacket] was put upon his trial." Red Jacket, however is reported to have exculpated himself, speaking in his own defense for three hours and accusing Handsome Lake of manufacturing his visions and his charges of witchcraft for the purpose of restoring the fallen fortunes of his discredited brother Cornplanter. The sympathy of a small majority of the council lay with Red Jacket, and he was exonerated, although the council did endorse the prophet's opposition to witchcraft.[27] Handsome Lake's response was to immortalize, in dubious color, his rival Red Jacket in the Code. In a vision Handsome Lake saw Red Jacket in torment in Hell:

> Then the messengers pointed out a certain spot and said, "Watch attentively," and beheld a man carrying loads of dirt and depositing them in a certain spot. He carried the earth in a wheelbarrow and his task was a hard one. Then he knew that the name of the man was Sagoyewatha, a chief. Then asked the messengers, "What did you see?" He answered, "I beheld a man carrying dirt in a wheelbarrow and that man had a laborious task. His name was Sagoyewatha, a chief." Then answered the messengers, "You have spoken truly. Sagoyewatha is the name of the man who carries the dirt. It is true that his work is laborious and this is for a punishment for he was the one who first gave his consent to the sale of Indian reservations. It is said that there is hardship for those who part with their lands for money or trade. So now you have seen the doom of those who repent not. Their eternity will be one of punishment."[28]

According to Seneca tradition, Handsome Lake's "slanders" against Red Jacket, both at home and in Washington, for a time cost him his status as Seneca tribal speaker and ultimately prevented his elevation to a sachemship.

The major action of the council was to prohibit the use of liquor and to appoint Handsome Lake "High Priest, and principal Sachem in all things Civil and Religious."[29] In the Code it is recorded that "all the people assembled and with one accord acclaimed that Ganio'dai'io' should lead them and that they should never murmur." As one of the chiefs expressed it, Handsome Lake had been "deputed by the four Angels to transact our business" and the people "have perfect confidence in Handsome Lake are willing to lend an Ear to

his instructions and yield Obedience to his precepts. To him they
have entrusted all their Concerns to be governed by his direction,
wisdom and Integrity."[30] Cornplanter, presumably satisfied that the
Delaware witches had repented, told the Munsee that "He had swept
their beds clean, that they might lie down in peace—that he had
swept clean before their doors, that they might go out and in without
molestation."[31] The Delaware band, however, was so disillusioned by
the whole episode that they migrated en masse to the more tolerant
atmosphere of Buffalo Creek and later to the Grand River Reservation in Canada.

Handsome Lake's position now was virtually, if only briefly, that
of a dictator. He could claim that the Cornplanter girl's survival and
the relaxation of tension between the Seneca and the Delaware were
the result of his forthright stand against the witches. He prepared,
therefore, to destroy the power of witchcraft among the Seneca,
with virtually full approval, or at least acquiescence, of the entire
Seneca nation. The virulence of Handsome Lake's hatred for witches
was unbounded. He believed that, as the angels told him, witches
were the agents of the Evil Spirit, responsible for almost all sickness
and disease and working to destroy the world itself. If they were not
checked by good men who believed in Handsome Lake's message,
the world would come to an end. Although no one as yet, since the
killing of June 13, 1799, had been executed for witchcraft, according
to tradition Handsome Lake now proceeded to hunt out the witches.
There are, however, no specific, documented accounts of executions
during Handsome Lake's sojourn at Jenuchshadago, and in all probability not many women (for Handsome Lake's charges were generally made against women) were killed there. Local legend recalls
one execution, but this case is sufficiently reminiscent of the killing of
June 13, 1799, to be possibly a distorted recollection of that event.
According to the story Handsome Lake diagnosed the illness of a
woman as being the result of witchcraft. He accused an old lady who
lived by herself and did her own planting. When Handsome Lake and
his cohorts visited her and voiced the charge, she merely replied,
"How do you know?" He took her hand and pointed to a mark on
it that indicated that she was a witch. Then she asked him, "What do
I use to bewitch people? You are a prophet. Show me plainly so that
I can see." He could only repeat, "You *are* a witch." So he told his
men to kill her. There was a fierce struggle, for she was a big woman

and could fight like a man; she seized the blade in the hands of her executioner and her hands were cut. At last they killed her.[32] The probable reason for the rarity of such events was that Handsome Lake's revelation allowed witches the opportunity to confess and repent. Thus accused persons or persons who feared accusation could publicly, or privately before Handsome Lake, "confess" their sin and receive his absolution.

THE POLITICS OF
EVANGELISM:

The Second, or Social, Gospel

B EGINNING IN THE FALL OF 1801 AND INCREASINGLY IN THE YEARS
thereafter until his death in 1815, Handsome Lake presented a
second gospel, which emphasized the value in daily life of temperance, peace, land retention, acculturation, and domestic morality. His
ideas on these subjects were drawn in part from the progressive, pro-
acculturation faction among the Allegany Seneca, in part from the
federal officials who backed his movement, and in part from the local
Quaker model. The social gospel was something of a departure from
his first, extremely conservative position, however, and it earned him
the opposition of the conservatives. In the end his own political
situation became precarious as his demand for dictatorial power
alienated the progressives, the Quakers, the federal establishment, and
even conservative Indians, and he was even forced for a time to leave
Cornplanter's band. But although his political fortunes failed, he and
his disciples continued to carry the good word to other Iroquois
reservations, and even other tribes, and initiated a dramatic renaissance of Iroquois society.

· *Concessions to the Progressive Faction* ·

ALTHOUGH IN PIOUSLY CONDEMNING WITCHCRAFT and alcohol Handsome Lake was in tune with traditional Seneca morality, people from

the beginning had questioned the wisdom or even the rightness of particular executions. He had aroused criticism by his ambivalence about the adoption of European arts. Cornplanter had long favored extensive acculturation. Henry O'Bail, his son—the only "educated" man among the Seneca—had taken the Quaker advice seriously to heart and was now a sober man, owner of a herd of "eleven horned cattle." In the fall of 1801 O'Bail was found by the visiting Friends' committee splitting rails for an acre of cleared land on which he intended to plant wheat. He had moved from Jenuchshadago to the neighborhood of Genesinguhta and planned to build a house next spring. Henry O'Bail had been at the great witch council at Buffalo Creek along with his brother Charles Halftown and some others of the men who had been friendly with the Quaker visitors. At this council, despite the weight of the chiefs' opinion in favor of Handsome Lake, Henry O'Bail and four other young warriors had spoken out publicly against his advice. Handsome Lake had declared "that they should not allow their children to learn to read and write; that they might farm a little and make houses; but that they must not sell anything they raised off the ground, but give it away to one another, and to the old people in particular; in short that they must possess everything in common." On his return to Jenuchshadago Henry told his father Cornplanter that "he thought it would be much better for them to hold Councils about making fields than about witchcraft & dances & such things."

This kind of opposition enraged Handsome Lake's more ardent followers, for opposition was in itself a sign to them of evil, perhaps even of witchcraft. One of the "younger" men was quickly brought "under trial for some disrespectful expressions relating to the business." Cornplanter himself was caught neatly in the middle. His brother had to a degree usurped his former power and now was undoing much of the work of civilization that Cornplanter so laboriously had nourished, particularly in the area of education. He had been, apparently, somewhat uneasy about the Delaware witchcraft case and came back from the Buffalo Creek council with a less than cheerful countenance. For two months the two men seem to have maintained a silent struggle. The denouement was finally precipitated by the renewed request of the Friends that the children and young men be instructed in reading and writing. In October 1801, a council to discuss the matter was held, at which Cornplanter—whose "mind was become quite different from what it was two months ago"—spoke in favor of education. Handsome Lake opportunely conceded that "the white people were going to settle all around them; that they could not live unless they learned to farm, and follow the white people's ways, etc."[1]

Handsome Lake had little choice. Whatever their religious feelings, the majority of the Seneca favored technical acculturation. The strategy of the majority of the Seneca chiefs was to secure grants in aid of civilization in return for making certain minor adjustments in the boundaries of the reservations to accommodate the government or the land companies. Although Handsome Lake was opposed to land sales on principle and had a distaste for the white man's customs, the credibility of his role as political leader would be compromised if he maintained a minority opinion before the councils. To be sure, he had been publicly appointed to be the censor of the Seneca nation. But the Seneca were not accustomed to censors and were not prepared to obey a dictator against their own better judgment.

And so Handsome Lake acceded to the proposal, announced by Red Jacket as chief speaker of the Seneca nation at a council at the Genesee River in November 1801, to exchange various minor bits and pieces of land in New York for reforms in the annuity system and for a federally supported program of technical aid. The Iroquois were willing to sell the strip of land at Black Rock that had occasioned the bitter dispute between Handsome Lake and Red Jacket earlier that year. They would surrender to the Holland Land Company the small reservations along the Genesee River in return for adjustments in the boundaries at Cattaraugus and Buffalo Creek. They wished to have their annuity goods paid henceforth in coarse warm cloth like flannel rather than fine broadcloth, in order to keep the old men, women, and children from the cold winds and snow of winter; and they wanted all the cash annuities from the various treaties regularly deposited in a national fund in the Bank of the United States rather than diffused in useless small payments to individuals. And they wanted to be civilized (although not Christianized). Specifically, they requested oxen to plow the ground ("which would relieve our women from digging"), pigs, sheep, cows to provide milk, butter, and cheese, farming equipment to raise wheat and other grain, and spinning wheels. Neither Handsome Lake nor his rival Red Jacket was inclined toward Christianity, and the Christian party had not yet formed.

· *The Visit to Washington* ·

IN ORDER TO PRESS THIS PROPOSAL FURTHER, in the winter of 1801–02 representatives of each of the Six Nations, excepting the Mohawk, made plans to visit the new seat of the federal government in Washington, D.C.[2] This visit would increase the pressure on Handsome Lake to support the progressive faction by acquainting him directly with the President of the United States and his interest in the civilization of the Indians. It also focused his attention on the need to concern himself with other social issues, particularly the unsettled land issues. A preliminary letter was written to President Jefferson in January, and Jefferson replied with a cordial invitation to come to the seat of government to discuss land questions and technical assistance. The leader of the Seneca delegation was Handsome Lake, and with him traveled Cornplanter, the Tonawanda chief Blue Sky, and several warriors. Some of the young men, the Delaware in particular, enjoyed a gay time on arrival in Washington, and their Quaker hosts remarked that "their Conduct has been such as we very much disapprove in various Aspects."[3] The general purpose of the visit was to secure from the United States the promise of technical aid; and in this the visit was successful. Plows, oxen, yokes, chains, milch cows, sheep, carding and spinning equipment, were ordered to be distributed among the several reservations, and the Congress appropriated $15,000, to be renewed annually, to "civilize" the Indians of the United States.[4]

But Handsome Lake's plans reached beyond the securing of material aid for the nation. He made this visit the occasion for securing the blessing of the government of the United States on his new religion and his pretensions to leadership of the Seneca. Such an endorsement would, if obtained, not merely constitute additional validation of his mission; it would also serve to block his rival, Red Jacket, from obtaining federal support in the internecine struggle. Furthermore, he wanted the Oil Creek Reservation assigned to him as a personal estate.

Handsome Lake's first address to the President was, significantly, couched in egalitarian terms. "Brother," he began, "I thank the Great Spirit above that I have a very bright day to talk with the Great Chief of our white Brothers. It is the Great Spirits doing." Having thus pointed out how the Great Spirit favored his enterprises even in small details like the weather, he went on to explain his divine commission: "The Great Spirit has appointed four Angels and appointed me the fifth to direct our people on Earth. I thank the Great Spirit that the Great Chief of my white Brother is well and hearty. This is the first year since the Great Spirit appointed me to guide my people and give them knowledge, good from bad. He directed me to begin with my own people first and that is the Reason why I have been so long in coming to my white Brother."

He next took note of the problem of intergroup relations, pointing out that whisky and land cessions were the root of the troubles. Both parties were at fault. "I am very much troubled," he observed, "to find that my Brothers and my White Brothers have gone astray." The guilt of the Indians lay in drunken quarreling. Drink was the reason why whites and Indians did not live like brothers. "I have now come forward to make us love one another again with your assistance." The white people, for their part, were guilty because of their seizure of the Indians' land, and "the Great Spirit has told me to come and tell them of it." He asked for "a Writing on Paper for it, So that we can hold it fast." Handsome Lake also pointed out to the President that there was some urgency to his demands. "If we do not Settle all our business that we are now on, the Great Spirit will send a Great Sickness among us all. But if we can Settle all our Business, Health and Happiness will come and the Seed of the People and the Fruit will come forward."

Having thus let President Jefferson know in outline what the Great Spirit expected of him, Handsome Lake went on to expound his apocalyptic doctrine further. His revelation, he explained, was by no means intended only for Indians: it was the duty of all the people of the earth to attend carefully and to obey, on pain of divine punishment. The President of the United States, as leader of a great nation, had a special obligation to heed the prophet's requests and to negotiate only with those persons appointed by him as the "fifth angel" and the director of mankind:

Our lands are decaying because we do not think on the Great Spirit, but we are now going to renew our Minds and think on the great Being who made us all, that when we put our seeds in the Earth they may grow and increase like the leaves on our Trees. The four angels appointed with me to direct the People on Earth to tell me that if any Man whatever he may be will look on the Great Being above us all and do his will on Earth, when his days are out and the angels find he is a good man they will grant him more days to live in the World and if he lives a good Man, doing no Evil in those days, when these days are out the Great Being will take him to himself. The like of this was never known before these four angels empowered me to relieve any man of any wickness whatever it may be, if he be a good man, who looks up to the Great Spirit above but if he be a bad man and does not look up to the Great Spirit, I cannot relieve him and he cannot be helped if he be fond of liquor.

Dear Brother, the Lord has confidence in your people as well as ours, provided we can settle all our Business. He will take care of us first, and you afterwards if you will Take Notice of the voice of the Angels. The four Angels desired me to pick out two young men of my people, that I know to be sober, good young men, to take care of all our Public business. They are Charles O Beal and Strong. Here is my Brother Captain Cornplanter. He is cried down by the Sachems of Buffalo Creek which you very well know. But it is not my wish for I very well know that he has done his Endeavour for the Benefit of our nation. He is a Sober man and endeavours to make all our young men Sober and good—the Sachems at Buffalo Creek are all drunken men and dislike him. I, who am now Talking to you, would wish you to know, that half of my Spirit is here on Earth yet, and the other half is with the Great Spirit above and I wish you to consider my Business and my Nation well, that we may Continue friends and Brothers and when that takes place I will be thankful to the Great Chief of my white Brothers and to the Great Spirit above us all. We will be good friends here and when we will meet with the Great Being above we shall have bright and happier Days. Dear Brother, that is all I have got to say because I know you have got the Word of the Great Spirit among you.[5]

The President's reply was conveyed by his secretary of war, Henry Dearborn, on March 10. Dearborn began by telling his "Brothers"—Handsome Lake and the Seneca and Onondaga delegations—that their "father and good friend, the President of the United States," had thought over their message carefully "since you took him by the Hand three days ago." The President declared that if all the red people followed the advice of their friend and teacher Handsome Lake and were "sober, honest, industrious and good," there was no doubt that the Great Spirit would make them happy. He accepted the admonitions of the prophet concerning the evils of strong drink and reported that the Congress was considering a law to prohibit the use of alcohol by Indians resident within the United States. And he agreed to provide a "writing on paper" that guaranteed that their land could not be taken by anyone except by their own consent.

Encouraged by this friendly and cooperative response, Handsome Lake and his colleagues went on to more particular issues in a second address, delivered two days later. These issues chiefly concerned land, and Handsome Lake now revealed the increasing anxiety that he felt about the territorial security of the Iroquois. "The Four Angels have directed," he announced, that the Indians should receive "separate Deeds" for each reservation. An existing deed to the Cattaraugus and Allegany reservations and a map showing the survey lines had been lost, and he wanted a copy lest the occupants, unable to prove ownership, be dispossessed. He wished to be given a personal deed to the Oil Spring Reservation, "of ten miles square for the exclusive use, benefit and comfort of myself." The Great Spirit himself expected him to be "importunate" about securing the territory of the Indians. But if the matter could be satisfactorily concluded, then "the remainder of our days will be devoted to agriculture and such other pursuits, as are calculated to render life comfortable to ourselves and pleasing in the sight of the Great Spirit."

The President's second response, again communicated to the prophet and his associates by the secretary of war, was equally friendly. He proclaimed officially that all Seneca and Onondaga reservations established by treaty, convention, or deed of conveyance were Indian property, protected by the laws of the United States, and that the Indians could, if they wished, hold them "forever." He promised to look into Handsome Lake's claim to the Oil Spring Reservation (and eventually it was secured to the Seneca).

The Seneca party now set off on their return to the Allegheny, armed with copies of the speeches by the secretary of war, the territorial guarantee, a civil and military passport, one hundred dollars, and an order on the commandant of Fort Pitt to supply the travelers with money, provisions, and a shirt, axe, and hoe to each and every Indian.[6]

But Handsome Lake's anxieties about the territorial security of the Seneca were still active when he reached home. Some time late in the summer he wrote a letter (unfortunately now lost) through the local subagent, Callendar Irvine, to the President, again complaining about whiskey and iniquitous land sales of the recent past, particularly the sale of parts of the Oneida, Cayuga, and Onondaga reservations. The Secretary of War replied at once with praise for Handsome Lake's temperance program and with defense of the cessions, pointing out in the latter connection that it "must be presumed that your Chiefs would not have sold any part of your land unless they were satisfied that the sale would meet the approbation of the majority of the nation."[7] And a week later, on November 3, 1802, President Jefferson himself wrote to Handsome Lake on the matter:

Washington, November 3, 1802. Brother Handsome Lake: I have received the message in writing which you sent through Capt. Irvine, our confidential agent, placed near you for the purpose of communicating and transacting between us whatever may be useful for both nations. I am happy to learn you have been so far favored by the Divine Spirit, as to be made sensible of these things which are for your good and that of your people, and of those which are hurtful to you; and particularly that you and they see the ruinous effects which the abuse of spiritous liquors have produced upon them. It has weakened their bodies, enervated their minds, exposed them to hunger, cold, nakedness, and poverty; kept them in perpetual broils, and reduced their population. I do not wonder then, brother, at your censures, not only on your people, who have voluntarily gone into these fatal habits, but on all the nations of white people who have supplied their calls for this article. But these nations have done to you only what they do among themselves. They have sold what individuals wish to buy, leaving to everyone to be the guardian of his own health and happiness. Spirituous liquors are not in themselves bad. They are often found to be an excellent medicine for the sick. It is the improper and intemperate use of them, by those in health, which makes them injurious, but as you find that your people cannot refrain from an ill use of them, I greatly applaud your happiness

to place the paltry gain on the sale of these articles in competition
with the injury they do you; and as it is the desire of your nation
that no spirits should be sent among them, and I am authorized by
the great council of the United States to prohibit them, I will
sincerely co-operate with your wise men in any proper measures
for this purpose which shall be agreeable to them.

You remind me, brother, of what I have said to you when you
visited me the last winter, that the land you then held would remain yours and should never go from you but when you should
be disposed to sell. This I now repeat, and will ever abide by. We,
indeed, are always ready to buy land; but we will never ask but
when you wish to sell; and our laws, in order to protect you
against imposition, have forbidden individuals to purchase lands
from you; and have rendered it necessary, when you desire to sell,
even to a state, that an agent from the United States should attend
the sale, see that your consent is freely given, a satisfactory price
paid, and report to us what has been done, for our approbation.
This was done in the late case of which you complain. The
deputies of your nation came forward in all the forms which we
have been used to consider as evidence of the will of your nation.
They proposed to sell the state of New-York certain parcels of
land, of small extent, and detached from the body of your other
lands. The state of New-York was desirous to buy. I sent an agent
in whom we trust, to see that your consent was free, and the sale
fair. All was reported to be free and fair. The lands were your
property. The right to sell is one of the rights of property. To
forbid you the exercise of that right would be a wrong to your
nation. Nor do I think, brother, that the sale of lands is, under all
circumstances, injurious to your people; while they depended on
hunting, the more extensive forests around them, the more game
they would yield. But, going into a state of agriculture, it may be
as advantageous to a society as it is to an individual who has more
land than he can improve, to sell a part and lay out the money in
stocks and implements of agriculture, for the better improvement
of the residue. A little land, well stocked and improved, will yield
a great deal more [than] without stock or improvement. I hope,
therefore, that, on further reflection, you will see this transaction
in a more favorable light, both as it concerns the interest of your
nation, and the exercise of that superintending care which I am
sincerely anxious to employ for their subsistence and happiness.
Go on, then, brother, in the great reformation you have under-
taken. Persuade our red men to be sober and to cultivate their

lands; and their women to spin and weave for their families. You will soon see your women and children well fed and clothed; your men living happily in peace and plenty, and your numbers increasing from year to year. It will be a great glory to you to have been the instrument of so happy a change, and your children's children, from generation to generation, will repeat your name with love and gratitude forever. In all your enterprises for the good of your people you may count with confidence on the aid and protection of the United States, and on the sincerity and zeal with which I am animated in the furthering of this humane work. You are our brethren of the same land; we wish your prosperity as brethren should do. Farewell!

Th. Jefferson[8]

This correspondence—copies of which were treasured and displayed—was of supreme importance to Handsome Lake and to his followers, for it proved the sanction of his mission by the highest authorities of the land.

· *The Quaker Model* ·

THE QUAKER MISSIONARIES maintained a silent pressure on the prophet and on the rest of the Seneca by constantly presenting both a model of impeccable personal conduct and an example of economic and intellectual enterprise whose practical advantages were vividly manifest. This Quaker program the prophet adopted almost—but not quite—in its entirety. It was consistent and cumulative. Friends rigidly adhered to a policy of refusing any opportunity to profit personally from their transactions, giving much equipment and instruction gratis and lending or selling other items at cost. Rather than take up Indian land, they bought a tract off the reservation for the model farm. This absence of economic self-interest, together with a general discreetness in their criticism of native religious beliefs (including the belief in witchcraft), made more palatable their forthright opposition to other areas of custom, such as drunkenness, social dances, illiteracy, and inefficient technology. The core of the program was presented in 1798 and remained constant; new elements and additional rationalization were offered as needed. This program may be analyzed as follows:

1. Presentation of the model of an advanced white rural community

The major part of the energy spent by the Quaker mission was devoted to constructing and operating a model farm (at first at Genesinguhta, on the reservation, and then, from 1803 on, nearby at Tunessassa on land purchased from the Holland Land Company). The farm was self-supporting to the extent that the occupants lived on their own produce; but it maintained economic relationships with the surrounding white and Seneca communities, particularly in buying hardware and cattle from white traders down the river and dispensing surplus farm produce and equipment to the Seneca. In order to facilitate this local trade, the Quakers advised the Indians to construct serviceable roads. Furthermore, the Quakers established various special facilities and services essential to a rural white community: a sawmill and a gristmill at Tunessassa, a spinning and weaving shop, and a smithy. At the farm the Quakers maintained barns, stables, and a complete set of farm equipment, including not only field tools but carpenter's, mason's and cooper's tools as well. They lived in a well-constructed two-story, pine-shingled, painted dwelling-house with cellar, stone and clay chimney, and glass windows. There the Indian visitor could see, handle, and feel the material apparatus of white rural life: scythes, bar iron, nail rods, cartwheels, sickles, felling axes, drawing knives, mill picks (to make grindstones), shoemaker's tacks, dishcloths, camp kettles, towels, soap, plow irons, augers, spinning wheels, looms, beds, chairs. . . . Furthermore, they could observe the Quakers as they went about their various tasks: the men felling trees, building fences, plowing, sowing, reaping, caring for livestock, making and repairing equipment, keeping written accounts; the women dairying, cooking and preserving foods, making soap, laundering, housecleaning, knitting, spinning and weaving, repairing clothes; the children (after a few years) doing their chores. They were able to see the apportionment of these tasks to those properly responsible, according to the seasons of the year and to the appropriate times of the day, and to note at close range the personal habits of cleanliness, sobriety, punctuality, and orderliness that were virtues in this way of life.

2. Keeping a formal school of the three R's and the manual arts

In the winter of 1798–9 Henry Simmons opened a grammar school
in one of the rooms of Cornplanter's house at Jenuchshadago. In 1799
a separate schoolhouse was built near the village, but it was abandoned
as a school at the time of the Delaware witchcraft crisis and apparently was never reopened, the building being used thereafter by the
Indians as a council-house. Simmons's early-winter class of elementary
pupils ranged from twelve to twenty-five persons, including several
adults, but seasonal movements, suspicion of education as an alienat-
ing influence, and the practical inconvenience that school attendance
meant for the families of the pupils combined to make formal English
education the least successful of the Quaker enterprises during early
years of the mission. In 1802 the Indian committee in Philadelphia,
at Seneca request, offered to educate four boys, taking them at about
age fifteen and returning them to the reservation at twenty-one, to
live near Philadelphia in Quaker farmhouses. Here, it was thought,
they would learn the rudiments of formal education and the trade of
farmer or other useful country occupations, but "the chief object of
our undertaking their education will be to bring them up in habits of
industry as our Children are in well ordered families in the country."
Although formal schools for Indian pupils were reopened at Tunessassa in 1814 and at Cold Spring in 1816, the hiatus in schooling lasted
during most of the remainder of Handsome Lake's life along the
Allegheny. The farm at Tunessassa did, however, establish a program
of training in the manual arts, taking Indian boys as boarders for
periods of up to six months and teaching them farm trades, and holding regular instruction sessions for girls and women in soap-making,
spinning, and weaving.

3. Technical assistance in specific Seneca projects

Various Seneca individuals, and the Allegany community as a whole
from time to time, wished to make improvements in their manner of
living that required either capital or instruction or both. The Quakers
initially offered to help the Seneca on such occasions and did in fact
spend much time and large amounts of money in this way. Part of the
program was devoted to giving out small hardware, such as needles

and thread, scissors, combs, spectacles, and other consumer goods
that were already known to the Indians but in short supply. Indian
women were allowed to keep the soap and cloth that they manufactured while learning the arts on Quaker equipment at Tunessassa.
But the major part of the technical assistance was directed toward
improvements: house construction, field clearing and fencing, plowing and seeding, roadbuilding, sawmill construction, the building of
a council house at Cold Spring. For these large jobs, the Quakers
provided tools, seed, paint, and livestock as required, helped with the
labor, and instructed the interested Indians in how to use the tools
and carry on the work. At first, the tools were presented to the
Indians after the initial job was done; later, in order to curtail an
increasingly dependent and demanding attitude, a store was set up
at which the Quakers sold hardware at cost. The most impressive
consequence was the abandonment of the old fenced settlement at
Jenuchshadago and the construction of new painted frame houses
with hung doors and glass windows in a more dispersed settlement
pattern. By 1805 three new communities had been developed: one
south of Jenuchshadago, one around the first Quaker farm at Gen-
singhuta, and a third at Cold Spring. Individual Indian households
cleared, plowed, and fenced their own fields, no longer in the
communal fenced area, but in association with the homestead. The
community built a road upriver under the cliffs from Jenuchshadago
to the tribal reservation in New York and constructed a sawmill on
a better millsite north of the state line. New crops were introduced
including wheat, hay for the cattle, and flax for cloth. And the
Indians were advised to invest tribal and individual income from
annuities in useful and productive materials, such as clothing, livestock, and plow irons, rather than in economically useless items such
as cheap jewelry and whiskey, and to enlarge their income by increasing production rather than by selling off any more of their only
remaining major capital asset, the land.

4. Preaching of the Protestant ethic

The Quakers did not come to the Seneca to convert them to Christianity and enroll them in an Allegany Yearly Meeting. Hence
they did very little in the way of reciting Christian dogma and
history, reading from the Bible, or threatening sinners with damna-

tion. The general tolerance of Seneca religious belief and custom was based on the Quaker conviction that every human being, not merely the Christian, entertains an inner light that evinces itself as the voice of natural conscience. Since this inner light is the mystic presence of divinity in every man, the Seneca were in no danger of damnation if they but heeded the voice. The conscience, of course, in true eighteenth-century fashion was assumed to represent universal human values, and many of these values were intimately connected with what has been called the Protestant ethic. This ethic emphasized sobriety, marital fidelity, observance of contract, hard work, orderliness, a respect for equipment and livestock, cleanliness, the duty of patiently helping back to duty those who strayed from the path of virtue rather than killing or otherwise retaliating upon them with violence. With considerable sophistication the Quakers understood that the construction, maintenance, and growth of a self-supporting democratic rural community of small independent farmers depended very largely on the widespread acceptance of precisely these ethical values and thus addressed themselves from the outset to awakening or reinforcing them in the Seneca. It was, in the Quaker view, axiomatic that these values were expressed by the inner light and thus needed only to be drawn to the Indians' attention rather than implanted afresh. But it was also understood by the Quakers that because of the fabric of private vested interests, institutions could not be changed overnight. The consequence of this dual conviction—that Indians were human beings of the same moral stature as white men, and that when local politics was involved, it was best to work quietly—was a unique method of approach. Where no major political interests appeared to oppose them, the Quaker representatives were bluntly forthright in denouncing what they regarded as bad practice. Thus they roundly condemned even cherished local customs, such as the social dances, the traditional sexual division of labor, and the spending of relatively large sums of money on vain personal finery, and they became almost fiery in their exhortation of idolaters, whiskey drinkers, and gamblers. But where politics was involved, as in the Seneca opposition to a public school and in the witchcraft issue, they remained remarkably silent, waiting for a more opportune season to press their convictions and contenting themselves in the meantime with partial measures. On some matters, even where political opposition was not an obstacle, these preachments failed; they were unable, for instance, to persuade the Seneca, either by instruction or example, to observe the weekly day of rest ("First Day"). Their success was most marked in those areas of behavior where there already existed, on a high level of generality, an influential body of opinion consonant with their own, as was the case with respect to economic reorganization and temperance. In such areas, once agreement was established on the major abstract goals, Quaker advice on the technical necessities for attainment was apt to be readily accepted, even if it required wholesale abandonment of custom, as was the case with regard to settlement pattern and sexual division of labor. The Quakers were always careful to insure that superficial and playful imitation was not substituted for deep learning, and thus they emphasized both the communication of concepts, rather than mere rote procedure, and the assurance of rewards of praise and of substance. Prizes were given in cash and kind for successful accomplishment, and the Indians were encouraged to keep the finished products of joint labors (thus Indian women were given the cloth woven by the Quakers from the flax or wool that the Indians had spun on the Quaker wheels).[9]

· *The Social Gospel* ·

THE THEME OF THE FIRST VISION of Handsome Lake had been preeminently apocalyptic, and the immediate aim of the prophet was simply to rescue souls from the storm of judgment. Thus, although worry about the welfare of Seneca society no doubt played a role in inspiring the first vision and prompted the classification of sins given in the early revelations, the fear of imminent doom at first had diverted attention from the long-term problem of establishing an enduring society and directed it toward the immediate necessity of ritual purification of a world on the brink of annihilation. But the principles of what may be called a social gospel, particularly as it concerned temperance, were latent even in the primary vision, and they became increasingly manifest during the period from 1801 to 1803. After 1803 most of the prophet's pronouncements concerned social matters. The main values that the social gospel inculcated were temperance, peace and unity, land retention, acculturation, and a revised domestic morality.

Temperance remained a prime concern throughout Handsome Lake's mission. The social disorders other than witchcraft to which whiskey contributed were matters of daily recognition both by Handsome Lake and by other responsible Seneca. The prohibition of whiskey thus came willy-nilly to have meaning as social policy in addition to its significance in Handsome Lake's eschatology, and it therefore may be regarded as the first tenet of the strictly social gospel. Handsome Lake was not content merely to condemn drinking as a sin; he went to some pains to explain just what were the social evils attendant upon drinking: family quarrels, mistreatment of children, lowered economic productivity, and mayhem and murder at drinking parties. He used logical argument as well as his religious authority to convince the skeptical of the evils of drink:

Good food is turned into evil drink. Now some have said that there is no harm in partaking of fermented liquids.

Then let this plan be followed: let men gather in two parties, one having a feast of food, apples and corn, and the other have cider and whiskey. Let the parties be equally divided and matched and let them commence their feasting at the same time. When the feast is finished you will see those who drank the fermented juices murder one of their own party but not so with those who ate food only.

The second tenet of the social code was peace and its correlate, social unity. Handsome Lake deplored the tendency for chiefs to bicker, for the result was disunity among the people, and spoke out against the factional tendency in matters of politics and religion. In the vision of the sky journey he had been told that "all the Chiefs of the Six nations should put their minds together and all be of one mind."[10] In 1800 he was still talking about the problem of unity, complaining to the Quakers that "I always try to instruct the chiefs and others to do right and to be of one mind and it is the will of the Great Spirit that all people should be of one mind but some of them will not listen to what I say. . . ."[11] This concern for unity was, of course, given institutional form in 1801 when he became the moral censor of the Seneca nation and principal leader of the Six Nations. Furthermore, he came to disapprove of capital punishment and publicly expressed regret for having caused the death of two women convicted of witchcraft, for "the Creator has not privileged men to punish each other."

Another aspect of the tenet of peace and amity was the preservation of good feelings toward the whites. The whites were pictured as neither good nor evil in themselves, but simply different from Indians. Thus, for example, whiskey was permissible for white men, for whom it had been created to use as a medicine and to strengthen themselves after work. Indians, to whom it was injurious, ought not to be jealous of the white man's freedom to drink.[12] He willingly accepted Jesus as his counterpart among the white people and considered the teachings of Jesus to be the equivalent of his own but intended for whites.[13] In fact, Handsome Lake apparently was willing for Indian converts to Christianity to remain with their new faith, provided they were conscientious in obeying its prescriptions. The Oneida pagan priest, Doctor Peter, in August 1806, reported that in a conversation he had recently had with the Seneca prophet, "the man of God" said "that we who have ministers of the written holy book must attend to their instructions and obey them, for that these ministers derive all their knowledge from the written holy book, and that he [i.e., Handsome Lake] receives his from the same source from which that originated." Doctor Peter therefore warned those Indians who "had had water sprinkled upon them in the name of the white people's more immediate Savior, strictly to observe all the precepts pertaining to water baptism, or they would miss their way and finally perish." And he advised all the Indians "to live in peace and love one another and all mankind, white people as well as Indians."[14] Handsome Lake reassured his people that their fears of extermination by the whites were groundless; their doom would be brought upon them by their own sins.[15] Throughout his mission he spoke well of and encouraged the Quakers. It would then appear that he was anxious to cool the angry passions of those who hated and blamed the whites for all the ills of the Indians, recommended love and understanding between the races, and counseled mutual respect for the differences that (apart from technological acculturation) had been ordained by the Great Spirit. Each race had now had its own savior, commissioned by the same God: Jesus for the whites, Handsome Lake for the Indians; each savior had a message for his own race, but one that it was well for the other race to heed. Men of good will among whites and Indians could make their joint occupancy of the earth a happy time, but, he felt, the white men were even more commonly alienated from their own savior than the Indians from theirs.

The third tenet was the preservation of the tribe's land base. This principle seems not to have become articulate as part of the prophet's message until the third vision (February 1800) but the sources of his concerns are easily enough discerned in historical perspective. He was the outstanding proponent of an embargo on further extensive cessions. But he was not opposed to profitable exchanges of land. He favored a general consolidation of Indian land holdings into large reservations and was willing to sell or trade the smaller tracts on the Genesee for equivalent land next to the big reservations at Buffalo Creek and Cattaraugus (including his own lands at Cuba Lake). He was motivated in this by a desire to bring the dissolute Indians on the small reservations, exposed to equally dissolute white settlements, under the control of the larger village communities. This would both promote moral reform and reduce the likelihood of piecemeal alienation of Seneca land.

The expansion of the social gospel to include as its fourth major tenet a pro-acculturation policy required that the prophet take a firm position on issues about which at first he had been indifferent or ambivalent. By 1801 he had made up his mind that English schooling was desirable for at least some of the children. In that year and again in 1811 the prophet and Cornplanter joined in requesting that the Quakers reopen the school (unsuccessfully, for the school was not opened again until 1814). In 1803 he is reported to have opposed a mission school at Buffalo Creek, objecting to "the building of the house, receiving any books from the white people for the instruction of their children, or hearkening to the gospel and maxims of civilization." But on the other hand, he is also reported to have finally agreed, albeit reluctantly, to the building of the school and the instruction of the children, provided they were not prevented from celebrating the Seneca religious festivals at Midwinter and Green Corn.[16] The Code itself asserts, concerning "studying in English schools,"

Now let the Council appoint twelve people to study, two from each nation of the six. So many white people are about you that you must study to know their ways.[17]

It would appear, in the final analysis, that Handsome Lake recognized a value in formal English schooling, but a value that was limited: the protection of the interests of the tribe from white lawyers and officials whose documents the Indians must be able to read for themselves in order to avoid being cheated.

With respect to the learning of white farming and domestic technology, Handsome Lake had little problem, and when his attention turned to these matters in the summer of 1801, he saw no difficulty in advising the people "that they might farm a little and make houses; but that they must not sell anything they raised off the ground, but give it away to one another and to the old people in particular in short that they must possess everything in common." In October he and Cornplanter announced that they saw the white people were going to settle all around them; that they could not live unless they learned to farm and follow the white people's ways.[18] During the trip to Washington in 1802 he openly endorsed a pro-acculturation policy. In 1803 he spoke on behalf of all the Allegany Seneca in urging the Quakers not to remove their settlement from Genesinguhta, and he added significantly, "I myself have been advising our people to pursue the course of life you recommend to us and we have fully concluded to follow habits of Industry, but we are only just beginning to learn." He went on to ask that the Quakers sell them the tools and clothes necessary for the new way of life.[19] In 1807 the *Evangelical Intelligencer* reported that the "Seneca Prophet" was adjuring his followers to "cultivate their lands" and to "live industrious lives."[20] The Code itself unambiguously praised the abundant harvests, animal labor, and warm houses that white technology could provide and urged the people to learn the white man's ways in these matters (providing only that there be no pride in material wealth). Thus, there can be no question that the prophet gave emphatic encouragement to the transformation of the Seneca economic system from a male-hunting-and-female-horticulture to a male-farming-and-female-housekeeping pattern.

But on the other hand, Handsome Lake was not in favor of pell-mell, indiscriminate acculturation. The educational and technological customs of the whites were to be integrated into a Seneca society that retained as a social value the village communalism, reserved land title to the nation itself, and depended upon traditional reciprocal gift-giving rather than commercial sale as the mechanism of internal distribution. The moral restraints of modesty and of kindness to animals were levied in such a way as to preclude, in theory at least, the development of the profit motive and rural capitalism. Furthermore, many white culture traits were proscribed in the Code: whiskey, mixed social dancing to the music of the violin, gambling with cards, and punishment of evildoers by the state (symbolized by handcuffs, whips, the hangman's rope, and prisons). And of course religious and ethnic identity were to remain Indian. Thus the society envisioned by the prophet was to be an autonomous reservation community, using white technology, but retaining its Indian identity, rejecting the centralization of police powers and the private profit motive as social evils, and condemning the more conspicuous vices of white society (drunkenness, the sexual promiscuity to which he felt mixed dancing by couples led, and gambling). He had nothing to say about the fate of those aspects of white technology that had long ago been adopted by the Seneca (e.g., metal household containers to replace pottery, guns to replace the spear and the bow and arrow, metal knives and axes to replace stone, etc.): these were by now an integral part of the Iroquois way of life and were not singled out as alien because of their ultimate origin in another land. Indeed, it would seem that Handsome Lake's attitude toward acculturation was remarkably rational, in the sense that he saw no peculiar virtue either in cultural nativism or cultural assimilation and made decisions about acculturation without the dogmatism that was aroused by such issues as whiskey, witchcraft, and land sales.

The fifth major tenet of the social gospel was a revised domestic morality. Like many reformers, Handsome Lake felt that personal salvation, social betterment, and postponement of the apocalypse all depended upon the establishment and pursuit of certain principles of personal behavior. If these principles were followed, then all good things would be realized. Most of the Code, both in early versions and later ones alike, was devoted to explicating these principles of personal morality and to describing the torments in the afterlife of those who violated them.

The earliest principle of the moral gospel to be enunciated by Handsome Lake was the duty of sons to obey their fathers. He expressed this principle in his second vision in August, 1799, in allegorical form, describing the angry dispute between Cornplanter and his son Henry and the neglect of Handsome Lake by his own son.

The second principle of domestic morality to be emphasized by the prophet was the duty of mothers not to interfere with their daughters' marriages. Handsome Lake was deeply concerned by the fragility of the classic Iroquois nuclear family and devoted much of his preaching to homilies on domestic tranquility. The "Great Message" contains, in Parker's published version of the Code, about 130 sections. The first four sections define the four cardinal sins: drinking whiskey, practicing lethal witchcraft, using magical charms, and using medicines to sterilize a woman. Three of these four bear directly on the nuclear family, for drunkenness led to quarrels between husband and wife, the magical charms included love charms that facilitated promiscuity, and sterility unnaturally limited not only the numbers of a woman's descendants but also the number of children in the household. In the latter case, Handsome Lake singled out the mother-daughter relationship as the central problem. He condemned the mother who ignored her child's warnings against wrongdoing and who advised her married daughter to abort and become sterile or to leave her husband. "The Creator," he said, "is sad because of the tendency of old women to breed mischief." These cautions, together with the implication that older women were particularly apt to practice witchcraft and to influence their daughters to do the same, amounted to a direct challenge to the primacy of the kind of exclusive mother-daughter relationship that was essential to the old quasi-matriarchal system.

The third major principle of domestic morality was the sanctity of the husband-wife relationship, which in Handsome Lake's thought now took precedence over other kinship ties. By 1806 his disciple at Oneida was reported by Kirkland to have "spoken upon the duties of husbands and wives, and the great sin of divorce."[21] In 1807 he himself was reported in the *Evangelical Intelligencer* to insist to his followers "that they put not away their wives."[22] And in a number of undated revelations he delineated his conception of how the members of the nuclear family should and should not behave. He condemned the man who deserted a series of women in order to avoid the responsibilities of fatherhood. He condemned the woman who was jealous of her husband's love for his children. He condemned quarreling between husband and wife. He condemned scandalous gossip about the misbehavior of wives while their husbands were away hunting. He praised the wife who forgave her husband who strayed, but condemned the erring husband. He condemned philandering men. He condemned the punitive mother. He condemned the drunken father. He urged the childless couple to adopt children of the wife's sister rather than separate. He condemned gossiping women who spread rumors that a woman's husband was not the father of her child. And he urged grandchildren to care for aged and helpless grandparents.

The remainder of the Code contains a number of admonitions concerning the reciprocal social and economic roles of men and women. A woman should be a good housewife: generous, serving food to visitors and neighbors' children, never a petty thief, always helping the orphaned of the community, and avoiding gossip. A man should "harvest food for his family," build a good house, and keep horses and cattle.

In review of Handsome Lake's moral admonitions, it is plain that he was concerned to stabilize the nuclear family by protecting the husband-wife relationship against abrasive events. A principal abrasive, in his view, was the hierarchical relationship between a mother and her daughter. Mothers, he believed, were all too prone to urge their daughters toward sin by administering abortifacients and sterilizing medicines, by drunkenness, by practicing witchcraft, and by providing love magic. They set their daughters' minds against their husbands, condoned mothers' severity to their children, and were above accepting advice from their own offspring. Thus, in order to stabilize the nuclear family it was necessary to loosen the tie between mother and daughter. Furthermore, men were supposed to assume the role of heads of families, being economically responsible for their wives and children and not frittering away their energies on strong drink, gambling, dancing, and philandering, nor on mother-in-law trouble. Although he did not directly challenge the matrilineal principle in regard to sib membership or the customs of nominating sachems, he made it plain that the nuclear family, rather than the maternal lineage, was henceforward to be both the moral and the economic center of the behavioral universe.

· *Political Defeat* ·

THE YEAR 1803 began auspiciously for the prophet. A general council of the Seneca nation was held in January at Jenuchshadago, or Cornplanter's Town, with chiefs and warriors from all the villages represented, amounting to about two thirds of the whole adult male population. Acting on the basis of the policy formulated at the Buffalo Creek council of 1801, which had made Handsome Lake the supreme leader of the Six Nations, this group announced "that the Great Council fire for the Six Nations is now opened at this Place which is to Continue while they are a Nation, the old fire at Buffalo Creek to be intirely extinguished." Nicholas Rosencrantz and Henry O'Bail were appointed official interpreters, and delegates were dispatched, with Handsome Lake's approval, to Philadelphia and Washington to secure economic aid for the Seneca at Tonawanda and to rescind the recent sale of the lands at Black Rock.[23]

This effort to move the council fire of the Six Nations was perhaps the high-water mark of Handsome Lake's political fortunes. At Jenuchshadago he was supported by kinsmen who functioned as administrative chiefs: his brother Cornplanter, the local political "boss"; his nephew Charles O'Bail, and his fellow clansman Strong, two "sober, good young men" whom he had appointed "to take care of all our [i.e., the Allegany band's] publick business";[24] and another nephew, Henry O'Bail, who had just become an official interpreter. Of the sixteen to twenty chiefs of the local band, no less than four, including himself, were members of the Wolf clan (the others being Cornplanter, Blacksnake, and Strong) and four more were members of the Snipe clan of Cornplanter's wife (including Henry and Charles O'Bail, his nephews). Thus nearly half of the local chiefs were closely associated by kinship with the prophet, and a number of others were solidly in his favor.[25]

But there were those who did not support the move. Brant and his Mohawks and the other Iroquois tribes at Grand River in Canada claimed that the council fire was at the Onondaga village there; the principal chiefs at Buffalo Creek insisted that it was still at Buffalo Creek. Agent Chapin claimed that although the warriors and women supported the prophet, the chiefs opposed him, and he started the rumor (which became widespread in later years) that the whole movement was a scheme of Cornplanter's "to take the lead of the Nation." He insisted that Buffalo Creek was the place of business for the Six Nations. And Handsome Lake himself traveled to Buffalo Creek in May with Cornplanter's son John to collect the annuities for the Allegany band. (And so he did in the spring and summer for many years thereafter.)

The issue as to where the council fire really was, insofar as the Seneca were concerned at least, was settled once again in August 1807, when a large council of the chiefs of the Six Nations (presumably including Handsome Lake) met at Buffalo Creek to revitalize the confederacy. According to the official report of the local Indian agent the meeting was called principally by the Seneca chiefs "for the purpose of renewing and confirming, the former confederacy of the six Nations." More Iroquois chiefs from all the tribes assembled than at any time since the Treaty of Canandaigua in 1794. The meeting was a success. "They have," said the agent, "according to their own antient customs, have pledge themselves Nationally to each other, to be United let what will happen, peace or war." Thus Handsome Lake was able to see the realization, in one institution at least, of his dream of unity—but it came at the expense of his own political interests. One chief could not dominate the confederacy. The great council fire had burned fitfully at Jenuchshadago; now it burned again even brighter than before at Buffalo Creek, where Handsome Lake's rival Red Jacket held sway.[26]

The prophet's dominion at Cornplanter's Town now also came rapidly to an end. In the fall of 1803 he presided over the local council meeting where the removal of the Quaker farm from Genesinguhta was discussed. The Quakers wanted to relocate it at Tunessassa, a few miles away off the reservation. Handsome Lake made a warm reply to this proposal. Speaking as "the united voice" of the chiefs, the warriors, and the women, he praised the Quakers as peaceable and honest people and urged them not to move too far away. "We want you to be near us," he said, "that you may extend further assistance and instruction."

Friends Tewastie—I myself have been advising our people to the course of life you commend to us as we have fully concluded to follow habits of industry but we are only just beginning to learn, and we find ourselves at a loss for tools to work with, we now request you to bring on plenty of all kinds you think will be usefull, then such of our peoples as are able will buy for themselves and such as are poor, we wish you to continue to lend and they shall be returned to you again—we also want you to bring on usefull cloths, and sell to us, that we may get some necessary things without having to go so far for them—In looking forward we can limit no time for you to live beside us, this must depend on your own judgement....

The prophet also requested that the blacksmith who was teaching the men remain a while longer because he was the best smith they had ever seen and they wished to learn more from him. In a secondary role Cornplanter backed up the statements of his brother. It was an amicable meeting with the Quakers, and the relocation of the farm and various other questions were agreed on easily.[27]

But a few months later Handsome Lake and Cornplanter quarreled, and Handsome Lake and his adherents moved from Jenuchshadago to build a new town at Cold Spring, on the reservation in New York. The underlying source of the trouble was personal jealousy of the "old chief" by Handsome Lake and some of the younger men, particularly Blacksnake, who for some time had resented the high-handed manner in which Cornplanter had managed the affairs of the Allegany band. But the immediate issue was land and money. Cornplanter had built his private sawmill at a bad place; much of the year it was useless, either flooded or dry. He proposed to move his sawmill to a site within the reservation where he would lease it as before to a white man and take the profits himself. Many of the Indians thought this was unreasonable and refused to sanction the arrangement. Cornplanter in a rage declared that if the tribe refused to let him use the national land (the reservation), he would not let them use his private land (the grant), and he ordered everyone off. The band's response to this was to displace him from the office of chief, to lease the sawmill site in question to one of Cornplanter's white millwrights (for a rental of sixty thousand board feet of lumber yearly, payable to the band), thus setting up a competing sawmill at a better location than Cornplanter's, and to leave the grant. The leaders in the move were nominated to serve on the council. Cornplanter, reduced to the status of a common warrior, was left to sulk with a few loyal families at Jenuchshadago.[28]

Having thus lost his most powerful political ally, Handsome Lake now began to lose credit with the Quakers. They wanted the Indians to give up the old way of living in small villages and to disperse among the fields in the settlement pattern typical of rural white America, with houses built up to a mile apart, each surrounded by its own fenced fields and woods. But Handsome Lake, to the Friends' considerable annoyance, rejected this advice and persuaded most of the Indians to construct a new, tightly organized village on four acres of wooded knoll close to the river at the mouth of Cold Spring Creek. The men worked in gangs, cutting the timber off the village site and opening a prospect to the river, constructing log houses of rough-hewn lumber with clapboard roofs and earth floors. (Chimneys, paneled doors, and glass windows were added later.) Individual households were allowed to choose their own fields around the village to raise corn and build cabins in the summer. The prophet's reason for insisting on this settlement pattern was religious. In order to carry on "their yearly dances & sacrafices . . . they must build a town to live in, in winter seasons." The Quakers opposed this manner of proceeding as not being "the nearest road to distinct property" but only a few families followed their advice and built separate farmsteads along the bottom lands up the river. After all, they had found that at least five members of the council—Blue Eyes, Mush, Silver Heels, John Snow, and Henry O'Bail—were living apart from Cold Spring and had to be called from their homes by the blast of a horn. "To these," said the Quakers, "our advice flows freely & generally acceptable to them. the other party that are huddling together (are Indians yet) are not beginning right in our view."[29]

The result of these events was a division of the Allegany band into three mutually resentful fragments: a few families, kinsmen of Cornplanter, remaining with him on the grant; a number of Quaker-influenced families, more progressive than Handsome Lake's policy allowed, settled on the other side of Cold Spring; and the Handsome Lake faction, by far the largest, composed of an uneasy combination of progressives and conservatives, "huddling together" in the village at Cold Spring under the leadership of the prophet and Black-snake, whom he had "for his privy Counsellor."[30] It was an unstable situation, which Handsome Lake was unable to control. The Quakers covertly criticized his judgment in regard to the Cold Spring settlement and openly objected to the dirty, flea-infested Indian houses there. Some of the people felt that Cornplanter had been unjustly treated and favored bringing him, now that he behaved contritely, back as chief. In 1806, when a Quaker delegation from Philadelphia visited Cold Spring, Handsome Lake was still presiding over the council, and Blacksnake was full of laudatory remarks; the settlements were prospering with new houses, new fields, a new road along the river. But the Quakers sensed an undercurrent of dissatisfaction and experienced "some apprehensions that one or two of their young Ambitious chiefs was a little uneasy in their minds. . . ." There were rumors of whiskey being brought onto the reserve again. Some of the speeches had been a trifle sarcastic. Handsome Lake was also on edge, saying plaintively, in response to the Friends' exhortation to eschew whiskey and gambling, that some of the people would not obey him. Anxious now to find support from the Quakers, he was in the forefront of those greeting the visitors. He concurred in the Quaker plan to send two Indian youths every six months to live on the farm at Tunessassa "to be instructed in the farming business or learn to manage the Mills." And Blacksnake gave a short speech recommending him to their favor:

> All the Indians and white people know that the Great Spirit talks with our Prophet it is now Seven years since he began first to talk with him, & he tells the Indians they must leave off drinking whisky, & they have declined the use of it. . . .

> Brothers you must tell your friends, when you go home to make their minds easy, for we are determined never to let the whisky rise again and also to persue habits of industry and never decline it—Your young men and us are like one, when we want anything Done we Consult them and they assist us—and our Profit tells us what to do, and we get instructs from both. . . .[31]

While difficulties for Handsome Lake were accumulating along the Allegheny, further political intrigue against him was maturing among the chiefs at Buffalo Creek. Led by the eloquent and loquacious Red Jacket, the Buffalo Creek sachems spread rumors among both Indians and their white confidants that Handsome Lake was a false prophet.³² It was not that these chiefs disagreed with the policies that he proposed. They all agreed with him, in principle at least, about the evils of whiskey, all believed in the traditional religion, all opposed Christian evangelism, all desired that the benefits of an English education and white technology should be made available to the Indians. But even though the Great Council had appointed him supreme leader, his earlier witchcraft accusations and his current pretensions to authority created bitter resentment. Red Jacket deliberately planted rumors that the prophet was a fraud perpetrated upon the Indians by Cornplanter, who "having lost the confidence of his countrymen, in order, as it is supposed, to retrieve his former standing, . . . persuaded his brother to announce himself as a prophet, or messenger from heaven, sent to redeem the fallen fortunes of the Indian race." When Handsome Lake appointed conjurors to designate witches and sentence them to death, the sachems insinuated that the witch hunt was "an artful expedient to render his enemies the objects of general abhorence, if not the victims of an ignominious death."³³ Personally, he was characterized as "formerly a great drunkard despised by the Indians themselves, as an ignorant, idle, worthless fellow." (His standing as one of the forty-nine chiefs of the council was conveniently passed over in these slanders.) After his reformation it was conceded that he appeared to be "meek, honest and innofensive" but "those best acquainted with him" were said to report that he was "deficient in intellect." "He converses but little. His countenance does not indicate much thoughtfulness. When questioned, however, his answers are pertinent and his public speeches are sensible. . . . At the meeting of commissioners with the Senecas, for the purpose of purchasing a tract of land at the Black-rock, this Indian was present, and opposed the sale of their lands. He related the communications, which he said he had received from the Great Spirit. Some of the communications he could not recollect, and asked his brother Cornplanter. When asked how he could forget such communications, he said at the time the Great Spirit told him these things, he related them to his brother: and that he was told so many things, he did not remember all. . . . To one, who expressed his doubts of his having such communications, and used some arguments to show him he had not, he replied with his usual simplicity, 'I think I have had such communications made to me!' " And even after the break with Cornplanter became known, the suggestions that he was merely a front man for a family conspiracy continued. The alleged conspirators now were his nephews Blacksnake and Henry and Charles O'Bail, who, being both "sensible" and "men of great renown . . . use their influence in his favour." Indian agent Chapin reported in 1807 that Handsome Lake was "consulted as the principle chief of the nation; but Red Jacket, a cunning and subtile chief at Buffaloe Creek, does not believe in him, but in his public transactions he pays him respect, as he is popular with the nation. He observed to the agent for the Six Nations, that when the prophet made his speeches, his nephews sat contiguous to him on the right and left. On a certain occasion he had taken care to place some others next to the prophet, and he was not able to say any thing."[34]

Handsome Lake was aware of a current of opposition in the Allegany band and of the enmity of Red Jacket and the other chiefs at Buffalo Creek. His tendency was, when in difficulty, to imagine that its origin lay in the malevolence of witches, and now, when he found himself in trouble at Cold Spring, he began to think about witchcraft again as the explanation. One of his opponents at Cold Spring, a mentally ill man who had on at least one occasion stood in the doorway of the council-house and, in the classic Indian gesture of disrespect to a speaker, farted at the conclusion of the prophet's homily, wandered off alone into the forests. A search party found him after three days, lost in a swamp across the river. He was sitting on a nest of branches, devouring snakes. "He was not in his right mind," the prophet concluded. They took him home, but he died soon after.

The prophet proceeded to blame the man's insanity for his disrespect to the prophet's teaching and to blame the insanity on witchcraft. He accused a Cattaraugus woman and her daughter of secretly administering poison. The chief's council met and decided to punish the women by whipping them, one stroke to be given by each chief. (There were from sixteen to twenty chiefs.) Handsome Lake agreed with this judgment after consulting with the four angels, believing (or at least so he later claimed) that they would survive the lashing. The women were whipped, and they both died as a result of it.[35]

People began to murmur. In 1807 Cornplanter was restored to his position as a member of the chiefs' council.[36] And soon after that a religious dispute began to develop over the restrictions the prophet had placed on the medicine-societies. In 1807 there was, according to tradition, an epidemic that caused a number of deaths. Many people secretly believed that the outbreak of illness was the result of a neglect of the medicine-company ceremonies. Handsome Lake, when asked the cause of the epidemic of deaths, according to oral tradition is reputed to have declared (perhaps cautiously) that a large underground animal was causing the deaths (such subterranean monsters were a common Iroquois belief). If the people would go to a certain place across the mountains and dig there, they would find the animal. A group of men, planning to kill the monster, went to the prescribed spot and dug a huge hole. But they found no animal. The people continued to die, and at last Handsome Lake declared that it must be witchcraft. Several oral traditions agree that a council was held at which many people were present. Handsome Lake pointed the finger at at least one old woman, who was killed on the spot. But the woman had dissatisfied relatives; and that night at a council of chiefs and dissidents charges were aired: that Handsome Lake was killing off only those who did not believe in him; that those whom he accused were not guilty; that it was not witchcraft, but neglect of the medicine ceremonies, that was the root of the difficulty.[37]

Handsome Lake now was convinced that although the people revered him, the chiefs were in a witch-inspired conspiracy against him, and he confided this belief to his disciples. One of these disciples, "one of the most distinguished of their young men," told a white man that "the prophet would yet be persecuted and put to death, as the wicked put to death the Lord Jesus Christ."[38]

The denouement came in 1809; and again the issue was witchcraft. Cornplanter was absent when an Onondaga woman accompanied by her husband and a few relatives arrived at Cold Spring for trial as a witch. Handsome Lake's supporters convened in council. "It was a very small Council but on looking into her hands she was pronounced Guilty of the Charge by Connudiu." An aged chief named Old Fatty now declared, "If he was a young Man & able for war as he once was he would put en End to her—on which Sun Fish immediately caught up an Axe & knocked her in the Head & among them they compleated the Massacre." According to tradition, the stunned woman survived the first blow of the hatchet, recovered consciousness, and groaned; then her throat was slit. But the woman's relatives at Onondaga were not satisfied that she was a witch: "the Relatives of the Woman threaten revenge (Blood for Blood) if ever they catch Sun Fish." When Cornplanter returned and learned of the affair, he privately told people that he disapproved of it.[39] When a Quaker committee arrived a few months later and also disapproved of the killing, he stated publicly in council, "I hope we shall be careful in future how we take the lives of any for witchcraft without being sure that they are guilty, and he thought it very difficult to prove it." Later he voiced the opinion that it would be better to invoke the death penalty against a chief for selling any more land than for witchcraft, because the one could be proved and "the other he had his doubts about."[40] And Henry O'Bail, one of Handsome Lake's chiefly nephews, now also openly took sides against the prophet. Earlier, in 1802, he had with the council's permission tumbled the rotting wooden statue of Tarachiawagon into the Allegany River; in this he had been supported by the Quakers, who regarded it as an example of "idolatry." Handsome Lake, perhaps preferring to be himself the central object of religious respect, had not objected. More recently Henry O'Bail had been among those who publicly objected to the burning of the white dog. This was one of the sacred rituals and was annually being practiced at Cold Spring under Handsome Lake's direct supervision. Now he was publicly stating that "Witchcraft . . . does not exist."[41]

Handsome Lake was now virtually without friends among the Allegany band. The Quakers were against him. His brother Cornplanter and his nephew Henry were against him. The local kinsmen of the witches whom he had accused were against him. The witches not yet discovered were against him. He secretly pondered escape. But where could he go? He could not go to Cattaraugus Reservation because there lived members of the Delaware band whom he had accused of witchcraft. He could not go to Buffalo Creek because there lived Red Jacket and the chiefs who were conspiring against him. He could not go to Onondaga because there lived the kinfolk of the woman whom he had just executed, and they were vowing revenge. He could go to Tonawanda, but that was a poor and demoralized community. He began to think again of death. At last he had another vision. As he told it later,

Now it was that when the people reviled me, the proclaimer of the prophecy, the impression came to me that it would be well to depart and go to Tonawanda. In that place I had relatives and friends and thought that my bones might find a resting place there. Thus I thought through the day.

Then the messengers came to me and said "We understand your thoughts. We will visit you more frequently and converse with you. Wherever you go take care not to be alone. Be cautious and move secretly."

Then the messengers told me that my life journey would be in three stages and when I entered the third I would enter into the eternity of the New World, the land of our Creator.[42]

And so, in the late fall or winter of 1809, Handsome Lake suddenly left Cold Spring, accompanied by a few faithful disciples, including the minister Joiise.[43] The departure was dramatic and is remembered even today among the Indians at Cold Spring and Cornplanter's Town. At Tonawanda he found refuge and a base from which he could continue his evangelical work. But he had no local political power. And so after tempers cooled, he returned to Allegany, more quietly than he had left. There he found that the chiefs' council had officially resolved "to take no more lives under a suspicion of witchcraft."[44] He remained a member of the chiefs' council, but his brother Cornplanter resumed the position of presiding chairman, which Handsome Lake had held. In 1811 he, along with ten other chiefs of the council, signed a letter replying to the Quakers that they did indeed wish to have their children taught in a school. The council had, in fact, conducted a house-to-house survey questioning parents about their views, and the community there, as well as the council at Buffalo Creek, was favorable.[45]

The prophet's last political stratagem to counteract the influence of Red Jacket and Cornplanter was only partially successful. He undertook the role of "peace prophet" during the War of 1812. During the years preceding the war the New York Iroquois had been repeatedly solicited by representatives of the revived western confederates, under the leadership of Tecumseh and his brother the Shawnee Prophet (the "war prophet"), to join them and the British in a frontier campaign to recover their lost lands. The New York chiefs unanimously opposed joining any such conspiracy, and in a council at Jenuchshadago in the summer of 1812 the chiefs of the

Allegany band, including Cornplanter and Handsome Lake, specifically reassured the whites from Warren and Meadville of their intentions to remain at peace.[46] Officially the United States also encouraged the Iroquois to remain neutral. But a number of Brant's Mohawks from Grand River did enlist in the British forces. This action prompted the United States to solicit "volunteers" to the number of 150 to 200 warriors. The Indian agent at Buffalo Creek argued, "I know of no Instance where Indians have ever lain still when war came near them" and he expressed fear that if the United States did not recruit the warriors, the British would. The Six Nations Council at Buffalo Creek tacitly permitted the recruitment. But Handsome Lake now intervened, organizing a council of the Iroquois of New York "at their ancient council fire at Onondaga." This council, attended by representatives of the Oneida, Onondaga, Stockbridge, Tuscarora, and Seneca, sent to the President of the United States a speech complaining "that a few of the Indians got together at [Buffalo Creek] and were invited to take up the hatchet —this they say is contra to the advice of Genl Washington and contra to the Wishes of their great Prophet, who attended this Council." They suggested that any request for military services by the Indians be addressed to councilors of the League at Onondaga.[47]

This action did not deter the United States from recruiting Indian volunteers. During the two years of war from 1812 to 1814 the muster roll of New York Iroquois who enlisted in the war in defense of what many of them now called "our country" numbered over six hundred officers and enlisted men. Some twenty were eventually given commissions, including Handsome Lake's chief disciples Blacksnake and Henry O'Bail and other Allegany council chiefs, among them Cornplanter, Black Chief, and Strong.[48] But Handsome Lake nonetheless had a measurable effect in slowing down the mobilization of the Iroquois, and federal officials resented his meddling. When Handsome Lake visited Buffalo Creek on his way back from the meeting at Onondaga, he insulted agent Erastus Granger, who signed up the volunteers, by failing to call on him. "If I can see him before he goes home," wrote Granger, "I shall tell him to stay at Alleghany till the War is over."[49] Against the wishes of federal Indian agents, the Onondaga warriors who were recruited in 1812 insisted on stopping off on their way at Allegany. The agent told them "not to call on the Old Prophet, for he must not interfere with the wishes of our great chiefs. The chiefs [said] that they *would* go that way; but it was for a religious purpose; they should stay there but a short time, and then go on to Buffalo." By the summer of 1813 the two reservations under Handsome Lake's greatest personal influence—Allegany and Tonawanda—had still turned out a total of only seven warriors; at Buffalo Creek nearly all the men had already taken up arms. Next year the chiefs from Allegany and Tonawanda were still reported to be reluctant about the war.[50]

The peace council at Onondaga did have another effect. It represented a temporary victory for Handsome Lake in his continuing effort to move the Six Nations council fire away from Buffalo Creek, far from the influence of his rival Red Jacket. Although the fire remained officially at Buffalo Creek until the reservation itself was sold a generation later, the fire did at long last come back permanently to its old hearth at Onondaga.

· *Evangelical Triumph* ·

IN THE POLITICS OF THE CHIEFS' COUNCIL, despite the eminence of his titles, Handsome Lake failed, mired in personal jealousies and tribal factionalism and unable to call upon an efficient bureaucracy for the administration of his policies. Such a failure, indeed, was in a sense ordained by Iroquois culture, for a correlate of the theme of freedom was an extreme sensitivity to issues involving personal dominance. Pretenders to greatness, like Logan and Sturgeon, were sometimes assassinated on behalf of an offended community faction by members of their own family (a procedure which aborted the revenge process); leaders like Cornplanter, Red Jacket, and Brant were apt to suffer rejection or assault; factionalism was pervasive; and the intense ambivalence about dominance was traditionally expressed in the polarity between the politeness of day to day encounters and the violence that erupted in drunken brawls, witchcraft accusations, and, in older times, the torture rituals. The prophet thus, by his very success in achieving the role of moral censor, guaranteed his own political defeat.

But as an evangelist Handsome Lake was a triumphant success. In the intensely personal but stereotyped relationship between him and his followers, he played his role with skill and grace. His head-quarters were at Cold Spring, except for the brief sojourn at Tona-wanda, and there at the big council house and in his dwelling a few yards away he had his visions, consulted with Indian visitors from tribes for hundreds of miles around, and on occasion made speeches. In person he made a vivid figure on ceremonial occasions. In 1809 he was described as he presided at a council meeting: "Old Conudiu had a blaze of vermillion [paint] from the Corner of each Eye—his ears were cut round in their manner & extended a considerable length, on each Ear were two silver quills, one about 3½ & the other 2 Inches. The erect one having a tuft of Red Feathers tuck in the lower end—part of his forehead & on big Crown were also painted red & being nearly bald & a very grave countenance, he looked venerable—on his arms were wide silver bracelets—his leggings were of Red Cloth & his covering a Blanket over all—which he threw off in Council & took up his long Pipe. . . ."[51] And from Cold Spring he regularly set off on foot, accompanied by a few disciples, on an annual circuit of visits to other reservations and to the Great Council at Buffalo Creek, preaching, inquiring into local circum-stances, and castigating sinners.[52]

The calendar of visits to the prophet at Cold Spring begins with the great Six Nations Council in 1803. In the spring of 1804 he re-ceived a delegation of men and women from Onondaga, who re-ported on their progress in the new religion.[53] In the same year an Indian woman came from the Mohawk and Seneca towns at San-dusky, Ohio, and heard the word; she took it back to the pagan Sandusky Indians, advising them to continue their old worship of "the Warrior god" Tarachiawagon, whose red-painted statue stood in their village beside the council-house. (They told a Christian missionary then visiting that "they do not consider it a God, but have it there to put them in mind of their God."[54] In 1806 he him-self visited the Wyandots at Sandusky, darkly warning that "judg-ments are coming on the nations, unless they reform." His fame as a foreteller of doom had recently been given widespread popular con-firmation by the disastrous flood along the Allegheny in the spring of 1805, which washed away many of their improvements.[55] By 1807 the agent Granger reported to Dearborn, the Secretary of War, "the old Seneca Prophet, whom you once saw in Washington, strange as it may appear, has acquired an unbounded influence over the Six

Nations—his fame has long since reached some of the western Indians, and for two years past they have been sending Messengers to him, requesting his personal attendance in their Country, that they might hear the words of the Great Spirit from his mouth." In 1807 a delegation from the west, "consisting of Shawonees & others," even asked him to return directly with them, but the prophet "declined going at present."[56] Next summer a delegation of Seneca and Wyandot came from Sandusky. And later the same summer, in pursuit of a plan concocted by Granger to use him as a peace prophet ("the old man if managed right might be made subservient to the interest of the United States"), Handsome Lake did head a delegation of chiefs of the Six Nations on a visit to the western Indians. He was accompanied by Red Jacket, Cornplanter, and eight other distinguished Seneca chiefs from various reservations, and a large number of warriors. Handsome Lake kindled a fire and held a council with the western Indians at Sandusky, advising peace between them and the United States. Granger, not knowing of the prophet's earlier trip or his plans to visit the western Indians again, and failing to anticipate the prophet's opposition to the participation of his fellow tribesmen in a war on the side of the United States, congratulated himself on the success of his intrigue to use Handsome Lake as a peace prophet.[57]

Among the Six Nations the prophet's evangelical journeys were frequent but he chose carefully which places to visit. To Buffalo Creek and nearby Tonawanda he came annually from as early as 1801 for both evangelical, financial, and political purposes, for here the annuity moneys were paid and here meetings of the Seneca chiefs and of the Six Nations Council were held. He avoided Tuscarora, where a mixture of Christian and pagan Indians, the latter led by a female prophet, were developing a syncretic religion.[58] But Buffalo Creek had the disadvantage of being both the home of his political enemies and close neighbor to a white village where much whiskey was sold. Onondaga he visited annually from about 1803 and 1804, and in 1809, as we saw earlier, Onondaga delegations visited him at Allegany. "He harangued and exhorted them continually, and became distinguished among them for his powers and abilities. Business transactions were conducted under his direction and advice. On all occasions of difficulty, he was looked up to as the only individual who could restore things to a proper degree of order."[59]

There is no record of his having ever visited the Oneida and Stockbridge Indians. The people of this band were divided into a Christian faction headed by the missionary Samuel Kirkland, and a pagan faction inspired by the Mohawk prophet who had moved there from the Grand River and instituted a modified form of worship of Tarachiawagon that substituted a deer for the white dog. Knowing of the presence of these two religious movements, which agreed with his views on the importance of temperance, universal love, and domestic tranquility, and even expressed sympathy for each other, he advised these Indians "to listen to the instructions of the missionary" and follow the Bible. The missionary, in turn, was careful never to condemn Handsome Lake in public, although privately he was critical of his reputed tendency, whenever he wanted "a new revelation, to answer any particular purpose," to "cover his head with a bear skin for an hour or two, then lay it aside, muse awhile," and then disclose a heavenly message. A garbled version of Handsome Lake's teaching was circulated at Oneida. The prophet was said to have been in a trance three days and three nights and to have asserted that even one swallow of whiskey was a deadly sin if not repented of, although it was all right for white people to drink it, and Indians should not feel jealous or resentful of them because they used it so freely. "It was God who made rum, and made it for the white people to use as a medicine to strengthen them after labor." The prophet, it was said, urged them to love one another, whites and Indians alike; husbands and wives must love one another; and divorce was a sin. The pagans at Oneida adopted the Christian sabbath, meeting in church from nine in the morning to four in the afternoon, when they required confession and absolution and made speeches. "They are careful" said Kirkland, "to mention the prophet and refer to him frequently in every speech, seldom mentioning his Indian name, which is Kanyadaligo (a beautiful lake). The titles by which they honor him are Kawegago, Saongwida, God's man and God's friend; and Soyadadogeahre, the holy man, Sagwakonwanea, our chief man."[60]

By 1806 Handsome Lake considered his evangelical program well established at Cold Spring, Cattaraugus (which was nearby), Onondaga, Oneida, and Tonawanda. The trouble lay at Buffalo Creek and on the small reservations along the Genesee River. The Genesee was notorious as the resort of "bad Indians." The proximity of white settlers selling whiskey and exploiting the Indians economically, and the absence of substantial Indian communities that could exercise any restraint, had made of these places the scene of the kind of unrestrained drinking, brawling, and murder which Mary Jemison, who lived on one of them, described in her autobiography. In 1801 and 1802 Handsome Lake had taken part in negotiations to trade off these little reservations (including his own at Cuba Lake) for equivalent areas annexed to Cattaraugus and Buffalo Creek and, in spite of considerable Indian resentment, had personally signed the deeds to change the boundaries at Cattaraugus and to sell Little Beard's Town. But most of the little reserves remained. In the summer of 1806 he decided to evangelize them and led a company of his followers from Allegany to the little towns on the Genesee, preaching industry and temperance. The mission to the Genesee concluded at a general religious council on the Genesee River. The presence of so many Indians in one place prompted a rumor that the Indians were plotting to massacre all of the white settlers in the Genesee. The nearby Indian agent attended and found that the settlers' fears were unfounded; on the contrary, it was a very peaceful occasion, as he reported to the secretary of war:

> I have constantly attended this counsil every day, from the time of their first meeting, until they dispersed, and so little cause is there for alarm, that I never, on any former occasion observed them so quiet and peaceably disposed.—the object of their meeting was to agree on some mode and form of religion, and some other internal regulations, among themselves. this council was called by the prophet (a half Brother to Corn Planter), who is religiously engaged in endeavoring to inculcate certain religious doctrines amongst the Six Nations and to prevent them from drinking the use of ardent spirits three days was set apart by the Indians to confess their sins, of their past lives to the prophet, who has become their confessor. these were the only matters of consequence that took place at the late council. The Chiefs sent a runner to me requesting me to attend their council, the principal business with me was to solicit my influence in preventing the merchant tavern keepers and other persons from selling whiskey to the Indians.[61]

But despite the success of the Genesee revival, the long-term results were disappointing. Next fall the prophet and his disciples declared to the Quakers, "We have extended a great deal of labour towards our neighboring Indians, to persuade them to leave off the use of whiskey, and though *our* young men have generally declined it, yet we are almost discouraged about our Brothers at Buffalo and Genesee River."[62]

As the years went by, a clear pattern began to emerge: Handsome Lake, despite his position as a chief of the League, a member of the Allegany council, and the declared leader of the Six Nations, was not able to control the actions even of those chiefs who subscribed to his gospel. He was widely popular as an evangelist among many chiefs, warriors, and women, and his influence was particularly great at Allegany, Cattaraugus, Sandusky, Onondaga, and Tonawanda. He was not widely followed at Buffalo Creek, where Red Jacket, without visions and in avowed opposition to the prophet's pretensions, supported a similar program of religious conservatism coupled with secular progress. At Oneida a garbled mixture of his teachings, those of the Mohawk prophet, and Christianity held sway. Tuscarora also was partly Christian and under the influence of one of Kirkland's converts from Oneida. Through the declining years of his life, therefore, he concentrated his missionary energies on visiting those communities which liked him best and followed his teaching most closely. Every summer he left his house by the council building at Cold Spring and trudged to renew the warm fellowship of *Gaiwiio* in the dark, wooded hollows at Tonawanda and Onondaga. Here he met devotees, personal converts who had undergone intense emotional experiences in the course of conversion, had been strengthened to forsake whisky and other sins, and looked to Handsome Lake as their personal savior.

These conversions were not casual matters. The Indians traversed the same mystic path to *Gaiwiio* as white converts to Christianity; and the converts retained an intense devotion to the prophet who gave them the strength to achieve salvation. "One of the Onondagas, when asked why they did not leave their drunken habits before, since they were often urged to do it, and saw the ruinous consequences of such conduct replied, they had no power; but when the Great Spirit forbid such conduct by their prophet, he gave them the power to comply with their request."[63]

But Indian converts to Christianity were less sure of their power. The Oneida and Tuscarora reservations were unhappy places, for the Christian converts could not, as Handsome Lake's could, hold to temperance. And the Christian group at Sandusky, bedeviled by the witch-hunting and war prophecies of the Shawnee Prophet on the one hand and inspired by the preaching of Handsome Lake on the other, were a troubled people. A tragic account was given of a Christian convert named Barnet at Sandusky. In 1806 he was appointed one of the executioners of four women accused of witchcraft. They were "four of the best women in the nation" and the executioners refused to perform the task. Nor could he accept the teachings of Handsome Lake. In 1810 he came to the Christian mission and said that he was "much troubled about his relatives; in particular about four of them who listened to the Seneca-prophet, and are led astray by him. He had tried to convince them of their error, and to persuade them to forsake the prophet; but finds that he can have no influence on their minds. They appear in his view, to be bent on their own destruction. He is at a loss to know whether he should say anything more to them or not." Barnet became so sick and uneasy in his mind that he could not hunt, and his wife and children were in danger of perishing for want of warm clothing. They told the missionary that "it is his trouble about sin, makes him sick." Barnet was baptized a Christian in 1811 and was so happy that he could not sleep for joy. But next year he was depressed again and said he could "compare it to nothing, but to two constantly fighting within him." He feared that he would die.[64]

To Handsome Lake's converts, by contrast, came a feeling of peace, confidence, and strength. It is no wonder, as the Christian missionaries enviously said, that he was "held in great veneration by the people."[65]

⬱ 10 ⬳

RENAISSANCE

Handsome Lake's preaching was remarkably effective. Inspired by their prophet and taking advantage of the educational and technological aid offered by religious and government organizations, the Iroquois quickly began to implement the recommendations of the social gospel. A true renaissance occurred on many of the reservations in the years between 1799 and 1815. This renaissance affected the lives of the Iroquois most conspicuously in matters of temperance, technology, and religious observance.

Thus, long before his death in 1815 Handsome Lake was able to see both a spiritual and a profane reformation among his people. But the political strife that had plagued his own career continued and intensified after his death. It was not until after a generation of political disorder that his old disciples, sickened by the endless contention and threatened by the aggressive proselytizing of the Christian missions, collated and revived his words and made them into the code of a new religion, a religion that survives today as *Gaiwiio*— The Old Way of Handsome Lake.

· *Temperance* ·

The implementation of the prophet's demand for temperance was not left to individual conscience. The political structure of the several communities and of the Great League itself was mobilized to exact conformity to the discipline of sobriety. As we have seen, village, tribal, and League councils early met to discuss the prophet's Code and uniformly supported the condemnation of alcohol. At Allegany it was said that "they . . . seldom held a council without some animadversions of their baneful effects" (i.e., of spiritous liquors).[1] At many of these councils Handsome Lake appeared to exhort the people to follow the Code, but his presence was not necessary for his views were widely known and his revelations constantly cited. The Quaker journals and letters and the minutes of their meetings with the Indians were filled with formal declaration of the intention of the chiefs and principal men and women of individual communities to oppose the drinking of liquor. These council resolutions did not, to be sure, have the force of law in the European sense, for there were no police or courts to enforce the resolution; but the council members made it their business to harass nonconformists into sobriety. If the chiefs found out that someone had gotten drunk "when they were out in the white settlements, they were sharply reproved by the chiefs on their return, which had nearly the same effect among Indians, as committing a man to the workhouse among white people."[2]

The temperance program moved ahead most rapidly, of course, in the Seneca towns along the Allegheny River, where drunkards were continually under the watchful and reproving eye of Handsome Lake himself. The Quaker reports provide a year-by-year monitoring of the situation there. In May 1799, even before Handsome Lake's first vision, a council in Cornplanter's settlement had resolved not to permit any more whiskey to be imported into the town, and two young men had been appointed "petty chiefs" to enforce the resolution. By the month of September, after the vision, Cornplanter was able to report that the Allegany Seneca "now drank much less than formerly." By 1801 it was reported that "the Indians," including Handsome Lake himself, "now became very sober, generally refraining from the use of strong liquor, both at home and when abroad among the white people. One of them observed to Friends, 'no more get drunk here, now this two year.' "[3] By 1802 under the pressure of the charge that "the Whiskey is the great Engine which the bad Spirit uses to introduce Witchcraft and many other evils amongst Indians," sobriety was "in some degree spreading to other settlements of the Seneca Nation."[4] In 1803

Handsome Lake was praised as being principally responsible for curing the Seneca of "the misuse of that dreadful manbane, distilled spirits."[5] When the Quakers visited the Allegany in 1806, they learned that the surrounding white settlers were amazed by the fact that the Seneca would "entirely refuse liquor when offered to them. The Indians said, that when white people urged them to drink whiskey, they would ask for bread or provisions in its stead."[6] Black-snake informed the Quakers that the Indians still refused to drink whiskey and were "determined never to let the Whisky rise again."[7] Next year the Allegany chiefs, including Handsome Lake, reported again that their young men had generally given up the drinking of whiskey.[8]

The profit motive, however, which the Quakers were endeavoring to encourage, had mixed effects in regard to the general question of drinking. Two young chiefs in 1807 bought some whiskey and hid it, not for their own use, but for the purpose of selling it to the white people." But this conduct was "much disapproved by the Indians generally."[9] In 1809 it was reported by Allinson that an enterprising white trader, who succeeded in making a number of Seneca drunk on cider royal, was driven away from the Indian settlements: "A White Trader about 5 Months back had bought a Load of Goods up the River and among the rest some Cyder and Cyder Royal—stopping at Cold Spring he offered them for sale and the Indians not aware of the effects of Cyder-Royal many of them purchased & Drank particularly a few of their chiefs who collecting in their council Houses alarmed many of the Sober Indians—who threatened to Stave his Casks & let out the Liquor if he did not go away—they however thought it best first to come & advise with Friends & with this View several of their Warriors Came down to Tunassasa—on their Representation Joel Swain & Jacob Taylor went with them to their Town but the Trader probably alarmed with the threats of the Indians and removed his Canoe Further up the River where it is expected he disposed of his Liquors among the White People." Allinson included his observations on Allegany Seneca drinking in 1809 on a positive note: "The Indians of this Settlement generally abstain from the use of Spiritous Liquors so that it has become very rare to see one of them Intoxicated—since which they seldom quarrel or fight among themselves but live in Harmony to-gether—this disposition they endeavour to Cultivate among the

Children & hence they rarely differ as is very common with Boys.
. . . They are naturally avaricious and saving & not being so liable to
Imposition as when they drank Spirits, some of them are growing
rich."[10]

Indian storekeepers continued to contribute to backsliding from
temperance for many years, and Handsome Lake was unable completely to suppress the traffic in liquor. His prophecies of doom and
damnation were used to good effect in reducing it to minor proportions, however. In the fall of 1811 the prophet had been issuing grave
warnings of divine retribution "if they fell into their former bad
practices." During the winter several earthquake shocks were felt
along the borders of Lake Erie and the Niagara frontier "which
gave the Indians such alarm that they believ'd the predictions of
their prophet was going to be fulfil'd upon them. . . . They believ'd
it to be the voice of the great Spirit, that he had now spoken so
loud as to be heard and that some great event would follow." Resolutions against whiskey-selling were immediately reasserted. And in
1814 one of the principal Indian whiskey-sellers died of a lingering
illness. He had kept a "kind of store" where "from the love of gain"
he kept liquor to sell. "In a time of great affliction of body, and distress of mind, he acknowledged that Selling whisky and other bad
practices had brought him to that situation—this with the more
thoughtful part of the Indians had a serious effect, and in consequence thereof many of their leading characters became again animated to discourage the use of strong drink among them."[11]

On other Seneca reservations, particularly at Cattaraugus and
Tonawanda, the temperance movement was also notably successful.
In 1801 Red Jacket, as "Chief Speaker of the Seneker Nations," declared that "we have all agreed to quit the use of liquor which you
must be in some measure convinced of from what you see at the
present meeting" (which was for the purpose of receiving the
annuities, and was held at the Genesee River).[12] At Cattaraugus the
Quakers were told in 1806 that the chiefs' council "had taken up
strong resolutions against the use of Whisky and Strong drink & that
all that was then present were Chiefs & each of them kept a daily
watch over the rest of the Indians to caution them against drinking
Whisky playing ball or other Bad practices which they believ'd
was not pleasing to the Great Spirit—but were of the mind that the
Great Spirit was better pleas'd when they took hold of the ax or the

hoe and set to work—that since they had got their eyes open to see they were sensible that strong drink had done them a great deal of mischief and kept them poor but now they had got hold of it and was determined never to let it rise again & that they were in hopes that the Indians of the Six Nations would in time become master of it."[13] Even more direct was the information given the Quakers at the same settlement in 1809: the Cattaraugus Seneca "had done with the use of spiritous liquors every man, but there were yet three women who would sometimes become intoxicated, yet they did not intend to cease labouring with them till they became reformed."[14] At a council of Seneca from various reservations held at Jenuchshadago in January 1803 it was announced by a chief from Tonawanda that his people too had renounced the use of strong drink.[15]

The other tribes also joined in temperance, inspired by Handsome Lake. In 1803 a missionary reported of the Onondaga that they had "for two years greatly reformed in their intemperate drinking. . . . The Impression he made was so powerful, that different tribes held several councils on the subject, and finally agreed to leave off the intemperate use of strong liquors."[16] The effect of the prophet's preaching on the Onondaga is vividly described in the recollections of a trader and whiskey-seller named Webster. One day eighteen of the principal chiefs and warriors of the Onondaga nation called at the trading post saying that they were just setting out to attend "a great council of the six nations, to be held at Buffalo." Mr. Webster treated them to a drink all round, and they left in high spirits. In due time the delegates returned and again stopped off at Webster's trading post. The trader put a bottle of liquor before them, but to his "utter astonishment . . . every man of them refused to touch it." At first he thought that this was a sign of hostility and feared for his life, "for he could imagine that nothing short of the most deadly resentment (or a miracle), could produce so great a change." But he was quickly reassured. "The chiefs explained, that they had met at Buffalo, a Prophet of the Seneca nation, who had assured them, and in this assurance they had the most implicit confidence, that without a total abstinence, from the use of ardent spirits, they and their race would shortly become extinct; that they had entered upon a resolution, never again to taste the baneful article, and that they hoped to be able to prevail on their nation to adopt the same salutary resolution. Many at this early day adopted the temperance principles, it is said at least three fourths of all the nation; and of all those who pledged themselves to the cause, not an instance was known of alienation or neglect; but to a man, they religiously adhered to their solemn pledge. The consequence was, that from a drunken, filthy, lazy, worthless, set of beings, they became a cleanly, industrious, sober, happy, and more prosperous people. At this period, it was considered one of the most temperate communities in the land; only a very few of the nation indulging in the intoxicating cup, and these were treated with contempt by their more sober companions."[17] On another occasion an Onondaga, on being asked why they had not abandoned their drunken habits before (as they had often been urged to do by white missionaries and others, and which they knew to have ruinous consequences), explained that earlier "they had no power but when the Great Spirit forbid such conduct by their prophet, he gave them power to comply with his request."[18] In 1809, Quakers reported, the Onondaga "had totally refrained from the use of ardent spirits for about 9 years, and . . . none of the natives will touch it."[19]

The effect on the Oneida was equally striking. The Oneida had for many years been served by a harried schoolmaster, by Quaker missionaries, and by Samuel Kirkland, who had formed a congregation of more or less loyal Christians. In 1799, as we remarked earlier, the Oneida had been swept by a revival of the pagan religion recommended by a Mohawk prophet from the Grand River. But by August 1806, the full import of Handsome Lake's revelation had been communicated to them, even to the Christians, by a member of the Christian congregation, the Reverend Mr. Kirkland's Oneida helper, Doctor Peter. After Kirkland's sermon Doctor Peter stood up and spoke about "the late revelations from the Seneka prophet, or man of God, as they stile him." Doctor Peter spoke "with great zeal and eloquence."

He said the prophet enjoined the strictest temperance and sobriety upon all Indians, and commanded them to abstain from the use of ardent spirits, which was never made for Indians; and for any Indian to drink a single glass or one swallow would be a deadly sin if not repented of. (Here in his great zeal he overstepped the mark, and this bold assertion was apparently displeasing to many.) He then exhorted them to live in peace and love one another and all mankind, white people as well as Indians. He then spoke upon the duties of husbands and wives, and the great sin of divorce.

The pagans, according to Kirkland, although they became converts to Handsome Lake's Code, were not overly successful in their adherence to the rule of temperance; but Kirkland's flock of Christians were not always sober either. In any case, the Seneca prophet was quoted in December 1806, as insisting that total temperance was necessary to salvation. "He forbids their feeling envious or resentful towards the white people because they so generally and freely use it, forbids them to reproach the white people with being the inventors of rum. This would be very offensive to the Great Spirit, for it was God who made rum, and made it for the white people to be used as a medicine to strengthen them after labor!" But he reported that fewer among the pagan Oneida were temperate than among the Onondaga. Despite the uncertainty of their sobriety, however, even Kirkland certified that the pagan party "absolutely forbid the use of rum, and assert that no Indian can be a good man who takes even a spoonful."[20]

The temperance movement was least effective at Buffalo Creek, at Tuscarora, and on the Genesee, where Iroquois settlements were closest to major white population centers. Buffalo Creek, furthermore, was the headquarters of Red Jacket, who although a defender of the old pagan religion of the Iroquois and an opponent of demon rum, was not favorably disposed toward the pretensions to power of Handsome Lake. Red Jacket himself drank, and so did Young King, another Buffalo Creek resident, one of the most influential of the Seneca chiefs, before his conversion to Christianity in the 1820's. In 1807 Handsome Lake and other Allegany Seneca leaders declared, "We are almost discouraged about our Brothers at Buffalo and Genesee River," on account of their persistence in intemperate habits.[21] And in 1809 Allinson on his visit to Buffalo said: "There are several Indian Towns with in a few miles & the Indians are too often here to give hope, on National Ground, of their general reformation from the use of Spiritous Liquors, & yet we were told that many of them have abandened this Destroyer & stand firm against Temptation." At Tuscarora nearby, where by 1809 the chiefs had committed the nation to Christianity, the council declared "we mean to keep sabath, and hear Gospel, and try to persuade all our Nation not Drunk Whiskey—we shamed any of our People get Drunk."[22]

The overall impression provided by many observers between 1800 and 1810 is that the Iroquois in New York had substantially reduced their consumption of alcohol. In 1806 Halliday Jackson was able to sum up his impressions to this effect: "I . . . have noted with satisfaction that in the course of our travels among all the Indians on the Allegheny River, or either of the Villages at Cataraugus we have not seen a Single individual the least intoxicated with Liquor—which perhaps would be a Singular Circumstance to Observe in traveling among the same number of white Inhabitants."[23] And Jacob Taylor in 1809, when he was at Buffalo Creek to attend a meeting of the Council of the Six Nations, remarked, "I think I never saw so many Indians together before that conducted with so much propriety— the number could not be well ascertained, but it was thought there were about One Thousand, and I dont remember to see one Drunken Indian amongst them."[24]

· Technology ·

BY 1799 THE IROQUOIS had for a generation been living in a state of economic limbo, unable any longer to hunt extensively or even very effectively to continue the traditional agriculture. During the war years, they had been largely dependent upon military stores for rations, clothing, and equipment; after the war, they had relied heavily on handouts from Indian agents and missionaries and on the annuities paid to the tribes and to individual chiefs. Now, and suddenly, they embraced the rural technology of the white man and became a nation of farmers. The effective causes for this cultural transition were, as in the case of the relinquishment of alcohol, certainly multiple. Advice and general example had been provided for many years, but agriculture by men had been resisted as an effeminate occupation with the women themselves taking the lead in ridiculing male farmers as transvestites. "If a Man took hold of a Hoe to use it the Women would get down his gun by way of derision & would laugh & say such a Warrior is a timid woman."[25] The final realization of the irrevocability of reservation life, occurring simultaneously with Handsome Lake's explicit sanctioning of the farmer's role for men and the provision of tools and instruction in their use by Quakers and other whites, made the change possible.

The Quaker observers provide anecdotal, and sometimes even statistical, measures of the pace of agricultural reform among the Iroquois. The initial approach of the Allegany Seneca to the proposed new methods was cautious and sometimes even rigorously scientific. "It was in the spring of 1801, that the Indians first began to use the plough for themselves. They took a very cautious method of determining whether it was likely to be an advantageous change for them or not. Several parts of a large field were ploughed, and the intermediate spaces prepared by their women with the hoe, according to former custom. It was all planted with corn; and the parts ploughed (besides the great saving of labour), produced much the heaviest crop; the stalks being more than a foot higher, and proportionably stouter than those in the hoed ground."[26] The support that the chief women at this time gave to Handsome Lake and to the Quakers was indispensable, for it released the men from the embarrassment of being called effeminate when they worked in the fields. By the end of the year 1801 the agricultural revolution along the Allegheny was well underway. Individual fields were being fenced (about 18,000 fence rails were sawed and split in that year alone). Instead of clusters of cabins near the river, now there were well-made log houses with shingled roofs scattered among the fields and meadows. The trail along the river was widened, and soon some twenty miles of roads, usable by wagons, connected all settled parts of the reservation. The tinkling of cowbells could be heard in all directions, and corn fodder and mown hay were stored to feed the cattle through the winter. In 1801 thirteen or fourteen new farming lots were laid out, and in 1803 some seventeen new houses were constructed. By 1806, when a Quaker inspection team arrived to survey the work of the preceding eight years, they found that both the settlement pattern and house type had dramatically changed. Now the Allegany Seneca lived in a hundred or so log cabins, of which about thirty were concentrated at Cold Spring village and the rest distributed among approximately one hundred individually fenced farms. Many of the houses were roofed with shingles and had panel doors and glass windows. A number of these farms had barns and were equipped with carts and wagons. The fencing was a good eight to ten rails high. The carpentry work had been mostly done by

Indians, including the corner-notching of the logs; "scarcely a vestige remained of the cabins they occupied when Friends first settled among them [in 1798]."[27] Standards of cleanliness had improved, and there was some modern furniture. The Quaker inspection team was entertained in the house of Cornplanter's son Henry. It was the local showpiece: "It was a good house and well finished with a Piazza in front pallisaided round, and altho' its internal furniture still bore some marks of Indian housWifery, they were furnished with a good feather bed enclosed with Callico Curtains."[28] The Minister's house, up the river from Cold Spring, was painted red and white and surrounded by a red paling fence "& at a Distance looks very smart."[29] Many of the chiefs at both Allegany and Cattaraugus built two-story houses. The council-house, at the center of Cold Spring village only a few yards from Handsome Lake's house, was forty feet long by twenty wide and the largest structure in the town. It was built of boards. All dwelling houses, however, still had earthen floors and were infested with fleas, bedbugs, and other insects, and dogs and pigs wandered through the open doors.

In 1826 the total Seneca population of 469 persons in the Allegany band was assigned by the Quakers to one or another of 80 "families" (presumably meaning nuclear households); thus the average family size was approximately six persons.[30] This suggests that the combined effect of the new settlement pattern dictated by the needs of rural technology and of the social gospel preached by Handsome Lake, emphasizing the focal moral importance of the nuclear household, had within a generation been able to complete the transition from the ancient matrilineal household to the nuclear family. Eventually, also, these families became patrilineal with respect to name and inheritance, the Indian men taking on an English name, or an English translation of an Indian name, as a surname, and transmitting this name, along with inheritance rights to real estate, in the white style.

The new agriculture was productive and diversified. By 1801 the yield of corn had been increased tenfold. Spring wheat was planted between 1801 and 1806, and by 1806 the Indian farmers were adding to the traditional staples (corn, squash, beans, and tobacco) such other new crops as oats, buckwheat, potatoes, turnips, and flax. Grain was ground at the Quaker mill; the old wooden mortars fell into disuse. The production of flax was tied to the arts of spinning and weaving, which took hold firmly about 1807; by 1813 many of the Indian women were operating their own spinning wheels and producing over the winter sufficient thread to keep two Indian weavers busy making some two hundred yards of cloth, including both linen and wool, from which they made blankets and other useful cloth; some surplus was even sold to whites off the reservation. So profitable were the farms that some Seneca were able to invest in livestock. By 1803 there were well over a hundred head of cattle and by 1806 over a hundred horses; by 1810 there were at least five yoke of oxen available for heavy farm labor, such as hauling firewood and clearing fields of stones and stumps; by 1814 there was a considerable stock of swine being kept. By 1816 all but four families had "horned cattle," and the number of such cattle in the community reached four hundred. The Indians were learning to tan hides and salt the beef. Sheep still could not be managed because of the incursions of wolves.

Inevitably, various cultural consequences flowed from the fundamental new economic transformation. Progress in public health measures was an early effect. By 1805 the Indian women were learning to make soap, and standards of personal and household cleanliness were rising. During the War of 1812 the Quakers were able to avert a threatened epidemic of smallpox by vaccinating over a thousand Seneca at Allegany and Cattaraugus.[31] The Quakers emphasized the virtue of cleanliness so strongly that some of the Indian women, when white visitors approached "would immediately begin to sweep their houses, and appear somewhat disconcerted if friends entered their doors before they got their apartments in order." But the absence of surgeons to mend broken bones and stitch cuts and the general inability of both Indian and white medicine of the day to cope effectively with infectious and degenerative diseases meant that there were relatively large numbers of older people whose bodies bore the scars and deformities of a lifetime without effective medical care. Battered, aging hulks, half blind, or lame, or crippled in hand or foot or disfigured from the lack of minor surgery, they nonetheless worked as their infirmities allowed.

A specialization of labor among Indian artisans developed, with individual Indian men setting up shop as weavers, blacksmiths, shoemakers, and carpenters. Some Indian farmers were said to be getting rich, and others, who for a time had clung to hunting as their means of support, had with the decline of the small remaining local fur trade about 1810 been forced to hire themselves out as farm laborers to the well-to-do. A few of the men were adding to their income by renting out their land and by working part time as smiths, carpenters, and shoemakers, and everyone, of course, had access to timber and grazing meadows on the "national land," which was held in common by the tribe and could be used by anyone so long as he did not interfere with anyone else's use. Some of the Indians even complained of the pace of work and resented the comparative leisure of their domestic animals. "An Industrious Indian" at Cattaraugus testified that "he had become very uneasy on thinking he had so much to do to provide for his horses and that they had done nothing to assist him that he had lost considerable of Sleep on the occasion and was determined in future to make them assist him work."[32] The Quakers were well pleased with the progress made at Allegany, and in 1814 observed that "their improvements rather exceeded, in divers respects, those made in some new settlements of white people on the frontiers, in the same length of time."

The economic structure of the Indian farm household was described in detail in 1820 by the Quaker historian of the Tunessassa mission. He compiled individual data on a sample of thirty-five families (nearly half of the community). His figures showed that the average Indian family had cleared and fenced ten acres of ground, putting four in corn, two in oats, one in potatoes, and using the rest for meadow, orchard, or vegetable garden; owned a plow and either a pair of horses or a yoke of oxen; and kept five cows and eleven pigs. Only four households had less than five acres of cleared ground and only three more than fifteen. By 1826 the eighty families at Allegany were working 699 acres of improved land, raising thereon corn (239 acres), oats (116), hay (70), potatoes (42), wheat (38), besides a quantity of buckwheat and various vegetables. These families possessed 479 head of cattle, 58 horses, and 350 hogs. The agricultural revolution had become the way of life for the next generation.[33]

Although the Quaker vocational school, conducted in the Seneca language, thus was remarkably effective in transforming the economic basis of Seneca society, comparable progress was not made in academic instruction. The Friends had in the winter of 1798–9 opened their school to instruct Indian children—in English—in reading, writing, and arithmetic, and although about twenty pupils had attended on and off, they proved irregular scholars. The project of academic, as opposed to vocational, education, was abandoned for ten years, and instead a few—perhaps half a dozen—Indian youths were sent from time to time to live with Friends in Philadelphia for several years, there to absorb English letters, Quaker values, and the manual arts. In 1810 a census of the households revealed that most of the parents wanted their children to attend a summer school. But still very few of the Allegany Seneca spoke English, and instruction in reading, writing, and arithmetic could be conducted only with great difficulty. A Quaker school at Tunessassa was not firmly established until 1822. Throughout the period from 1799 to about 1825, despite the occasional presence of a schoolmaster, not more than twenty children were regular pupils at any one time, and it may be doubted whether the schools accomplished much more than rudimentary instruction in English speech. As the Quakers observed about 1811, "very few of them had yet acquired the English language so as to be able to understand what they did learn."[34]

Technological progress was faster at Allegany, which received the concentrated attention of both Handsome Lake and the Quakers, than it was on the other reservations. But all were moving in the same direction. The Quakers frequently visited Cattaraugus and donated mill irons and plows; the Cattaraugus Seneca soon were building two-story board houses, fencing their farms, and keeping livestock. The Quakers also gave sawmill irons to Red Jacket for building a mill at Buffalo Creek, and they and Kirkland's mission had earlier helped the Oneida. And Handsome Lake was urging economic acculturation everywhere. Allegany was merely the spearhead of the movement to abandon the traditional technological and economic structure and to adopt the white man's customs.

· *Religious Observance* ·

HANDSOME LAKE DID NOT CONSIDER that his revelations and the gospels that issued from them constituted a new religion. He believed rather that he was commissioned to revive in a pure, full, and correct form the traditional religious observances of the Iroquois and thereby to guide his people toward a better life in this world and salvation in the next. Although later his disciples, in codifying the prophet's teachings, did in effect create a new religious institution, during his lifetime such innovations as he proposed were added to the body of Iroquois belief in the spirit of free incorporation of dream-inspired religious observance that was characteristic of Iroquois culture. At no time, despite his difficulties in political affairs, did he have to confront a conservative *religious* opposition except in the matter of the medicine-societies.

The religious renaissance among the Iroquois thus was essentially a renewal of popular observance of the traditional communal religious rituals. The major innovation in belief—the idea of divine judgment and an afterlife in heaven or hell—was readily palatable and quickly and widely accepted because it was similar in form to the old belief in the cosmic bargain between the Good Twin and the Evil Twin. There were few important innovations in ritual adopted as a result of the prophet's teaching. The old annual calendar—including the white dog ceremony—was celebrated without any modification except, at Allegany, the abandonment of the statue of Tarachiawagon.[35] The old medicine-societies—including the False Faces—continued their rituals despite the prophet's qualms about them.[36] His emphasis upon the four sacred ceremonies—Thanksgiving Dance, Great Feather Dance, Personal Chants, and Bowl Game—did not imply that all other observances should be abandoned; it was merely an endorsement of the central themes in existing ritual. The pantheon remained unchanged except for the addition of a new scene of action for the struggle between the creative and destructive principles, represented traditionally by the Good Twin and the Evil Twin, Tarachiawagon and the Great World Rim Dweller, in the domain of heaven and hell, where the same protagonists bore different names (Haweniyu or the Great Spirit, and Ganosge' or the Tormentor). The ritual of confession, which later became a central feature of the religion of Handsome Lake, was in his own time simply an application of the traditional practice of requiring confession of a suspected witch, and Handsome Lake's central role as accuser and confessor was an amplification of the old responsibility of the shaman. The prophet directly supported the Minister at Cold Spring who for years had been calling the people together for the ceremonies, and he indirectly supported any other traditional religious leader whom he could find. Even his own temporary position as great leader was an extension of custom, for in times of crisis the Iroquois were used to the nomination of powerful war-captains or political leaders (like Brant among the Mohawk and Cornplanter among the Seneca) who were made responsible for mobilizing the village, tribe, or League to action.

Thus, in the first decades of the nineteenth century, when the Quaker missionaries and Mary Jemison, the white captive, described the religious rituals among the Seneca and Kirkland wrote his accounts of the pagan ceremonies of the Oneida, they delineated a ceremonial and belief system already hundreds of years old with minor modifications of content, emphasis, and terminology recently suggested by Handsome Lake. Furthermore, each Iroquois tribe, and even each band or reservation community, maintained its own more or less variant form of this general system. Handsome Lake, under the circumstances, simply could not introduce a new religious system standardized for all the reservations. As we shall see, it was not the prophet but the prophet's disciples who created the new, relatively uniform institution known as the Longhouse Religion or the New Religion of Handsome Lake, with its own unique beliefs, rituals, organization, and ceremonial paraphernalia, and who determined the relation this new institution should have to the old religion that Handsome Lake himself had practiced.

There was, for a time, some religious doubt expressed by various critics of the prophet who, as he put it, would say, "We lack an understanding of this religion." Most of this doubt did, as one might expect, focus on the introduction of the concept of divine judgment and an afterlife in heaven or hell. Handsome Lake answered the critics who asked why no one had known these things before by suggesting that not everything was known even to the angels, who told him, "even we, the servants of the Creator, do not understand all things." When asked where the ancestors had gone, he replied,

Now it is said that your fathers of old never reached the true lands of our Creator nor did they ever enter the house of the tormentor, Ganosge'. It is said that in some matters they did the will of the Creator and that in others they did not. They did both good and bad and none was either good or bad. They are therefore in a place separate and unknown to us, we think, enjoying themselves.[37]

But rather than propose new ritual, Handsome Lake applied these new principles of belief as sanctions for the observance of old custom. It was, he said, man's duty to follow the traditional ceremonies; it was the Evil Spirit who kept him away from the performing the ancient religious observances of the Iroquois.

Thus the religious innovations of Handsome Lake were modifications of belief whose function was to ensure the dedication of the people to conservative ritual. He was in his own eyes as the messenger of God, necessarily the defender of the faith. And at his behest hundreds of lukewarm pagans and half-converted Christians returned to the council-house to hear once again the prayers of thanksgiving, to burn the white dog, to tell their dreams, and play the Sacred Bowl Game—the cosmic game of chance forever being renewed in the endless and balanced struggle between the Spirit of Good and the Spirit of Evil.

· The Death of Handsome Lake ·

HANDSOME LAKE DIED on August 10, 1815, while on a visit to Onondaga. He had for some time had intimations of approaching death. In the spring at Allegany he had had a vision:

> The day was bright when I went into the planted field and alone I wandered in the planted field and it was the time of the second hoeing. Suddenly a damsel appeared and threw her arms about my neck and as she clasped me she spoke saying, "When you leave this earth for the new world above, it is our wish to follow you." I looked for the damsel but saw only the long leaves of corn twining round my shoulders. And then I understood that it was the spirit of the corn who had spoken, she the sustainer of life. So I replied, "O spirit of the corn, follow not me but abide still upon the earth and be strong and be faithful to your purpose. Ever endure and do not fail the children of women. It is not time for you to follow for Gaiwiio is only in its beginning."[38]

That summer he went again on his annual visit to the other reservations, walking first the seventy-five miles to Tonawanda, where he received a formal invitation from Onondaga to visit there and preach to the people. Again he had a vision foreboding death.

The prophet was depressed, and his thoughts were muddled with voices and frequent visions. "I must now take up my final journey to the new world," he thought, and he "longed for the home of his childhood and pined to return." In response to a command from the angels he called together the children and told them that he would die. They pleaded with him not to go. Then the prophet "rose and exhorted them to ever be faithful and a great multitude heard him and wept." He started out afoot on the 150-mile trip to Onondaga accompanied by a number of followers. At Canawaugus, on the Genesee River, the place where he was born, they stopped and here performed the Thanksgiving Address. Then he spoke to his followers, saying, "I have had a dream, a wondrous vision. I seemed to see a pathway, a trail overgrown and covered with grass so that it appeared not to have been traveled in a long time." The company stopped again at the head of Seneca Lake, and again Handsome Lake performed the Thanksgiving Ritual and reported another dream: "I heard in a dream a certain woman speaking but I am not able to say whether she was of Onondaga or of Tonawanda from whence we came."

When they came near the Onondaga Reservation line, they stopped to eat lunch. After they had entered the reservation and were near the council-house, Handsome Lake discovered that he had lost his knife. He was disturbed and announced, "I have forgotten my knife. I may have left it where we stopped and ate last. I can not lose that knife for it is one that I prize above many things. Therefore I must return and find it." He went back alone along the trail to find the knife while the others went on to the council-house to wait for him.

He became sick while he was searching for the knife and with great difficulty struggled back to the Onondaga village. He was not able to reach the council-house "for he was very sick and in great distress," and took refuge in a small cabin some distance away, along a creek at the foot of the hill. The formal council was canceled; without the prophet the meeting was, to use the old form of words, "only a gathering about the fire place." The prophet remained in the cabin, ill and in pain, for several days. The chiefs sent a messenger to bring Henry O'Bail from Allegany. The people tried to amuse him by playing a game of lacrosse in his honor. "It was a bright and beautiful day and they brought him out so that he might see the play. Soon he desired to be taken back in to the house."

Near the end he addressed the crowd gathered about the cabin: I will soon go to my new home. Soon I will step into the new world for there is a plain pathway before me leading there. Whoever follows my teachings will follow in my footsteps and I will look back upon him with outstretched arms inviting him into the new world of our Creator. Alas, I fear that a pall of smoke will obscure the eyes of many from the truth of Gaiwiio but I pray that when I am gone that all may do what I have taught.[39]

He died soon after this, before his nephew could reach him, but attended by three persons who swore to keep the details of his last moments a secret. The story was given out by his three attendants that when he died, "he said he was going home, & then passed away without sickness."

The body of Handsome Lake was buried in the center of the council-house. In due course the ceremony of condolence required by his office as a chief of the League was performed, and his successor to the title—probably a fellow council chief from Allegany named Snow[40]—was installed. The news of his death reached Buffalo on August 27, when Indian agent Erastus Granger, his old rival, wrote vindictively, "You say the prophet is dead, and I say amen."[41] But the death notice in the *Buffalo Gazette* of October 3 was more charitable:

. . . died . . . at the Onondaga Castle, in the 66th year of his age, the Allegheny Chief, known throughout the Indian territories as the *Peace Prophet,* to distinguish from *Neemeser,* the brother of Tecumseh. Until fifty years old he was remarkable only for his stupidity and beastly drunkenness.—But about eighteen years since he fell in a fit—continued insensible for several hours; and was considered dead. He, however, recovered and exclaimed, *"Don't be alarmed. I have seen Heaven: call the nation together that I may explain to them what I have seen and heard."* The tribe was collected, and he told them he had in his trance seen four beautiful young men, sent by the Great Spirit, and who addressed him thus: *"the Great Spirit is angry with you, and all the red men, and unless you immediately refrain from drunkenness, lying and stealing, you shall never enter the beautiful place which we will now show you."* He then said, he was conducted to the gate of Heaven, which was open, but which he was not allowed to enter: that it was beautiful beyond description, and the inhabitants perfectly happy:—that he was then brought back, and the young men on taking leave promised to pay him a visit yearly to witness the effect of their mission. The chief immediately abandoned his habits, visited the tribes,—related his story—which was believed, and the consequence has been, that from a filthy, lazy, drunken set of beings, they have become cleanly, industrious, sober, and happy. The Prophet continued, he says annually to receive his celestial visitants: annually made his visits to the tribes: and was on one of them when he deceased.[42]

· *The Years of Trouble* ·

THE THIRTY YEARS between the death of the prophet and the formation of a new church dedicated to his name were a new time of continuously mounting pressure for the New York Iroquois. The time of trouble culminated in a disastrous land sale and the division of the nation into Christian and "pagan" factions. The pressures upon the Indians took three forms: white settlement and economic penetration, white missionary activity, and the purchase of Indian land.

After the War of 1812 the frontiers of western New York were rapidly occupied by white farmers and entrepreneurs. All the northerly reservations were encircled by settlements, and even the old asylum along the Allegheny, which except for the area actually occupied by the Seneca was little suited for farming, was gradually surrounded by little villages and individual farms located on the isolated tracts where by hard work a family could scratch out a living. Sometimes these people pastured their cattle on Indian lands, to the considerable irritation of the Indians. Others, taking advantage of the vast stands of white pine, about this time began the logging industry, floating big rafts down the river past the village at Cold Spring to the sawmills at Warren. Although the Indians used their own sawmill for squaring logs and cutting boards for their own use, and had sold small quantities of cut lumber, they too began now to cut the big pines and float the rafts down to sell at the mills. All of these activities, coming so soon after the war, tended to expose the Indians again to whiskey and to contemptuous white men and somewhat to distract them from the process of reform that the Quakers and the prophet had launched. And in 1830 the first steamboat anchored at Cornplanter's village on its way upstream.[43]

Even more threatening to the integrity of the reservation communities was the intrusion of Christian evangelists. The social gospel of Handsome Lake had prepared the Iroquois to cope with the economic problems of life on the reservations. It had not, however, equipped them to deal successfully with the challenge of missionaries who sought to make converts. The religious people they had admitted into their communities—the Quakers at Allegany and Cattaraugus and Jabez Hyde, a Presbyterian schoolmaster at Buffalo Creek—from 1811 to 1818 had acted only as secular advisers and teachers and had not attempted to convert the Indians to Christianity. But the evangelical missionary movement, springing up in the first decade of the nineteenth century, began seriously to turn its attention to the native Indians of New York in the second. By 1814 other and more sanctimonious Christian denominations than Quakers were taking an interest in the Seneca Indians. In that year Cornplanter, resentful of Quaker criticism of him for taking up drinking, invited the Western Missionary Society to set up a school on the grant. This school lasted from 1814 to 1818 and served as the entering wedge for evangelism, for circuit preachers appointed by the society annually visited the settlement during those years to bring the word of God to the heathen.[44] In 1816 the Reverend Mr. Timothy Alden, representing the Society for the Propagation of the Gospel among the Indians of North America, visited Cornplanter's Town and the school there. He found that the schoolmaster had already succeeded in persuading the seven households still located on the grant to discontinue the annual calendar of religious ceremonies and no longer to profane the sabbath "by hunting, amusements, nor any kind of labor. Such already is the happy effect of the example set by Mr. Oldham and his family." Next year, when Alden returned to preach in Cornplanter's house, with Henry O'Bail as interpreter, he found that the schoolmaster was holding religious services every Sunday. Cornplanter told him that he was convinced the Christians must be right "because you have the words of the Great Spirit written in a book." Alden that year also visited Cold Spring and preached to the Seneca farther up the river; he gave a sermon to Red Jacket and some of the chiefs at Buffalo Creek. In 1818 he preached again at Cornplanter's Town, Cold Spring, Buffalo Creek, and Cattaraugus. In 1820 he preached at Cattaraugus and Tonawanda.[45]

About this time, at the other end of the Seneca country, the

United Foreign Missionary Society, taking over responsibility for the Seneca field from the New York Missionary Society, which had succeeded only in maintaining a school, began an aggressive campaign of evangelism. At Buffalo Creek some of the Indians were persuaded in 1818 to accept a "preacher of the Gospel," and Hyde's day school became a boarding school where the pupils would be safe from pagan influences. This Buffalo Creek missionary group fanned out quickly, dispatching a schoolteacher to Tuscarora and a missionary to Cattaraugus, and including Allegany on the annual circuit of the missionaries regularly assigned to Buffalo and Cattaraugus. A Baptist missionary was already established at Tonawanda (although he was physically ejected in 1822). The Oneida and Tuscarora were already nominally Christianized. Indian churches were organized at Buffalo in 1823, at Cattaraugus in 1827, and in 1830 at Allegany. The Allegany Christian congregation grew apace, and by 1844 it had grown to 144 members in regular standing. In 1829 the Gospel of Luke, the Sermon on the Mount, and several hymns were printed in the Seneca language. In 1831 the Reverend Mr. Asher Wright commenced his mission at Buffalo Creek and transferred it to Cattaraugus when the Buffalo Creek Reservation was abandoned in 1845. He and his wife learned Seneca and were able to maintain both a church congregation and a distinguished boarding school, the Thomas Indian School.[46]

The third source of pressure was the demand that the Indians of New York sell their reservations. In 1810 the Holland Land Company had sold to the Ogden Land Company the preemption right to the Seneca reservations. After the war the local agents and shareholders of this company, who included such prominent landowners as James Wadsworth of the Genesee and General Peter B. Porter of Buffalo, congressman and later Secretary of War, worked to persuade the Indians to sell their lands and move to the west. By 1817 the Seneca were seriously discussing such a move and even sent a delegation to Sandusky to investigate the possibility of joining their kinsmen in Ohio. But the advantages of such a removal appeared to be slight, and few if any of the Indians wished to leave New York, where there appeared to be every prospect of peaceful relations with the surrounding white community and of continuing advance in their material welfare. Nonetheless, by bribes, threats of dire punishment for refusing to obey the supposed wish of the United States government for such a move, and deliberate misrepresentation of the facts to federal authorities, Seneca and other Iroquois chiefs were brought unwillingly to sign treaties by which some of the reservations were sold to the Ogden Land Company and the State of New York. In 1821 part of the Oneida reserve was lost, and many of the pagans removed to Wisconsin. In 1826 the Seneca sold to the Ogden Land Company all five of the remaining Genesee River reservations, most of Tonawanda, about a third of Buffalo Creek, and a fifth of Cattaraugus. Pressure to remove the Indians entirely west of the Mississippi now began to form in Washington, and despite bitter complaints about the 1826 treaty almost half of the chiefs of the Indians of New York residing on the Seneca reservations in 1838 were persuaded to sign another treaty, by which they agreed to emigrate to Kansas and vacate the reservations. A party of nearly two hundred did go to Kansas, where nearly half died; nearly all of the survivors returned, complaining about the climate, the lands, and the hostility of the Indians already resident there. So much resentment was aroused by this treaty, and so many whites, including Quakers, worked to negate it, that it was finally renegotiated in 1842. By the terms of 1842 the Seneca were left in possession of Allegany, Cattaragus, and Oil Creek reservations. Buffalo Creek was evacuated in 1845, the residents finding refuge at Cattaraugus and Allegany, and at Grand River. The Tonawanda Seneca simply refused to move, and after prolonged litigation they were confirmed in possession of a small part of their original reservation. And the Onondaga, whose lands were not involved in the interests of the Ogden Land Company, also remained on their reservation.[47]

The combined effect of the pressures of settlement, missionary work, and land negotiations was to split the Seneca into two factions: the "Christian" party and the so-called "pagan" party. The missionaries had an immediate and surprising success in making converts and by 1830 probably had secured the adherence, in sympathy if not by baptism, of half the population. Probably the ratio of occasional but convinced church attenders to baptized converts was on the order of ten to one—an unfavorable ratio, from the missionary standpoint, but not an important distinction to many Seneca, who were not accustomed to think in terms of exclusive church "membership." At Allegany alone in 1819 several of the chiefs favored the gospel; by 1828 there were about 180 "Christians," including five chiefs.[48] The Christians were no more eager to sell land than the pagans, for they could not look forward to any improvement in either spiritual or material condition if they removed westward, away from their missionaries, into rough and turbulent frontier regions. The missionaries on their part sought earnestly to protect their charges, both Christian and pagan, from eviction. But the Christian Indians were apt to be more conformist, trusting, and submissive in the face of demands from land agents and government officials, who claimed to be fellow Christians. And at the urging of their ministers, who were evangelists seeking to make converts, they were also less tolerant of the pagan party in religious and political matters than the pagan party was of them.

The leader and chief spokesman of the Christian party was a Buffalo Creek chief named Young King. Young King was the maternal nephew of Old Smoke and, like Handsome Lake, was regarded among white men as a "heavy, dull, unambitious, but honest man." He was a big man physically and a respected warrior who had been wounded by a musket ball in the leg during the War of 1812. He was also a heavy drinker and in 1815, in the course of a drunken brawl, had lost an arm when a white man swung at him with a scythe. As early as 1815 he had been willing to have some Indian children educated in school and instructed in the Christian religion. During the 1820's he became an avowed Christian sympathizer and a temperance advocate; pointing to his arm, he would say, "Look what whiskey has done for me." He formed a temperance society (such societies were the Christian counterpart of Handsome Lake's admonitions), helped to support the church at Buffalo Creek by cutting wood, favored an English education for the young, and fenced and plowed on his own farm. In 1832 he and his second wife joined the Church. He died in the cholera epidemic in 1835 at the age of sixty-nine.[49]

There was, in fact, not much to distinguish the Christians from the pagans individually in regard to gross circumstances of personal history or tribal standing. All had been brought up in the old religion. All stood for similar policies in regard to temperance, education, land retention, and material progress. The difference probably lay in the fact that, for one reason or another, the Christians tended to seek assurances of worth from powerful and apparently benevolent white men like ministers and Indian agents, and the pagans aggressively rejected white men as a source of emotional support, insisting upon retaining their native identity and referring their conduct to native models. Thus Captain Pollard, another of the leaders of the Christian party (he had joined the church in 1824), asserted in council that his party "were meek & humble—the other proud and stubborn." He rejected the pagan party's citing of the prophet's advice against selling land without sanction from the Great Spirit, saying sarcastically, "The other side declared that they should dispute all power to sell their Lands, until the Claimants, should show that they had been to Heaven with their flesh on." And looking toward the future, he declared that his party "will obey & follow his [i.e., the white man's] advice because it is good. For when those who are in active life shall have passed away, their posterity will be more closely allied to the White man—they will assimilate to him in language conduct & Religion & the Gate of Heaven will not be closed against them."[50]

This trusting identification with white men was bitterly resisted by most of the leaders of the pagan group, who clung to the fact that they were Indians and sought for the most part to find in the memory of Handsome Lake a figure with whom they could identify. Red Jacket was now the recognized leader of the pagan party, for despite his earlier (and perhaps continuing) jealousy of Handsome Lake as a man, he firmly insisted that the Iroquois retain their own religion. Although, as he said, like the Christians he "believed in *One God*" and in heaven and hell, he had found little understanding on the part of the Christian missionaries, who after all were "dressed and fed by White men," and he alluded contemptuously to the ignorance of Indian religion by the ministers. "He has attended meeting," he reported, "when the stripling Priest has represented him as not knowing whether a cat or a dog was his God." Red Jacket was still reputed to be an overly ambitious man, and a story was circulated that in attempted imitation of Handsome Lake he announced that "the Great Spirit had made known to him in a dream, that their Nation would never prosper, until they made of him a Sachem." He would attribute epidemics, land sales, and "all the Misfortunes of the Nation" to the persistent failure of the Seneca to recognize him as a chief of the League. His Christian wife left him, and in 1827 the Christian chiefs deposed him as chief; but in 1828 he was reinstated as "the head Sachem of the Wolf tribe." Nonetheless, Blacksnake, the old "privy counselor" of Handsome Lake, thought well of him and was reported to have "more reverence for Red Jacket than for any other Indian" (except the prophet).[51]

Blacksnake was the leader of the pagan party at Allegany. Less hostile to the whites than Red Jacket, he strictly followed "the principles of Con-ne-di-yeu," urging temperance, morality, education, and adherence to the old religion.[52] But others of the Allegany pagans were, like Red Jacket, motivated as much by resentment against overbearing white ministers as by devotion to the old religion. Cornplanter in particular had for years been inspired by mingled and confused feelings of jealousy of both Handsome Lake and Red Jacket and even of the Quakers and Presbyterians—whom he himself had invited to Allegany. But in 1818, disturbed by the rumors of land cessions, he began to oppose all Christians and to reidentify with the pagan group. At first his program was rational. He proposed seriously that the Indians on the Allegany Reservation abandon the old system of usufruct holdings and divide their lands into private farms and that these holdings be secured by legal deeds valid under federal jurisdiction, thus at once precluding the sale of the reservations by the chiefs and advancing the agrarian reform already underway. But the women objected because their garden plots were widely scattered, and many of the young men objected because they wished to cut pine logs on the tribal lands and feared that private lots would not contain sufficient timber. At the last minute, with the surveyor on the ground, the old chief changed his mind, and the council refused to permit the division of the land into private lots.[53]

Gradually Cornplanter became morose and withdrawn. In December, 1820, he experienced the first of a series of visions. The Great Spirit told him that he was to have nothing further to do with white people or with war. He announced that "the white people were crazy, and the Indians were doing very wrong to follow their customs; he said it was wicked for the Indians to have cattle, cows, and hogs; cows in an especial manner were very injurious to the Indians: their children drinking the milk when they were very young, caused them to have misfortunes, and prevented them from being a useful people."[54] He was commanded to burn all his old trophies of war, including his captain's commission, a flag, medals, belts, a military hat, and a highly prized sword, which he immolated on a huge pile of logs. Many of his revelations were repetitions or echoes of the teachings of Handsome Lake: liquor had not been created for Indians, and they were commanded not to drink it; war and scalping were evil and had been introduced by the whites; the Indians were the true owners of the land, and the whites "should always consider that they live on borrowed soil"; Indians should sell no more land; Indian men should take care of their wives and children and were ordered "not to lust after any woman but my own"; Indians need not observe the sabbath; Indians must observe their old religion, for "if we would quit our old way we should get into confusion and something would happen or befall us so that we should lose our lives." But the old man was constantly disturbed by personal disappointments. As he said, "his wife . . . is now settling with her old husband on the Allegheny in distressful circumstances," a result of the wars brought by white men. He felt guilty about killing seven men in battle: "I was a great sinner to kill so many persons." He worried about the future of his idiot son and wanted him "to go with me and it seemed to be granted [by the Great Spirit] that we should both go together"; he vowed to take this son with him on all his journeys. He felt that his obedience to the Great Spirit had added ten years to his life. The most bizarre feature of his code was the claim that cow's milk had been cursed by Jesus. "When the Savior was on the Earth he was slain by wicked high tempered people and after his death he put his revenge on the cows milk and wicked man and woman that quarrel and fight when they use this milk then the milk and their bad temper puts them out of their senses." He claimed to be the only true living prophet of God. "I mean to be governed by the great man that speaks to me from above and no other person can hear or understand him and I am a mind to do as he tells me for I believe *him* to be my Maker and if he tells me wrong I cannot help it and he tells me not to pay any tax or have anything to do with law or war or Sabbath Days." When the tax collector arrived, Cornplanter met him with a bodyguard carrying guns. In deference to his past services to the state, the legislature agreed to exempt his lands from taxation. But the Indians thought he was deranged. They declined to close the Quaker school at his demand or to give up keeping chickens and selling eggs for cash. When he sang his speeches at council meetings, at the command of the Great

Spirit, to a tune of his own composing, the audience laughed. He changed his name to Nonuk—"Cold" or "Dead."[55]

But the derangement proved to be temporary, and his mind cleared. At the time of his death in 1835 he was still an awesome figure—like Young King, a battered wreck of a man. Nearly six feet tall, gray-haired, bearded, with one eye missing and the empty socket covered by the drooping brow, a limp hand rendered useless by a severed tendon, one earlobe torn and hanging down on his shoulder like a rag, he stood like a scarred oak among saplings. He lived in poverty on the grant in a decaying two-story log house without household furniture except wooden benches covered with deerskins and blankets and a few wooden spoons and bowls. Around him, however, lived fifty of his kinsmen in eight or ten houses.[56] In the year of his death he took his farewell of the Seneca nation at annuity time at Buffalo Creek. Just before the fire was covered, he stood up and solemnly made his last speech.

[He] recounted the principal events of his life, as connected with the interests of his nation. He said he had endeavored conscientiously to discharge his whole duty to his people. Whatever errors he might have committed were errors of judgment and not of the heart. If he had done any wrong or in any way given offence to anyone present, without just cause, he desired the aggrieved party to come forward and be reconciled. It was his wish to be at peace with all men . . . and he added "When I leave this place, most of you will have seen me for the last time." He then gave them advice and counsel for the future; went from one to another and took them by the hand, saying a few parting words to each; passed out of the door, mounted his horse, called his traveling companions, and left, never to return.

When Cornplanter died, the old team of Cold Spring council members, who had, along with Handsome Lake, been managing the Allegany renaissance between 1804 and 1809, was already dispersed and divided. It had been a kind of primitive Camelot, dedicated to the salvation of a people and the defense of the faith. Now, of the prophet's fifteen original colleagues, some were dead and some had moved away; some remained faithful to the old religion, some had forsaken it for Christianity. From the Wolf clan, Handsome Lake and Cornplanter had died; Blacksnake still lived along the Allegheny and was a chief and the leader of the pagan party; Strong had moved to Cattaraugus, where he was a leading figure in the Christian party. From the Bear clan, John Pierce and Halftown remained as chiefs at Cold Spring but were members of the Christians, and Crow had moved to Cattaraugus. From the Snipe clan, Henry O'Bail had died. He had remained a pagan, but because of his "bad practices" his father had disowned him and sent him to live with his mother along the Genesee; he died in a drunken fall. Charles O'Bail, a pagan, still lived at Allegany on the grant. From the Turtle clan, Blue Eyes still lived at Allegany where he was one of the Christian chiefs; Mush had died. From the Crane clan, Silver Heels had joined the Christians. The replacements for the dead and the living who had moved were divided; the old unity was no more.[57]

· The Formation of the Handsome Lake Church ·

ALTHOUGH TEMPERANCE and the economic reforms enjoined by Handsome Lake's gospel endured as commonly accepted norms by almost all of the New York Iroquois, his hopes for political unity and for domestic tranquility were not fully realized during his lifetime nor in the years after his death. Indians, Quakers, and evangelists alike deplored the still too common Indian custom of "putting away their wives." And as we have seen, the rise of the Christian party stimulated bitter factional dispute. At Allegany the quarrel became so intense that the pagan party, against its own better judgment, for a time opposed the Quaker school at Cold Spring and forced its closing. There was talk among the pagans of separating from the Christians and living on a different part of the reservation or even of emigration to the West. About fifty in number, the Christian faction were driven from Tonawanda and took refuge at Buffalo Creek; the hundred Christians at Onondaga fled to Allegany. Old loyalties were broken: Strong, a member of the Wolf clan, who had been one of the two young men appointed by Handsome Lake to oversee the people at Jenuchshadago and who had become a member of the council at Cold Spring, turned Christian. Another of the prominent men at Allegany, James Robinson, also joined the Christians and for a time was presiding chief of the Seneca tribal council.

The strong feelings generated by this division into parties reached their peak between 1818 and 1822. At that time emotion drove many of the members of the pagan party into extremely nativistic positions. Since the missionaries were demanding the abandonment of an Indian identity and calling the conservatives by the opprobrious term "pagan," some of those who chose to retain pride in being Iroquois felt forced to oppose everything any missionary proposed —not merely psalm-singing and sabbath-keeping, but also secular schooling and even further material improvements. Although the Quakers themselves opposed the evangelists, they too were resented in the general wave of nativistic feeling. Bizarre antiwhite prophecies began to circulate, which violated both the word and the spirit of Handsome Lake's preaching. Cornplanter, as we have seen, for a time appeared as a nativistic prophet. Farther up the river another Allegany prophet, Ganaego, had visions in which the Great Spirit instructed the Indians not to send their children to school and foretold disaster for those who did. Among other things he predicted that a great snake would go down the Allegheny River and make the water unfit to drink.[58] Fear of witches became more intense among the pagans, and women were executed at Buffalo Creek and at Tuscarora. Whites and Christian Indians called this murder, and when a pagan chief's children at Tuscarora died, they said it was in punishment for this sin.[59]

The responsible leaders of the pagan group disapproved of this panicky retreat into nativism. Blacksnake at Allegany, Jemmy Johnson at Tonawanda, Red Jacket at Buffalo Creek, took measures to restore balance to the adherents of the traditional religion. They were concerned not merely to retain the loyalty of the people to the old way, but also to counteract the increasingly nativistic tone of the new pagan prophets. A policy of uncompromising refusal to accept *any* white customs would be destructive for its adherents, would deepen the schism within the tribes, and would drive many reasonable people into the hands of the Christian faction. As the Tonawanda pagans succinctly put it, the Indians needed more education, not less.[60]

Beginning in 1818, therefore, leaders of the pagan party undertook to define the form and spirit of the old religion. In order to do so they called upon the memory of the great prophet, Handsome Lake, whose position with regard to religion had been firmly traditional but who had also been in favor of education, of economic progress, and of social harmony, and who had refused to condemn Christianity, hoping for mutual tolerance and respect among people of different faiths. Their effort to consolidate the old religion by appealing to the well-remembered teachings of the prophet gradually produced between 1818 and 1845 a new religious institution—a church—devoted to the preservation and propagation of the prophet's message.

The first step in this process was the convocation of a two-day religious council at Tonawanda in the summer of 1818. It was held in an old council building, fifty feet long and twenty wide, furnished exactly in the old longhouse style with two layers of bunks on each side, furnished with skins and blankets below and peltry, corn, and hunting gear above. The ceremonial fire and an outside temperature of ninety degrees kept the room oppressively hot. As an introductory ritual a form of Handsome Lake's confessional was held. Anyone who had done anything wrong was invited to come forward and confess his faults. The only one to step forward was a little girl ten or twelve years old. She stood before the chiefs and said she had done something wrong. "What is it?" asked one of them. She replied that one day she was in the trader's store and stole a paper of two rows of pins from the counter. She had never done anything bad before and was sorry she stole the pins. The chiefs decided that she should pay the trader four cents for the pins, and so the girl went to the trader and gave him four cents.

But the main purpose of this council was "to revive the moral instructions formerly received from GOSKUKKEWAUNAU KONNEDIEUY, the prophet, Kiendtwokhe's half brother, who died about the year 1815. The Indians seem now to think much of these instructions, and are desirous of having them recalled to mind, and redelivered for the benefit of the rising generation." Many speakers repeated the lessons of the prophet and urged their importance upon the listeners in the crowded building. Two of the most impressive speakers were John Sky, who spoke for three hours in a voice so loud "that every word might have been distinctly heard at a distance of a quarter of a mile." At great length he repeated the moral truths taught by Handsome Lake, emphasizing the duty of parents to set a good example to their children and expatiating on the evils of "drunkenness, lying, cheating, stealing, and other pernicious practices." He concluded eloquently: "You must not do anything bad; you must not think anything bad; for the Great Spirit knows your thoughts, as well as your words and actions. *This* is what the prophet taught us. You know it—and this is according to the word of God! ...."

The other principal speaker was a minor prophet who gravely recounted a vision confirming the apocalyptic preachings of Handsome Lake:

I have had a dream, which in my sleep, I was directed to relate in council. I dreamed that the sun in the firmament spoke to me. He told me to go to the Indians, and to tell them that the Great Spirit is very angry with them for their wicked ways. Tell them, they must repent of their wicked ways and forsake them, or the judgments of the Great Spirit will come upon them. If they do not repent and forsake their wicked ways, when the corn is in the cob, this year, there will be a storm, which will lay their corn flat on the ground and destroy it. If they do not then repent and forsake their wicked ways, next winter, there will be such a rain as they never saw before. The flood will be so great as to bury their houses in the water.[61]

Although the consolidation of the pagan views at this and perhaps other similar meetings tended for a time to sharpen the line of division between the Christians and the pagans, in the long run it reduced antagonism. More secure in their faith, and focused upon the image of the prophet as their great leader, the pagans were less sensitive to slight and more tolerant of their Christian neighbors. The Christians, particularly at Allegany, developed their own versions of the life and teaching of Handsome Lake, stories that grew more lurid and distorted with every year. He was accused of having slaughtered as many as one hundred suspected witches at one meeting; of having gotten his whole message from the Bible, either translated for him by his nephew Henry O'Bail or read to him by a mythical gray-haired missionary hermit in the woods across the river; of having recanted and professed Christianity during his last agonizing hours at Onondaga, while he bit through his lips to keep from screaming in pain, and steam came from under the blankets. But the pagans, increasingly secure and tolerant—more tolerant than the Christian converts—smiled and went their own way.

Throughout the twenties and thirties the followers of Handsome Lake cherished and repeated his sayings. The ministers harangued the people at Green Corn and New Year's with recitals of the prophet's moral commands. The validity of his visions was confirmed by two prophets, one at Tonawanda and one at Buffalo Creek, who received annual visits from the four angels. During the emigration crisis, when there was a proposal to move the Iroquois to the plains of Kansas, the angels took the Buffalo Creek seer on a tour of hell. "He passed over an immense prairie & at the distant end beheld an enormous stone ediface, without doors or windows, but the guide who accompanied him being a special messenger from the Great Sp[irit] knocked against the wall & instantly an opening was made from which issued a blaze that ascended hundreds of feet above the roofs, & he beheld within huge potash kettles, filled with boiling oil & moulten lead, & there were the wicked rising & falling & tumbling over in the bubling fluids & ever & over as the heads of some were thrown above the top of kettles they gave a horrid yell & down they plunged again. There he was told would be punished all the chiefs who advocated emigration." This vision virtually repeats Handsome Lake's earlier image of the domain of the Tormentor. The Tonawanda prophet, also echoing Handsome Lake, said that "there are four angels which are annually sent to him by the great spirit whose special duty it is to take charge of the Seneca Indians & that they inform him of what errors the Indians fall into, the vices they indulge in & the crimes they commit & what it is necessary for them to do to please the great spirit, & present the calamities which will befall the nation unless there is a reformation of conduct. He has recently told the Tonnawanda Indians, that a terrible sickness was coming from the rising sun, which would exterminate them unless they had a great feast & dance & all took a particular kind of medicine, which he had been instructed how to prepare. This has been done & the Indians are now safe from the disastrous evils, with which they were threatened."[62]

By the 1840's the constant recitation of the prophet's teachings and the accumulation of confirming dreams and visions by minor prophets had produced a large body of legend and text, more or less accurately recounting events in the prophet's life and his various visions and moral lessons. Individual preachers who knew this material well were able to recite versions of this Code in detail and were called upon at the two great annual festivals to serve as preachers. One of these men was Blacksnake, now an old man, still living at Allegany. Blacksnake in the mid-1840's had formulated a specific version of the Code, beginning with an account of the first vision and going on to organize the prophet's moral teachings in the form of twelve commandments prohibiting whiskey, witchcraft, love magic, divorce, adultery, premarital sex, refusal of the wife to live with her husband's parents, failure of parent to discipline unruly children, unwillingness to love all men, enmity, and gossip.

Farther north, at Tonawanda, a fuller and somewhat different version of the Code was developing, and it was here that the church took definite form. Here Jimmy Johnson, Handsome Lake's grandson Sosheowa, was the preacher in the 1840's. Annually in October he recited the Code of Handsome Lake on the mornings of four days, in a version very close in form and details of content to the later-published *Code of Handsome Lake*.[63] The Tonawanda version was to become the standard by which other speakers' versions were judged, and it was this version that was carried from village to village in the fall of each year in the Six Nations Meetings. It was at Tonawanda that the architectural form of the church building was defined, modeled after the old longhouse, but with wooden benches substituted for the two-tiered bunks, and wood stoves instead of earthen hearths. Here was kept the wampum belonging to Handsome Lake (probably the official belts and strings associated with his office as sachem in the League, for the current holder of the title remained the custodian). Here the annual ceremonial calendar, including the burning of the white dog and dream-guessing, was carried on conscientiously, along with the other major rituals recommended by the prophet. And here, on the most pagan of all the reserves, the chiefs refused to join the rest of the Seneca in the republican form of government adopted after the debacle at Buffalo Creek, preferring to stand by old political customs. Thus, from Tonawanda in the 1840's, under the guidance of Handsome Lake's grandson Jimmy Johnson, spread a new renaissance of traditional Iroquois religion. Now, however, it was crystallized in a new ritual form, the Six Nations Meeting, and invoked the prophet himself as the spiritual guide of the followers of the old religion. A renewed assertion of the sacredness of the family, expressed in heavy emphasis on those parts of the social gospel that condemned adultery, separation, and the other domestic vices, reflected the concern of the Seneca to complete the last major social reform that the prophet had urged upon the people. But now, in addition to its manifest content, the new religion of Handsome Lake conveyed a second message: that the Great Spirit, through his messenger Handsome Lake, supported and loved those who wished to remain Indians. The Indians on the reservations in New York and Canada who attended the Six Nations Meetings and the recitation of the Code at the major annual ceremonies were gaining membership in a group that, in contrast to the Christian denominations, supported identification with Indians rather than with whites.

The forms of the Handsome Lake Church were set about 1850 and have changed little since then. The dream-guessing rites and the white dog sacrifice, which aroused the indignation of white people, were gradually left out of the annual ceremonies and were no longer performed by the early part of the twentieth century. But these are not essential to the institution. Now the adherents of the Old Way are sometimes called conservatives or old-time people. What was revolutionary in the prophet's day is now, one hundred and fifty years later, the extreme of traditionalism. Today most of the men support their families by wage work in various mechanized industries: the railroads, the gypsum mines, the great industrial complex at Buffalo, high-steel work all over the country; the women, when they work outside the home, may serve as schoolteachers, secretaries, factory operatives, domestic servants. Housing, except for a few old structures, is modern. All children go to the state-supported schools. And the transformation of domestic life, which Handsome Lake promoted by teaching the virtues he felt essential to the nuclear domestic unit, has long been completed: the family names are English and are transmitted patrilineally, the man is the provider, and the old clan-and-lineage system, while not extinct, is blurred and not essential to most social relationships.

Thus the Old Way now contains little that can be pointed to as distinctively white and modern; the *Gaiwiio* today refers to values and beliefs that, whatever their ultimate origin, are now traditionally Iroquoian. Furthermore, with the fading away of the sharp antagonisms between Christian and pagan, the Christian denominations and *Gaiwiio* bear a relationship not unlike that in white society between Protestant denominations and Catholicism. Being a follower of Handsome Lake today is an expression of a somewhat nostalgic and deeply emotional identification with Indianness itself, with the group of "real" Iroquois people, as opposed to identification with white men and white-dominated organizations, and in some cases of a desire for the personal spiritual salvation achievable by renunciation of sin and acceptance of the leadership of Handsome Lake and the Great Spirit.

Now, along the Allegheny, the river rises high behind the new dam at Kinzua and covers the sites of the old towns at Jenuchshadago and Cold Spring, where Handsome Lake preached. The people have moved away to prefabricated bungalows on higher ground. No longer do the old gray houses stand among the patchwork of pale green fields and dark green forest, with thin smoke spires rising above and the lacy web of paths and roads running among them all. No longer do the flies buzz in the long grass down on the flats, or the elms and walnut trees wave softly in the wind that flows gently down from the hills. But the words of Handsome Lake still resound in the longhouses, for as the prophet said, "Gaiwiio is only in its beginning."

BIBLIOGRAPHY

AND

NOTES

Notes and References

SCHEDULE OF ABBREVIATIONS

APS: American Philosophical Society

ASPIA: American State Papers, Indian Affairs

BAE: Bureau of American Ethnology, Smithsonian Institution

BHS: Buffalo Historical Society

CCHS: Chester County Historical Society

CL: Clements Library

DC: Draper Collection

DRCHNY: O'Callaghan, E. B., ed., *Documents Relative to the Colonial History of the State of New York*

HAMC: Hamilton College

HAVC: Haverford College

HL: Huntingdon Library

HSP: Historical Society of Pennsylvania

LC: Library of Congress

LR: Letters Received

LS: Letters Sent

MHD: Merle H. Deardorff

MHS: Massachusetts Historical Society

NYHS: New-York Historical Society

OR: O'Rielly Collection

PA: *Pennsylvania Archives*

PHC: Pennsylvania Historical Commission

PYM: Philadelphia Yearly Meeting Archives (located at Friends' Book Store)

RBIA: Records of the Bureau of Indian Affairs

SC: Swarthmore College

SHSW: State Historical Society of Wisconsin

UM: University of Michigan

7 STAT.: Peters, R., ed., *The Public Statutes at Large of the United States of America*, Volume VII

WD: War Department

CHAPTER 1: THE OLD WAY OF HANDSOME LAKE

1. The following description of aspects of current religious practice among followers of the Old Way of Handsome Lake refers to the Allegany Seneca specifically and is based largely on my field notes recorded in 1951 and 1952 at Cold Spring Longhouse.

2. Parker, 1913 (reprinted, with an introduction by W. N. Fenton, in Fenton, 1968). The version printed by Parker was written down in the Seneca language by Chief Cornplanter (Sosondowa), a Handsome Lake preacher on the Cattaraugus Seneca Reservation, about 1903 and was translated by William Bluesky, the native lay preacher of the local Baptist church. Sosondowa's version is embedded in Cattaraugus tradition and is supposed to have descended from Chief John Jacket's version of about 1863. There are at least three untranslated versions of the Code filed with the BAE: a Grand River Onondaga text, BAE MS 449, dated c. 1889; a Grand River Mohawk text from Seth Newhouse, BAE MS 3489, dated c. 1880; and one or more New York Onondaga texts, BAE MS 2585, dated c. 1908. There is also an untranslated text from the New York Onondaga at the Syracuse University Library, copies of which are held by the BAE and APS. Historical sources provide several abridged or shortened versions: an Allegany Seneca version recorded by the Christian Benjamin Williams, probably from Governor Blacksnake, Handsome Lake's nephew and apostle, c. 1846 (SHSW, DC, Brant Papers, 16 F 266); a Seneca version of Jimmy Johnson, as recorded by Ely Parker for L. H. Morgan, at Tonawanda in 1845 (Parker, 1919); and another version of Jimmy Johnson, as recorded in several drafts by Ely Parker for L. H. Morgan, at Tonawanda, October 1848 (Fenton, 1951; Morgan, 1951). A new version of the Code is being recorded and translated by Wallace Chafe.

3. The following description of the confession is largely drawn from an already published account: A. Wallace, 1952b.

Part I: The Heyday of the Iroquois
CHAPTER 2: THE SENECA NATION OF INDIANS

1. NYHS, OR, Vol. XV, d3 (recollections of Thomas Morris).
2. Beauchamp, 1916, pp. 67–84.
3. Jackson, 1830b, p. 19.

4. This section is drawn from a paper entitled "Handsome Lake and the Decline of the Iroquois Matriarchate," which was read at the Wenner-Gren symposium at Burg Wartenstein, Austria, on Kinship and Behavior in the summer of 1966. The concept of dominant kin relationship is developed in Hsu, 1965.

5. Kenton, 1927, Vol. II, pp. 78–80.

6. Seaver, 1824, p. 104–6.

7. Kenton, 1927, Vol. II, pp. 87–8.

8. SHSW, DC, 16 F 227 ("Cornplanter's Talk").

9. SHSW, DC, 16 F 32 ("Life of Governor Blacksnake").

10. Hamilton, 1953, p. 320.

11. Lafitau, 1724, Vol. I, p. 393.

12. Jackson, 1830b, p. 20.

13. *Ibid.*

14. *Ibid.*

15. Fenton, 1940, p. 429.

16. Kenton, 1927, Vol. II, p. 90.

17. Jackson, 1830b, p. 19.

18. Kenton, 1927, Vol. II, p. 90 n.

19. The description of the local council and its relation to the "tribal" councils is based on Seneca data recorded by the Quakers and federal officials in the first half of the nineteenth century. The dependence of the tribal council on the village councils becomes clear in the name lists of both, e.g., Bonsall's 1803 and Atkinson's 1809 lists of the Allegany Seneca chiefs (CL, Bonsall Journal, 1803, and HAVC, Allinson Journal, 1809) and the lists of treaty participants and signatories of the period (7 STAT. and ASPIA).

20. The sketch of the maturation of the Seneca child and youth is drawn from several sources; and not all of the instances are specifically Seneca, some being based on Huron data and others on Onondaga and Mohawk. The general cultural similarities of all these Iroquoian-speaking tribes, however, are sufficient to make possible the crosstribal use of most sorts of general information. Particularly useful sources were: Carse, 1949; Fenton, 1941b and 1951; Hamilton, 1953; Jackson, 1830b; Kenton, 1927; Morgan, 1851; Murdock, 1934; Parker, 1913; Pettitt, 1946; Quain, 1937; Randle, 1951; Speck, 1945; Wainwright, 1947.

21. The structure, function, rituals, and origin myth of the League of the Iroquois have been discussed at length in Morgan, 1851; P. Wallace, 1946 (from whose work the quotations in this section are drawn); and Thwaites's edition of the Jesuit Relations. There exists a large literature on the political history and institutions of the Iroquois; the principal studies are cited in the bibliography.

The classic study of Iroquois polity is of course Lewis H. Morgan's *League of the Ho-de-no-sau-nee, or Iroquois,* first published in 1851 (Morgan, 1901). Later researches have not substantially changed his description of the formal organization, but they have shown that its efficiency as a decision-making assembly, especially in matters of war, was not so high as Morgan's respect for the Iroquois had led him to believe.

CHAPTER 3: THE RITUALS OF HOPE AND THANKSGIVING

1. The major sources from which the foregoing brief and synthetic account of the Seneca annual economic and ceremonial cycle was drawn are: Fenton, 1936; Jackson, 1830b; Shimony, 1961; Chafe, 1961; Morgan, 1851; Murdock, 1934; Quain, 1937; Speck, 1945; and the author's own field notes, particularly those taken at the Midwinter Festival at Cold Spring (Allegany Seneca) in January and February, 1952. This summary necessarily presents a modal portrait to which the events of any given year in any given village did not necessarily conform. The ceremonies, for instance, varied not only from one community to another (or at least they do today) but also from one year to another in the same community, in response to dream-required innovations and to the pressure of circumstances, such as food supply, war, and the presence or absence of particular persons.

2. Jackson, 1830b, p. 28.

3. Fenton, 1953, p. 126.

4. HL, Parker Collection 1802–46, Ely S. Parker MS. (no date) on Medicine Men and Indian Dances.

5. This section is reprinted with minor changes from the author's article by the same title, published in the *American Anthropologist,* 1958, Vol. LX, pp. 234–48. Except where otherwise noted, the data and quotations are taken from the selections of the Jesuit Relations reprinted in Kenton, 1927, particularly the relations of Fathers Fremin, De Carheil, Ragueneau, Jouvency, Le Mercier, Le Jeune, De Quen, Bressani, Lalemant, and Bruyas. See also Blau, 1963.

CHAPTER 4:   THE RITUALS OF FEAR AND MOURNING

1. NYHS, OR, Vol. XV, Thomas Morris to Richard Morris, September 9, 1796.

2. Hamilton, 1953, p. 317.

3. SHSW, DC, 16 F 107–219 ("Life of Governor Blacksnake").

4. W. Stone, 1838, Vol. I, p. 28.

5. Data on Iroquois witchcraft is contained particularly in BAE, Gatschet MSS., 1883–5; BAE, Goldenweiser MSS., 1912–13; BAE, Hewitt MSS., 1880–90; Morgan, 1851; Erminie Smith, 1883; Decost Smith, 1888 and 1889; and Shimony, 1961.

6. The Iroquois creation myth exists in numerous texts and summaries. Each of these differs from the next, sometimes not only in minor detail. Some of the differences are tribal: the Huron legends of the seventeenth century are not quite the same as Seneca and Onondaga, for instance. Versions differ also according to the particular informant's idiosyncrasies of emphasis and innovation and according to the patience and thoroughness of the ethnographer, interpreter, or historian. The version recited here is based on the brief "Cornplanter's Talk" of February 1821 (SHSW, DC 16 F 227) and on the long text, in very bad reservation English, recorded by the Seneca Benjamin Williams about 1846, probably from the words of Blacksnake or Brooks Redeye (SHSW, DC, 22 F 23–44). The Williams version (which recapitulates and expands Cornplanter's) is no more nor less authentic than any other; but it is almost certainly the version that Handsome Lake knew. It has been paraphrased by this writer, and some repetitious passages have been eliminated or briefly summarized. Supplementary data were taken from J. N. B. Hewitt's articles "Tawiskaron" and "Teharonhiawagon" in Hodge, 1906; from Hewitt, 1903, 1928; and from Curtin and Hewitt, 1918, since the Williams version skimps the creative activities and rivalry of the twins. The legend that identifies the giant prototype and progenitor of the Faces is found (again with minor variation) in Speck, 1949, p. 71; Fenton, 1941a, pp. 418–19; and in my own field notes at Grand River Reservation, December, 1946 (interview with the Cayuga sachem, Deskaheh). Deskaheh explicitly identifies the Great World-Rim Dweller as the Evil Twin, and this identification of the False Face with the Evil Twin is implied in all versions by their common interest in disease, windstorm, witchcraft, and winter; in their common desire to be recognized as the Creator; in their shared antipathy for the Good Spirit; in the fact that

in some versions the Evil Twin, defeated in battle by his brother, is transformed into the mountains, while in others the giant says he comes from the mountains. One version of the creation myth, however, has the False Face as the *father* of the twins. All efforts to "identify" the characters in myths by making this sort of logical equation are, in one sense, wasted, because myths are like dreams not only in their fantastic content but also in their variability from one version to the next. Nevertheless, the functional identification of the prototypical False Face with Tawiskaron, the Evil Twin, is in my opinion substantial enough to require pointing out. One might speculate that this is a syncretism: that the Iroquois, in a sense, invented *two* evil spirits, first the Evil Twin and then the False Face, and have only recently felt the need to relate them to one another.

7. BHS, Box "Indians," Parker gift, pencil notes by Asher Wright.

8. The quotations from the condolence ritual are taken from Hewitt and Fenton, 1944, and Fenton, 1946. The Iroquois Condolence Council has been extensively described in other sources, including Morgan, 1851; Hale, 1883 and 1895; Shimony, 1961; and Beauchamp, 1905.

9. The form of the Dekanawidah myth, which like other myths exists in several versions, used here is drawn from the interpretation of P. Wallace, 1946, and my own reinterpretation in terms of revitalization movements in A. Wallace, 1958.

10. Jackson, 1830b; PHC, Skinner MSS.

11. Curtin and Hewitt, 1918, pp. 458–9.

12. Relation of Father Le Jeune, 1639, in Kenton, 1927, Vol. I, p. 389.

13. Relation of Father Le Jeune, 1636, in Kenton, 1927, Vol. I., pp. 257–8.

14. Relation of Father Le Jeune, 1637, in Kenton, 1927, Vol. I, pp. 336–48.

Part II: *The Decline of the Iroquois*

CHAPTER 5: THE LAST WARS IN THE FOREST

1. The play-off system and its interruption by the French defeat in the French and Indian War are detailed in the many records of commercial, diplomatic, and military relations between the whites and the eastern Indians for the period 1701–63. See particularly Sullivan, 1921–65; P. Wallace, 1945; Downes, 1940. The description of Teedyuscung's belt is to be found in A. Wallace, 1949, pp. 111–13.

2. The general material on the Pontiac Wars of 1763 is taken from Peckham, 1947. The information on the traditionally known role of Guyasuta and others of Handsome Lake's kinfolk in the affairs at Fort Franklin and the Devil's Hole, and Handsome Lake's participation in these events, comes from the testimony of Seneca informants interviewed by Lyman C. Draper in 1850 (SHSW, DC, Draper's Notes, 4 S *passim*).

3. The account of Pontiac's role in the conspiracy of Pontiac and the revelations of the Delaware Prophet is taken from materials given in Peckham, 1947, pp. 98–100, 101, 112–16, 120, 187–8; Heckewelder, 1819, pp. 291–3; Schoolcraft, 1839, Vol. I, pp. 239–48.

4. Sullivan, 1921–65, Johnson Papers, Vol. X, pp. 505–6.

5. SHSW, DC, 4 S 58–73. See also Mary Jemison's and L. S. Everett's accounts of the Devil's Hole massacre in Seaver, 1824, pp. 63–4, 154–8.

6. The Iroquois negotiations at Fort Stanwix in 1768 and their subsequent diplomatic difficulties are summarized and documented in Downes, 1940. Many of the primary documents are to be found in the Johnson Papers, Sullivan, 1921–65, and Thwaites, 1904.

7. The account of Logan and Lord Dunmore's War is taken from W. Stone, 1838, Vol. I, pp. 38–48, and from materials in SHSW, DC, 4 S 67, 98–9. Further materials on Lord Dunmore's War and Six Nations' unofficial participation in but official avoidance of it are to be found in Thwaites, 1904, in the Kirkland Papers at Hamilton College, and in Sullivan, 1921–65.

8. The material on the various negotiations with the Six Nations, culminating in the Albany Council of 1775, is taken largely from W. Stone, 1838, Vol. I, Chs. iv and v and App. No. 12 (Proceedings of the Albany Council). See also Mohr, 1933, and Harmon, 1941, pp. 1–2.

9. The maintenance of the neutrality position from 1775 until the fall of 1776 is documented in W. Stone, 1838, Vol. I, Chs. iv, v, vi, and vii, and in the narratives of the councils at Fort Pitt and Albany given by Blacksnake to Lyman C. Draper (SHSW, DC, Brant MSS., 16 F). Guyasuta's pronouncement is quoted by Sipe, 1927, pp. 402–3. See Savelle, 1932, for an account of the Fort Pitt councils.

10. The abandonment of the neutral position at Niagara in 1776 is noted in Mohr, 1933; W. Stone, 1838, Vol. II, pp. 3–4 n.; and the Draper MSS., 4 S 16. The preceding events are described in W. Stone, 1838, Vol. I, Chs. vi, vii, and xiii.

11. The council at Oswego is described briefly in W. Stone, 1838, Vol. I, pp. 186–8, and at some length in accounts by Blacksnake, who was there,

recorded by and for Draper (16 F, 4 S 17, 73). Its date apparently was in May (Beauchamp, 1905), p. 354.

12. The account of the Oriskany battle is based on Seaver, 1824, pp. 76–7; W. Stone, 1838, Vol. I, pp. 209–64; and SHSW, DC 16 F, Blacksnake memoirs I and II and 4 S, Draper's notes of February 11, 1850.

13. SHSW, DC, 16 F (Blacksnake memoirs).

14. The account of the 1778 campaign is based on W. Stone, 1838, Vol. I, and on the Blacksnake memoirs in SHSW, DC, 16 F.

15. PA, first ser., Vol. VII, p. 593.

16. The spring campaign of 1779 is described in W. Stone, 1838, and in PA, first ser., Vol. VII.

17. W. Stone, 1838, Vol. I, p. 404.

18. Sullivan's raid has been copiously described in W. Stone, 1838, Vol. II, and Brodhead's expedition in Downes, 1940, and Deardorff, 1941. Blacksnake gives some incidents of these campaigns in his memoirs in SHSW, DC, 16 F.

19. Brodhead, 1857, p. 797.

20. Norris, 1879; PA, first ser., Vol. VIII, p. 157.

21. The campaigns of 1780 to 1783 and their effects on the frontier settlements are generally described in W. Stone, 1838, Vol. II; PA, first ser., Vol. VIII; DRCHNY, Vol. VIII; Downes, 1940; and in the Blacksnake and Bucktooth memoirs in SHSW, DC, 16 F and 4 S respectively.

CHAPTER 6: THE COLLAPSE OF THE CONFEDERACY

1. Ford, 1904, Vol. XXV, pp. 680–91 (October 15, 1783).

2. Harmon, 1941, pp. 2–9.

3. The conquest theory is outlined in PA, first ser., Vol. X, pp. 53–4, 126; W. Stone, 1838, Vol. II, pp. 240–3; Hough, 1861, Vol. I, p. 74; SHSW, DC, 16 F, Blacksnake memoirs (account of Fort Stanwix treaty); Ford, 1904, Vol. XXV, pp. 680–91. The various treaty journals and correspondence of 1784, 1785, and 1786 also contain explicit assertions of the theory. For a general review, see Mohr, 1933.

4. For events of the Treaty of Fort Stanwix in 1784 and its subsequent repudiation, see accounts in SHSW, DC, 11 F 7 (Commissioner Lee to

J. Reed, October 1784); Hough, 1861; Mohr, 1933; W. Stone, 1838; and Blacksnake's detailed account in SHSW, DC, 16 F.

5. The negotiations at these three treaties are described in a number of sources: Harmon, 1941; Mohr, 1933; ASPIA; Manley, 1932; MHS, Pickering Papers; SHSW, DC, 23 U; Hough, 1861; Ketchum, 1865; Evans, 1941.

6. The numerous cessions are recorded in Hough, 1861.

7. SHSW, DC, 23 U, Butler to Spt. Genl., August 3, 1788.

8. Hough, 1961, Vol. I, pp. 119–28 *et passim;* Flick, 1933, Vol. V, p. 156; NYHS, OR, 15 d 3.

9. Hough, 1961, Vol. I, pp. 160–2; NYHS, OR, Vol. V, p. 92 and 15 d 3; ASPIA, Vol. I, pp. 211–15.

10. W. Stone, 1838, Vol. II, p. 249; Shipman, 1933; SHSW, DC, 23 U 27–31. The organization of the northern confederacy is revealed in the speeches of Indian participants. See particularly SHSW, DC, 23 U 41–2, 51, 66–73, 172–87, Aupaumut, 1827, entry of September 17, 1792; Cruikshank, 1923–31, Vol. I, p. 219.

11. NYHS, OR, Vol. V, p. 77; W. Stone, 1838, Vol. II, pp. 265–9; Shipman, 1833; SHSW, DC, 23 U 38–51.

12. Several monographs treat the tricornered conflict of interests in Ohio among Indians, British, and Americans: Mohr, 1933; Downes, 1940; Shipman, 1933; Harmon, 1941; W. Stone, 1838.

13. Aupaumut, 1827, pp. 127–8.

14. NYHS, OR, Vol. V, p. 88; Stone, 1838, Vol. II, pp. 273–9; SHSW, DC, 23 U 173.

15. Details of preparations for the Fort Harmar Treaty are given in Ford, 1904, Vols. XXXIII and XXXIV; NYHS, OR, Vol. V, p. 86; Shipman, 1933; and W. Stone, 1838, Vol. II.

16. John Heckewelder as quoted in Shipman, 1933, pp. 40–5, from Pickering Papers in MHS.

17. 7 Stat.; ASPIA, Vol. I, pp. 4–12; Kappler, 1904, Vol. III, pp. 698–701.

18. Quoted in Mohr, 1933, pp. 135–7.

19. NYHS, OR, Vol. VI, p. 16.

20. Shipman, 1933, pp. 46–55.

21. W. Stone, 1838, Vol. II, p. 278 (quoting Brant to Langan, October 7, 1788).

22. See Wildes, 1941, and Shipman, 1933, for a summary of political and military events in the war for the Northwest Territory.

23. NYHS, OR, Vol. VI (Knox to Washington, June 15, 1789; ASPIA, Vol. I, pp. 53–4; Harmon, 1941, pp. 10–19).

24. W. Stone, 1838, Vol. II; Shipman, 1933, p. 56.

25. Brant's activities in the affairs of the western confederacy are most fully described in W. Stone, 1838.

26. Schenck, 1887, p. 102.

27. Hough, 1961, Vol. I, p. 165.

28. Schenck, 1887, p. 98.

29. ASPIA, Vol. I, p. 158.

30. Field notes, Grand River Reservation, Ontario, winter 1947–48.

31. PA, second ser., Vol. IV, pp. 569–70.

32. Colonel Proctor's journal, 1791, in ASPIA, Vol. I, pp. 159–60; PA, second series, Vol. IV, pp. 569–70.

33. There are four major accounts of this extended meeting: Hendrick Aupaumut's journal of his mission on behalf of the U.S. (Aupaumut, 1827); Blacksnake's narrative (SHSW, DC, 16 F); reports in the Simcoe Papers (Cruikshank, 1923–31, Vol. I); and correspondence and report of the Six Nations emissaries, November 1792, NYHS, OR Vols. VIII and IX. It should be noted that the date "1793" given on the published version of Hendrick's journal is incorrect; Hendrick's mission was made in 1792.

34. PHC, Skinner MSS., pp. 121–2.

35. NYHS, OR, Vol. VIII, p. 45, and Vol. IX, p. 34; W. Stone, 1838, Vol. II, pp. 295, 313, 405, and App., pp. xiii–xxvi; PA, second ser., Vol. IV, p. 557. Today the descendants of these emigrants are known as the Seneca-Cayuga of Oklahoma.

36. SHSW, DC, Blacksnake Papers, 16 F, pp. 68–9, 117–21.

37. Rossman, 1952; NYHS, OR, Vol. X, Docs. 31, 35, 40, 41, 43, 50, 54, 57; W. Stone, 1838, Vol. II, pp. 378–9.

38. W. Stone, 1838, Vol. II, pp. 378–9; NYHS, OR, Vol. X, Doc. 31; PA, first ser., Vol. VI, p. 819.

39. Hough, 1861, Vol. I, pp. 168–71.

40. HSP, MS. Division, Journal of John Parrish to the Treaty at Newtown Point, Am 565.

41. W. Stone, 1838, Vol. II, p. 275.

42. NYHS, OR, Vol. X, p. 69; 7 STAT., p. 61.

43. W. Stone, 1838, Vol. II, pp. 394–424, and App., p. xv. Stone's assumption that Brant remained "at the head of the Confederacy, until the day of his decease" is not justified by the evidence. The council at Niagara evidently was held on Canadian soil and amounted to a rejection by Brant and his people of the claims of the New York Iroquois to control of the lands in Canada. Brant did, however, remain at the head of the Grand River Iroquois, who have continued to maintain a separate roster of League chiefs and conduct independently their own condolence and installation ceremonies (cf. Fenton, 1946).

44. SHSW, DC, 4 S, 109–11.

45. *Ibid.*, 4 S 117–21 (conversations with Charles O'Bail, Cornplanter's son).

46. NYHS, OR, Vol. VIII (Chapin's copy of Pickering's Census of the Six Nations, November 12, 1792).

47. ASPIA, Vol. I, pp. 153–4 (Proctor's Journal of 1791).

48. The locations and periods of occupation of the Allegany Seneca after the Revolution must be inferred from scattered primary sources. The following have been of particular use: Proctor's 1791 Journal in ASPIA, Vol. I, pp. 149–62; Pickering's Census of 1792 in NYHS, OR; Draper's Notes and the Blacksnake Papers in SHSW, DC, 4S and 16 F; Kirkland's 1789 Census of the New York Iroquois, HAMC; and various maps, particularly John Adlum's 1798 map of the Seneca towns in the Record Room of the Philadelphia Yearly Meeting.

49. Hough, 1861, Vol. I, pp. 110–28, 160–63; Flick, 1933, Vol. V, p. 156.

50. PA, second ser., Vol. VI, pp. 782–3.

51. The definitive history of Cornplanter's private real-estate transaction is given in Deardorff, 1941.

52. Hough, 1861, Vol. I, p. 165.

53. NYHS, OR, Vol. VI (Seneca Chiefs to Governor of Pennsylvania, August 12, 1790).

54. Schenck, 1887.

55. Cornplanter in Philadelphia was most eloquent about Fort Stanwix. The story of his visit is given in PA, fourth ser., Vol. IV; NYHS, OR, Vol. VI, August 12, 1790, Doc. 33, Vol. VIII, Doc. 3, Vol. XV, Doc. 3d; Hough, 1861, Vol. I, pp. 110–16, 161–76; and SHSW, DC, 16 F, Blacksnake memoirs. Objections had also been made in 1784, 1785, 1786, and

1787. The whole matter of the Fort Stanwix lines was not settled until the Treaty of Canandaigua in 1794 (7 STAT., pp. 44–7).

56. NYHS, OR, Vol. XV, Red Jacket to Pickering, November 25, 1790; Hough, 1861, Vol. I, pp. 160–3.

57. PA, ser. 2, Vol. VI; Meginness, 1887; Rossman, 1952, p. 233; ASPIA, Vol. I, pp. 521–2.

58. NYHS, OR, Vol. VIII, J. Parrish to I. Chapin, November 27, 1792; Hough, 1861, Vol. I, pp. 161–8.

59. Hough, 1861, Vol. I, p. 161.

60. NYHS, OR, Vol. VI, Seneca Chiefs to Governor of Pennsylvania, August 12, 1790; Schenck, 1887, pp. 99–102, 105; PA, second ser., Vol. IV, pp. 546–7; W. Stone, 1838, Vol. II, pp. 326–31.

61. Hough, 1861, Vol. I, pp. 161–71.

62. *Ibid.*

63. PA, fourth ser., Vol. IV, p. 160–4; Deardorff, 1941.

65. *Ibid;* but see also Red Jacket's lack of enthusiasm for culture change, as recorded by John Parrish in his journal of the 1791 conference at Newtown Point (HSP, MS. Division, Am 565).

66. Hough, 1861, Vol. I, pp. 168–71.

67. NYHS, OR, Vol. VIII, Chiefs of Six Nations to "General" Chapin, August 1792, and Vol. IX, Minutes of Council at Buffalo Creek, October 8–10, 1793; W. Stone, 1838, Vol. II, *passim;* Cruikshank, 1923–31, Vol. I, p. 219.

68. This reversal of policy is stated clearly in Knox's memorandum to Washington on Indian affairs of June 15, 1789 (NYHS, OR, Vol. VI), and culminated in the abortive treaty negotiations of 1793 (see Shipman, 1933).

69. Hough, 1861, Vol. I, 165–71; PA, fourth ser., Vol. IV, 160–5; Deardorff, 1941; PA, ser. 2, Vol. VI ("Papers Relating to the Establishment of Presqu'isle"); NYHS, OR, Vol. XV, Doc. 3 (Concerning delay in Morris's plans to purchase western New York); 7 STAT., pp. 44–7 (Treaty of Canandaigua, 1794); ASPIA, Vol. I, pp. 140–215.

70. PA, second ser., Vol. IV, pp. 549–50, and fourth ser., Vol. IV, pp. 109–10; Hough, 1961, Vol. I, pp. 165–8; 7 Stat., pp. 44–7; NYHS, OR, Vol. VIII, July 7, 1792, November 1797 (correspondence of I. Chapin concerning punishment of white murderer and indemnification of his victim's family). N.B. also the provisions of the laws governing the

Northwest Territory and the system of licensing under bond traders and other entrants into Indian territory.

71. PA, fourth ser., Vol. IV, pp. 109–10; Hough, 1861, Vol. I, pp. 165–8; 7 STAT., pp. 44–7.

72. NYHS, OR, Vol. XV, R. Morris to T. Morris, August 1, 1797.

73. Ibid.

74. NYHS, OR, Vol. XV, T. Morris to R. Morris, May 29, 1797.

75. NYHS, OR, Vol. XV, pp. 54–68 (Journal of Treaty of Big Tree).

76. NYHS, OR, Vol. XV, Doc. 3, Memoir of Thomas Morris.

77. Except as otherwise noted, the account of the Big Tree negotiations is taken from Wilkinson, 1953 (which is based largely on NYHS, OR, Vol. XV).

78. 7 STAT., pp. 601–3; Royce, 1899.

79. Specification of the reservations and their sizes from 7 Stat., pp. 601–3; Royce, 1899; NYHS, OR, Vol. XV, List of Reservations, September 16, 1797; and Oil Spring Reservation, Cat. Co., pp. 81–2, and Congdon, 1967.

CHAPTER 7: SLUMS IN THE WILDERNESS

1. Schenck, 1887, p. 332.

2. The history of early frontier settlement in the Allegheny Mountain area surrounding the Cornplanter grant is derived from a number of local histories, particularly those concerned with Warren County, Pennsylvania, and Cattaraugus County, New York. See in particular Schenck, 1887; Cattaraugus County, 1879; and Warren Centennial, 1897.

3. A detailed description of place names and related activities of the Cornplanter Seneca is in Fenton, 1945–46.

4. The names and reputations of most of the chiefs, warriors, and leading women of the Allegany Seneca at this time are provided principally by Adlum, 1794 (as edited and annotated by Kent and Deardorff, 1960); by John Decker in his recollections for Draper, preserved in the SHSW, DC, 4 S; and by the Quaker diarists of 1798 and thereafter, particularly MHD, Sharpless, 1798; SC, Simmons; the several Jackson journals at SC and CCHS; and Jackson, 1830a.

5. A detailed description of the houses, the economy, the diet, the religious beliefs and observances, and the alcoholic excesses of the Allegany Seneca in 1798 is given in MHD, Sharpless, 1798; SC, Simmons Letter Books, 1798–99; and Jackson, 1830b. Their accounts are based on personal observation during visits to the town in 1798 and 1799.

6. No precise casualty figures are available, of course, but an examination of W. Stone's (1838) life of Brant and of Draper's interviews with Blacksnake and other Seneca informants (SHSW, DC, 4 S and 16 F) reveals that the Six Nations lost heavily in the Oriskany battle and various numbers at the many subsequent engagements both major and minor. Two hundred fatal casualties is probably a conservative estimate when one considers the difficulties of the time in treating infections of various kinds in casualties at first reported merely as wounded, or perhaps not even reported.

7. HAMC, Kirkland Papers, Census of the Five Nations (filed with correspondence under date of October 20, 1789).

8. For details of the destruction accomplished by Sullivan, Brodhead, and Van Schaick, see W. Stone, 1838, Vo. II; PA, first series, Vol. VII; R. Stone, 1924; and any of several other accounts of these expeditions including the various journals of officers and men.

9. Seaver, 1932, p. 75; Harris, 1903, p. 423. See W. Stone, 1838, Vol. II, p. 54; Ketchum, 1865, Vol. II, p. 1; Hough, 1861, Vol. I, p. 133; and PA, first ser., Vol. VIII, p. 152, concerning the weather.

10. SHSW, DC, 16 F, Blacksnake memoirs; Turner, 1849, p. 281.

11. NYHS, OR, Vol. IX, p. 46 (August 12, 1793) and Vol. X, p. 5 (February 1, 1794); Collections of the MHS, first ser., Vol. V, p. 28.

12. W. Stone, 1838, Vol. I, p. 176.

13. Harris, 1903, pp. 433–4.

14. Brodhead, 1857, p. 780.

15. MHS, Pickering Papers, Vol. LXII, p. 250; NYHS, OR, Vol. VIII, census of November 12, 1792; Vassar College, Parrish Papers, No. 55; HAMC, Kirkland Papers, census of the Five Nations (filed with correspondence under date of October 20, 1789); Morse, 1822, App., p. 76.

16. Sullivan, 1921–65, Vol. IV, pp. 240–1; Beauchamp, 1903, p. 342. Total population is generally calculated as four or five times the number of warriors.

17. Quoted in Pearce, 1953, p. 69.

18. Kent and Deardorff, 1960, pp. 265–324, 435–80.

19. Hough, 1961, Vol. I, pp. 21–5. See also Ford, 1904, Vol. XXVI, pp. 152–5.

20. The behavior of the white delegates at Fort Stanwix is described by Evans, 1941, and in Manley, 1932, and Shipman, 1933. Blacksnake was present, and his account documents the discomfiture of the Indians at being confronted with the American policy (SHSW, DC, 16 F).

21. Manley, 1932.

22. Fitzpatrick, 1925, pp. 400–4.

23. SHSW, DC, 23 U 42.

24. Cf. A. Wallace, 1949.

25. Evidence for serious alcoholism among prominent Iroquois of this period is to be found in many sources, such as NYHS, OR; SHSW, DC, 4 S and 16 F; Deardorff, 1951; W. Stone, 1838; Parker, 1912; ASPIA.

26. Ketchum, 1865, Vol. II, p. 149.

27. NYHS, OR, Vol. IX, Calking to Chapin, June 20, 1793.

28. *Ibid.*, Vol. VIII, p. 70, and Vol. XV, Doc. 3.

29. *Ibid.*, Vol. XV, pp. 54–69.

30. W. Stone, 1838, Vol. II, pp. 464–6.

31. SC, Jackson Journal, 1800, pp. 4–5.

32. Seaver, 1824, pp. 97–101 119–22, 127–34.

33. Jackson, 1930b, p. 34.

34. NYHS, OR, Vol. XII, p. 33 (Chapin to secretary of war, September 4, 1796).

35. BHS Publications, Vol. VI, p. 245.

36. SHSW, DC, 4 S and 16 F; Wildes, 1941, p. 411. Fenton's study of Iroquois suicide (Fenton, 1941b) does not record any cases during our period.

37. PHC, Skinner, MSS., pp. 121–5; Seaver, 1932.

38. Parker 1913, pp. 17–18.

39. Brant's acculturation policy is described in W. Stone, 1838, Vol. II, pp. 287–9, 398–405, 430–45, 489; and in Lydekker, 1938, Chs. VII and VIII.

40. Hough, 1861, Vol. I, pp. 165–71.

41. NYHS, OR, Vol. XII, pp. 21, 45–45A.

42. Kent and Deardorff, 1960, pp. 465–6.

43. PYM, Indian Committee, Vol. I, Cornplanter to Brother Onas, n.d. but *c.* 1791.

44. Sipe, 1927, p. 465; Warren Centennial, 1897, claims that the first (white) sawmill in Warren County was built on Jackson Run in 1800 and that the first raft of lumber floated down the Allegheny was sawed there. Cornplanter's mill was farther upstream, just above the New York State line.

45. NYHS, OR, VOL. XV, Doc. 3 (T. Morris's recollections of Red Jacket).

46. HSP, MS. Department, John Parrish' Journal at Newtown Point, 1791, AM 565.

47. BHS Publications, Vol. VI, No. 4 (Letters of Holmes from Fort Niagara, 1800).

48. S. Drake, 1837, pp. 98–100.

49. Mathews, 1908, pp. 62–63.

50. Kirkland's account of the revival of the white dog ceremony at Grand River and Oneida is at HAMC, Kirkland Papers, February 26, 1800, and May 30, 1800. See also Blau, 1964, and Tooker, 1965.

51. The depressed condition of the south-west New York and north-west Pennsylvania frontier is amply described in several printed collections and digests of primary source materials, particularly Harpster, 1938; Buck, 1935; Buck and Buck, 1939; Wright and Corbett, 1940; BHS Publications, Vol. V.

52. NcNall, 1952, pp. 3–5 (citing Dwight's Travels of 1804).

53. Agnew, 1887; PHC, Pennsylvania Population Co., MS.; Harpster, 1938, pp. 267–70.

54. Henderson, 1936, p. 159, *et passim.*

55. PHC, Pennsylvania Population Co., MS.; McNall, 1952, pp. 18–21; "Andrew Ellicott" in the Dictionary of American Biography. See also Turner, 1849, and Ketchum, 1865.

56. The relationship of the Israel Chapins, Sr. and Jr., to Phelps and Gorham is developed in NYHS, OR, Vol. V, Docs. 1, 5, 14, 33, 38, 40, 94, 98; Vol. VI, Docs. 2, 3, 4; Vol. VIII, Doc. 17, and Phelps to Chapin, November 3, 1792, and in various other documents scattered through O'Rielly's notebooks. These relationships among the principal white men at Big Tree are also revealed in O'Rielly's notebooks, particularly NYHS, OR, Vol. XV, Doc. 3, and in McNall, 1952.

57. Cattaraugus County, 1879, pp. 45–51.

58. *Ibid.;* PHC, Pennsylvania Population Co., MS.

59. The extended family system of settlement is made evident in the local histories. See Schenck, 1887, and Cattaraugus County, 1879.

60. NA Letters received by secretary of war 1812–15, December 3, 1801.

61. McNall, 1952.

62. The distribution of missionary effort is described in Cross, 1950; Buck and Buck, 1939; Hotchkin, 1848; Cattaraugus County, 1879.

63. The major treaties and agreements are published in 7 STAT., and Hough, 1861. See also Kappler, Vol. II, p. 1027 for date on the original annuity of 1792.

64. Act of January 4, 1790.

65. Harmon, 1941, pp. 10–19.

66. NYHS, OR Vol. VI, p. 36.

67. MHS, Collections, ser. 1, Vol. 5 (1798), "Report of a Committee, Who Visited the Oneida and Mohekunuh Indians in 1796," p. 30.

68. Hough, 1861, Vol. I, pp. 48–69, 165–8.

69. Cotterill, 1954, p. 124.

70. Kappler, Vol. II, p. 1027.

71. NYHS, OR, Vol. VIII; "List of Goods delivered . . . November 1792"; Vol. IX, p. 37.

72. See A. Wallace, 1949.

73. PYM, Minutes of Indian Committee, 11 month, 3rd 1795 to 3rd month 8th 1796.

74. NYHS, OR, Vol. XII, Doc. 17.

75. The chronicle of Quaker preparations recited above is based, except as otherwise noted, on the Minutes of the Indian Committee, found at PYM, Friends Book Store.

76. This is the phrase used by Jackson (in A. Wallace, 1952a) to describe the arts and crafts taught by the Quakers.

77. The initial negotiations between the Cornplanter Seneca and the Quakers are described in MHD, Sharpless, 1798, and PYM, Pierce and Sharpless Journal, 1798, May 18.

78. The events of the fall and winter are described in Jackson, 1830a, and SC, Simmons Letter Books, 1798–99.

79. Parker, 1913, p. 20. According to legend Handsome Lake had been bedridden for four years when in June 1799, he had his vision. Although he may not have been in good health, it is highly improbable that he was bedridden earlier than a few weeks before his vision. The evidence for this conclusion is as follows. First, the Code (in Parker, 1913) begins with a description of a winter's hunting trip down the Allegheny in 1798 and a drunken return in the spring of 1799—not just a description of a drunken orgy *after* the return of the hunting party. The language suggests a participant's recollections. The allusion to "four years of sickness in bed" in Parker's (1913) Code is attributed to Handsome Lake's daughter and son-in-law. Blacksnake's memoir of the first vision (SHSW, DC, 16 F 226) begins with the words: "The year [1799] Certifies that from a personal Aquanted called good lake that year he was sick confined to his bed. . . ." Jackson's journal (in A. Wallace, 1952a) merely says: "in these days [i.e., spring of 1799] . . . one of the Heathen (the Brother of Cornplanter the Chief lay upon his bed sick. . . ." Simmons (in A. Wallace, 1952a) asserts that at the time of the vision, Handsome Lake "had been on the decline of life for several years . . ." but does not claim he had been bedridden throughout that time. Additional information is available, moreover, about Handsome Lake's official role. In July 1795, the surveyors at Presqu' Isle were escorted by "one . . . who belongs to the Nobility, he is a nephew to King Guia Shuthongn and stepson to Chitteaughdunk!" (Mathews, 1908, pp. 120–1). The only official "Nobility" among the Iroquois were the *royaner*, or League chiefs, one of whom held the title Handsome Lake, and the only League chief who was also a nephew to Guyasuta, to my knowledge, was *this* Handsome Lake. A Handsome Lake also signed the Big Tree Treaty in 1797 and later a message to the government of New York State drafted at Geneseo on November 21, 1798 (NYHS, OR, Vol. XIII, p. 34). While any man who held this League chieftainship would bear the titular name Handsome Lake, it is probable, because of the early reference to Guyasuta's nephew, that this Handsome Lake was the bearer of the name between 1795 and 1799. If Cornplanter's brother *was* Handsome Lake by 1795, then he cannot have been bedridden for four years, because he was present at Presqu' Isle in 1795, at Big Tree in 1797, and Geneseo in 1798. On the other hand, even if he was not made a League chief until after 1795, he would have had to be in sufficiently sturdy health to be capable of participating in the condolence ceremony and of qualifying as a chief, and the "four years bed-ridden" legend is again disqualified.

80. The foregoing account of Simmons's work in the late winter and spring of 1799 is taken from his second diary, which commences February 3, 1799. A copy of this diary was made by Mr. M. H. Deardorff,

and I have used this copy. The original was owned by Mr. Robert S. Ewing of West Grove, Pennsylvania, and it is now in the possession of Swarthmore College Library. Parts of this diary are reprinted in A. Wallace, 1952a.

81. Parker, 1913, pp. 20–1.

82. The increased interest in acculturation in the spring of 1799 is described in SC, Simmons Journal; in Jackson, 1830a, p. 35; and in SC, Simmons Letter Books, 1798–99, Simmons *et. al.* to the Indian Committee, March 24, 1799, and June 16, 1799.

83. SC, Simmons Journal; Jackson in A. Wallace, 1952a.

Part III: The Renaissance of the Iroquois
CHAPTER 8: PREACHING TO REPENTANCE:
The First, or Apocalyptic, Gospel

1. The external circumstances of the vision are given by several sources: Parker, 1913, pp. 22–4 (the Handsome Lake traditional code); Blacksnake's own recollections in SHSW, DC, 16 F 226; and the Simmons and Jackson diaries and notes printed in A. Wallace, 1952a. These sources do agree on the essential course of events, but disagree on the duration of the trance (Blacksnake says four days, Simmons two hours) and the severity of his prior illness (as we have seen, the Code in Parker, 1913, implies in one interpretation that he was bedridden for four years, but the early material and Simmons suggest that he had been declining for some time but not that he was bedridden). The text of the Code clearly implies that Handsome Lake, sick or not, had been a member of the drunken hunting party that came back from Pittsburgh in May. Blacksnake claimed (years later) to have seen the three angels talking with Handsome Lake when the latter came out of the door. Possibly he (and Handsome Lake) misperceived Handsome Lake's daughter and her husband.

2. SC, Simmons Journal, entry of "Sixth Month 15th," and Jackson, in A. Wallace, 1952a, give almost identical versions of the vision and the subsequent events.

3. Simmons in A. Wallace, 1952a.

4. *Ibid*.

5. The vision of the sky journey is described at length in one section of Parker's version of the Code. A comparison of this Code with Simmons's contemporary account demonstrates, first, that the assemblers of

the Code, who were piecing together the recollections of the prophet's disciples, placed some of the revelations acquired during this vision of August 8, 1799, out of context in other parts of the Code (a process of randomization evident in other topics as well); and second, that Handsome Lake cautiously avoided telling Simmons about that part of the journey in which the prophet toured the domain of punishment for sinners (doubtless fearful of offending the sensibilities of white men, who frequently criticized Indians for torturing prisoners). The reconstruction given is cast as much as possible in the language of the sources that purport to quote the prophet: i.e., the Code (in Parker, 1913) and Simmons's journal (in A. Wallace, 1952a).

6. Parker, 1913.

7. Simmons in A. Wallace, 1952a.

8. Parker, 1913.

9. SC, Simmons Journal, entries under "5th Month" and "8 Mo. 28th."

10. Parker, 1913.

11. *Evangelical Intelligencer*, Vol. I (1807), pp. 92–3.

12. HL, Parker Collection, MS. of Ely S. Parker concerning Indian medicine men, n.d. (from microfilm at APS).

13. *Evangelical Intelligencer*, Vol. I (1807), pp. 92–3; Speck, 1935, pp. 159–60.

14. Parker, 1913, pp. 27–30, n. 3; pp. 49–50, n. 2.

15. Parker, 1913.

16. HSP, Penn MSS., Indian Affairs, Vol. IV, p. 56 (Cornplanter *et al.* to Mead *et al.*, n.d. [c. January, 1801]); PYM, Pierce Journal, 1801, D 10 A.

17. There are several accounts of this affair, both traditional and contemporary, from which the account given in the text is derived. See Fenton, 1946, pp. 52–5; HL, H. M. 20461 (Mead to O'Bail, February 2, 1801); Jackson, 1830a, pp. 42–3; and personal communication from M. H. Deardorff, based on his work with Seneca informants.

18. P. Wallace, 1945, p. 299.

19. PYM, Indian Committee, Box 1, Baylor, Swayne, and Thomas to Indian Committee, June 28, 1801.

20. HSP, Penn MSS., Indian Affairs, Vol. IV, p. 56.

21. NA, WD, LR, C-51(1), April 14, 1801.

22. Jackson, 1830a, p. 42; PYM, Pierce Journal, 1801, Department of Records, D 10 A; HSP, Logan Papers, Vol. XI, p. 70 (unsigned letter from Friends at Genesinguhta, January 18, 1802).

23. BHS Publications, Vol. XXVI, pp. 122–3 (Joseph Ellicott's Letter Books).

24. BHS Publications, Vol. XXVI, pp. 122–3.

25. NA, WD, LR, C-73 (1) and C-83 (1).

26. *Evangelical Intelligencer*, Vol. I (1807), pp. 92–3.

27. Clinton, 1812, pp. 39–40.

28. Parker, 1913, p. 68.

29. PYM, Pierce Journal, 1801, D 10 A; NYHS, OR, Col. XIV, p. 12 (Council of November 12, 1801).

30. Jackson, 1830a, pp. 42–3.

31. HSP, Logan Papers, Vol. XI, p. 76 (Handsome Lake *et al.* to Dearborn, March 15, 1802).

32. Fenton, 1946.

CHAPTER 9:   THE POLITICS OF EVANGELISM:
The Second, or Social, Gospel

1. PYM, Pierce Journal, 1801, D 10 A.

2. NA, WD, LR, C-29 (1), C-34 (1), C-38 (1), C-124 (1); Ibid., SW, RBIA, LS, Vol. A, pp. 164–6.

3. PYM, Indian Committee, Box 1 (March 9, 1802).

4. NYHS, OR, Vol. XIV, p. 14; Cotterill, 1954, p. 226.

5. HSP, Logan Papers, Vol. XI, p. 74 (Handsome Lake to President of United States, March 10, 1802).

6. Parker, 1919, 250 App.; NA, RBIA, SW, LS, Vol. A, pp. 193–4.

7. NA, RBIA, SW, LS, Vol. A, p. 286.

8. W. Stone, 1841, pp. 447–9. A draft copy of this letter is in HSP, Daniel Parker Papers, Box 2, and it was referred to in an accompanying letter to Callendar Irvine of November 5, 1802, a copy of which is in NA, RBIA, SW, LS, Vol. A, p. 289.

9. The synoptic description of the strategy and course of the Quaker mission on the Allegheny is taken from a number of sources. PYM contains

a number of valuable manuscripts bearing on the mission, particularly Records of the Indian Committee, Boxes 1 and 2; the sixteen volumes of "Indian Records"; Indian Notes, 1791–1878; and the journals of Joshua Sharpless and John Pierce to the Seneca in 1798 and 1801 respectively. The Haverford College Library holds the Journal of William Allinson to the Seneca in 1809. The Chester County Historical Society, in West Chester, Pennsylvania, has a number of useful documents, including Halliday Jackson's "A Short History of My Sojourning in the Wilderness" (published in *Pennsylvania History*, Vol. XIX, 1952, pp. 117–147, 325–49, under the title "Halliday Jackson's Journal to the Seneca Indians, 1798–1800"), journals of Halliday Jackson and others to the Seneca in 1806, 1814, and 1817, a tabulation of Seneca "improvements" from 1810 to 1818, and miscellaneous correspondence between the missionaries among the Seneca and their families and friends in the Philadelphia area. Swarthmore College Library has the Henry Simmons journal and letter books and Halliday Jackson's "Some Account of My Residence Among the Indians," 1800. Among the privately owned materials, copies of which were loaned to the author by Mr. M. H. Deardorff, were Joshua Sharpless's journal to the Allegany Seneca in 1798 (owned by Dr. W. T. Sharpless of West Chester, Pennsylvania) and the letters and journals of Henry Simmons, 1796–99 (owned by Mr. Robert H. Ewing, West Grove, Pennsylvania, and now in the possession of the Swarthmore College Library). Among published works, of course, the most valuable primary source is undoubtedly Jackson, 1830a.

10. A. Wallace, 1952a, p. 344.

11. PYM, Journal of John Philips to the Seneca, 1806, entry of September 16, p. 31.

12. HAMC, Kirkland Papers, Journal of December 27, 1806.

13. Parker, 1913, pp. 67–8.

14. HAMC, Kirkland Papers, Journal of August 3, 1806.

15. Parker, 1913, p. 35.

16. Covell, 1804.

17. Parker, 1913, p. 38.

18. PYM, Pierce Journals, 1801, entries of October 16, p. 42, and October 21, p. 60.

19. PYM, Records of the Indian Committee, Box 2, Speech of Handsome Lake to Friends, August 30, 1803.

20. *Evangelical Intelligencer*, Vol. I (1807), pp. 92–3.

21. HAMC, Kirkland Papers, Journal of August 3, 1806.

22. *Evangelical Intelligencer,* Vol. I (1807), pp. 92–3.

23. PYM, Indian Committee, Vox 2, Letter of Handsome Lake, January 1, 1803.

24. HSP, Logan Papers, Vol. 9, p. 74.

25. The membership of the Allegany Council is listed for 1803 in CL, UM, Isaac Bonsall Journal, 1803, and for 1809 in HAVC, William Allinson's Journal.

26. The dispute over the location of the council fire is mentioned in W. Stone, 1841, Vol. II, pp. 408–29, and App., pp. 39–44. Handsome Lake's signature is found on annuity receipts in NA, RBIA, SW, LR, and Parrish's letter to Secretary of War Dearborn in NA, WD under date of September 3, 1807.

27. PYM, Indian Committee, Box 2, Letter of Handsome Lake and Cornplanter, August 20, 1803.

28. The removal to Cold Spring and the deposing of Cornplanter are described in three letters from Friends at Tunessassa to the Indian Committee in Philadelphia, dated March 24, June 9, and August 29, 1804 (PYM, Indian Committee, Box 2). See also Jackson, 1830a, pp. 49–50.

29. PYM, Indian Committee, Box 2, Letter of March 24, 1804.

30. PYM, Indian Committee, Box 2, Letter of June 9, 1804.

31. The Quaker visit of 1806 and the councils at Cold Spring on that occasion are described in CCHS, Jackson Journal, 1806; SC, Jackson Journal published by Snyderman, 1957; and CL, UM, Isaac Bonsall Journal, 1806–07.

32. Red Jacket's personal opposition is mentioned as early as 1803. See Cram's Journal, April 2, 1803 (*Massachusetts Missionary Magazine,* Vol. I (1804), pp. 68–9.

33. Clinton, 1812, pp. 39–40. See also NYHS, OR, Vol. XIV, Doc. 19, Chapin to Dearborn, July 6, 1802, for an early reference to the Handsome Lake-Cornplanter conspiracy theory.

34. *Evangelical Intelligencer,* 1807, Vol. I, pp. 92–3.

35. Parker, 1913, pp. 40–7.

36. Jackson, 1830a, p. 53.

37. The circumstances of Handsome Lake's exodus from Cold Spring are not given in any of the Quaker records that I have seen, nor are they described very fully in Parker's version of the Code. The account of the

difficulty concerning the epidemic is based on PHC, Skinner MSS., interview with S. C. Crouse, a nephew of Blacksnake, from whom Crouse claimed he got the story; from M. H. Deardorff's notes of conversations with Eber L. Russell, March 2, 1950; and from W. N. Fenton's notes of conversation with Henon Scrogg, September 5, 1935.

38. *Evangelical Intelligencer*, 1807, Vol. I, pp. 92–3.

39. HAVC, Journal of William Allinson, September 17, 1809; SHSW, DC, 4 S, interview with Benjamin Williams; Turner, 1849, p. 509.

40. PYM, Box 2, Journal of Lee, Brown, Stewardson, and Allinson, September 25, 1809.

41. HAVC, Journal of William Allinson, Book 2, p. 15.

42. Parker, 1913, p. 47.

43. Parker, 1919, p. 18.

44. CCHS, Jackson Journal, 1810–18, pp. 14–15, 51.

45. PYM, Indian Committee, Box 2, Letter of June 4, 1811.

46. Schenck, 1887, pp. 136–7.

47. Ketchum, 1865, Vol. II, pp. 419–35; NA, WD, LR, G-147 (6), letter of September 10, 1812; Vassar College, Jasper Parrish Collection, No. 36, Granger's Letter of October 24, 1812.

48. Vassar College, Jasper Parrish Collection, No. 23, Military census of February 14, 1814.

49. Vassar College, Jasper Parrish Collection, No. 36, Granger's Letter of October 24, 1812.

50. Ketchum, 1865, Vol. II, pp. 419–35.

51. HAVC, Journal of William Allinson, Book 2, p. 44.

52. The annual circuit is specifically mentioned by Clark, 1849, pp. 103–109 and may be inferred from the frequency with which he is recorded as being at Buffalo Creek, Onondaga, Tonawanda, and the Genesee.

53. PYM, Indian Committee, Box 2, Letter of March 24, 1804.

54. *General Assembly's Missionary Magazine*, 1805, Vol. I, pp. 401–6.

55. *Evangelical Intelligencer*, 1807, Vol. I, pp. 92–3; Jackson, 1830a, p. 50.

56. Babcock, 1927, pp. 23–4.

57. Schenck, 1887, p. 136; Babcock, 1927, pp. 23–5; Stone, 1866, pp. 298–9; PYM, Indian Committee, Box 2, Letter of April 25, 1806.

58. *Massachusetts Missionary Magazine*, 1804, Vol. I, pp. 68–9.

59. Clark, 1849, Vol. I, pp. 103–9.

60. HAMC, Kirkland Papers, Journal for 1806.

61. HL, Parrish Collection, Letter of July 29, 1806; NYHS, OR, Vol. XIV, p. 7.

62. PYM, Indian Committee, Box 2, Letter of November 6, 1807.

63. *Evangelical Intelligencer*, 1807, Vol. I, pp. 92–3.

64. *Connecticut Evangelical Magazine*, 1811, Vol. IV, pp. 315–19.

65. *Evangelical Intelligencer*, 1807, Vol. I, pp. 92–3.

CHAPTER 10: RENAISSANCE

1. Jackson, 1830a, p. 51.

2. Jackson, 1830a, pp. 45–6.

3. SC, Simmons Journal, entries under "5th Month" and "9 Mo. 11th," 1799; Jackson, 1830a, pp. 35–44.

4. HSP, Logan Papers, Vol. XI, p. 70 (unsigned letter from a Friend at Genesinguhta, January 18, 1802).

5. LC, British Archives, Gilbert's Journal.

6. Jackson, 1830a, p. 51.

7. CCHS, Jackson Journal, 1806; SC, Jackson Journal (published in Snyderman, 1957), September 16, 1806.

8. PYM, Indian Committee, Box 2, Speech to Indian Committee by Conudiu *et al.*, November 6, 1807.

9. CL, UM, Isaac Bonsall Journal, 1806–07, entry of September 18, 1807.

10. HAVC, William Allinson Journal, Vol. I, p. 26, 38–9, (September 17, 1809).

11. CCHS, Jackson Journal 1810–18, pp. 14–15, 41.

12. NYHS, OR, Vol. XIV, p. 12 (Council at Genesee River, November 12, 1801).

13. CCHS, Jackson Journal, 1806; SC, Jackson Journal (published in Snyderman, 1957), pp. 60–6.

14. HAVC, William Allinson Journal, Book 3, p. 7, September 29, 1809.

15. PYM, Pierce Journal, 1801, entry of October 16, p. 42; and Indian Committee, Box 2, 1803–15, Letters of August 30, 1803, and June 4, 1811.

16. *Massachusetts Missionary Magazine*, 1804, Vol. I, pp. 68–9.

17. Clark, 1849, Vol. I, pp. 103–9.

18. *Evangelical Intelligencer*, 1807, Vol. I, pp. 92–3.

19. *The Friend*, 1844, p. 163.

20. HAMC, Kirkland Papers, Journal for August 3 and December 27, 1806.

21. PYM, Indian Committee, Box 2, Speech to Indian Committee by Conudiu *et al.*, November 6, 1807.

22. HAVC, William Allinson Journal, 1809, Book 2, pp. 34–5, and Book 3, p. 20.

23. CCHS, Jackson Journal, 1806; SC, Jackson Journal (published in Snyderman, 1957), p. 72 (September, 1806).

24. HAVC, William Allinson Journal, Book 2, p. 32 (letter of September 19, 1809).

25. HAVC, William Allinson Journal, 1809, Book 1, p. 42.

26. Jackson, 1830a, pp. 43–4.

27. Jackson, 1830a, p. 52.

28. CCHS, Jackson Journal, 1810–18, p. 54.

29. HAVC, William Allinson Journal, 1809, Book 1, p. 35.

30. Jackson, 1830a, p. 89.

31. Parker, 1919, p. 297.

32. CCHS, Jackson Journal, 1910–18, pp. 37–8.

33. The statistical information about Seneca agricultural technology and other aspects of their economic transformation is given in systematic and detailed form in Jackson, 1830a, pp. 85–9 *et passim*.

34. CCHS, Jackson Journal, 1810–18, pp. 11–13.

35. Although the white dog is not burned today by Handsome Lake followers, and some of them say that he disapproved of it, the sacrifice was still being carried out under his direct sponsorship at Allegany in 1809 (HAVC, William Allinson Journal) and was continued in the "pagan" communities in New York and Canada until it died out under the pressure of white disapproval late in the nineteenth and early in the twentieth centuries.

36. Again, although the prophet criticized the conduct of the societies and purged them of their ritual use of alcohol, their ceremonies were

publicly practiced under his eyes at Allegany in 1809 (HAVC, William Allinson Journal) and have been continued by his followers ever since.

37. Parker, 1913, p. 56.

38. *Ibid.*, p. 47.

39. *Ibid.*, p. 79–80.

40. Treaty of Buffalo Creek, August 31, 1826, in Records of the U.S. Senate (RG 46) Sen 19B-C6, 19th Congress, second session.

41. Vassar College, Jasper Parrish Papers, E. Granger to J. Parrish, August 27, 1815.

42. *Buffalo Gazette*, October 3, 1815.

43. The progress of settlement and the increasing involvement of the Seneca with whites are detailed in the country histories, particularly Schenck, 1887, and also in the Quaker records, particularly Jackson, 1830a; CCHS, Jackson Journal, 1817; CCHS, Jackson MS. 1818; and PYM, Indian Committee, Box 3.

44. PHC, transcript of the Original Records of the Western Missionary Society.

45. Alden, 1827.

46. The history of the missions to the Iroquois in New York is summarized in Howland, 1903. Original missionary narratives are published in Severance, 1903, and Asher Wright's own summary of this work is printed in Fenton, 1957.

47. The treaties of 1826, 1838, 1842, and 1857 are to be found in, respectively: Records of the U.S. Senate, RG 46 Sen 19B-C6, 19th Congress, second session; Peters, 1856, 7 STAT. 550; Peters, 1856, 7 STAT. 586; anl 11 STAT. 735. The Quaker records after 1817 record the political intrigues as they involved the Allegany Seneca in great detail. Journals and correspondence concerning these land negotiations throughout the period are retained in NA, RBIA, RG 75. See also Ellis, 1879.

48. J. Hyde in Seeverance, 1803, p. 269; Morse, 1822, App., pp. 83–4; NA, RBIA, RG 75, LR, "Report of Council of Seneca Indians with R. L. Livingston, June 25th, 1828."

49. NYHS, OR, Vol. XIV, d3; PHS, Publications, Vol. III, pp. 81–2; BHS, Box "Indians" (Parker gift); Vassar College, Jasper Parrish Papers, E. Granger to J. Parrish, July 20, 1815; *Buffalo Gazette*, April 16, 1816.

50. NA, RBIA, RG 75, LR, "Report of Council of Seneca Indians with R. L. Livingston, June 25th, 1828."

51. *Ibid.;* Manley, 1950.

52. SHSW, DC, 4 S.

53. The plan to allocate the Allegany Seneca lands in severalty is chronicled in PYM, Indian Committee, Box 3.

54. *The Friend,* Vol. XXII, p. 374.

55. Cornplanter's visions and their reception by the Indians are recorded in several versions, which agree in essentials: SHSW, DC, 16 F 277; Sipe, 1927, pp. 467–8; Alden, 1827; PHC, Index of Indian Records, pp. 215–22. Other materials cited on his nativistic period are contained in *The Friend,* Vol. XXII, p. 388, and Deardorff, 1841.

56. Schenck, 1887, pp. 149–50.

57. The fate of all the members of the 1809 Council cannot be determined. Materials used come from SHSW, DC, Draper's Notes (4S), and from treaty signatures and treaty journals in the 1826–38 period.

58. PYM, Elkinton Journals; PYM, Indian Committee, Box 3.

59. *Niagara Journal,* May 8, 1821; Tuttle, 1834, pp. 40–62.

60. PYM, Indian Committee, Box 3, Letter of November 21, 1824.

61. Alden, 1827.

62. Dearborn, 1904, pp. 55, 90–1.

63. The Tonawanda version of the 1840's was recorded by Ely S. Parker on two occasions, in 1845 and 1848, and his unpublished notes were used by Lewis Henry Morgan as the basis for his published account of the Handsome Lake religion in 1851. Parker's notes were later published by his descendant, Arthur Parker (Parker, 1919) and by W. N. Fenton, 1951. The Tonawanda version agrees remarkably well in many details with the Allegany-Cattaraugus version, which was formulated, according to tradition, at a council at Cold Spring about 1860, at which all speakers of the Code came together to compare versions and decide on an official one. This version was published by Parker in 1913. The quotations used in this book came largely from the Parker 1913 version. No explicit attempt has been made here to reconcile discrepancies or to label parts of the various published and unpublished versions of the Code as later additions and interpretations, but the author has not quoted or cited certain sections that apparently were added to the Code by speakers who did not always distinguish between the words of the prophet and their own historical and editorial comment. Thus the existing Code includes both the words of Handsome Lake and exhortations, historical introduction and commentary by later speakers, and miscellaneous interpretations, applications, and perhaps new prophetic material.

Bibliography

Manuscript Collections

ALLEGHENY COLLEGE
  Timothy Alden Papers

AMERICAN PHILOSOPHICAL SOCIETY
  Ely S. Parker Collection

BUFFALO HISTORICAL SOCIETY
  Box: "Indians"
  Indian Papers 1811–1893, Erie County, Niagara County

BUREAU OF AMERICAN ETHNOLOGY (SMITHSONIAN INSTITUTION)
  Manuscript Collections

CHESTER COUNTY HISTORICAL SOCIETY
  Halliday Jackson Journals, 1806, 1810–1818, 1814, and 1817

CLEMENTS LIBRARY, UNIVERSITY OF MICHIGAN
  Journals of Isaac Bonsall, 1803 and 1806–1807

MERLE H. DEARDORFF
  Transcripts of Henry Simmons's Journals and Letter Book, Joshua Sharpless' Journal, 1798, and other privately owned manuscript materials

HAMILTON COLLEGE
  Samuel Kirkland Papers

HAVERFORD COLLEGE
  William Allinson Journal, 1809

HISTORICAL SOCIETY OF PENNSYLVANIA
  Logan Papers
  Daniel Parker Papers

HISTORICAL SOCIETY OF WESTERN PENNSYLVANIA
  Methodist Collection

HENRY E. HUNTINGDON LIBRARY
  Parrish Collection
  Parker Collection

MASSACHUSETTS HISTORICAL SOCIETY
  Henry Knox Papers
  Pickering Papers

MUSEUM OF THE AMERICAN INDIAN, HEYE FOUNDATION
  De Cost Smith, field notes, Onandaga, 1889

NATIONAL ARCHIVES
  War Department Records: Bureau of Indian Affairs

NEW-YORK HISTORICAL SOCIETY
  O'Rielly Collection
  Baroness Hyde de Neuville's Sketches of American Life, 1807–1822

PENNSYLVANIA HISTORICAL COMMISSION
  Transcripts of the Records of the Western Missionary Society (copy
    of thesis by Edward I. George)
  Transcripts of Indian Records
  Skinner Manuscripts

PHILADELPHIA YEARLY MEETING, ARCHIVES (located at Friends' Book Store)
  Indian Committee Collection (10 boxes)
  Joseph Elkinton Journals, 1810–1828
  John Pierce and Joshua Sharpless Journal, 1798
  John Pierce Journal, 1801
  John Philips Journal, 1806
  Miscellaneous boxes of Indian material

PRESBYTERIAN HISTORICAL SOCIETY (Philadelphia)
  Early Missionary Magazines

STATE HISTORICAL SOCIETY OF WISCONSIN
  The Draper Collection (microfilm copy at Princeton University
    Library)

SWARTHMORE COLLEGE, FRIENDS' HISTORICAL LIBRARY
  Monthly Meeting Records
  Halliday Jackson Journal, 1800
  Henry Simmons Journal, 1798–1800
  Henry Simmons Letter Books, 1798–1799

VASSAR COLLEGE
  Jasper Parrish Papers

PUBLICATIONS

Early Magazines and Newspapers

The Adviser or *Vermont Evangelical Magazine*
Buffalo Gazette
Connecticut Evangelical Magazine
The Friend
General Assembly's Missionary Magazine or *Evangelical Intelligencer*
Massachusetts Baptist Missionary Magazine
Massachusetts Missionary Magazine
The Mental Elevator
New York Missionary Magazine
Niagara Journal
Pittsburgh Gazette
Western Missionary Magazine

Published Primary Historical Materials

ALDEN, TIMOTHY *An Account of Sundry Missions Performed Among the Senecas and Munsees, in a Series of Letters with Appendix.* New York, J. Seymour. 1827

ALLEN, ORLANDO "Personal Recollections of Captains Jones and Parrish, and of the Payment of Indian Annuities in Buffalo." *Buffalo Historical Society Publications*, VI: 539–46. 1903

AMERICAN STATE PAPERS, INDIAN AFFAIRS

ASHE, THOMAS *Travels in America, Performed in 1806, for the Purpose of Exploring the Rivers Allegheny....* London. 1808

AUPAUMUT, HENDRICK "A Narrative of an Embassy to the Western Indians." *Memoirs of the Historical Society of Pennsylvania*, II: 61–131. 1827

BADGER, REV. JOSEPH *A Memoir of Rev. Joseph Badger, Containing an Autobiography and Selections from His Private Journal and Correspondence.* Hudson, Ohio. 1851

BEAUCHAMP, WILLIAM M., ed. *Moravian Journals Relating to Central New York, 1745–66.* Syracuse, Onondaga Historical Association. 1916

BLAIR, EMMA HELEN, ed. *The Indian Tribes of the Upper Mississippi Valley and Region of the Great Lakes.* 2 vols. Cleveland, Arthur H. Clark Co. 1912

BRODHEAD, JOHN R. *Documents Relative to the Colonial History of the State of New York*. E. B. O'Callaghan, ed. Vol. VIII. Albany, Weed, Parsons & Co. 1857

CENSUS, BUREAU OF *Heads of Families: First Census of the United States, 1790.* Vol. VII: State of New York; Volume VIII. State of Pennsylvania. Washington. 1908

CLINTON, DEWITT *Discourse Delivered Before the New-York Historical Society, at Their Anniversary Meeting, 6th December, 1811.* New York, James Eastburn. 1812

COVELL, LEMUEL *A Narrative of a missionary tour through the western settlements of the State of New York and into the southwestern parts of the province of upper Canada . . . in the fall of 1803.* Troy, New York. 1804

CRUIKSHANK, E. A., ed. *The Correspondence of Lieutenant-Governor James Graves Simcoe, with Allied Documents Relating to his Administration of the Government of Upper Canada.* Toronto, Ontario Historical Society. 1923–31

DEARBORN, HENRY A. S. "Journals of Henry A. S. Dearborn." *Publications of the Buffalo Historical Society*, VII, 1904. 1838

ELKINTON, JOSEPH "Journals at Tunessassa, 1815–64" (extracts). *The Friend*, XXII, XXIII. 1827–49

EVANS, GRIFFETH "Journal of Griffeth Evans, Clerk to the Pennsylvania Commissioners at Fort Stanwix and Fort McIntosh, 1784–85." *Pennsylvania Magazine of History and Biography*, LXV: 202–33. 1941

FENTON, WILLIAM N., ed. "The Hyde de Neuville Portraits of New York Savages in 1807–1808." *New-York Historical Society Quarterly*, XXXVIII: 119–37. 1954
"Seneca Indians by Asher Wright (1859)." *Ethnohistory*, IV: 302–21. 1957
"The Journal of James Emlen Kept on a Trip to Canandaigua, New York . . . 1794." *Ethnohistory*, XII: 279–342. 1965

FITZPATRICK, JOHN C., ed. *George Washington, President of the United States, Diaries 1748–1799*, 4 vols. Vol. I, 1748–1770. 1925

FORD, W. C., et al., eds. *Journals of the Continental Congress*, Vol. I–XXV, 1774–84. Washington. 1904

HAMILTON, MILTON W., ed. "Guy Johnson's Opinions on the American Indian." *Pennsylvania Magazine of History and Biography*, LXXVII: 311–27. 1953

HARPSTER, JOHN W., ed. *Pen Pictures of Early Western Pennsylvania.* Pittsburgh, University of Pittsburgh Press. 1938

HECKEWELDER, JOHN *History, Manners, and Customs of the Indian Nations.* . . . Philadelphia, Historical Society of Pennsylvania, 1876. 1819

HOUGH, FRANKLIN B., ed. *Proceedings of the Commissioners of Indian Affairs.*. . . 2 vols. Albany. 1861

JACKSON, HALLIDAY *Civilization of the Indian Natives.* Philadelphia, Gould. 1830a
Sketch of the Manners, Customs, Religion and Government of the Seneca Indians in 1800. Philadelphia, Gould. 1830b

KAPPLER, CHARLES J. *Indian Affairs: Laws and Treaties.* 3 vols. Washington, U.S. Government Printing Office. 1904

KELLOGG, LOUISE P., ed. "Frontier Advance on the Upper Ohio." *Wisconsin State Historical Society Collections,* Vol. XXIII. 1916
"Frontier Retreat on the Upper Ohio." *Wisconsin State Historical Society Collections,* Vol. XXIV. 1917

KENT, DONALD H., AND MERLE H. DEARDORFF, eds. "John Adlum on the Allegheny: Memoirs for the Year 1794." *Pennsylvania Magazine of History and Biography,* LXXXIV: 265–324, 435–80. 1960

KENTON, EDNA, ed. *The Indians of North America.* 2 vols. New York, Harcourt, Brace. 1927

KETCHUM, WILLIAM *An Authentic and Comprehensive History of Buffalo.* Buffalo, New York, Rockwell, Baker & Hill. 1865

LAFITAU, JOSEPH *Moeurs des sauvages Americains.* 2 vols. Paris. 1724

LA POTHERIE, BACQUEVILLE DE *Histoire de l'Amerique septentrionale.* Paris. 1722

LINCOLN, GENERAL BENJAMIN "Journal of a Treaty Held in 1793, with the Indian Tribes North-West of the Ohio, by Commissioners of the United States." *Collections of the Massachusetts Historical Society,* Ser. 3, V: 109–176. 1836

MASSACHUSETTS HISTORICAL SOCIETY. *Collections,* Ser. 1, Vol. V. 1798

MEGINNESS, JOHN F., ed. *Journal of Samuel Maclay, while surveying the west branch of the Susquehanna, the Sinnemahoning and the Allegheny Rivers, in 1790.* Williamsport. 1887

MORSE, JEDIDIAH *A Report to the Secretary of War of the United States on Indian affairs, comprising a narrative of a tour performed in the summer of 1820.* New Haven. 1822

NORRIS, MAJOR "Journal of Sullivan's Expedition." *Buffalo Historical Society Publications,* I: 217–52. 1879

O'CALLAGHAN, E. B., ed. *Documents relative to the colonial history of the state of New-York.* Vols. VIII, IX. Albany, Weed, Parsons & Co. 1853–87

PENNSYLVANIA ARCHIVES Ser. 1, Vols. VII, VIII, X, XI, XII; Ser. 2, Vols. IV, VI (Papers Relating to the Establishment at Presqu' Isle). 1874–1935

PETERS, RICHARD, ed. *The Public Statutes at Large of the United States of America.* Volume VII, *Indian Affairs 1778–1842* ("7 Stat"). Boston, Little, Brown. 1856

PITTSBURGH GAZETTE "Letter of January 16 concerning economic conditions in western Pennsylvania in 1790." Reprinted in 1933 in *Western Pennsylvania Historical Magazine,* XVI: 48–52. 1790

PROCTOR, COLONEL THOMAS "Narrative of the journey of Col. Thomas Proctor to the Indians of the North-West, 1791." *Pennsylvania Archives,* 2nd ser., IV: 551–622. 1876

SCHERMERHORN, JOHN F. *Report respecting the Indians, inhabiting the western parts of the United States.* Boston, Massachusetts Historical Society Collection, Ser. 2, Vol. II. 1814

SCHOOLCRAFT, HENRY ROWE "Algic Researches: Comprising Inquiries Respecting the Mental Characteristics of North American Indians." *Indian Tales and Legends,* Ser. 1, 2 vols. New York. 1839

SEAVER, JAMES E., ed. *A Narrative of the Life of Mary Jemison, the White Woman of the Genesee.* New York, New York Scenic and Historic Preservation Society, 1932. 1824

SEVERANCE, FRANK H., ed. "Narratives of Early Mission Work on the Niagara Frontier and Buffalo Creek." *Publications of the Buffalo Historical Society,* Vol. VI. 1903

SHARPLESS, JOSHUA "A Visit to Cornplanter in 1798: Extracts from the Diary of Joshua Sharpless." Published in 1930 in Warren, Pennsylvania, *Times-Mirror* (original MS. owned by W. T. Sharpless, West Chester, Pennsylvania). 1798

SLOANE, JAMES "Early Trade Routes: Adventures and Recollections of a Pioneer Trader with an account of his share in the building of Buffalo Harbor." *Buffalo Historical Society Publications,* V: 215–37. 1902

SNYDERMAN, GEORGE S., ed. "Halliday Jackson's journal of a visit paid to the Indians of New York (1806)." *Proceedings of the American Philosophical Society,* CI: 565–99. 1957

STERN, B. J., ed. "The Letters of Asher Wright to Lewis Henry Morgan." *American Anthropologist*, XXXV: 138–45. 1933

SULLIVAN, JAMES, *et al.*, eds. *The Papers of Sir William Johnson*. 14 vols. Albany. 1921–65

THWAITES, REUBEN GOLD, ed. *The Jesuit Relations and Allied Documents* ... *1610–1791*. 73 vols. Cleveland, Burrows. 1896–1901
Documentary History of Dunmore's War, 1774. Madison, State Historical Society of Wisconsin. 1904

TUTTLE, SARAH *Letters and conversations on Indian Missions at Seneca, Tuscarora, Cattaraugus, in the State of New York, and Maumee, in the State of Ohio*. Boston, Massachusetts Sabbath School Society. 1834

WAINWRIGHT, NICHOLAS B., ed. "The Opinions of George Crogham on the American Indian." *Pennsylvania Magazine of History and Biography*, LXXI: 152–9. 1947

WALLACE, ANTHONY F. C., ed. "Halliday Jackson's Journal to the Seneca Indians, 1798–1800." *Pennsylvania History*, XIX: 117–47, 325–49. 1952a

WRAXALL, PETER *An Abridgement of the Indian Affairs ... in the Colony of New York, 1678–1751*. C. H. McIlwain, ed. Cambridge, Harvard University Press. 1915

WRENSHALL, JOHN "The manuscript autobiography of John Wrenshall, early Pittsburgh merchant, trader and Methodist leader, in 1803." *Western Pennsylvania Historical Magazine*, XXV: 81–3. 1942

Primary Ethnographic Documents

BEAUCHAMP, WILLIAM M. "The New Religion of the Iroquois." *The Journal of American Folk-Lore*, X: 169–80. 1897
Civil, Religious and Mourning Councils and Ceremonies of Adoption of the New York Indians. Albany, New York State Museum, Bulletin 113. 1907

CHAFE, WALLACE L. *Seneca Thanksgiving Rituals*. Washington, Bureau of American Ethnology, Bulletin 183. 1961
Seneca Morphology and Dictionary. Washington, Smithsonian Press. 1967

CURTIN, JEREMIAH, and HEWITT, J. N. B. *Seneca Fiction, Legends, and Myths*. Washington, Bureau of American Ethnology, 32nd Annual Report. 1918

FENTON, WILLIAM N. *An Outline of Seneca Ceremonies at Coldspring Longhouse*. New Haven, Yale University Publications in Anthropology, No. 9. 1936

"Masked Medicine Societies of the Iroquois." In Smithsonian Institution Annual Report, Publication 3624: 397–430. 1940

"Tonawanda Longhouse Ceremonies; Ninety Years after Lewis Henry Morgan." Bureau of American Ethnology, Bulletin 128: 140–66. 1941a

"Iroquois Suicide: A Study in the Stability of a Culture Pattern." Bureau of American Ethnology, Bulletin 128: 80–137. 1941b

"Place Names and Related Activities of the Cornplanter Senecas." *Pennsylvania Archaeologist*, XV: Nos. 1–4 and 1946; XVI: No. 2. 1945

"An Iroquois Condolence Council for Installing Cayuga Chiefs in 1945." *Journal of the Washington Academy of Sciences*, XXXVI: 110–27. 1946

"Seth Newhouse's Traditional History and Constitution of the Iroquois Confederacy." *Proceedings of the American Philosophical Society*, XCIII: 141–58. 1949

The Roll Call of the Iroquois Chiefs: A Study of a Mnemonic Cane from the Six Nations Reserve. Washington, Smithsonian Miscellaneous Collections, III: No. 15. 1950

The Iroquois Eagle Dance: An Offshoot of the Calumet Dance. Washington, Bureau of American Ethnology, Bulletin 156. 1953

FENTON, WM. N., ED. *Parker on the Iroquois: Iroquois Uses of Maize and Other Food Plants; the Code of Handsome Lake, the Seneca Prophet; the Constitution of the Five Nations.* New York State Study Ser., II, Syracuse University Press. 1968

GOLDENWEISER, ALEXANDER A. *On Iroquois Work.* Summary Reports of the Geological Survey of Canada, 1912 and 1913. 1914

HALE, HORATIO *The Iroquois Book of Rites.* W. N. Fenton, ed. Toronto, University of Toronto Press, 1963. 1883

"An Iroquois Condoling Council." *Proceedings and Transactions of the Royal Society of Canada*, Ser. 2, I: 45–65. 1895

HEWITT, J. N. B. *Iroquoian Cosmology.* Washington, Bureau of American Ethnology, Annual Reports 21 and 43. 1903–28

"The Requickening Address of the Iroquois Condolence Council." *Journal of the Washington Academy of Sciences*, XXXIV: 65–85. 1944

MORGAN, LEWIS H. *League of the Ho-De-No-Sau-Nee or Iroquois.* New York, Dodd, Mead & Co., 1901. 1851

Systems of Consanguinity and Affinity of the Human Family. Washington, Smithsonian Institution. 1871

MYRTLE, MINNIE *The Iroquois: or the Bright Side of Indian Life.* New York. 1855

PARKER, ARTHUR C. "Secret Medicine Societies of the Seneca." *American Anthropologist*, XI: 161–85. 1909

· *Bibliography* ·

The Code of Handsome Lake, the Seneca Prophet. Albany, New York State Museum, Bulletin 163. 1913
The Constitution of the Five Nations. Albany, New York State Museum, Bulletin 148. 1916

RANDLE, MARTHA "Iroquois Women, Then and Now." In W. N. Fenton, ed., *Symposium on Local Diversity in Iroquois Culture.* Washington, Bureau of American Ethnology, Bulletin 149. 1951

SCOTT, DUNCAN C. "Traditional History of the Confederacy of the Six Nations." *Proceedings and Transactions of the Royal Society of Canada,* Ser. 3, V: 195–246. 1912

SHIMONY, ANNEMARIE A. *Conservatism Among the Iroquois at the Six Nation's Reserve.* New Haven, Yale University Publications in Anthropology, No. 65. 1961

SMITH, DE COST "Witches and Demonism of the Modern Iroquois." *Journal of American Folk-Lore,* I: 184–93. 1888

SMITH, ERMINIE, ed. *Myths of the Iroquois.* Washington, Bureau of Ethnology, 2nd Annual Report.

SPECK, FRANK G. *Naskapi: The Savage Hunters of the Labrador Peninsula.* Norman, University of Oklahoma Press. 1935
Midwinter Rites of the Cayuga Long House. Philadelphia, University of Pennsylvania Press. 1949

Secondary Sources

AGNEW, DANIEL *A History of the Region of Pennsylvania North of the Ohio and West of the Allegheny River.* . . . Philadelphia, Kay & Brother. 1887

ALVORD, CLARENCE WALWORTH *The Mississippi Valley in British Politics, A Study of the Trade, Land Speculation, and Experiments in Imperialism Culminating in the American Revolution.* 2 vols. Cleveland, Ohio. 1917

BABCOCK, LOUIS L. *The War of 1812 on the Niagara Frontier.* Publications of the Buffalo Historical Society, 29. 1927

BEAUCHAMP, WILLIAM M. *A History of the New York Iroquois.* Albany, New York State Museum, Bulletin 78. 1905

BERKHOFER, ROBERT F. *Salvation and the Savage: An Analysis of Protestant Missions and American Indian Response.* Lexington, University of Kentucky Press. 1965

BLAU, HAROLD "Dream Guessing: A Comparative Analysis." *Ethnohistory*, X: 233–49. 1963
"Function and the False Faces: A Classification of Onondaga Masked Rituals and Themes." *Journal of American Folk-Lore*, LXXIX: 564–80. 1966

BRISTOW, ARCHIE *Old Time Tales of Warren County*. Meadville, Pennsylvania, Tribune Press. 1932

BRYANT, WILLIAM C. "Orlando Allen: Glimpses of Life in the Village of Buffalo." *Buffalo Historical Society Publications*, I: 329–71. 1878

BUCK, ELIZABETH HAWTHORN "Social Life in Western Pennsylvania as Seen by Early Travelers." *Western Pennsylvania Historical Magazine*, XVIII: 125–38. 1935

BUCK, SOLON J., and BUCK, ELIZABETH HAWTHORN *The Planting of Civilization in Western Pennsylvania*. Pittsburgh, University of Pittsburgh Press. 1939

CAMPBELL, WILLIAM W. *Annals of Tryon County; or, the Border Warfare of New-York, During the Revolution*. New York, Harper. 1831

CANFIELD, W. W. *The legends of the Iroquois told by "The Cornplanter."* New York. 1802

CARSE, MARY ROWELL "The Mohawk Iroquois." *Bulletin of the Archaeological Society of Connecticut*, XXIII: 3–53. 1949

[CATTARAUGUS COUNTY] *History of Cattaraugus County, New York*. Philadelphia, L. H. Levers. 1879

CLARK JOSHUA V. H. *Onondaga; or Reminiscences of Earlier and Later Times. . . .* 2 vols. Syracuse, Stoddard and Babcock. 1849

CLEVELAND, C. C. *The Great Revival in the West, 1797–1805*. Chicago, The University of Chicago Press. 1916

CONGDON, CHARLES E. *Allegany Oxbow: A History of Allegany State Park and the Allegany Reserve of the Seneca Nation*. Little Valley, New York, Straight Publishing Co. 1967

COTTERILL, R. S. *The Southern Indians: The Story of the Civilized Tribes Before Removal*. Norman, University of Oklahoma Press. 1954

CRAIG, NEVILLE B. *The Olden Time*. Pittsburgh. 1846–48

CRIBBS, GEORGE ARTHUR "The Frontier Policy of Pennsylvania." *The Historical Society of Western Pennsylvania*, II: 5–35, 72–106, 174–98. 1919

CROSS, WHITNEY R. *The Burned-Over District*. Ithaca, Cornell University Press. 1950

· *Bibliography* ·

CRUIKSHANK, E. A. *The Employment of the Indians in the War of 1812.* Annual Report of the American Historical Association. 1895

DAHLINGER, CHARLES W. "Old Allegheny." *Western Pennsylvania Historical Magazine,* I: 161–223. 1918

DEARDORFF, MERLE H. "The Cornplanter Grant in Warren County." *Western Pennsylvania Historical Magazine,* XXIV: 1–22. 1941
"Zeisberger's Allegheny River Indian Towns: 1767–1770." *Pennsylvania Archaeologist,* XVI: 2–19. 1946
"The Religion of Handsome Lake: Its Origin and Development." In W. N. Fenton, ed., *Symposium on Local Diversity in Iroquois Culture.* Washington, Bureau of American Ethnology, Bulletin 149. 1951

DONEHOO, GEORGE P. *A History of the Indian Villages and Place Names in Pennsylvania.* Harrisburg, Telegraph Press. 1928

DOWNES, RANDOLPH C. *Council Fires on the Upper Ohio: A Narrative of Indian Affairs in the Upper Ohio Valley until 1795.* Pittsburgh, University of Pittsburgh Press. 1940

DRAKE, BENJAMIN *Life of Tecumseh, and of his brother the Prophet, with a historical sketch of the Shawanee Indians.* Cincinnati. 1841

DRAKE, SAMUEL G. *Biography and History of the Indians of North America.* Boston. 1837

ELLIS, FRANKLIN *History of Cattaraugus County, New York, with Illustrations and Biographical Sketches of Some of its Prominent Men and Pioneers.* Philadelphia, L. H. Everts. 1879

EVANS, P. D. *The Holland Land Company.* Publications of the Buffalo Historical Society, 28. 1924

FENTON, WILLIAM N. "Problems Arising from the Historic Northeastern Position of the Iroquois." *Smithsonian Miscellaneous Collections,* C: 159–251. 1940
"Seth Newhouse's Traditional History and Constitution of the Iroquois Confederacy." *Proceedings of the American Philosophical Society,* XCIII: 141–58. 1949
"Iroquois Studies at the Mid-Century." *Proceedings of the American Philosophical Society,* XCV: 296–310. 1951
The Iroquois in History. Paper read at Wenner-Gren Symposium, Burg Wartenstein, Austria, August 7–14, 1967. 1967

FERGUSON, RUSSELL J. "A Cultural Oasis in Northwestern Pennsylvania." *Western Pennsylvania Historical Magazine,* XIX: 269–80. 1936

FLICK, ALEXANDER C. *History of the State of New York.* 10 vols. 1933–37

GIPSON, LAWRENCE HENRY *The British Empire Before the American Revolution.* 13 vols. New York, Knopf. 1954–67

HALE, NELSON R. "The Pennsylvania Population Company." *New York History,* XVI: 122–30. 1949

HALSEY, FRANCIS WHITING *The Old New York Frontier: Its Wars with Indians and Tories, Its Missionary Schools, Pioneers and Land Titles 1614–1800.* New York, Charles Scribner's Sons. 1912

HARMON, GEORGE DEWEY *Sixty Years of Indian Affairs.* Chapel Hill, University of North Carolina Press. 1941

HARRIS, GEORGE H. "The Life of Horatio Jones: The True Story of Hoc-Sa-Go-Wah, Prisoner, Pioneer and Interpreter." *Publications of the Buffalo Historical Society,* VI: 383–514. 1903

HENDERSON, ELIZABETH K. "The Northwestern Lands of Pennsylvania, 1790–1812." *Pennsylvania Magazine of History and Biography,* LX: 131–60. 1936

HODGE, F. W., ed. *Handbook of American Indians North of Mexico.* Washington, Bureau of American Ethnology, Bulletin 30. 1906

HOTCHKIN, JAMES H. *A History of the Purchase and Settlement of Western New York, and of the . . . Presbyterian Church in that Section.* New York. 1848

HOUGHTON, FREDERICK "History of the Buffalo Creek Reservation." *Publications of The Buffalo Historical Society,* XXIV: 3–181. 1920

HOWLAND, HENRY R. "The Old Caneadea Council House and Its Last Council Fire." *Publications of the Buffalo Historical Society,* VI: 97–124. 1903

HSU, FRANCIS L. K. "The Effect of Dominant Kinship Relationships on Kin- and Non-Kin Behavior: A Hypothesis." *American Anthropologist,* LXVII: 638–61. 1965

HUNT, GEORGE T. *The Wars of the Iroquois: A Study in Intertribal Trade Relations.* Madison, University of Wisconsin Press. 1940

IBBOTSON, JOSEPH D. "Samuel Kirkland, the Treaty of 1792 and the Indian Barrier State." *Proceedings of the New York State Historical Association,* XXXVI: 374–91. 1938

KELSEY, RAYNER WICKERSHAM *Friends and the Indians 1655–1917.* Philadelphia, the Associated Executive Committee of Friends on Indian Affairs. 1917

LOTHROP, S. K. "Life of Samuel Kirkland, Missionary to the Indians." In Jared Sparks, ed., *Library of American Biography,* Ser. 2, XV: 137–308. Boston, Charles C. Little & James Brown. 1848

LOUNSBURY, FLOYD G. "The Structural Analysis of Kinship Semantics." In Horace G. Lunt, ed., *Proceedings of the 9th International Congress of Linguists*. The Hague, Mouton & Co. 1964

LYDEKKER, JOHN WOLFE *The Faithful Mohawks*. New York, Macmillan. 1938

MACLEAN, JOHN P. "Shaker Mission to the Shawnee Indians." *Ohio Archaeological and Historical Quarterly*, XI. 1903

MANLEY, HENRY S. *The Treaty of Fort Stanwix, 1784*. Rome, New York, Rome Sentinel Co. 1932
"Buying Buffalo from the Indians." *Proceedings of the New York Historical Association*, XLV: 313–98. 1942
"Red Jacket's Last Campaign and an Extended Biographical and Biographical Note." *New York History*, XLVIII: 149–68. 1950

MATHEWS, CATHARINE VAN CORTLANDT *Andrew Ellicott, His Life and Letters*. New York, The Grafton Press.

MCNALL, NEIL ADAMS *An Agricultural History of the Genesee Valley, 1790–1860*. Philadelphia, University of Pennsylvania Press. 1952

MOHR, WALTER H. *Federal Indian Relations, 1774–1788*. Philadelphia, University of Pennsylvania Press. 1933

MURDOCK, GEORGE P. *Our Primitive Contemporaries*. New York, Macmillan. 1934

PARKER, ARTHUR C. "The Senecas in the War of 1812." *Proceedings of the New York State Historical Association*, XV: 78–90. 1916
"The Life of General Ely S. Parker: Last Grand Sachem of the Iroquois and General Grant's Military Secretary." *Publications of the Buffalo Historical Society*, XXIII. 1919
"An Analytical History of the Seneca Indians." Rochester, New York, *Researches and Transactions of the New York State Archaeological Association*, Vol. VI, Nos. 1–5. 1926
"Notes on the Ancestry of Cornplanter." Rochester, New York, *Researches and Transactions of the New York State Archaeological Association*, Vol. V, No. 2. 1927

PEARCE, ROY H. *The Savages of America: A Study of the Indian and the Idea of Civilization*. Baltimore, Johns Hopkins Press. 1953

PECKHAM, HOWARD H. *Pontiac and the Indian Uprising*. Princeton, Princeton University Press. 1947

PETTITT, GEORGE A. *Primitive Education in North America*. Berkeley and Los Angeles, University of California Press. 1946

QUAIN, BUELL H. "The Iroquois." In Margaret Mead, ed., *Cooperation and Competition Among Primitive Peoples.* New York, McGraw-Hill. 1937

ROSSMAN, KENNETH R. *Thomas Mifflin and the Politics of the American Revolution.* Chapel Hill, University of North Carolina Press. 1952

ROYCE, CHARLES C. *Indian Land Cessions in the United States.* Washington, Bureau of American Ethnology, 18th Annual Report. 1899

RUSSELL, EBER L. "The Lost Story of the Brodhead Expedition." *New York History,* XXVIII: 252–63. 1930

SAVELLE, MAX *George Morgan: Colony Builder.* New York, Columbia University Press. 1932

SCHENCK, J. S. *History of Warren County, Pennsylvania.* Syracuse, D. Mason & Co.

SCHOOLCRAFT, HENRY R. *Notes on the Iroquois.* New York. 1846
Historical and statistical information respecting the history condition, and prospects of the Indian tribes of the United States. 6 vols. Philadelphia. 1851–57
Archives of Aboriginal Knowledge: Information Respecting the History, Condition and Prospects of the Indian Tribes of the United States. 6 vols. Philadelphia. 1860.

SHIPMAN, FRED WALDO *The Indian Council of 1793: A Clash of Policies.* Clark University, M.A. thesis MS. 1933

SIPE, C. HALE *The Indian Chiefs of Pennsylvania.* Butler, Pennsylvania, The Ziegler Printing Co., Inc. 1927

SMITH, JOSEPH *Old Redstone, or Historical Sketches of Western Presbyterianism and Its Early Ministers.* Philadelphia. 1854

SNYDERMAN, GEORGE *Behind the Tree of Peace: A Sociological Analysis of Iroquois Warfare.* Ph.D. Dissertation, University of Pennsylvania. 1948; published in *Pennsylvania Archaeologist,* Vol. XVIII, Nos. 3–4. 1948.
"A Preliminary Survey of American Indian Manuscripts in Repositories of the Philadelphia Area." *Proceedings of the American Philosophical Society,* XCVII: 596–610. 1953

SPECK, FRANK G. *The Iroquois: A Study in Cultural Evolution.* Bloomfield Hills, Michigan, Cranbrook Institute of Science. 1945

STONE, RUFUS B. "Brodhead's Raid on the Senecas." *Western Pennsylvania Historical Magazine,* VII: 88–101. 1924

STONE, WILLIAM L. *Life of Joseph Brant—Thayendanegea.* 2 vols. New York, Blake. 1838

The Life and Times of Red Jacket, or Sa-go-ye-wat-ha; being the Sequel to the History of the Six Nations. 2 vols. Albany, Munsell. 1866

THATCHER, B. B. *Indian Biography, or an historical account of those Individuals who have been distinguished among the North American Natives....* New York. 1840

TOOKER, ELIZABETH "The Iroquois White Dog Sacrifice in the Latter Part of the Eighteenth Century." *Ethnohistory,* XII: 129–40. 1965
"On the New Religion of Handsome Lake." *Anthropological Quarterly,* XLI: 187–200. 1968

TRELEASE, ALLEN W. *Indian Affairs in Colonial New York: The Seventeenth Century.* Ithaca, New York, Cornell University Press. 1960

TURNER, O. *Pioneer History of the Holland Purchase of Western New York.* Buffalo. 1849
History of the Pioneer Settlement of the Phelps and Gorham Purchases. Albany. 1852

WALLACE, ANTHONY F. C. *King of the Delawares: Teedyuscung.* Philadelphia, University of Pennsylvania Press. 1949
"Handsome Lake and the Great Revival in the West." *American Quarterly,* Summer, pp. 149–65. 1952b
"Mazeway Resynthesis: A Biocultural Theory of Religious Inspiration." *Transactions of the New York Academy of Sciences,* XVIII: 626–38. 1956a
"Revitalization Movements: Some Theoretical Considerations for their Comparative Study." *American Anthropologist,* LVIII: 264–81. 1956b
"Stress and Rapid Personality Change." *International Record of Medicine,* CLXIX: 761–74. 1956c
"The Origins of Iroquois Neutrality: The Grand Settlement of 1701." *Pennsylvania History,* XXIV: 223–35. 1957
"Dreams and the Wishes of the Soul." *American Anthropologist,* LX: 234–48. 1958a
"The Dekanawidah Myth Analyzed as the Record of a Revitalization Movement." *Ethnohistory,* V: 118–30. 1958b
"Cultural Determinants of Response to Hallucinatory Experience." *AMA Archives of General Psychiatry,* I: 58–69. 1959
"Cultural Composition of the Handsome Lake Religion." In W. N. Fenton and John Gulick, eds., *Symposium on Cherokee and Iroquois Culture.* Washington, Bureau of American Ethnology, Bulletin 180. 1961
Religion: An Anthropological View. New York, Random House. 1966

WALLACE, PAUL A. W. *Conrad Weiser, 1696–1760: Friend of Colonist*

and Mohawk. Philadelphia, University of Pennsylvania Press. 1945
The White Roots of Peace. Philadelphia, University of Pennsylvania
Press. 1946
"Historic Indian Paths of Pennsylvania." *Pennsylvania Magazine of
History and Biography*, LXXVI, No. 4. 1952
Indian Paths of Pennsylvania. Harrisburg, Pennsylvania Historical and
Museum Commission. 1965

WARREN CENTENNIAL *An Account of the Celebration at Warren, Pennsylvania . . . 1895*. Warren, Pennsylvania, Warren Library Association.
1897

WHITE, EMMA SIGGINS *Genealogical Gleanings of Siggins and other
Pennsylvania Families*. Kansas City, Tiernam-Dart Printing Co. 1918

WILDES, HARRY EMERSON *Anthony Wayne, Trouble Shooter of the
American Revolution*. New York, Harcourt, Brace & Co. 1941

WILKINSON, NORMAN B. "Robert Morris and the Treaty of Big Tree."
Mississippi Valley Historical Review, LX: 257–78. 1953

WILSON, EDMUND *Apologies to the Iroquois*. New York, Farrar, Straus,
and Cudahy. 1960

WRIGHT, J. E., and CORBETT, DORIS S. *Pioneer Life in Western Pennsylvania*. Pittsburgh. University of Pittsburgh Press. 1940

YOUNG, ELEANOR *Forgotten Patriot: Robert Morris*. New York, Macmillan. 1950

INDEX

(iii)

A NOTE ABOUT THE AUTHOR

Anthony Wallace was born in Toronto, Canada, in 1923 and did both his undergraduate and graduate work at the University of Pennsylvania (Ph.D., 1950). He has been Chairman of the Department of Anthropology at the University of Pennsylvania since 1961. In addition to his present position, Mr. Wallace is Medical Research Scientist at the Eastern Pennsylvania Psychiatric Institute where he was formerly Director of Clinical Research. He has written three books, *King of the Delawares: Teedyuscung* (1949), *Culture and Personality* (1961), and *Religion: An Anthropological View* (1966). He lives in Philadelphia with his wife and their four children.

A NOTE ON THE TYPE

The text of this book was set on the Linotype in Janson, a recutting made direct from type cast from matrices long thought to have been made by the Dutchman Anton Janson, who was a practicing type founder in Leipzig during the years 1668–87. However, it has been conclusively demonstrated that these types are actually the work of Nicholas Kis (1650–1702), a Hungarian, who most probably learned his trade from the master Dutch type founder Kirk Voskens. The type is an excellent example of the influential and sturdy Dutch types that prevailed in England up to the time William Caslon developed his own incomparable designs from these Dutch faces.

This book was composed, printed, and bound by
The Book Press, Brattleboro, Vt.

Typography and binding design by
GUY FLEMING